$19.95

7 98

Creative Parenting

Creative Parenting

How to use the new continuum concept to raise children successfully from birth through adolescence

by William Sears M.D.

Illustrated by Monique Trempe-Tardy

NEW YORK   **EVEREST HOUSE**   PUBLISHERS

Library of Congress Cataloging in Publication Data:
Sears, William, M.D.
Creative Parenting.

Includes index.
1. Infants — Care and hygiene. 2. Children — Care and hygiene.
3. Parenting. I. Title.

RJ61.S4418   649′.1   82-4998

ISBN 0-89696-179-6   AACR2

Copyright © 1982 by William Sears, M.D. and Optimum Publishing
International Inc.

Published in the United States of America by Everest House, 33 West 60th
Street, New York, N.Y. 10023

Published simultaneously in Canada by Optimum Publishing International
Inc., Montreal

Manufactured in Canada

Edited by Jill Davidson-Schichter
Designed by Suzanne Vincent-Poirier

First American Edition

DEDICATION

To my family:
Martha
James
Robert
Peter
Hayden

ACKNOWLEDGMENT

Most of the credit for this book goes to the thousands of parents and children who have shared their feelings with me during my practice of pediatrics.

I also wish to thank two of my former professors who have had a deep influence upon my pediatric career and therefore upon this book: Dr. Richard Van Praagh, Professor of Pediatrics at Harvard Medical School and Dr. Harry Bain, Professor of Pediatrics of the University of Toronto.

A special thanks to Michael Baxendale, President of Optimum Publishing International Inc., who recognized the need for the messages contained in this book; to my editor, Jill Davidson-Schichter, whose patience and insight were greatly appreciated; to Dr. George Owen, Professor of Nutrition at the University of Michigan for his critique of the Nutrition section; to Dr. Kalman Baruch of Savannah, Georgia for his critique of the Orthopedic section; to my nurse, Diane Rasmussen who was very dedicated to helping me finish this book; to Mr. Donald Wood for his critique of the Language section; to Dr. Joseph MacInnis and the crew of the Spirit of Apollo with whom I have spent many hours at sea and profited by their encouragement.

Finally, a sincere thanks to my wife, Martha, who has made a profession of mothering and with whom I have shared the joy of our own creative parenting.

FOREWORD

Growing with your infant and child can provide a lifetime of happiness and satisfaction for both of you. With growth comes knowledge as well as wisdom. Sometimes we learn from our mistakes, but it is preferable to learn in order to avoid mistakes.

The last decade has witnessed the gratifying emergence of ever increasing numbers of parents who want to learn about what is best for their infants and children. They are not content to learn just what their doctor tells them. They have become active rather than passive learners. They seek out answers so they can make their own decisions.

Social mobility has produced isolation for some parents, isolation from extended families - no grandparents or wise aunts to turn to for advice and information about raising your own offspring.

It is precisely for the parents who wish to know as much as possible about their infant and child that this book is written. Dr. Sears has prepared a book that truly meets the needs of the parents of the eighties—the needs of those who need to know.

This book is far more comprehensive than virtually any other book on the subject of parent education. It is not a primer but an eminently readable encyclopedia. I enjoyed reading it and I believe you will also.

If you don't already have children, reading this book will make you want to have them, to understand them, and to love them. Every problem is anticipated, every common illness discussed. Most importantly, it is not just a book on taking care of a sick child but a book on caring for, observing and understanding the well child.

Frank A. Oski, M.D.
Chairman of the Department of Pediatrics
State University of New York

INTRODUCTION

During the past ten years, we have seen the emergence of medically educated parents who, by challenging traditional methods of health care delivery, are having an enriching effect on the current medical system. "Artificial" is becoming a bad word. Mothering "devices" are being put aside in deference to feeling, touching and self-involvement. "Cookbook" pediatrics are giving way to the more valuable maternal intuition. A child's feelings are becoming as medically important as his stuffy nose. Breastfeeding is finally replacing the bottle and the mathematics of formula preparation is becoming passé. The importance of nutrition in general health and behavior has produced a generation of label readers. The increasingly popular prepared childbirth classes have defined the dual role of the "pregnant couple," and the importance of the long-neglected father involvement in childbirth has finally been recognized and is being given its proper priority. Cries from expectant couples of "we deserve better" have stimulated the proliferation of family-oriented maternity centers and alternative-birthing environments.

Traditional male-female and mother-father roles are being challenged both at home and in the market place. Birth control devices have enabled parents to plan their families conveniently. Attacks on the traditional roles of motherhood and the family unit both by the media and the women's liberation movements have produced more frustrations than freedom. The single parent, the working mother and the daycare center have put a strain on contemporary mothering. Economic constraints have produced the double income dilemma whereby the value of the second car is being weighed against the value of time with your child. This book is written for thinking, feeling, intuitive parents who place top priority on their professions as parents.

CREATIVE PARENTING admittedly sets high standards, but I make no apologies, because I believe that the ideal can be achieved by most parents.

Much of this book is written with the help of Marti, my wife and the mother of our four children. Marti is a certified teacher of the International Childbirth Education Association and a leader in the La Leche League International. I hope this female connection adds a deeper understanding of mothering, as written to mothers by a mother.

How to Read This Book

This work is intended to be a **complete book of child care**, with an emphasis on the most common questions parents ask and the most common problems children have. I am writing to both mothers and father and I hope both of you will read each chapter carefully.

Although CREATIVE PARENTING is primarily a reference book to consult when you have a specific problem, it is not meant to be used solely as a reference source. Child rearing is a "continuum" and this book is also written as a continuum. Certain parenting practices and childhood problems of one stage are intimately related to those of the preceding stage. Therefore, I advise readers who wish to get the most out of this book to read the entire text first, to pay particular attention to those sections which pertain to your family and your philosophies of parenting, and to disregard what you feel is irrelevant.

If after reading this book you have appreciated two messages—the dignity of your child as a person and the dignity of parenting as a profession—then preparing this book has been worthwhile.

The Concept of Continuum Parenting

Continuum parenting is an uninterrupted, nurturing relationship, specifically attuned to a child's needs as he passes from one developmental stage to the next. The two principles of continuum parenting which are elaborated upon throughout this book are "immersion" mothering and "involved" fathering. Immersion mothers and involved fathers convey such deep love to their child that he feels right, which naturally brings forth desirable behavior and sends a message of love to the parents.

Stimulated by their child's reactions, continuum parents also feel right and consequently increase their immersion mothering and involved fathering. This mutual giving raises the entire parent-child relationship to a higher level. The concepts of continuum parenting are illustrated below:

THE CONTINUUM CONCEPT

Immersion mothering

Parenting your unborn child

A positive pregnancy experience

A positive birthing experience

A breastfeeding relationship with infant-led weaning

Discipline through loving guidance

Giving your child an educational advantage at home

Family recreation

Parent-child mutual respect

Involved fathering

CONTENTS

CHAPTER I

PREGNANCY TO DELIVERY

Getting The Right Start

Since I have been involved in pediatrics, I have noticed that some couples adapt to parenting more easily than others.

Parents who get the right start seem to follow a similar path through pregnancy and delivery. They look to support groups for advice and support during pregnancy and in the early postpartum period. They attend prepared childbirth classes together. After delivery, mother and baby stay together until both are discharged from the hospital. Most of these mothers breastfeed their babies and wean them only when the infant shows he is ready (infant-led weaning). Fathers of these couples involve themselves in the pregnancy, delivery and care of the child, and wisely and attentively mother the mother, as she mothers the child.

These parents are more observant of their infant's behavior and they more intuitively respond to their infant's cues. They have a higher tolerance for their infant's fussiness and are better able to cope with undesirable behavior. They usually show a greater commitment to parenting and less of a desire to escape when the going gets tough. Finally, these prepared parents seem to enjoy a more harmonious relationship with their baby. Couples who get the right start are the ones who are most successful as parents.

You will find throughout this book the parenting practices which will get you off to the right start as parents.

Basic Decisions

Very early in your pregnancy you should ask yourself six questions:

1. What support groups are available in my community?
2. Who will be the best obstetrician for me during my pregnancy?
3. Who will be the best pediatrician for my baby?
4. Which hospital should we have our baby in?
5. What are the alternative birthing environments for delivery?
6. What classes on prepared childbirth are available in my community?

Choosing a Support Group

Support groups consist of experienced parents whose sole purpose is to help other parents. They enhance the entire pregnancy experience by acting as an extended family and by helping you develop your own parenting philosophy. There are many excellent support groups available to you. I have listed some of them below:

● **The La Leche League International (LLLI)**

This is a volunteer organization, composed of women members and group leaders, all of whom strongly advocate breastfeeding. Each leader, besides having practical breastfeeding experience, has special training in counselling new mothers about common concerns of child care. A "League Mother" enjoys access to a lending library, a board of medical consultants and continuing input from other members through monthly meetings. At this writing, there are approximately 13,000 league leaders, and 4,200 groups to join in 45 countries. (Although the LLLI moto is "Good mothering through breastfeeding," I find the philosophy of this group is simply good mothering in all aspects of childcare).

● **The International Childbirth Education Association (ICEA), The American Society for Psychoprophylaxis in Obstetrics (ASPO) and The American Academy of Husband-Coached Childbirth (The Bradley Method) (AAHCC)**

These groups focus on the pregnant couple during the childbearing year and especially stress father involvement. What these groups can do for you is discussed under the section **Childbirth Classes** on page 37.

Choosing Your Obstetrician

Choosing an obstetrician and pediatrician is somewhat different from choosing other medical specialists because obstetricians and pediatricians are involved in a normal process in your life rather than at a time of sickness. In perhaps no other medical specialty is the art of patient-doctor communication so important. Friends or local support groups can provide you with the names of supportive physicians. This is a good base from which to comparison shop.

When making your first appointment, let the obstetrician's receptionist know you are making the appointment solely to discuss the doctor's philosophy of childbirth and his attitudes toward your needs. **Both** parents-to-be should attend this first appointment. Let the doctor know why you are there, tell him what you want, what your feelings are and how you wish to have your baby. You are intelligent people asking him to support your

Choosing your obstetrician. Both parents-to-be should attend this first meeting. To facilitate patient-doctor communication, prepare a list of questions beforehand.

desires and to do everything within his medical and personal competence to support both your obstetrical and personal needs. Discuss with your obstetrician alternative birthing environments, medication and various hospital policies such as father involvement and rooming-in. Ask about childbirth education classes in your local community and especially about his attitude towards these classes.

Because of the emergence of prepared and thinking parents, most obstetricians are becoming increasingly flexible about offering alternative methods of birthing to fit the parents' requests. Because the person you are speaking with is a highly trained medical professional with justified pride in his profession and an extreme interest in the medical safety of your childbirth, you will probably receive an answer somewhat like "I respect your desires completely but I must, for the best medical interest of yourself and your baby, reserve the right to medically intervene should the need arise . . . and I must expect you to trust my judgment." In other words, your doctor is asking of you the same respect and flexibility that you are asking of him.

Choosing Your Pediatrician

The selection of a pediatrician basically follows the same guidelines as choosing an obstetrician: the doctor's competence and communication abilities. Usually the first visit between mother and pediatrician takes place in the hospital shortly after delivery. This initial patient-doctor communication is often compromised by a busy hospital ward and an extremely tired mother. Therefore, it is beneficial for you, the father and your pediatrician to meet each other prior to delivery. My own practice has always been to see prospective parents (mother and father) about two weeks prior to the anticipated delivery. This interview between parents and pediatrician gives the pediatrician an idea of what you really want. Your visit also increases his respect for you as prospective parents.

One day, expectant first-time parents came into my office at a particularly busy time and, after surviving a one-hour wait in the Romper Room, took refuge in my office and queried, "Why do we need you?" This is a question all first-time parents should ask themselves. What do you really want and need from your "baby doctor?" Are you a dependent person who is not completely comfortable exercising your basic intuition as a parent and therefore need periodic reassurance that what you are doing and feeling is the best for your baby? Or are you experienced, self-confident and comfortable exercising your own intuition and will therefore only need your doctor when your intuition tells you that things are not quite right? After you have determined what your needs are, you must communicate them to your doctor. If the doctor seems to appreciate your needs and you seem to be on the same wavelength during this initial office visit, then he is the pediatrician for you and your child.

Choosing a Hospital

Throughout this century the goal of modern obstetrical medicine has been to decrease the incidence of maternal and infant sickness and death. The emphasis has been on safety — delivering a healthy infant and maintaining a healthy mother. Psychological benefits were considered a bonus. Since 1950, the maternal death rate has decreased tremendously and the newborn death rate has been cut in half.

We are now entering an era of obstetrical medicine in which the safety of the mother and infant are still foremost in the physican's mind, but in which the psychological needs of both mother and baby are also considered. Evidence exists that consideration of psychological needs actually improves the health of mother and baby. These needs, therefore, should no longer be just a bonus, but a right.

The new options in obstetrical care which have begun to emerge in the last ten years, largely as a result of the demands of involved parents rather than at the initiative of the medical profession, have been termed **alternative birthing concepts**.

These maternity and newborn facilities of the future allow families to deliver in a family-centered environment where professional attendance is available should unanticipated medical complications arise. Today the two main hospital obstetrical alternatives remind me of the advertising slogans: "We Do It All For You" and "Have It Your Way."

The "We Do It All For You" philosophy goes something like this: Childbirth is an "illness" and we are going to "relieve" you of this illness by a surgical procedure in a hospital. You will be shaved and scrubbed until you are clean as in a routine surgical case, and then you will be taken to a labor room where you will be medicated. Your baby will be monitored by a machine to ensure his safety. This is necessary because some of the medication may not be good for him. The father, meanwhile, can wait in the Fathers' Waiting Room where a TV set has been thoughtfully provided. Actually, this is a good time for him to go to the Administration Office and complete the necessary papers.

If your labor is not progressing conveniently for all concerned, we will "induce" your labor by a little drip into your vein. When your baby seems ready to be delivered we will wheel you into a surgical suite and place you on a table. You must remain on your back with your legs up in stirrups (even though this is the position of maximum pain and discomfort) because it is easier for us to deliver your baby that way. (Stirrups, I feel, are a carry-over from the days when women were so heavily medicated and so unprepared that they lost control during childbirth). When your baby is born, we will take him directly to a plastic box to keep him warm. He will then be taken to our nursery where experts will care for his needs and help him recover from his birth. He may be a little sleepy until the medication wears off. Your baby may cry a little but don't worry, he will soon adjust to our nursery routine. Meanwhile, your husband can view his baby in the plastic box through the glass windows of the nursery. As are all surgical patients, you will be taken to a Recovery Room and from there to your own room. You will be very tired after this ordeal so we will let you sleep in peace. After you are rested, we will bring your baby to you for a brief visit. Thereafter, he may only come at certain times, according to our routine. We will feed him a scientifically tested formula and care for his needs, as we are the experts and you are only his mother. In three or four days, you and your baby may go home.

Don't think, don't touch, don't relate, they'll "do it all for you."

The "Have It Your Way" philosophy goes something like this: Mary and Tom are expectant parents. They have carefully selected their obstetrician and pediatrician, in whom they have complete confidence. They have attended prepared childbirth classes and, with the help of various support groups in their community, have educated themselves in the alternative methods of childbirth. They have decided that parenting is top priority and Mary wants to be awake and aware during childbirth. They want professional medical guidance for the safety of mother and baby but they also want to enjoy this experience. Mary and Tom find a hospital that offers the maternity care which fits their needs.

When Mary's labor begins, or more accurately, when the couple begin their labor, both father and mother are admitted to what is called the "Birthing Room." Both the atmosphere of the room and the attitude of the nursing staff convey a respect for the parents. The room, pleasant and bright, contains a lounge chair, rocking chair and several windows. The bed resembles most hospital beds, but is adjustable for use as a delivery bed. All the necessary medical and surgical equipment is unobtrusively but efficiently placed around the room. The obstetrical nurse welcomes the laboring couple to this unit and tells them that this will be their room for their entire hospital stay. Mary will labor in this room, deliver in this room, postpartum in this room and be discharged from this room. Tom may visit at any time and stay as long as he wishes, because this is his baby too.

When Mary's labor begins, she is supported both by Tom and by trained obstetrical personnel. Mary's perineum is not shaved because studies have shown that the humiliating practice of perineal shaving does not reduce the incidence of infection. Mary is free to sit up, walk and lie on her side at any time during labor. (Lying on the back is not only usually the most uncomfortable position during labor but also is possibly harmful to the baby because it slows down uterine blood flow). Prepared by childbirth classes and constantly supported by Tom, Mary is able to control her labor pains and relax the appropriate muscles without the use of medication. At times the pain seems overwhelming and Mary is about to lose control. Tom gives her the supporting boost that only a caring partner can give. His respect for motherhood and Mary has never been so high. The long-awaited moment of delivery arrives and the baby is crowning. The bed is adjusted to facilitate the obstetrician's attendance and Tom is seated at the head of the bed, performing the role of an involved, caring mate. At the moment of birth, Tom notices an expression on Mary's face which he has never seen before, an expression which reveals joy and pain at the same time. It is an expression which he will hold in his memory forever.

Immediately following delivery, the lights are dimmed, the room is quiet, their daughter is placed on the warmth of Mary's abdomen and arms and put immediately to her breast. Their baby is in a state of quiet alertness and the next hour is spent touching, talking and suckling. Mary, Tom and Heather also spend the next few days getting to know each other, in peace and privacy. Heather is breastfed on demand, and her early newborn needs are cared for by her mother, infinitely more capable than paid personnel. During her periods of postpartum fatigue and uncertainty about newborn care, it is, however, reassuring to know that the hospital personnel are immediately available to help her when the need arises. On the third hospital day, Mary, Tom and Heather leave the hospital with a profound memory of a beautiful event, the birth of a family.

Alternative Birthing Concepts

It is important to remember that alternative birthing centers, or birthing units, are more than a physical facility. They represent the existence of attitudes of mutual respect between the hospital, the obstetrician, the parents and the pediatrician. They recognize that childbirth is not a disease and couples should have choices in childbirth. You are delivering a feeling person whose rights should be respected, particularly during his first contact with the outside world.

Alternative birthing concepts are not passing fads, but a growing reality. In 1978, the Inter-Professional Task Forces of Health Care of Women and Children responded to an increasing consumer demand and endorsed this concept with the following statement: "The American College of Obstetricians and Gynecologists, The American College of Nurse Midwives, The Nursing Association of The American College of Obstetricians and Gynecologists, The American Academy of Pediatrics and The American Nurses Association endorse the philosophy of family-centered maternity-newborn care. The development of this conviction is based upon a recognition that health includes not only physical dimensions, but social, economic and psychological dimensions as well . . . ."

By the time this book is published, I believe that if hospitals are going to stay in the baby business, the majority will be offering or considering family-oriented maternity care. Those that do not will find their obstetrical beds empty, because the "we do it all for you" philosophy leaves a couple very hungry.

● **Home Births**

In recent years, home births have become increasingly popular. Because of the possibility of unanticipated obstetrical complications, both The American Academy of Obstetricians and Gynecologists and The American Academy of Pediatricians advise against home births. Actually, the person who is at the highest risk — the baby — has no voice in this decision. The home birth movement arose because our current health care delivery system fails to fill an honest consumer need.

I can speak with some insight about this dilemma since I have had the opportunity to attend home birthing and it is, indeed, a beautiful human experience for parents and babies. I can truly empathize with parents who wish home birth. The answer to this dilemma is not, however, home birth, but a **home-like birthing environment in a hospital**.

Prepared Childbirth Classes

I prefer to use the term "prepared" childbirth classes, rather than "natural" childbirth classes. The emphasis of most childbirth education is on preparation. If you are properly prepared, your childbirth most often will naturally be "natural."

Most childbirth classes begin around the seventh month of your pregnancy and continue weekly for six to eight weeks. The classes are held towards the end of your pregnancy so that the knowledge will be fresh in your mind for your delivery. There are also "early-bird" classes for the newly-pregnant couple. The purpose of these is to discuss choices of birthing environments, emotional and physical changes which occur during pregnancy, exercise and nutrition, and habits to avoid. Reading material is also suggested. If you are uncertain about whether you should take the entire series of childbirth classes, attend the early-bird classes to see what prepared childbirth classes can do for you.

Childbirth classes usually start off by having each couple introduce themselves to the group. They tell the group why they are coming to class and what they expect to accomplish. The mother frequently answers that she wants to know more about what is happening in her body and hopes the classes will help her give birth in a way that is good for her and her baby. The fathers usually give one of the two following reasons: "To please my wife" or "I want to learn more about what is going on and how to help." Many fathers flatly state at the beginning that they are not too sure they will be able to "pull it off" — that is, actually be helpful at the birth. Mid-way through the series of classes these reluctant, insecure labor coaches start to realize the vital role they must play in the birth of their child. By the end of the classes they are bursting with the enthusiasm of an informed and well-practiced trainer and cannot wait to get things rolling. Here are some comments from fathers who "pulled it off": "This was the most exciting and rewarding experience and very meaningful for me as a husband and father — it didn't hurt me a bit"; "This is where becoming a father really begins"; "I can tell you I would never exchange those memories and am looking forward to being pregnant again"; "Had I not been exposed to prepared childbirth training, I would not have been able to help Susan during the difficult moments of labor when she needed my assistance most."

A good childbirth class covers physical preparation for delivery, increases your knowledge of pregnancy, labor, delivery and the postpartum period, and teaches you how to care for the baby.

● **Physical Preparation**

You will practice the relaxation and breathing techniques to be used during labor and delivery. You will learn about comfort measures such as the most comfortable positions and giving back rubs. You will rehearse labor and delivery with simulated contractions and will practice efficient "pushing."

Childbirth education classes help prepare you for delivery.

● **Knowledge of Pregnancy, Labor, Delivery and the Postpartum Period**

Classes will cover personal care throughout pregnancy. There will be lessons on the anatomy and physiology of pregnancy, labor, delivery and the postpartum period. The stages of labor will be taught. Various types of labors and deliveries will be discussed. You will learn how to help yourself during labor and delivery. You will be introduced to hospital routines and the way to cooperate with the obstetrical team. The use of analgesics and anesthetics will be outlined in a fair amount of detail and the pros and cons of various medications will be presented. Classes generally show movies to illustrate actual labor and delivery. Finally, a thorough discussion of the postnatal adjustment period is provided.

Perhaps the most valuable contribution the classes make is to help women break the **fear-tension-pain cycle**, as described by Dr. Grantley Dick-Read. He found a way to break the cycle at any one of several points, thus creating the possibility of an enjoyable childbirth. By eliminating fear of childbirth (especially fear of the unknown), by teaching women how their bodies work in labor and why they feel the way they do, by reducing the tension in muscles and minds produced by that fear, by teaching relaxation techniques and by showing them how to work with rather than against their bodies in labor, he showed the obstetrical world that most women do not have to either suffer greatly or be drugged to give birth.

● **How to Care for the Baby**

Time is also spent learning about the baby in utero, the appearance of the newborn and the importance of gentle birthing, bonding, and rooming-in. A good deal of time is set aside to discuss integrating the baby into your family and coping with common difficulties. A great deal of emphasis is placed on the topic of breastfeeding.

A postnatal "show and tell" class is usually held a few weeks after the birth of your baby. The purpose is to share your birthing experience with other couples and to discuss problems you may have encountered in adjusting to and caring for your baby. Family planning is discussed and postnatal exercises are taught.

While preparing for the birth of your baby, read everything you can find. Take advantage of classes in nutrition and parenting. Mother-baby classes and groups for postpartum couples provide an excellent way to avoid the isolation one can feel with a new baby at home. They act as an extended family, providing the support, and "mothering the mother," so vital in those early weeks and months of the baby's life.

Recent Advances in Obstetrical Care

● *Technology in Perspective*

There has been a flurry of magazine articles which question the wisdom and safety of using new medical technology during childbirth. Expectant couples are understandably confused about the benefits and risks of "technological childbirth" and "natural childbirth." Their confidence in the obstetrician is often undermined. Confidence in your doctor and your hospital is absolutely necessary to fully enjoy your childbirth experience. However, consumer questioning of technology is vital to keep technology in perspective, especially in such an important human event as childbirth. If you read something contrary to your doctor's practices (e.g. medications, fetal monitoring), discuss your concerns directly with your obstetrician. A magazine article must generalize and sensationalize. Your obstetrician may have an alternative viewpoint based upon your individual obstetrical situation.

In approximately 10 per cent of deliveries, complications could arise which may result in an obstetrical experience different from what you were prepared for (e.g. prematurity, prolonged labor, fetal distress). The safety of the baby and often also of the mother may necessitate a departure from the ''natural way.''

Ultra sound is a recent technological advance which may help your obstetrician make certain medical judgments about alternative methods of delivery. Using sound waves, this device can provide valuable information about the fetus—the possibility of multiple births, fetal maturity and the health and location of the placenta.

If your obstetrician suspects that your baby may be in distress during labor, he may undertake **electronic fetal monitoring (EFM)**. EFM is a device which is attached to your abdomen over your uterus (external fetal monitoring) or directly to the baby's scalp by means of wires (internal fetal monitoring). This device monitors your baby's heart rate changes during labor. Certain heart rate patterns indicate that your baby might not be receiving enough oxygen. Based on the information provided by the EFM as well as your labor progress, your doctor may judge that your baby could be endangered if your labor is allowed to continue. He may elect to perform a **Caesarian section** in order to deliver your baby more rapidly.

The number of Caesarian sections has been increasing at a concerning rate and the procedure now accounts for 10 to 20 per cent of all deliveries. Valid reasons do exist for the increase. The Caesarian section is becoming a safer surgical procedure. In certain circumstances (e.g. a breech position), delivery by Caesarian section is safer for the baby than a vaginal delivery. Considering this, as well as the fact that a child's health is at a greater risk during childbirth than at any other time in his life, your obstetrician may decide that the stress of a vaginal delivery may jeopardize the baby's health. (See **Bonding the Caesarian Baby**, page 50 .) If your doctor suspects obstetrical complications, he must make a professional judgment about the safest delivery for both mother and baby. Your desire for a natural childbirth notwithstanding, this is the time it is absolutely necessary to trust your doctor's judgment.

Recently, regional referral centers for delivery of babies

whose mothers have a high risk of obstetrical problems have been established. These are called **Perinatal Centers** (''peri'' means around and ''natal'' means birth). These centers are staffed by obstetricians and perinologists (specialists in the care of ill newborns) and use the latest discoveries in obstetrical medicine to lower the risk of health problems to both mother and baby. Besides providing newborn intensive care units, these specialists treat mother and baby before delivery to lessen the severity of a potential problem after delivery. For example, proper management of a diabetic mother during the last eight weeks of pregnancy lowers the risk of an ill newborn. Prior to the establishment of these regional centers, an ill newborn had to be immediately transferred to an intensive care unit in a children's hospital. Sick newborns do not travel well. The aim now is to identify mothers who have a high risk of obstetrical problems and to refer them to the appropriate regional center for prenatal care and delivery.

The choice between natural or technological childbirth should not be an either/or decision. I feel that obstetrical care should be a blend of parental intuition and medical science. Neither the parents nor the baby should be deprived of either.

Parenting Your Unborn Child

Pregnancy — The Changing Person

Pregnancy is not only growing a baby. It is the time when you are growing into a mothering person, physically and emotionally.

The physical changes are obvious, but with each physical change, there are accompanying emotional changes due to the effects of the hormones of pregnancy. For example, your breasts develop in order to nourish your baby. The hormone **prolactin**, responsible for these breast changes, also causes a change in your personality. You feel more maternal.

Pregnancy may also be considered a developmental stage, much like adolescence. It is a time of identity crisis. You ask yourself ''I am going to be somebody's mother, but what will happen to the me I know now?'' You feel definite body image changes which may be experienced in a positive way as a pride in your pregnancy, a proof of fertility or a delight in nourishing another life within your own body. Or you may have negative feelings, a fear of miscarriage, a fear of becoming less attractive to your husband, ambivalence about leaving your present job or worry about your capabilities as a mother.

Pregnancy also changes marriage. The responsibilty of a child adds a certain maturity to the marital relationship. Pregnancy is a major commitment to the marriage. If your marriage is on shaky ground you may be particularly vulnerable to the usual labile emotions of pregnancy and so it is not likely that a baby will stabilize your marriage.

Pregnancy is a time for sincere communication between husband and wife, a time to share positive and negative feelings about the present and about future role changes. A lack of appreciation of the emotional and physical changes during pregnancy can mean the difference between regarding pregnancy as a richly rewarding experience and seeing it as the low point of the marriage.

In the early months, the many sudden changes of pregnancy bring about combined stresses, a situation which severely taxes an individual's ability to cope. Learning to cope can be a maturing factor, a positive force that prepares you to deal with the many stresses and adjustments of parenthood.

The second trimester, like middle childhood, is a quieter period. The fear of miscarriage subsides and the discomforts of morning sickness and fatigue have passed. Feeling your baby move, experiencing the reality of your baby as a separate being, is the highlight of these months. The father is able to place his hand upon your abdomen and feel life inside. You both can begin to form the attachment bond to your baby. This feeling usually enhances the father's acceptance of the emotional and physical stresses of pregnancy. This feeling of life together, your hand upon his hand, both hands upon baby, often triggers an increased dependency upon one another. The wife feels an increased dependence upon her husband as protector and provider; the husband depends upon his wife to nourish the life within her.

By the sixth month, your pregnancy begins to show obviously and the status of pregnancy begins to reap social rewards. Be it a helpful arm or a seat on a bus, pregnancy guarantees you a "May I help you?" Despite the radiant glow many pregnant women show, you may not feel so radiant. In the third trimester, many women need constant reassurance from their husbands that they love them in this "state." Special attention to good grooming also aids your self-image at this stage.

Sexuality changes during pregnancy. Your sexual desires may go up and down because of the tremendous changes in the physical characteristics of the sexual organs and the fluctuations in hormone levels. Toward the end of pregnancy, most women experience diminished sexual desires due to the combination of feeling awkward as a sexual partner and a fear of inducing premature labor. Pregnancy itself may fulfill the sexual needs of some women. Near term, you may become increasingly aware of your husband's sexual needs and also of your inability to satisfy them. Inventiveness and sensitivity to each others' moods is most useful at this time. In the final month, anticipation runs high. Insomnia is common. Many women leave their jobs, although some keep right on working until the last minute to avoid the anxiety of anticipation. Ideally, the final months of pregnancy should be a time of peace and quiet, a time to relax, slow down and begin mothering your unborn child. This can be an early attachment stage vital to the continuum of parenting. A mother may begin to tune in to the child inside her and begin to experience her unborn child as a person within the family.

In the final weeks, you may experience a "nesting instinct," a sudden burst of energy to clean the house, to prepare the nursery and to have everything just right for your baby. This instinct is probably due to the same hormones which will enhance your mothering instinct after birth. Just be careful not to overdo it and wear yourself out. Laboring in an exhausted state is not an advantage. (Father feelings during pregnancy are discussed on page 85 .)

Nutrition During Pregnancy

Feeding your baby really begins before birth. Good prenatal nutrition, or the lack of it, has a profound effect on the development of your fetus.

Weight of baby	**7½ lbs.**
Weight of placenta	**1½ lbs.**
Weight of uterus	**3½ lbs.**
Weight of amniotic fluid	**2½ lbs.**
Weight of breasts	**1 lb.**
Weight of extra blood volume and extra fluids	**8½ lbs.**

How much weight should you gain during your pregnancy?

Up until the past few years, strict limits were placed on weight gain. Not looking pregnant was the fashion. Now we know the normal weight gain during your pregnancy should be around 24 pounds (22-27 pounds, 10-12 kg), which breaks down as shown on page 43.

A weight gain of 3 pounds during the first trimester followed by gains of 3.5 pounds per month is acceptable. If you are underweight to begin with then you may actually show an even larger weight gain, adding catch-up pounds early in your pregnancy. This is nature's message to you that you need more nutrition. What you eat is more important than how much you eat. The main extra nutritional requirements for all growing persons (in this case, mother and fetus) are proteins (75-100 gm/day), vitamins and iron. Each day you should eat the following: 2 eggs; 1 serving of fish, liver, lean beef or chicken (6-8 oz/170-227g); salad of fresh green leafy vegetables; 1 quart (1 litre) or more of milk (whole or skim, according to your liking and tolerance of milk); 1 serving of cheese or yogurt (more if milk is omitted from your diet); whole grain cereal; serving of yellow vegetables; citrus fruits or fruit juice. You should eat liver at least once a week and a whole baked potato every other day. It is very unlikely that you will put on too much weight by overindulging in the above foods. Most excessive weight gain during pregnancy is due to eating the wrong kinds of food. Avoid "junk food," excess salt, skipping meals and crash diets during your pregnancy. Your appetite and diet should parallel your pregnancy. During the last three months of pregnancy, you may be consuming an extra 500 nutritious calories a day without abnormal weight gain. Pregnant women are subject to certain cravings (e.g., pickles, ice cream, pizza), many of which are not high-protein nutritious foods. While you deserve to pamper an occasional craving, it is wise not to over-indulge constantly. If you are feeling well, eating properly, and do not have any physical evidence of abnormal water retention then a restriction on your weight gain is not usually necessary.

Bad Habits During Pregnancy

Chemicals which cause defects in your fetus are called **teratogens**. While there are only a handful of drugs which are proven to be teratogenic, our knowledge of the possible teratogenic effects of some drugs is incomplete. We know that a certain level of a specific teratogen such as alcohol (see below) can cause certain malformations. What we do not know is the minimum amount of a potential teratogen that may be taken without causing any harm to the fetus. In other words, if a lot of teratogen harms the fetus a lot, will a little harm the fetus only a little, and a very small amount not harm the fetus at all? The reason for our lack of knowledge of this "threshold effect" is that very low levels of a teratogen may cause very subtle malformations which may be difficult to identify.

For this reason, mothers should rely on common sense. When you take a drug, your fetus also takes a drug. Because the fetus is a rapidly developing organism with limited capabilities to get rid of a drug, the effect of the drug on your fetus may differ from its effect on you. An example of this type of drug is marijuana. At this writing, there are no known detrimental effects of marijuana on the fetus. We do know, however, that marijuana can damage brain cells and reproductive cells in experimental animals. Common sense should indicate that it would be a foolish risk to smoke marijuana during pregnancy.

● **Drugs**

Most drugs cross the placenta and therefore may enter your fetus. The basic problem is that most potentially harmful drugs taken during pregnancy are taken in the first month, before a woman knows she is pregnant. This is the time of highest risk to the fetus. Before you take an over-the-counter medication for supposed "flu" symptoms, consider whether your symptoms could be due to pregnancy. Even over-the-counter remedies (such as aspirin and nasal sprays) should not be taken without first consulting your physician. Addictive drugs such as heroin have been proven harmful to the fetus and should not be taken. Unless directed by your physician, refrain from taking any drug (stimulants, depressants, etc.) which alters your bodily functions to an unnatural state.

● **Smoking**

Smoking is detrimental to your baby's growth and health. This is a fact. **Don't smoke during pregnancy!** There is no compromise. Nicotine decreases the blood supply to the placenta and, therefore, to your baby. The risk of prematurity and diminished fetal and brain growth increases in proportion to the number of cigarettes you smoke each day. The effect on your "nerves" of giving up smoking during pregnancy will be much less than the effect on your nerves if you have an ill newborn.

● **Alcohol**

In the past few years, a condition called **fetal alcohol syndrome** has been recognized. In the early 1900s, physicians observed that an increased incidence of malformations occurred in babies

NO SMOKING

NO DRINKING

FETAL GROWTH
IN PROGRESS!

born nine months after certain European wine festivals. It was not until recently, however, that alcohol was recognized as one of the most widely used drugs as well as one of the most potentially harmful that could be taken during pregnancy. A broad spectrum of abnormalities results from the fetal alcohol syndrome, including diminished fetal growth, unusual facial features and mental retardation. Nearly every organ in the body may be affected by alcohol in the fetal blood and the greater the alcohol consumption the greater the severity of fetal malformations.

How much alcohol can you safely drink without damaging your fetus? As we discussed above, the answer to the "threshold effect" of many teratogens — alcohol is one — is not known. We do know, however, that five or more drinks on one occasion (binge drinking) or an average of two drinks per day throughout pregnancy can harm your fetus. The term drink is defined as one ounce of alcohol, which means one ounce of whiskey, one 12-ounce glass of beer or one 8-ounce glass of wine.

Unfortunately, many heavy drinkers are also heavy smokers, a combination which can be disastrous for the fetus. It is interesting that many mothers lose their desire for alcohol during pregnancy and reduce consumption by 50 to 90 per cent. This is also often accompanied by a natural aversion to cigarettes and caffeine, possibly a few of nature's own protective messages. It seems wise therefore to avoid any alcohol consumption during your pregnancy.

● **Caffeine**

At this writing there is no evidence that caffeine is harmful to the human fetus. But caffeine given to experimental animals may result in malformations in the fetuses. Until the caffeine question is settled, the Federal Drug Administration advises that, as a precautionary measure, pregnant women eliminate or limit their consumption of products containing caffeine, which in order of highest content of caffeine are: coffee, cola, tea, and chocolate. Some over-the-counter remedies also contain caffeine.

Entering the Hospital for Delivery

The time arrives for both of you to enter the hospital. You have taken prepared childbirth classes. You have previewed the hospital several months earlier and you are familiar with its routine. At this point, you realize how being a prepared parent has considerably lessened the anxiety of childbirth.

Upon entering the maternity ward, it is a good idea to introduce yourself to the head nurse or the nurse who will be assigned to you during your hospital stay. Let her know your degree of preparation, your anxieties and, above all, your specific needs. Be very explicit about what you hope to get out of your hospital stay. This frank and open dialogue with the nurse paves the way for better postpartum communication. The degree of preparation, the level of maternal anxieties and the nature of specific needs are so variable that many nurses are probably confused about their role in your childbirth. It is much easier for your nurse to help you if you make your needs known to her beforehand.

Moment of Birth — Parent-Infant Bonding

Healthy mothers and babies should be together from the time of birth until they are discharged from the hospital.

Many researchers are studying the importance of early parent-infant attachment, a process called **bonding**. I sincerely hope you put this concept into practice at the moment of your baby's birth. You have formed a bond with your baby probably from the first moment you found out you were pregnant, or certainly from when you first felt life. The intensity of this bond reaches its climax at birth and should not be interrupted unless overwhelming medical complications prevail. This early attachment at birth enables you to transfer your life-giving love for the

47

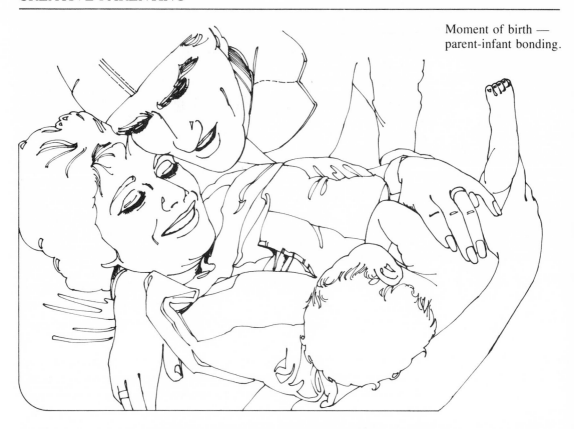

Moment of birth —
parent-infant bonding.

"inside infant" to the care-giving love for the "outside infant." Inside, you gave him your blood; outside you give him your milk, your eyes, your touch, your warmth and your voice. This family continuum should not be interrupted by trivial hospital routine or diluted by depressing medications.

Recent studies have shown that newborn babies are much more receptive than they were formerly thought to be. For approximately an hour after birth, your baby is in a state of "quiet alertness," and it is in this state that he is most receptive to parental input stimuli. In this early sensitive period, your newborn is ideally prepared for his first communication with you. Neither you nor your newborn should be deprived of this opportunity.

How does early attachment benefit your baby and yourself? Drs. Klaus and Kennell, notable researchers in the field, compared a group of parents who cared for their babies immediately after delivery to a group whose babies were temporarily separated from them and cared for according to nursery routines. The early-contact group was more successful at breastfeeding, spent more time in the face-to-face position of visual contact, and had more father involvement at a later stage. The early-contact babies cried less and laughed more. A follow-up study suggested that early-contact infants enjoyed a greater continued maternal-infant attachment and had more advanced language and learning scores. The researchers postulated that there is a sensitive period in the first hour after birth which is best for parent-infant attachment and that these early attachments may have long-lasting effects on parent-child relationships. Mothers who have been separated from infants during this early-contact period are less confident in exercising their intuitive mothering.

What about the baby who for some reason, such as prematurity, Caesarian delivery, or adoption, is temporarily separated from his mother? Is the baby permanently affected by loss of this early contact or can you make up for what he has missed? In other words, is delayed bonding possible? The answer to this question is not known for each individual infant but, in consolation to mothers who have, of necessity, been temporarily separated from their babies, I suspect that as soon as mothers and babies are reunited, a strong and sustained mother-infant attachment can adequately compensate for the loss of this early contact. Immediate bonding is not like glue which cements a mother-infant relationship forever. There are many steps which must be taken before a strong mother-infant attachment is achieved. Immediate bonding during this biologically sensitive period gives this attachment a head start. However, I have seen adopting parents who, upon first contact with their one-week-old newborn, release feelings as deep and as caring as those of a biological mother.

Bonding the Premature Baby

Newborn intensive care units have improved the quantity and quality of survival of sick and premature babies. Nonetheless, an unfortunate consequence of these units is the separation of sick newborns from their mothers during a very sensitive period. This separation often results in certain "diseases of non-attachment" in the mother which you should guard yourself against if this situation arises.

The mother who delivers a premature baby is deprived of the pregnancy feelings of preparedness and nesting that occur late in the third trimester (see **Pregnancy Feelings**, page 41 .) Instead of showering a mother with congratulations for delivering a full-term, healthy baby, the focus of attention is shifted from the mother to the baby. What is usually a joyous event becomes a crisis situation. You may experience a feeling of failure for being unable to carry the baby to term. If your newborn is very premature or very sick, you may doubt your baby's survival. To prepare yourself for the possibility of his death, you may detach yourself from your baby. What should be a period of attachment becomes a period of detachment. What should be a period of joy becomes a period of grieving. Follow-up studies of graduates of newborn intensive care units have indicated that some of these babies show features of ineffective mothering — poor weight gain, child abuse, being treated as fragile (the vulnerable child syndrome). Most of these disorders of mothering result from separating the mother and her newborn at a sensitive time.

Involvement in your baby's care is the key to soothing the pain of separation. The advantage of delivering your baby in a hospital which also has a newborn intensive care unit is that you can still have a bonding relationship with your newborn. This is not possible if your baby must be transferred to another hospital and you and your baby are no longer within touching and seeing distance of each other. (See **Regional Perinatal Centers**, page 41 .) In our perinatal center in Toronto, mothers and fathers were encouraged to participate in the care of their sick newborn as soon as possible. I encouraged mothers to sit "incubator side," stroke and caress their babies, attempt some eye-to-eye contact and talk to their babies. Infections did not increase in these "touched" babies. Parents are neither unclean nor inept. In fact, prematures who were stroked by their mothers had fewer "stop-breathing" episodes and thrived better. You are the most important person in the care of your sick newborn. Technology can never replace you. Mothers who took an active part in the hospital care of their premature baby became more effective mothers at home. (See **Breastfeeding Your Premature Baby**, page 118 .)

Bonding the Caesarian Baby

Some adjustments in the usual bonding process must be made for babies delivered by Caesarian section. Although Caesarian section is a surgical procedure, it is primarily a birth. Both the safety of the surgical event and the dignity of the birthing event should be respected. If you are having an elective Caesarian section (usually a repeat Caesarian section), discuss with your obstetrician prior to your delivery the options in anesthesia which may allow you to touch, feed, and see your baby soon after delivery. Many mothers experience a great deal of pain and fatigue after a

Caesarian section. I feel that the best "pain reliever" is an "injection" of your baby in your arms. The presence of fathers in the delivery room during a Caesarian birth is currently not allowed in most hospitals but, like father-presence at a vaginal birth, this is gradually being permitted. It is a beautiful sight to see your newborn lifted "up and out" during a Caesarian birth. If for some medical reason a healthy Caesarian section baby cannot be placed in the arms of his mother soon after delivery, **father bonding** should be encouraged.

How to Get the Most Out of Your Bonding Relationship

A positive childbirth experience seems to foster maternal bonding while a negative birth experience, in which fear and pain predominate, may adversely affect a mother's feelings toward bonding with her newborn. Prepared childbirth classes and a supporting father help to reduce many of the factors which contribute to a negative birth experience and therefore indirectly promote a positive bonding experience. It has also recently been noted that many of the sedatives and pain-lessening medications which are given to mothers during labor reduce both the mother's and the baby's receptiveness to the bonding experience. Mothers who have attended prepared childbirth classes usually require fewer (or no) drugs during labor.

When entering the world, infants have a limited motor system but have a very advanced sensory system. The following sensory stimuli will help to get the most out of your bonding relationship:

1. Touch your baby. Gently stroke your baby in a circular motion using your whole hand, beginning with the back and covering the entire body. The skin is the largest organ of the human body and its stimulation, or lack of it, can have a profound effect on your infant's behavior. Infants are best given completely nude to the mothers, thereby allowing complete body-touching.

2. Look at your baby in the en face position, the position in which your face is rotated so that your eyes and those of your baby meet in the same vertical plane. Your newborn can see you best within a distance of twelve inches. The feedback both of you receive by staring at each other is richly rewarding. One of the most popular scenes of Renaissance art is that of a mother suckling her newborn infant. This breastfeeding position lends itself beautifully to the en face relationship.

3. Talk to your newborn. Mothers tend naturally to speak to their newborn babies in a high-pitched voice. The newborn's auditory mechanism is naturally attuned to perceive speech at a pitch of high frequency and you may notice that your baby moves rhythmically in response to the rhythm of your voice.

4. Nurse your baby right after delivery. The sucking reflex is strongest in the first hour after birth. Put your baby immediately to your breast, touch his cheek with your nipple and notice his natural reflex to lick your nipple. Your baby is physiologically prepared for this early licking and sucking action. Licking and sucking on the nipple releases a hormone called **oxytocin** into your bloodstream, which increases uterine contraction and lessens the complication of postpartum bleeding. This early sucking also stimulates secretion of the milk-producing hormone, **prolactin**. Many researchers feel that the increase in these maternal hormones (love hormones), stimulated by early infant feeding, also enhances a mother's close feeling of attachment to the baby during the sensitive period the first few hours after birth.

One of the old objections to early infant-mother attachment in the delivery room is "baby may get cold." So, let's analyze this objection. Much heat is lost from the human body via radiation from the major abdominal organs (viscera) through the abdominal wall. The viscera are relatively large and close to the surface of the abdominal wall in newborns, thus allowing for easy heat loss. When a newborn baby is given to his mother immediately after birth, there is a natural tendency to place the baby skin-to-skin, abdomen-to-abdomen, that is, his abdominal wall touches the mother's abdominal wall, her arms are wrapped around his back and his head is nestled on her breast. This body surface contact is a great source of radiant heat for the baby and minimizes the baby's heat loss. Mother's lactating breasts are sources of heat which are certainly much more pleasant than, and just as effective as, the plastic box incubator. Recent studies have suggested that babies who are bonded immediately and continuously after birth show an earlier stabilization of temperature and breathing patterns than non-bonded babies.

See, touch, talk to, warm and feed your baby during this mutually sensitive period and you will find that you have begun to cement a beautiful maternal-infant bond.

The Postpartum Period in the Hospital

Hospital postpartum care depends on many factors: Whether this is your first baby; the extent of medical complications, if any; your own feelings of inadequacy or competence as a new mother; and financial considerations. The length of the hospital stay may vary from a few hours to a week, although currently it seems to be around three days. A custom which seems to be gaining in popularity is that of early discharge from the hospital, sometimes within a few hours after delivery. This so-called take-out delivery certainly requires that both mother and baby be entirely well, and that adequate facilities and help for the mother and baby are present in the home. The trend toward family-oriented maternity care may lessen this desire for early discharge.

Fathers, your role in the moment of birth and the postpartum rooming-in period is extremely important. You will find that early and extended contact with your baby in the hospital will release feelings of intense interest in your newborn, and pave the way for the development of a strong father-child relationship later on. You may find that your wife experiences a sudden increased dependency upon you. Offer her emotional support and encouragement during this sensitive time.

Mothers, you may find that during your early postpartum period you will be extremely sensitive. Trivial problems and inconveniences may seem like mammoth barriers to overcome. What causes these anxieties? You are probably questioning your adequacy as a new mother. You are often tired and your body is undergoing intense biological changes. The support and encouragement of your husband and the attending hospital staff will help you overcome these feelings. (See **Postpartum Depression,** page 73 .)

Rooming-In—The Natural Extension of the Bonding Experience

How you and your baby spend your postpartum period in the hospital depends basically on one question which you should ask yourself prior to delivery: Who will be the primary care-giver of my baby in the hospital — me or the hospital staff? If you elect to be the primary care-giver of your newborn infant then **rooming-in** is certainly for you. Rooming-in allows you to feed, clothe, change, warm, stimulate and interact with your baby. The hospital staff in the newborn nursery assume the role of secondary care-giver. They should advise but not take over. The other method of hospital care is to let the hospital staff assume the role of primary care-giver. Your baby will be brought to you at specified times, usually every three to four hours, or as you desire.

Which one of these alternatives is "best"? There is no doubt in my mind that the rooming-in method is best for your baby and, indirectly, for you. For personal or medical reasons, however, you may elect to modify the degree of rooming-in.

What are the advantages of rooming-in for you and your baby? Rooming-in is the primary key to successful

Rooming-in — The
natural extension of
the bonding experi-
ence.

breastfeeding. (We will talk more about this in the chapter on breastfeeding.) Rooming-in is the natural extension of the bonding period. It is the smooth transition from mother's womb to mother's room. In many species of animals, newborns acquire a permanent biological attachment to their first care-giver, a process called **imprinting**. Perhaps this imprinting is present to some degree in human newborns.

If this is your first baby then this first postpartum period is your first time together as a family; therefore, it should be enjoyed to its fullest. The constant presence of your baby allows you to become attuned to his needs. It allows the fullest expression of intuitive motherhood, uncluttered by any other responsibility. Rooming-in seems to be the best of both worlds. It allows you complete privacy but still affords you the luxury of attending medical personnel should the need arise. Rooming-in mothers actually seem to get more rest since they experience less separation anxiety, and most newborns spend most of their time simply eating and sleeping anyway. Your newborn will seem more content with the rooming-in arrangement because he interacts with only one care-giver, you. Rooming-in babies seem less confused than babies in the regular nursery who interact with several different care-givers and are cared for according to the nursery routine rather than their individual needs. Newborn infants who room-in cry less, and more readily organize their cycles of sleep and awakening than infants cared for by multiple care-givers according to nursery routines. A mother once related to me her feelings about having her baby with her: "My baby seemed so serene. She had never been held by someone who didn't love her." The rooming-in arrangement makes you feel your baby is truly your own. The peace and privacy allows you to respond intuitively to your newborn's cues. I have noticed that mothers who have roomed-in leave the hospital much more comfortable and much more confident about their own maternal intuition. They have less postpartum depression and fewer feeding problems. (And, incidentally, I receive fewer phone calls for advice from these mothers.)

If your baby could choose his hospital accommodations would he choose a plastic box in an impersonal nursery or, as anthropologist Ashly Montague states, would he choose "a womb with a view?"

Sibling Visits to the Hospital

Sibling visits should be encouraged in all hospital maternity units. When parents go to the hospital, there is a temporary disruption of the parent-child bond at home. By encouraging sibling visits, other children are included in the birth event and feel less abandoned. Encourage them to jump on the "bond wagon" with the new member of the family. (See **Sibling Rivalry**, page 272 for a discussion on preparation for the arrival of a new baby.)

Routine Hospital Procedures

Apgar Scoring

Immediately after delivery in most hospitals, there follows a procedure which reminds our little newborn that he is born into a quantitative world where humans are measured and scored from the moment of birth through their educational and employment years. The procedure is called the **Apgar Score**, developed by

Dr. Virginia Apgar nearly thirty years ago as a measure of the general health of newborn babies. The score, performed at one and five minutes after birth, is based on your newborn's heart rate, breathing pattern, color, muscle tone and activity. He gets from 0 to 2 "points" for each of these. Hospitals often tell parents the Apgar score and therefore I feel it is necessary to make some comments about the meaning of the number which may be attached to your baby.

APGAR RATING SYSTEM

Sign	Score		
	0	**1**	**2**
Color	blue, pale	body pink, limbs blue	completely pink
Respiratory effort	absent	slow, irregular, weak cry	strong cry
Heart rate	absent	slow, less than 100	over 100
Muscle tone	limp	some flexion of limbs	active movement
Reflex response to flicking foot	absent	facial grimace	cry

I find it curious that when I ask mothers to tell me what they feel was important concerning their baby's birth and delivery, many will often mention: "He scored 9 or he scored 8." The Apgar score is a scale of 0 to 10. Infants who are pink all over, have strong movements, cry lustily, breathe rapidly and have a rapid heartbeat are usually given a 10. In reality, most normal, healthy newborns do not achieve a score of 10 since it is quite usual for their hands and feet to be somewhat blue. It often takes a few minutes for the newborn's circulatory system to become adjusted to his postnatal environment. Your baby may be somewhat quiet immediately after birth and "lose points." In fact, the state of "quiet alertness" is more desirable than crying, although this would not be reflected in the Apgar score. A baby who scores 10, therefore, is not necessarily healthier than a baby who scores 7 or 8. The Apgar score is also only valid if it is done by a medical person trained in Apgar scoring who uses an accurate 1- and

5-minute clock and whose only function in the delivery suite is to do an Apgar score. Accurate, careful scoring is usually done in a university hospital for research. It is therefore likely that the usual Apgar score given to parents in a routine delivery of an apparently normal healthy baby has very little predictive value. A low score certainly should not be a source of anxiety, but it alerts the attending medical personnel to observe the baby more carefully for circulatory or respiratory problems over the next few hours.

Routine Injections and Medications

Immediately after birth, an injection of Vitamin K is given because most newborns are deficient in this vitamin, which enables normal blood clotting.

It is also customary to administer silver nitrate to both eyes in order to prevent infection of the newborn's cornea, which may result from a vaginal infection in the mother. In some hospitals, silver nitrate is being replaced with a milder, equally effective ointment.

These procedures are necessary to ensure the proper health of your newborn baby. However, in the light of current knowledge concerning the importance of the first hour after birth in the bonding process, I strongly recommend that these procedures be delayed until after mother, father and baby have had their initial visit.

Jaundice

Most newborns develop some degree of jaundice (yellow color of the skin and eyeballs). Jaundice is caused by the build-up in the blood of a yellow pigment called **bilirubin**, and the deposit of the excess bilirubin in the skin. Everyone normally produces some bilirubin from the breakdown of old worn-out red blood cells (newborns produce more bilirubin because they need fewer red blood cells than they needed in utero). This bilirubin is usually disposed of by our livers, and therefore does not usually reach levels high enough to "yellow" the skin. If too many red blood cells are broken down too fast or if the liver is unable to remove the bilirubin from the blood, the visual appearance of jaundice results.

Newborns are susceptible to two types of jaundice — normal and abnormal jaundice. I use the term "normal" jaundice (also called physiologic or ideopathic jaundice) because many babies have some degree of jaundice for no apparent reason. "Normal" jaundice is thought to be due to temporary immaturity of the liver. Within a few days, the liver matures and begins disposing of the excess bilirubin. Your pediatrician will tell you whether your baby's jaundice is normal. If he feels it is, he will tell you not to worry. Normal jaundice is the source of much unnecessary anxiety at a time when a new mother is very vulnerable to any suggestion that her baby might be abnormal. It is important that the attending medical personnel not present this normal jaundice as a medical illness to the mother. Mothers should understand that there is virtually never any reason to stop breastfeeding a baby if he has this normal type of jaundice.

An insufficient intake of calories can aggravate newborn jaundice. Mothers who begin breastfeeding on early demand, produce milk earlier. Consequently, their babies usually develop jaundice less frequently. (See **Getting the Right Start,** page 102 .)

A very rare and abnormal type of jaundice which is prolonged by breastfeeding does exist and it is this rare **breastmilk jaundice** that has caused some hospitals to advise mothers to stop breastfeeding until the jaundice disappears. In 99 per cent of jaundiced, but otherwise healthy, babies there is absolutely no medical reason to stop breastfeeding even temporarily, nor is there usually any medical reason to separate mother and baby.

The other type of abnormal newborn jaundice usually occurs within the first twenty-four hours after birth and is usually caused by a difference in your blood type or RH factor and your baby's. This causes the breakdown of more red blood cells than your baby's liver can handle, and the bilirubin builds up more quickly in his blood. Because this type of excess bilirubin can cause brain damage if allowed to rise too high, this type of jaundice is much more serious and appropriate medical treatment is usually administered right away. Treatment may consist of frequently testing his blood to monitor the level of bilirubin, or placing him under a **bilirubin light** which helps dissolve the bilirubin pigment in the skin and allows it to be excreted in his urine. In extreme cases, such as an RH incompatibility, an exchange transfusion may be necessary. But even in the case of the abnormal type of jaundice, after appropriate medical treatment has been administered, there is no reason you cannot breastfeed.

Other types of jaundice, as well as jaundice in premature babies, are special situations which will be explained to you by your pediatrician should they occur. In any case of newborn jaundice, it is very important that both the anxiety level in the mother and the bilirubin level in the baby be adequately diagnosed and treated.

PKU Testing

Phenylketonuria (PKU) is an extremely rare metabolic disorder occurring in approximately 1 out of 15,000 infants. If diagnosed shortly after birth, it can often be treated with a special diet but, if left untreated, it can result in brain damage. This test requires only a few drops of blood and is usually done just prior to discharge. I first became aware of the parental anxiety produced by this procedure when new parents brought their baby into my office one day when the baby was only several days old. They were upset that their baby had missed his "mental retardation test" because they had left the hospital the day after delivery, when it was too early to perform the test. This case illustrates the importance of properly explaining hospital procedures to parents. A simple statement by hospital personnel about the rarity of this condition and the fact that the blood test is required by most state laws would usually alleviate anxiety.

Thyroid Testing

Along with the PKU test, a drop of your baby's blood is analyzed for sufficient thyroid hormones. Congenital hypothyroidism, which may cause retardation if untreated, occurs in 1 out of 5,000 infants. The earlier this disease is detected, the more effective is the treatment.

The Circumcision Question

Circumcision is the surgical removal of the foreskin, the skin which covers the head of the penis. This is probably the oldest operation, dating back to Biblical times when it was (and still is) a ritual custom in some religions. Until the past few years, circumcision was considered routine and therefore most infant males were circumcised shortly after birth. As with so many other "routine" procedures in life, parents have recently begun to ask "Is circumcision really necessary for my infant?" This very wise and long overdue parental questioning has forced pediatricians to find good answers about whether the foreskin should stay or go.

The ancient custom of circumcising males probably began as preventive hygiene. Because of desert living, poor sanitation and the lack of medical care, it became customary to remove the foreskin to avoid the risk of infection of the secretions which accumulate underneath the foreskin. The question now is, "If the living conditions which prompted the custom of circumcision no longer exist, should circumcision still be performed?"

The American Academy of Pediatrics advises that routine circumcision is an unnecessary procedure. Since many parents ask their pediatricians to help them make a decision, I will present some considerations which may help you decide the fate of your son's foreskin. The following is not intended for parents for whom circumcision is a religious custom. Ritual circumcisions are performed with dignity.

● **Does circumcision make hygiene easier?**

The foreskin secretes a fluid called **smegma** (also secreted by girls). These secretions may accumulate beneath the foreskin and become irritating. Infection sometimes occurs. Removing the foreskin removes the secretions and makes care of the penis easier. What happens if the foreskin is left intact? At birth, almost all boys have a tight foreskin. It is impossible at birth to make a judgment about how tight the foreskin will remain. By one year of age, the foreskin loosens from the head of the penis and retracts completely in around 50 per cent of boys. By three years of age, 90 per cent have fully retractable foreskins. Once the foreskin retracts easily, it becomes a normal part of male hygiene to pull back the foreskin and cleanse beneath it during a bath. While it is true that infections of the secretions beneath the foreskin are more often a problem in uncircumcised males, simple hygiene can prevent this problem.

● **If the foreskin does not retract naturally, will he need a circumcision later on?**

Occasionally the foreskin does not retract. It sometimes becomes tight and obstructs the flow of urine, a condition called **phimosis.** In this case, circumcision is necessary. If circumcision for phimosis later in childhood or adulthood is necessary, the boy is involved in the decision process and anesthesia is given.

● **I don't want him to feel different.**

This should not be a reason for circumcision. The modern teenager has a much more mature outlook about individual differences than we give him credit for. Also, the number of circumcised boys has been steadily declining in recent years.

● **I want him to be like his father.**

In past generations, no one thought to question routine circumcision. Now is the time in your family continuum to ask why.

● **Doctor, how is the circumcision performed?**

The baby is placed on a restraining board and his hands and feet are secured with straps. The adhesions between the foreskin and the penis are separated. The foreskin is held in place by clamps while a cut is made into the foreskin to about one-third of its length. A metal bell is placed over the head of the penis and the foreskin is pulled up over the bell and cut circumferentially.

About one-third of the skin of the penis (called the foreskin) is removed.

● **Is circumcision a safe procedure? Does it hurt?**

Usually circumcision is a very safe surgical procedure. However, as with any surgical procedure, there are occasional problems such as bleeding, injury to the shaft of the penis, or infection of the circumcision site. Yes, it does hurt! If the skin is clamped and cut, of course it hurts. My experience has been that after the initial crying during the procedure, babies often fall into a deep sleep, as if withdrawing from a traumatic situation.

● **Do circumcised boys experience any particular problem?**

The foreskin acts as a protective covering of the head of the penis. Removal of this foreskin allows the head of the penis to come into contact with ammonia in the diapers. Sometimes this irritation causes sores on the tip of the penis which may cause pain and obstruction of urine.

● **What about cancer prevention?**

There is currently no convincing medical evidence that cancer of the penis in an uncircumcised male who practices proper hygiene is more frequent than in a circumcised male. Nor has it been proven that cancer of the cervix in the sexual partners of uncircumcised males who practice proper hygiene is more frequent.

● **How do I care for the foreskin?**

Unless your doctor advises otherwise, simply leave it alone until the foreskin begins to retract easily. Do not force the foreskin to retract. This may break the seal between the foreskin and the penis and allow the secretions to accumulate beneath the foreskin. As the foreskin retracts naturally (this may take one to two years), simply wash out the secretions beneath the foreskin. The older child should learn this hygiene as part of his bath-time routine.

The main purpose of the above discussion is not to state an opinion for or against circumcision, but rather to present some facts upon which you can base your decision. Discuss your views with your pediatrician. I advise you to consider circumcision as you would any other surgical procedure for your child.

Your Baby's First Check-Up

It is customary in most hospitals for a pediatrician to examine a baby shortly after birth. So that you appreciate what your doctor is looking for when he examines your baby, I will outline a typical head-to-toe examination of a normal newborn baby.

Your pediatrician forms an opinion about your baby's general health simply by looking at him. Is he alert, active, pink and breathing normally? Does he show signs of being premature, full-term or post-mature?

Next, the doctor examines your newborn's head for any excessive molding, skull fractures or bleeding within the scalp. Are the soft spots, the fontanelles, soft and flat? Your baby's head circumference is then measured and compared to his length, weight and maturity. Is his head proportionally large or small, or of normal size? Do the baby's eyes show the normal momentary contact with the examiner's eyes? There may be a few ruptured blood vessels in the whites of his eyes. These will clear up quickly. When the doctor shines a light into your baby's eyes, do the insides of his eyes look normal? Is his nose formed correctly? Can your baby pass air normally through both nostrils? When your doctor looks into your baby's mouth, he checks to see that the palate is fully formed. Are his ears properly formed? Are the ear canals open and do the eardrums appear normal? There may be a few areas of bleeding or purplish discoloration on the earlobes and cheeks from the delivery. This is normal and soon goes away.

Is his neck all right? Does his thyroid gland (in the middle of the neck in front of the windpipe) appear too large?

Your doctor also feels your baby's collarbones to be sure they were not broken during the squeeze of delivery.

He next listens to your baby's heart and records how fast it is beating. Are there any extra heart sounds (called **murmers**), caused by the blood flowing through the heart in a different way, giving a clue that the heart might not be structured properly? The doctor then listens to your baby's lungs to be sure that air is going in and out properly. He can tell much about the general health of your baby's heart and lungs by noticing your baby's breathing patterns.

The abdomen is next on the agenda. Your doctor gently massages the baby's abdominal muscles to relax them so that he can feel the liver, spleen and kidneys. In this way he can determine if they are too large or in the wrong position. Are there any unusual cysts or extra growths within the abdomen? Does the umbilicus seem clean? Is it healing normally? Next, he examines the genitalia. Are they clearly male or female? If your baby is a boy, are his testes descended? There is usually a large amount of water in the scrotal sac, giving the newborn's testicles a swollen appearance. Is the opening in his penis correctly formed or is it off-center? Sometimes, if the opening of the penis is too much off-center (called **hypospadias**), he should not be circumcised in case an operation is later necessary. If a girl, is the vaginal opening normal? There is normally some whitish and blood-tinged vaginal discharge, representing a sort of menstrual period left over from the maternal hormones around the time of birth. Next, your baby's anus is examined to be sure that it is in the proper position and open. Your doctor may check with the nurses at this point to be sure your baby has passed stools through the rectum and anus by this time.

Your baby's hips are examined to be sure that the leg bones do not slip out of the hip sockets, a condition called **dislocatable hips**. This condition is very easy to diagnose and treat in the newborn period but becomes increasingly difficult thereafter. While examining the hips, your doctor may feel femoral arteries, the large vessels running through the center of the groin to the legs. The strength of the pulsation of these large arteries gives a clue about any obstruction to blood flow in the major artery coming out of the heart. Are his legs and feet properly formed? A slight amount of inward bowing of the lower legs and feet is normal due to the squatting position in utero. His normal incurved feet should be easily stretched back to the center and the ankles should show free motion. If the front of the foot shows a fixed inward curvature and the ankle does not move easily, a condition called **clubfoot** may be present. Toes are a familial curiosity. Webbed-like, over-lapping, unusually-sized toes are common familial traits.

Usually by the time your doctor has gone through this head-to-toe examination, he also has a general impression of your baby's neurological development. Is he alert, moving all extremities well, opening and closing his hands normally, showing the usual newborn reflexes (see page 69) and good muscle tone? There are many other minor things your doctor will check during the course of your newborn's exam.

In addition to checking for any physical abnormalities, your baby's doctor reviews the birth events to see if any problem occurred which may require special attention later on (e.g. the baby turned temporarily blue and required oxygen post-delivery). He also checks your baby's blood type to see if any potential incompatibility exists between mother's and baby's blood. After your pediatrician has checked your baby and the birth records, he will either tell you that your baby is perfectly normal or he will discuss any medical problems he may have detected.

This newborn examination has a special meaning to the

doctor. It is the first in a long series of "check-ups." I have always felt that the newborn examination is the first meeting of what should be a long and meaningful friendship between doctor and patient so, if possible, keep the same doctor who initially examines your baby in the hospital.

CHAPTER II

THE AMAZING NEWBORN

Enjoyment of your new baby is enhanced by a thorough knowledge of his features. This section describes the amazing newborn — how he acts, how he feels, how he senses and how he will interact with you. Remember, there are extreme variations in the sense development and the behavior patterns of each newborn, and therefore the following description is meant only as a guide, to enhance appreciation of your new baby's capabilities.

As the head emerges from your birth canal, the obstetrician immediately sucks the mucus out of your baby's nose and mouth with a suction bulb so that when your baby takes his first breath this mucus is not drawn into his lungs. The clamping of the cord, his first cry and his first breath create fascinating changes in blood flow throughout his heart and lungs, allowing him to be free of his parasitic existence and to move his own life-giving oxygen by his own power.

Your newborn should be placed directly on your abdomen, covered if necessary, for you to love, hold and feed. This is the first "night out" in nine months and he really wants to enjoy it.

Features of the Newborn

Immediately after your newborn has been delivered, he certainly does not look like the model baby usually seen in books and pictures. For years, newborns have been unfeelingly described as looking like "prizefighters." This term was obviously coined by writers, certainly not by parents, because to you he will immedi-

ately appear beautiful. His face and eyelids are puffy, bluish and speckled with your blood. His ears are wrinkled and pressed tightly to his head. His fists are clenched, his arms and his legs flexed and his nose may be somewhat flattened. You will notice that his wrinkled, loose-fitting skin is covered with a cheesy, slippery material called **vernix**. This serves as a protective coating in utero and is also a lubricant during birth. The asymmetrical shape of his head is caused by a process called **molding**, which allows the bones of the skull to overlap and conform with the various contours of your birth canal. Shortly after birth, these bones spring back to form a rounded head shape. A new baby's scalp is swollen and sometimes contains large accumulations of fluid and/or blood. These accumulations may calcify into a small lump which may persist for months but will eventually disappear. A newborn has very fine, short, silk-like hair called **lanugo** on his back, shoulders, ears and cheeks. This hair disappears within a few weeks. His feet are markedly in-turned and his legs are bowed.

The full-term newborn weighs between 5.5 pounds (2.5

kg) and 8.5 pounds (3.8 kg), the average being 7.5 pounds (3.4 kg). He may be anywhere from 20 to 21.5 inches (50 cm to 54 cm) long. His head is proportionally bigger than the rest of his body, about two-thirds of his total weight. Your baby's head will naturally tend to bobble and therefore needs careful support for the first month. He breathes twice as fast as an adult and his breathing patterns may be extremely irregular. His heart beat is also about twice as fast as an adult's. He seems to urinate constantly and his bowel patterns are extremely erratic. The first stools, called **meconium**, are very dark and extremely sticky. They are composed of amniotic fluid and cellular debris which are present in the newborn's gut and are gradually passed during the first few days of life. His stools gradually change to a more mustard color toward the end of the first week. He sleeps from fourteen to eighteen hours a day and is usually alert for approximately 30 minutes in a four-hour period. This is the state of quiet alertness which we discussed previously; and it is in this state in which he is most receptive to parental stimuli.

You are probably asking yourself, "What can he do with his body, what can he see, what can he hear, what can he feel, how are all the usual bodily functions operating in this little human that I hold in my hands?"

How Much Can Your Baby See?

At birth, a baby's eyes are often closed, his pupils are small, his eyelids swollen. He squints as though trying to protect his eyes from too much light too soon. The sensitivity of a newborn's eyes to bright light gives rise to the custom of dimming lights shortly after delivery. When this is done, he opens his eyes wide and gazes intently. A newborn infant will follow moving objects best at a distance of twelve inches. Your baby will follow your hands if you move them slowly from side to side at this distance. He is very attracted to red and yellow objects as well as contrasting light and dark ones. Newborns also seem to attend well to patterns, such as stripes, more easily than to solid colors. It has long been known, however, that infants of all ages are most sensitive to objects with soft, rounded contours such as the human face. The late Walt Disney capitalized on this phenomenon by portraying most of his characters with abundant rounded cheeks, relatively large eyes and expressive smiles.

If you have an overwhelming urge to see your baby's eyes, there is a little trick which I use during a newborn examination. Hold your baby in front of you with one hand supporting his head and the other his bottom, approximately twelve inches from your eyes. Raise him from a lying position to a sitting position, or gently swing him through an arch of about 180 degrees with a not too abrupt stop. This creates a reflex in his visual system which will prompt him to immediately open his eyes. I cannot emphasize enough the importance of eye-to-eye contact, which begins at birth and which provides one of the most rewarding of human contact responses. We will dwell upon this subject throughout each stage of your child's development.

How Much Can Your Baby Hear?

Your baby can hear before he is born. Imagine the lulling quality of pulsating sounds that emanate from your womb, and the interesting sounds that he hears from outside your body. As previously mentioned, your newly born baby is especially attuned to high-pitched female voices and is particularly receptive to his mother's voice. Studies have shown that mothers tend to speak to their newborns in a unique cadence and a higher pitch than in ordinary conversation. Filming of this early dialogue shows that newborns move in a rhythm synchronous with the rhythm of their mother's voice, similar to the way an adult nods his head in tune with the speaker. The rhythmic feedback of the newborn's gestures and facial expressions in turn stimulate the mother to continue her communication. This first duet between you and your newborn is the foundation for continued parent-child communication.

Sudden, loud, irregular sounds startle while soft, steady, rhythmic sounds quiet your baby. Father, your newborn may not be as fascinated by your voice as he is by his mother's, but take heart, because there is something in this period of auditory communication for you too. Lie on a flat surface and place your newborn baby on your chest with his ear directly over your heart. You will notice that the combination of your heartbeat and the rhythm of your breathing movements will soon lull your baby to sleep. This is a practice which I have enjoyed with all of our babies. It seems to be easiest in the newborn period, when babies' relatively undeveloped motor capacities render them less likely to squirm and more content to nestle.

The Importance of Touching

We have discussed the importance of touching in our section on parenting and parent-infant bonding. The main point to appreciate is that touching will be your primary mode of communication with your newborn baby. How you exercise the art of this communication will profoundly affect your newborn's behavior during the first few weeks. The skin is probably your newborn's most well-developed sensory organ and it is therefore only natural to focus most of your stimulation on this powerful receptor. Touch is language for both you and your newborn, and how you handle him may often mirror your inner feelings for him. Your baby can sense what you are feeling by the way you touch, and his behavior may be altered dramatically by how you hold him. A gentle, confident, sometimes firm touch conveys and elicits calmness. (For further discussion on the importance of touching and stimulating the skin, see **Bonding, Bathing and The Fussy Baby**, pages 47, 80 and 162 respectively.)

Your Newborn's Reflexes

In previous sections we discussed your newborn's sensory capabilities. Let's now talk about how your newborn moves in response to sensory stimuli. In the first few weeks, newborn behavior is primarily guided by reflex responses to sensory stimuli. He does not yet function at the cognitive level of the higher brain centers. Until recently, all newborn behavior has been considered merely instinctive, similar to the behavior of lower animals. Much of a newborn's behavior does stem from the reflex brain centers but, fortunately, current research has raised the dignity of the newborn.

Throughout the first month of stimulus-response development, your newborn is setting up a pattern for future learning. He is learning to be selective, to blot out unpleasant and inappropriate stimuli, and to store and respond to appropriate stimuli. This selective ability leads to the development of preference. Usually by the end of the first month not only will your newborn have established his own preferences, but he will also have taught them to you. Your newborn's reaction to your various stimuli is a learning process for you as well as for him. Much of your newborn's reflex behavior should not be considered merely a curiosity to see if he does everything the books say he should do at a certain age, nor should it be considered instinctive, non-human behavior similar to that of a well-trained pet. Rather, consider your baby's response to various stimuli a learning and adaptive process, a foundation for later personality development. You should know how he moves his arms and legs in response to various sensory stimuli, the pitch and rhythm of voices he likes best, his favorite sleeping positions, his favorite facial expressions, where he likes to be touched, how he likes to be cuddled. A question I often ask at the one-month visit is, "What does he like?" rather than "What does he do?"

Below is a list of some of the more common body reflexes your newborn will show you.

Your newborn may show a **startle reflex** whereby he throws his arms forward and clasps his hands in response to frightening stimuli. This is considered a protective reflex, as if he is trying to grasp onto his mother for security.

Your newborn also possesses a very strong **grasp reflex**. Stroking the palms of his hands or the soles of his feet will elicit such a strong response that he can be lifted up by his own grasp. A tickling or painful stimulus to hands and feet will elicit an instinctive withdrawal of the affected limb from the unpleasant stimulus.

Stroking his cheek or the palm of his hand stimulates his **hand-mouth reflex**. He "roots" his mouth in the direction of the cheek stimulus, flexes his arm in the direction of his opening mouth and eventually his fingers find their way into his mouth, a feat of great accomplishment for your wise newborn.

If you place your awake baby on his abdomen on a flat surface, he will try to "right himself" by attempting to arch his back and keep his head up. With each ensuing week, he will arch his back more and keep his head up longer until he finally accomplishes the long-sought-after push-up position.

Newborns attempt to move from place to place. Hold your newborn upright above a table and gradually lower him onto the soles of his feet against the flat surface, or gently stub his toe against the edge of the table. You will notice the **stepping reflex;** he seems to be trying to walk. He may propel himself across a bed by serpentine movements of his trunk and "push-off" movements of his legs and arms.

Your newborn also possesses a very efficient **gag-reflex** to expel any substance from his throat, thus protecting him from choking while learning feeding and swallowing.

Tiny babies also protect themselves from overstimulation. A barrage of inappropriate and unpleasant stimuli often induce newborns into a deep sleep. (This method is not recommended to get your baby to sleep.) A baby is accustomed to continuous sounds in utero, so it is not necessary to tip-toe around and hush everyone in order to create a noiseless environment at sleeptime.

During the hospital period, you will develop a "feel" for all of these qualities in your newborn. By the time you are ready to go home, you will realize that your amazing newborn is becoming an amazing person.

Infancy — The Critical Period

How you parent during the first two years determines, in large part, your child's behavior in later years. Your commitment to parenting and your investment in the infancy period creates a strong parent-infant attachment which helps prevent problems in later years. Infancy is the critical period for establishing bonds of love and security, and a trust in the environment. An infant has all the capabilities to express love and trust, grief and happiness. Infancy is also the period of greatest vulnerability to negative parental input.

Personality traits are influenced by the patterns of input from the primary care-giver, usually the mother. If the infant receives a consistent, positive input from his primary care-giver, then he learns to love and trust both his care-giver and his environment. He also begins to develop a positive self-image.

Suppose an infant constantly receives negative input from his care-giver. For example, he is not fed when hungry or not consoled when crying. He grows up not knowing what to expect in a variety of circumstances, and learns that the world is not such a comforting place to be. This child is at high risk for developing what Selma Fraiberg calls **diseases of non-attachment** such as aggression and hate. These diseases of the ''ego'' begin during the formative first eighteen months. Can you imagine the snowballing effects on a child who has never learned to trust? They can last a lifetime, to the point that an infant's defective parent-model may be reflected in his own parenting principles years later.

Certain misconceptions, which I would like to clarify, exist about parenting in the first two years. First, you cannot ''spoil'' an infant. This term should be stricken from all baby books forever. Spoiled implies rotten. Have you ever seen a child turn rotten because of too much love? The ideas that too much approval and affection will give a child a ''swelled head'' or that too much attachment to his parents may make him ''too dependent'' are misconceived. Actually, the opposite is true. Infants thrive in an atmosphere of love and affection. They grow up very trusting, and when they are ready they will become independent, secure children.

Parents often say, ''I don't want my child to manipulate me.'' This misconception occurs when you attribute adult values to a tiny infant. Adults act at the **cognitive** level, infants act primarily at the **reflex** level. He doesn't think, ''Now I'm going to yell until I get my way.'' Rather, his behavior mirrors his emotional and physical needs in a reflex manner. No, you have not been had, he really does need you.

71

CHAPTER III

COMING HOME—
THE ADJUSTMENT
PERIOD

The adjustment period at home is somewhat different from the adjustment period in the hospital. The euphoria of the birth experience, the constant help and advice at the push of a button, and the absence of any responsibility except to yourself and to your baby all eased the adjustment period in the hospital. However, in coming home, reality hits. Let's first discuss some of the usual stresses which occur in varying degrees among most mothers in the first few weeks after birth.

The After-Baby Blues—Postpartum Depression

At least 50 per cent of all women giving birth in North American hospitals experience some degree of after-baby blues whose symptoms are the following: lack of energy, episodes of crying, anxiety, fear, headaches, worry about physical appearance and attractiveness, mild insomnia, confusion, and a negative attitude toward the husband. These feelings are generally thought to be caused by a rapid drop in the level of maternal hormones following childbirth. However, some researchers feel that there is a higher incidence of after-baby blues in the United States because of hospital policies which assign the role of the primary caregiver to experts rather than to the mother, resulting in maternal-infant separation. Our society often focuses so much attention on the baby that the mother is left feeling unimportant, very much a non-person. These let-down feelings usually occur from two to ten days after birth.

Between 10 per cent and 20 per cent of North American mothers experience not only the milder form of after-baby blues, but also actually develop a depression manifested by persistent insomnia, loss of appetite and making mountains out of mole-hills. What you should keep in mind about postpartum depression is that the problem is very common.

● **What causes postpartum depression?**

The feelings of postpartum depression are your body's signals that you have exceeded your physical and psychological capacities to adapt to all the recent changes and energy demands that have been put upon you. This does not imply a weakness on your part, only that you have exhausted your body's capacity to adjust to these changes.

Certain risk factors which predispose certain mothers to postpartum depression should be identified during pregnancy so that you, your doctor and your husband can take measures to prevent these feelings after delivery. The risk factors are the following:

1. An unhappy childhood due to abusive parents.

2. An unwanted pregnancy and persistent feelings about how a child will interfere with your current lifestyle.

3. A previous history of depression or of difficulty in managing stressful situations.

4. Marital discord and the unrealistic expectation that a child may solve your problems.

5. A prolonged and difficult labor.

6. An ill or premature baby.

7. Any situation which separates mother and infant, and interferes with the necessary maternal-infant bonding relationship which we have previously discussed.

Another factor causing postpartum depression is the disappointment that occurs when the whole birth and postpartum experience does not live up to expectations. For example, due to circumstances beyond your control, medical complications may arise and your expectations of childbirth may not be fulfilled. It is also possible that, to some extent, postpartum blues have been fostered by the multitudes of baby books and by the media which tell you that you should be a superwoman with endless energy. Actually, I think that most postpartum depression is due to total exhaustion.

Another common set of stressful feelings during the post-partum period are those of doubt and frustration—doubt about your mothering abilities and frustration at your apparent lack of success. These feelings may often lead to a state of despair which even may result in an occasional (but temporary) hatred of your baby, which in turn is quickly followed by a sensation of guilt for these seemingly terrible feelings. Remember that these are not abnormal feelings. It is very important to talk about them with a trusted person, preferably your husband or physician.

Tips on Preventing or Alleviating Postpartum Depression

1. Be aware that your feelings are shared by thousands of other women. Most mothers find a great deal of comfort in talking to friends who have experienced varying degrees of exhaustion. Local support groups such as the ICEA and the La Leche League may provide valuable advice.

2. If you have any of the above-mentioned "high risk factors," attempt to take preventive measures before the postpartum period.

3. Be flexible. When entering the hospital be prepared for the fact that all you have read or learned about the ideal childbirth may not come to pass and that some disappointments may occur.

4. Insist on an early bonding relationship and rooming-in in the hospital so that you and your baby get to know each other well. In this way, many of the tension-producing problems will be worked out in the hospital, not left to be worked out at home.

5. Avoid extreme fatigue at all costs. Obtain help at home, remembering that your main responsibility is to yourself and your baby. The housework, dishes, and meals can be handled by someone else (fathers, take note!), but no one can mother your baby as you can.

6. Recognize the early symptoms of insomnia and loss of appetite and seek help immediately if they occur.

7. Take a few hours each week to do something just for you. Take a short walk, allowing your mind to be at peace with yourself. Treat yourself to some physical exercise each day even if you have to force yourself to do this. Sometimes an intuitive friend will sense your need for occasional peace and privacy and give you the added boost that you need.

8. Keep yourself physically attractive. If you look good, you feel good.

9. Entertain visitors only when **you** wish to. You should have no social obligations except to yourself, your baby and to your husband.

10. Seek help from your husband and be specific in telling him what you need (e.g. housekeeper, laundry, more help with the older siblings). Many a well-meaning father may not consider that what are "little things" to him may seem like giant obstacles to a depressed mother.

11. Good nutrition is essential, even if you have to sometimes force yourself to eat.

12. Drugs are not the answer in treating postpartum depression, except perhaps in the case of very severe depression. They should then only be taken on the advice of your physician.

How Fathers Can Ease Postpartum Depression

1. A mother needs mothering too. Be sensitive to her physical and emotional needs. Compliment her frequently. Sympathize with her feelings. "You must feel very tired. I understand." Don't react in anger when she seems tired or irritable. In many cultures there is a wise custom of presenting the postpartum mother with a "doula" (from the Greek word "doulos," meaning bondservant). This is a person who can take over the household chores and free the new mother to concentrate on the baby. Anyone can be a doula, even a husband once in a while. Free your wife of unnecessary tasks which take her away from the baby. Small tasks such as a pile of dirty dishes may seem like a mammoth undertaking to a depressed mother. If friends ask,"Is there anything you need?" say "Yes, please bring over supper tonight."

2. Be sensitive to the early signs of exhaustion and depression. Your wife may not want to appear "weak" and may try to cover up her shaky feelings.

3. Respect the **nesting instinct**. Avoid making major changes around the time of childbirth. This is not the time to move into a new house or begin a new job. If possible, these changes should be made before delivery. Remember, the nesting instinct is very strong in a new mother. To upset the nest is to upset the mother.

4. Set strict visiting policies with friends and relatives, even if you have to set "visiting hours" at home similar to the system at the hospital.

5. Convey your love for your wife. Husbands often say, "Of course, I love you." But do you **show** your feelings? If your wife feels loved she is more comfortable in mothering your infant. The greatest gift you can give your child is to love his mother.

Preparing the Nest

There are as many ways to prepare your home for a newborn as there are homes and new babies. (Page 79 outlines **Layette Needs**.) Your nest and how you manage it reflects your parenting philosophy, and therefore this section will not read like a shopping list of what to buy for baby, but rather a thinking list on how to care for baby.

We have run the whole gamut of living arrangements with our four children. In the early days, when we were expecting our first baby, we were students and had to set aside dreams of a properly appointed nursery. Baby took up residence in a borrowed cradle in my study for the first six months, next to our bedroom; we were told that it was not good to have your baby in your bedroom. After that, we found a crib in an army surplus store and placed it in the hallway. Baby Two had a bassinet in the living room for three months, then shared big brother's bedroom. These boys voluntarily shared their bedroom until ages nine and eleven, at which point one room could no longer contain all the projects as well as personal belongings of two growing boys. By the time we were ready for our third baby, we were able to afford the long-dreamed-of nursery. Long hours were spent renovating, curtaining, furnishing. Once again, though, a borrowed cradle was our baby's first bed.

Cradles

Unless you have a family cradle which has been passed down from generation to generation and from child to child (which is a wonderful family custom), I believe in borrowing cradles because you only use them for four to six months, depending on how fast your baby grows and develops. Cradles are a wonderful invention. For nine months your baby is accustomed to constant motion, so newborns just don't like lying in a bed permanently fixed to the floor — it's too static. As your baby shifts his weight, a cradle sways slightly, lulling him back to a deeper sleep. You may find that the switch from cradle to crib brings about some disturbance in sleeping due to the absence of the rocking motion. The day you find your baby pulling himself up to peer over the cradle edge, you know the cradle is too small and he is ready to graduate to a larger bed. (For further discussion on baby's sleeping arrangements see **Sleep Patterns and Problems** page 170 , and the **Family Bed**, page 173 .)

Rocking Chairs   Rocking chairs have soothed a lot of tired babies and mothers. They are especially welcome when you have had your fill of carrying baby around, but he hasn't. A rocking chair is used most often at bedtime. Rocking and nursing your baby to sleep is a wonderful bedtime routine. Falling asleep in mother's arms is much nicer than being put to bed, ready or not, and being left alone to sleep. A teddy bear or cuddly blanket may be comfortable, but mother is infinitely nicer.

Baby Carriers   A baby carrier is another useful piece of equipment. Numerous devices are sold to keep your baby close to you while freeing your arms. There are slings, shawls, carriers, simple strips of cloth and complicated designs with padded shoulder straps. Baby carriers, as opposed to plastic baby seats, encourage body contact or "marsupial" mothering. (See **Carriers and Safety**, page 420 .)

Toys   I feel very strongly that you, mother and father, will be your baby's favorite toys. From the moment of birth he will be enthralled with just looking at your face, especially your eyes and your smile. As he gets older and begins reaching out, he will spend long moments playing with your hair, nose, chin and ears. His favorite place will be in your arms. His favorite music box will be your voice and your heartbeat. Money can be spent on both plain and fancy toys, and on artificial mothering devices such as bounce chairs, playpens, strollers and jumpers, but your baby's favorite source of stimulation will always be you. Mothers, however, naturally get tired and unattended babies naturally become bored. Mother substitutes may be necessary occasionally, especially when your infant is older and in need of increased stimulation. Besides, there has to be something for grandparents to buy for baby. With this in mind, here are a few suggestions just to start you off.

Babies concentrate with pleasure on light and motion. Watch his reactions to flickering candles and Christmas lights. Mobiles are a fascinating source of entertainment for baby and can be hung anywhere. Place a mobile nearby (8 to 12 inches from his eyes at first) for him to watch or hit. Place him in an infant seat near a window so that he can see natural and fascinating mobiles — rain splashing onto the window or trees moving in the wind. Even in the early weeks, your baby is able to discriminate patterns and colors. He sees red and yellow colors, and light and dark contrasting patterns best. Cut-outs of col-

LAYETTE NEEDS		
Clothing	• diapers (cloth)	3 dozen
	• diapers (disposable)	
	• rubber pants (loose-fitting)	4
	• receiving blanket	6
	• lightweight tops (saques and/or kimonos)	8
	• terrycloth sleepers and/or heavyweight saques	8
	• booties	3 pair
	• sunhats	2
	• warm hats	2
	• sweaters	2
	• undershirts (3-6 month size)	6
	• socks	2 pair
Supplies	• mild bath soap and shampoo	
	• mild laundry soap	
	• diaper pins (if using cloth diapers)	3 pair
	• diaper pail	
	• rectal thermometer	
	• cotton balls	
	• baby bathtub or molded bath aid	
	• diaper cream-zinc oxide	
	• cotton-tipped applicators	
	• rubbing alcohol	
	• petroleum jelly	
	• nasal aspirator with 2-inch bulb	
	• 8 oz. bottles for formula	
	• 4 oz. bottles for water	
	• bottle brush	
Linens	• flannel - backed rubber pads	4
	• crib or bassinet sheets	2
	• hooded baby towels	2
	• wash cloth	3
	• baby blanket	2-4
Equipment	• bassinet, cradle, crib	
	• storage chest for clothing	
	• infant seat	
	• front baby carrier	
	• changing table or padded work area	
	• carry bed	
	• diaper bag	
	• rocking chair	
	• vaporizer-humidifier	
	• night light	

Bathing is really playtime; babies don't get dirty enough to need a daily bath for cleanliness.

ored circles, squares, bull's-eye patterns and the like are simple visual stimuli that you can cut out and use to entrance your baby. Rattles that he can grasp and shake and chew are good after a few months. Look for rattles that have a head of no less than 1 3/8'' x 2'' (35 mm x 50 mm) in diameter.

Caring for Your Newborn's Bodily Needs

Bathing

In the early days before your baby's cord drops off, you will just give him a sponge bath. You need a warm, draft-free room, a basin of warm water and a thick towel on which to place your baby. Many babies cry if you undress them completely, making bath-time too upsetting for both of you. If this happens, undress and bathe the baby in stages. Other babies love the feeling of being free of clothing, and cry when you are ready to dress them. The cord and navel areas need to be swabbed well at least twice a day with a cotton-tipped applicator covered in antiseptic. Do this gently but thoroughly. Make sure you get down to the base of the cord stump and watch for developing yellow matter and/or redness. The dried cord stump usually falls off by two weeks of age. It is normal for a few drops of blood to be left on the navel when the last of his umbilical cord parts company. As soon as the cord is gone and the navel looks healed, you can start putting your baby into a tub bath.

Now the real fun begins. Most babies respond to immersion in bath water with great pleasure, much as a newborn reacts when placed in the LeBoyer bath. The warm water is a signal to baby to relax his muscles and feel the buoyancy. You will see pleasure on his face, probably a smile, and little floating movements of his arms and legs. Give yourself and baby lots of time to enjoy this ritual. Bathing is really playtime; babies don't get dirty enough to need a daily bath for cleanliness. For busy parents, this is good news. Twice a week (especially in the winter) is enough bathing as long as the diaper area is washed every time there is a bowel movement.

There are several types of baby bathtubs on the market. Some you place on a tabletop or on a counter, others sit in your big bathtub. Or you can simply use the kitchen sink, which makes great pictures for the baby book and really tickles the fancy of the other children. A little tip is to wear a pair of old white cotton gloves and rub a little baby soap on the wet glove. You have an instant wash cloth that automatically shapes itself to baby's body, and reduces the slipperiness of bare hands on soapy skin. Also, place a towel in the bottom of the sink or tub to prevent the baby from slipping. When washing baby's face, just use water. Soap in the eyes can really hurt. If your baby's facial skin is extremely oily (baby acne), then a little soap will be useful in drying up the excess oil and pimples. Cotton-tipped applicators are handy for cleaning little crevices in and behind his outer ear, but never try to clean inside his ear canal because damage to the canal or eardrum could result.

What happens if your baby screams every time you try to put him into his bath? Either it means that he is hungry, the water is too hot or too cold, or you have a baby who dislikes the feeling of being alone in the water — his security is threatened. A beautiful solution to this problem is to take your baby into your bath with you. Get the water ready, a little cooler than you usually have it, then undress yourself and undress your baby. Hold him close to you as you step into the water and then sit back and enjoy this glorious skin-to-skin contact. Mothers, don't be surprised if your baby wants to nurse at this time. It is a natural result of being held close to your breast. In fact, if your baby still fusses upon entering the water in your arms, put him to your breast first and let him nurse as you slowly ease your way into the bath. This is a special way to enjoy mothering and bathing your baby.

Massage

You may want to try giving your baby an oil massage before his bath. At age one month, your baby's skin, arms, legs and back are sturdy enough to accept a systematic, firm, gentle stroking. The entire procedure is described beautifully in Dr. LeBoyer's book, **Loving Hands**. Undress your baby completely, and sit on the floor with the baby lying on a thick towel on your outstretched legs. Using pure vegetable oil to lubricate your hands, gently massage his entire body. Conclude this ritual with some bending and stretching exercises.

Powders and Oils

What about the use of powders and oils in the care of your newborn? Generally, they are totally unnecessary. The skin of a healthy baby is rich in natural body oil. Avoid over-cleaning. Too much soap robs baby's skin of these oils. Powder easily cakes and builds up in skin creases and can actually cause skin irritation and rash. Powders which smell ''nice,'' are for the benefit of parents, not babies. Actually, scented oils and powders camouflage the sweet, natural baby smell which is so appealing to mothers. Many mothers find this baby scent irresistible, just as they find a baby's face and baby's cry.

Temperature of the Environment

''How warm or cool should his room be?'' and ''How heavily should I dress him?'' are common questions that parents ask. Premature or small babies under five pounds have incompletely developed temperature regulating systems at birth and therefore need very close temperature regulation to avoid cold stress. Full-term, healthy newborns, especially those of eight pounds, have enough body fat and a mature enough temperature regulating system to feel comfortable in an environment similar to that of the average adult. A room temperature of 68° F to 70° F is preferable and some attempt should be made to keep the temperature of baby's room as constant as possible, since some babies do not adjust well to marked swings in room temperature in the first few weeks. A commonly over-looked and equally important feature in a newborn's environment is the relative humidity in his room. Babies are more comfortable in an environment of circulating air with a humidity of at least 50 per cent. The low humidity and dry air of our central heating systems can cause a newborn's skin to become dry and flaky. He will be more prone to excessive pimple-type rashes, similar to teenage acne. More importantly, breathing low-humidity air for a long period of time may dry out and clog his nasal passages, resulting in sleep disturbances, as well as noisy, sniffly breathing and poor nursing. I strongly recommend that you put a humidifer in your baby's room during the months of central heating.

Clothing

Cultural influences and common sense will dictate how you dress your baby. A rule of thumb is to dress him in as much or as little clothing as you are comfortable in yourself. Cotton clothing is best because it absorbs body moisture and allows air to circulate freely. Clothing should be loose enough to allow baby's free movement. Periodically check to see that feet on sleepers, as well as elastic banding on play outfits, particularly around the waist and thigh, aren't too tight.

Taking Baby Outside

When can you take your baby outside? Basically use the same guidelines which are mentioned above. If he is a full-term, healthy baby, his temperature regulating system, especially by the time he is eight pounds, is mature enough to tolerate very brief exposure to extremes of temperature (e.g. house to car and back). Consistency of temperature is still necessary in the first month, as prolonged exposure to extreme temperature swings may not be tolerated by your newborn. Travelling from a heated house to a heated car maintains this consistency.

Environmental Irritants

Smoking is a common nasal irritant to a tiny baby which contributes to sniffles. Don't smoke near the baby. The newborn is a nose-dependent breather and his nasal passages are narrow. For this reason, try to keep his environment free of all possible nasal irritants (e.g. paint and gasoline fumes, lint from clothing, and hairsprays).

CHAPTER IV

FATHER FEELINGS

I strongly believe that over the next decade more fathers will begin redefining their priorities in life. They will become less concerned with their corporate or peer image and more concerned with their family image. The economic stimulus to work more and earn more is becoming less attractive since the extra money is worth less. An example of this trend can be seen in the push by organized labor for more fringe benefits rather than more money. Pilot studies have found that fathers with increased leisure time from a shorter work week spend a significant portion of it with their children. The following discussion will center around some of the common feelings fathers have, the concept of priority fathering, and some suggestions about increasing your involvement with your children.

Father Feelings During Pregnancy

The earliest father feelings are usually those of pride — pride in their masculinity as well as their fertility. As the reality of the concept of ''family'' sinks in, the father reflects on his increased responsibilities. Society puts great pressures upon the male to produce and the economic burden of ''another mouth to feed'' may weigh heavily upon the expectant father. Feelings of dependency on the part of the wife run high during pregnancy and some men may question their ability to both father the baby and ''mother the mother.''

Many fathers experience pregnancy-like symptoms during their wife's pregnancy, probably due to a subconscious desire to share the pregnancy. Other fathers do not envy pregnancy at all and may regard this period as a necessary nuisance toward having a child. There may be a tendency to focus on the arrival of the baby and to subconsciously ignore the pregnancy. The mother's constant physical and emotional changes, however, serve as a reminder of the reality of the family pregnancy.

In the second trimester, the father can feel his baby move, a feeling which is often a great thrill for the expectant father. Feeling his baby kick often arouses sexual interest and may initiate love-making. Father anxiety increases as the time of delivery approaches. He may become increasingly concerned about the health of mother and baby. Many fathers cannot visualize a newborn and often picture their baby at an older age. Feelings that "we are no longer a romantic couple" hit their peak in the last few months and fathers may often have ambivalent feelings about their baby's effect on the marriage.

Involvement is the key to handling uneasy father feelings and this involvement should begin very early in the pregnancy. Remember that as your wife is mothering your unborn child during pregnancy, fathering also begins before birth. The following suggestions are aimed at assisting nervous fathers in handling these common feelings during pregnancy:

1. Involve yourself with the many choices you and your wife will make early in pregnancy: Which doctor? Which hospital? Alternative birthing environments?

2. Accompany your wife on her visits to the obstetrician. You will learn a lot about your developing baby.

3. Attend prepared childbirth classes (see page 37). Father involvement in the childbirth event is one of the major topics in these classes. You will learn about your developing baby, about parenting in general and, incidentally, about your wife.

4. Be involved in the birth of your child (see **Alternative Birthing Concepts**, page 36, **Entering the Hospital for Delivery**, page 47.)

5. Attend your baby's check-ups. Pediatricians encourage fathers to attend these office visits. Unfortunately, fathers do not enjoy the same knowledge of and intuition about babies as mothers do and, because of this, pediatricians make a special effort to discuss particular stages of your baby's growth and development with you. I am greatly impressed with the depth of father intuition men have when they are given the opportunity to express it.

6. Become involved in the postpartum period as discussed in **Coming Home**, page 73.

A common father feeling which has been expressed to me by my caring and involved fathers is the feeling of being "left out" during the first year of their infant's life. This feeling may occur if your wife is breastfeeding, is practicing immersion mothering, and has such a strong mother-infant attachment that you wonder "What can I give my infant?" Take heart, there is still a very important role for you — the role of supporter, or motherer of the mother. It is both normal and healthy for infants to show a strong mother preference during the first two years. By mothering the mother, you are making your wife happy and relaxed, which enhances her relationship with your child. (See page 76 for tips on mothering the mother.) In this way, you are indirectly fathering your infant and the whole family profits. Even though your wife is your baby's primary care-giver, you can still do a lot with your baby the first year. You can change diapers, bathe him, burp him and play with him, carry him around and comfort him during fussy periods. Initially, you may not feel comfortable with these "mothering" activities, but remember our principle of continuum fathering: involvement increases comfort, comfort makes an activity more enjoyable, and your fathering operates on a higher level. (See **Working Mother**, page 184.)

Priority Fathering

There are many obstacles in the world of work which divert a father from the genuine joy of being with his children. Work competes with fathering, and modern corporate man is often forced to choose between his company, his peers or friends, and his children. The economic pressures on fathers make it unrealistic to simply say, "Choose your work or your child." I would like to propose a solution to this "time with your child" dilemma of contemporary fathering.

Many fathers leave for the office before their children awake in the morning and return home just in time to tuck their children into bed. Work thus relegates fatherhood to a weekend and holiday profession. These fathers miss many of the spontaneous joys of parenting that occur when a father is just not around. If you have this type of demanding job, stop and take inventory: What would I like to be in the eyes of my children? What am I in the eyes of my children? What should my role as a father be and am I fulfilling this role? Are there certain needs my child has at a particular age which the passage of time will not give me a second chance to fulfill? Some of the answers to these questions may necessitate a change in your direction in life. If fathering requires a reorganization of priorities (cutting down on your workload, changing jobs), as a sailor friend once said to me, "Have the courage to follow your compass." I speak from experience, having made a career decision which reduced the size of my practice and my teaching commitments so I could spend more time with my family.

Involve your children in your work. Children love being asked to help Daddy in his job. They feel that they are really worth something in the eyes of their father. I would take my son to the hospital to make hospital rounds with me and even let him write out an occasional prescription (his handwriting is better than mine anyway).

Institute the practice of a **special time** for each child. One morning each week I take one of my children to breakfast on the way to school. This one-to-one communication is very valuable to both father and child. As we have stated before, it is important for parents to convey their love to their children frequently by, for example, eye-to-eye contact and touching. Mothers do not have a patent on gentling a child. A hug, a kiss, a gentle touch from a caring father will do wonders for your rapport.

A father feeling often expressed to me is, "My wife is too attached to our baby. She won't leave him with a babysitter so we can get away." It is easy to convey subtle messages to your wife such as, "You owe me some time too" and "People will wonder why we bring our baby to the party." Fathers, trust your wife's intuition and support her feelings. Some babies are more separation sensitive than others and only his mother will know when and how long to leave your baby. (For further discussion on mother-infant attachment, see **Where's My Mommy?**, page 181.)

Family vacations are a valuable asset to a contemporary father. Years ago, my wife and I fell victim to the "relief holiday disease" when we would temporarily escape into the magic world of child-free make-believe. As our parenting priorities matured, we vowed to make future vacations family vacations. Such vacations increase understanding and acceptance. They allow both parents and children to step back and appreciate the good feelings that exist when one is part of a family.

Father Fun

Early in infancy, a child learns to regard mother as a care person and father as a play person. This "fun to be with" relationship should continue throughout childhood and adolescence and serve as an entrée to improved father-child communications. A feeling I have always treasured is the time my four-year-old son said to me, ''Dad, you're fun.'' If a person enjoys your company, he is at ease communicating with you. Doing fun things with your child opens an avenue of communication which improves your effectiveness as an authority figure and a wise counsellor in time of need. One of the most satisfying of all father feelings is sensing that your child feels comfortable seeking your help with a problem. If you have been a consistently involved father, and fun to be with, this father-trust will occur naturally.

Doing fun things with your child opens avenues of communication.

Fathers, as a final note, remember that you are a role model for your children, both sons and daughters. Children vividly remember their parents' involvement and are likely to carry these practices into their own parenting. Not only are sons likely to carry on your fathering example, but also daughters seem to have even more vivid recollections of their father's influence on their lives, and are likely to seek these values in their own husbands. A truly effective father may pass on his fathering practices through the continuum of many generations. Fathering is indeed a long-term investment.

CHAPTER V

INFANT FEEDING AND NUTRITION

The Choice — Breast or Bottle?

In order to appreciate the decline and fall of feeding and nutrition practices in the twentieth century, let's get some insight into this problem by going back in history and tracing the changes in feeding practices. In the early 1900s, there was no decision to make about infant feeding. As you nourished the fetus in your uterus for nine months, so you nourished your infant at your breast for at least nine months, or until he was ready to take his place at the family table. Infant feeding was then considered a natural maternal instinct rather than a scientific or mathematical exercise. In the 1920s, commercially packaged baby food and prepared formulas became extremely popular. Scientists and technologists took over infant feeding from the mother and widespread marketing of these products as antiseptic and pure gradually caused the breast and kitchen to be replaced by the bottle and jar. It is interesting to note that, whereas in the 1920s, formula-feeding became more "fashionable" among the upper socioeconomic groups and breastfeeding became the way of the "less enlightened," in the 1980s the reverse is true. Breastfeeding and homemade foods are on the increase, especially among better informed mothers in the middle and upper socioeconomic groups. Maternal instinct is finally bucking commercial marketing. Breastfeeding is in, blenders are whirring and I expect we will see a generation of healthier children.

In my practice, I customarily see expectant couples a few weeks prior to delivery. I never say, "How do you plan to feed your baby?" I always assume that the mother will breastfeed, and immediately begin to discuss the family preparation needed for a successful feeding relationship. Many patients have later confided that "We had not considered breastfeeding, but you seemed so positive about it that we chose to breastfeed, and all three of us are glad we did." Nearly all infants in my practice are breastfed, which illustrates that the physician's attitude toward the feeding relationship can play an influential role in this decision. My encouragement of breastfeeding is not intended to make a mother feel guilty if she chooses not to breastfeed her baby. I would be less than honest, however, if I were to make any statement other than the following: **Breastfeeding is the ideal feeding relationship for you, your baby and your family.** In the vast majority of cases, any alternative is second best. However, the nurturing relationship is more important than the type of milk you use. If you decide not to breastfeed, your decision should be respected. (Later we shall discuss tips on developing a good bottle-feeding relationship.) If you are undecided, I recommend you attend an entire series of La Leche League meetings (see page 30 for discussion of the La Leche League). They will tell you, as I do, that there is no substitute for mother's milk. If at baby's birth you are still undecided, I recommend you start breastfeeding. Unlike the decision to bottle-feed, this is not an irreversible decision. Your baby's psychological, immunological and nutritional needs will be better satisfied by breastfeeding and you will feel an overpowering sense of closeness to your baby.

Breastfeeding — The Ideal Relationship

Advantages to Baby

A basic concept you should understand is the principle of **biological specificity of milk**. Each species of mammal has formulated the unique substance called milk, which can satisfy all the nutritional requirements of its offspring until they triple their birth weight (in humans, this is around one year of age). This milk, like blood, has been perfected throughout the evolution of each species in order to ensure the adaptation of the species to its environment. Thus, human milk is ideally suited for the adaptation of the human species and cow's milk is ideally suited for the adaptation of the bovine species.

The underlying problem in substituting milk across species lines is shown through analysis of the following nutrients:

1. Protein. Human milk protein is suited to humans in a number of ways. The curd produced is smaller and more digestible than that of cow's milk. The high casein content of cow's milk protein forms a thick, ropy curd which is less digestible and contributes to gas formation, constipation and "sore bottoms" in human infants. The stools of breastfed infants are neither uncomfortable to the infant nor unpleasant to the parents. The amount of protein in cow's milk is four times that of human milk (since cows grow four times faster than humans in the first year) whereas the amino acid composition (the basic nutritional building blocks for growth) of human milk is uniquely suited for human growth.

2. Fats. Human milk, unlike pasteurized cow's milk or formula, contains enzymes which aid in fat digestion. The infant's immature intestines are deficient in these enzymes. Human milk fat is almost completely digested and absorbed, whereas some of the fat in cow's milk and formula is not digested and contributes to the unpleasant stools. Human milk is richer in the essential fatty acids uniquely formulated for human brain growth.

3. Carbohydrates. The predominant sugar in human milk is **lactose**, which is absorbed and utilized efficiently by the infant. Human milk is definitely sweeter than cow's milk because it contains more lactose, and the newborn's taste is sensitive to this natural sweetness. Lactose also favors the development of certain protective bacteria in the intestines, otherwise known as "ecology of the gut."

4. Minerals. The lower calcium and phosphorus content of human milk is better suited to the rate of bone growth of the human infant, which is lower than that of the calf. The lower amount of salt in human milk is easier on the immature kidneys of the young infant.

5. Iron. The iron of human milk best illustrates how milk is adapted to its own species. The iron content of human milk is low and on paper it would seem insufficient for the infant's needs. Experience has shown and science has confirmed that breastfed infants seldom become anemic, while infants fed on cow's milk do. The iron in breast milk is so ideally suited to the human intestines that it is almost completely absorbed, whereas approximately 90 per cent of commercially added iron passes through the intestines unused. It may even interfere with the bacterial ecology of the gut. The unique iron of human milk has thus far evaded scientific analysis and duplication in the laboratory.

● **Immunity**

The human infant needs a large supply of disease-fighting elements in his blood and tissues. These are called **immunoglobulins**, which are proteins unique to each species, designed to fight against the diseases most prevalent in that species. Human infants have fewer immunoglobulins than they need in the first few months. Your infant begins manufacturing his own immunoglobulins in the first few months, but these do not reach adequate levels until the age of six months to one year. To make up for this insufficient immunity, the mother "protects" the infant for the first few months in two ways:

1. By transferring her immunoglobulins into her infant across the placenta. These immunoglobulins are all used between the ages of six months and a year, after which time the infant can survive on his own immunoglobulins.

2. By receiving immunoglobulins through human milk. **Colostrum**, the first milk you produce, is rich in certain immunoglobulins which are different from those your infant received across the placenta. Colostrum complements the work of your blood in the protection of your newborn. Like your blood, colostrum is a living tissue which contains your living white cells. These act as infection fighters in your newborn's intestines. Mothers are usually very conscientious about not missing their baby's shots. Your colostrum can be considered your newborn's first immunization. Colostrum is the ideal transitional food (from placental nourishment to milk) as it contains immunity factors similar to those in your blood. This colostrum also has a laxative effect which aids in the expulsion of the thick meconium present in your infant's early stools.

Human milk also contains factors which promote growth of favorable resident bacteria within the gut. These bacteria suppress the growth of other pathogenic bacteria which may be harmful to your infant. Cow's milk and formula contain no such protective mechanisms.

It has also recently been discovered that human milk carries antibodies to newly acquired infections. If a new germ enters a mother's intestines, she produces antibodies to this germ. These antibodies are delivered to the infant through your milk, protecting him from the same germ. Milk immunization is a dynamic process. As new germs appear, new antibodies are made in your milk to continue your infant's protection. Thus, your breast functions after birth as your placenta did in utero; it is a source of nourishment and a source of protection from disease.

● **Effect on later health of your baby**

Breastfed babies have fewer respiratory and intestinal infections. The tendency to allergies in infancy and later in childhood is also less if the baby has been breastfed. It is also strongly suspected, but difficult to prove, that breastfeeding lessens the tendency to obesity.

● **Breastfeeding as a benefit to oral-facial development**

Your newborn's oral-facial construction is uniquely adapted to breastfeeding. His upper lip contains a blister-like ''sucking pad,'' his rounded cheeks are filled with abundant fat pads, his tongue is oversized and his palate high-arched. All these physical characteristics are designed to fit the contour of your breast. The facial and tongue muscles work very differently when breastfeeding and when bottle-feeding. A breastfed infant sucks more vigorously and orients the milk toward the back of his tongue and palate. He controls the flow of milk better. A bottle-fed infant sucks with the front of his mouth. Orthodontists feel that breastfeeding contributes to the proper alignment of your infant's jawbone, whereas bottle-feeding contributes to malocclusion. The saying ''Your infant's breastfeeding efforts will later be reflected in his face'' does indeed have a scientific basis.

● **Adaptability of human milk**

One of the advantages of a living source of nutrition such as breast milk is its ability to adapt its function to meet changing requirements. Your breast milk adapts to the changing requirements of your infant. Colostrum, a living tissue, is ideally suited for your infant's first feedings. Over the first few months, the fat, carbohydrate and protein content of the breast milk changes according to your infant's feeding requirements and the maturity of his intestines. There are even daily fluctuations in the fat content of your milk between the beginning and the end of each feeding, and between the milk produced in the morning and that produced in the evening. The reasons for these fluctuations in fat content are uncertain, but they may play an important role in appetite control.

What is more exciting than all the advantages I have discussed are the recent discoveries about human milk. Recent studies show that human milk contains more **taurine**, an amino acid essential to brain growth. Human milk contains **prostaglandins**, a hormone which benefits the intestines and circulatory system. Although the practical significance of these discoveries is still uncertain, I predict that over the next few years even more exciting discoveries will confirm the superiority of human milk for human babies. (See page 118 for discussion on the adaptability of human milk to the premature infant.)

Advantages to Mother

What are the advantages of breastfeeding for you as a woman and mother? Breastfeeding makes bonding your newborn much easier and the importance of this bonding relationship has been emphasized earlier (see **Bonding**, page 47). The **oxytocin** produced by breastfeeding helps to contract your uterus after birth and lessens the chance of postpartum bleeding. There has been much attention given lately to the possibility that the hormone **prolactin**, produced by continued breastfeeding, is a ''mothering hormone.'' Injection of this hormone into animals has induced mothering qualities even in males. It is entirely possible that prolactin greatly contributes to a mother's maternal instincts. The ''radiance'' which is described in breastfeeding mothers may also be a result of this hormonal influence. Mothers tell me that breastfeeding is a pleasant, sensual experience.

Our society is very conscious about protecting a mother's nerves. Breastfeeding does interfere with sleep and fatigue may be a problem. Your chances of postpartum depression are, however, actually much less if you are breastfeeding, possibly because of the increased production of prolactin.

There is a lower incidence of breast cancer in women who have breastfed. This may be an important consideration if there is a strong family history of cancer.

For the advocates of the ''Let's have babies conveniently philosophy,'' you may find that breastfeeding is actually more convenient. Many mothers find that the instant availability and proper temperature of the milk (especially at night and while travelling) makes breastfeeding less time-consuming and difficult than the mathematics of formula preparation and its accompanying paraphernalia.

Advantages to Family

Natural child spacing is possible with breastfeeding. Although not a foolproof method of contraception, breastfeeding does suppress ovulation in many women, but only if you breastfeed frequently and totally.

Breastfeeding also has certain economic benefits. Your baby will probably be healthier and so you will have fewer medical and dental bills. In addition, you will save money by not buying formulas and canned baby foods. Breastfeeding mothers have one free hand with which to mother another sibling or two. On occasion, nursing can become story time for a toddler or just a time to sit and cuddle-talk. This free hand of mother's can go a long way in easing feelings of being left out. As a matter of course, other family members are automatically and casually introduced to a beautiful, natural life process.

How Your Breasts Make Milk

A successful breastfeeding relationship requires a thorough knowledge of the anatomy and physiology of breastfeeding. Success requires knowledge, knowledge provides comfort and comfort is the foundation of success. With these principles in mind, we shall discuss the breastfeeding relationship.

Figure 1.
Structure and function of the breast

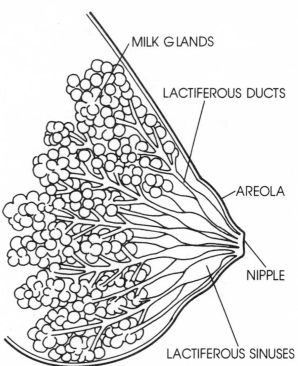

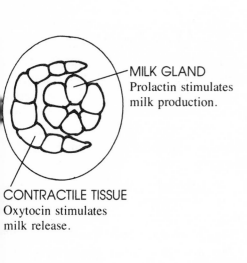

MILK GLAND
Prolactin stimulates
milk production.

CONTRACTILE TISSUE
Oxytocin stimulates
milk release.

The breasts or mammary glands are illustrated in Figure 1. Milk production occurs in tiny cells called **alveoli**, which are arranged in grape-like clusters around a central ductule into which milk drains. These ductules merge into dilated milk reservoirs called **lactiferous (milk-carrying) sinuses**. These sinuses begin at the areola of your breasts (pigmented area surrounding your nipple) and from these sinuses, milk empties into between fifteen and twenty openings in your nipple. Surrounding each

97

milk-producing alveolus is contractile tissue which, upon hormonal stimulation, squeezes milk out of the alveoli into the ducts. Sucking stimulates the nerve endings in your nipple, which stimulate the pituitary gland to secrete the hormone called prolactin, which stimulates the alveoli to produce and secrete milk. The first milk secreted, called **foremilk**, is the first milk your baby receives at each feeding. It is somewhat thin, like skim-milk, because of its lower fat content. Continued sucking causes the pituitary gland to produce another hormone called oxytocin. This stimulates the band of contractile tissue surrounding the alveoli to contract like a rubber band and squeeze a large supply of milk from the aveoli into the sinuses. This later milk, or **hindmilk**, has much greater nutritional value because it has a much higher fat content and slightly higher protein content. This sudden outpouring of hindmilk is called **the letdown reflex** because of the "letting down" of a large amount of creamier milk from the alveoli into the sinuses. This is also called the **milk ejection reflex**.

I have chosen to use the term "milk ejection reflex" in this book rather than the term "letdown reflex" because of an incident which occurred in my first year of medical practice. While making hospital rounds one day, I entered the room of a new mother nursing her baby and asked if she had any problems. She thereupon exclaimed, "Yes, I haven't experienced any letdown yet." I had no idea what she was talking about but assumed that it had something to do with depression and so I said something like, "Oh, that's all right. Some mothers do and some mothers don't." It was only later after asking my wife about the term "letdown," that I learned my patient was referring to her breasts and not to her mind. At that point, I realized that in all those years of medical training, I had been taught nothing about mammary function, perhaps because it was not considered very scientific. Later, when I became a teacher of medical students, I vowed that this glaring lack of knowledge about such a beautiful human function would not be passed on to the next generation of physicians. Because I find the usual term "letdown reflex" somewhat depressing, I will use the term "milk ejection reflex."

A successful milk ejection reflex is a fundamental key to successful breastfeeding. Oxytocin release is affected by fear, tension, pain and fatigue. If oxytocin is not released in sufficient quantities, the milk ejection reflex is faulty and the infant receives mostly foremilk, which is insufficient in quality and quantity for his nutrition and satisfaction.

Milk production works on the supply and demand princi-ple; the more your infant sucks, the more you will supply, until you have both negotiated a proper balance. Your baby develops a ''timer'' to his feedings, and your breasts and pituitary also develop an automatic timer synchronized to your baby's timer. For example, a mother may feel milk ejection reflex (her timer) at the same time her baby cries for a feeding, although the two may be miles apart. Breastfeeding problems occur when this timer and the supply and demand relationship is upset.

How Your Infant Sucks

Aroused by the touch of your nipple to his cheek and the scent of your milk, the infant's lips grasp the areola of your breast and the tongue thrusts forward to draw the nipple into and against the roof of the mouth. The infant's lips and jaw compress the areola and underlying milk sinuses, pushing milk toward the nipple. The infant's lips and large fat pads in the cheek provide an effect-ive seal, creating negative pressure within the mouth. The infant's tongue then ''milks'' the nipple in a rhythmic motion toward the back of the tongue, and little squirts of milk are then swallowed. (Sucking milk from a bottle through a rubber nipple is a different process. Because milk flows more easily from a bottle nipple, jaw compression and negative pressure are less necessary and the milking action of the tongue is different. The different sucking actions required by breast and bottle nipples may lead to **nipple confusion** if the baby is switched from one to the other.)

Tips for a Successful Breastfeeding Relationship

● **Breast Preparation**
Remember, just as parenting begins before birth, so does prepa-ration for breastfeeding. Childbirth education classes will instruct you in the anatomy and physiology of milk production, the techniques of breastfeeding and ways of overcoming com-mon problems. The many visual aids accompanying these clas-ses are extremely beneficial to understanding breastfeeding. Attending an entire series of La Leche League meetings is extremely valuable, both to prepare for breastfeeding and to acquaint yourself with a valuable support group, which you may need to call upon for advice and support during your first few months of breastfeeding.

Preparation of your breasts, particularly your nipples, is extremely important for successful breastfeeding. Women with fair skin, especially redheads, experience more difficulty with nipple soreness. It is wise to devote some time to conditioning your nipples during the last months of pregnancy. Gentle friction of your nipples at regular intervals over a long period of time serves to toughen them. Do this by rubbing your nipples with a bath towel, and also by wearing a nursing bra and dropping the flaps, to expose your nipples to the gentle friction of your clothing. Glands in the areola of your breast secrete natural oils which cleanse and lubricate; therefore do not remove these natural emollients with soap. Plain water is sufficient. Frequent exposure of your nipples to air and sunshine is also a good way to condition your nipples.

Inverted nipples require some special preparation prior to breastfeeding. Normally there is a generous supply of elastic and erectile tissue in the areola and nipple which allows the baby to stretch the nipple into his mouth during sucking. Some women have a different type of elastic tissue in their nipples which causes the nipples to invert when stimulated rather than become erect, making it difficult for the baby to grasp the nipple by himself. In order to determine whether your nipples are really inverted or just slightly flat, squeeze the areola of your breast between thumb and forefinger. An erect or flat nipple will protrude more, whereas an inverted nipple will retract. If your nipples do invert, the following nipple stretching exercises are important:

1. While supporting your breast with the palm of your hand, grasp the base of the nipple and some areola and stretch the nip-

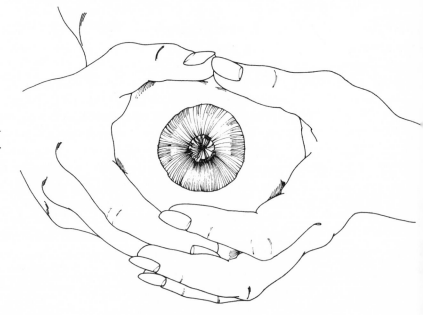

Figure 2.
Breast massage is the first step towards manual expression of milk.

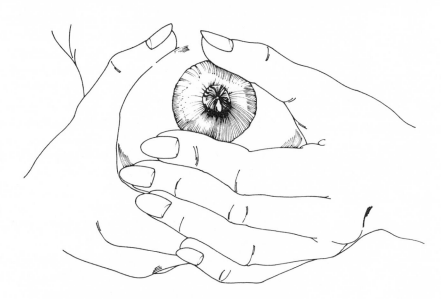

Figure 3.
Technique of manual
expression.

ple outward with your thumb and forefinger.

2. Roll your nipple clockwise and counterclockwise while holding the base of your nipple between your thumb and forefinger.

3. Stretch the areolar tissue at the base of the nipple by pulling the areola at right angles outward from the nipple (**the Hoffman technique**).

4. The use of a breast shield worn in the last six weeks of pregnancy encourages the nipple and areola area to protrude more. This type of shield, and instructions for its use, can be obtained from your local La Leche League.

Priming the pump, the manual expression of colostrum during the last six weeks of pregnancy, helps prepare your breasts to give a rich colostrum meal during your baby's first breastfeedings. I advise you to start this priming after you have devoted a few weeks to conditioning your nipples. The technique of breast massage and manual expression is shown in Figures 2 and 3. The first step in hand expression is a good breast massage. Cup your breasts with thumbs together above and fingers together below. Gently squeeze and massage the breast in an inward and downward direction toward the nipple. Continue this massage until the breasts feel warm and appear flushed. Then, while supporting your breast with one hand, place the thumb and forefinger of the other hand around the edge of your areola. While pressing inward toward the chest wall, squeeze thumb and forefinger together gently until secretion is obtained. Do not produce friction by sliding thumb and forefinger against the skin toward the nipple. Rotate your hand around the areola in order to reach all the milk sinuses which radiate from your areola toward the nipple.

Alternate sides every few minutes and make sure to carry out this manual expression very gently twice a day. It may take a while to see any colostrum at all and some mothers never do. But don't worry. It will be there when your baby nurses. For further illustration on the technique of manual expression of breast milk, see the book **Womanly Art of Breastfeeding**, published by the La Leche League. Breast preparation also helps some women overcome a personal reluctance to manipulate their breasts. Women who feel uncomfortable handling their breasts may have similar feelings about allowing their babies access to their breasts.

In addition to preparing your body for breastfeeding, preparing your mind is equally important. A comfortable attitude toward breastfeeding is necessary, especially if your confidence as a new parent is a bit shaky.

● **Getting the Right Start**

Early, frequent feeding on a demand basis combined with early hospital bonding and rooming-in, are the keys to successful breastfeeding. Begin breastfeeding immediately after birth if possible (see **Bonding**, page 52) and let your baby nurse as long and as frequently as he wishes. Don't clock watch! Mothers are often advised to begin nursing only a few minutes at a time and to gradually build up, but this is usually unnecessary. If your nipple conditioning has been adequate, you should not feel sore. Your baby seldom has such a ravenous appetite the first day anyway. Your breasts are softer and less engorged in the first twenty-four hours and babies learn to suck more easily on softer breasts. Your baby should determine the time and duration of his feeding, not the hospital. Although your baby has a natural instinct to root toward your nipple and to suck, he may need a little direction during the first few days. Use the two finger technique to make your nipple easier to grasp.

Grasp your breast just above the areolar margin with thumb and forefinger or first and second fingers and press slightly harder above the nipple. This method increases the nipple protractility and tilts the nipple slightly upward towards the roof of the baby's mouth. You may also use this technique to squeeze a little milk into his mouth if your infant is a bit uncooperative. He will use his tongue to draw your nipple into his mouth. Position your areola in his mouth so that the main pressure is applied to your areola (where the milk reservoirs are located) rather than entirely on your nipple. Be sure his nostrils are clear and unobstructed so that he can breathe easily while nursing.

Establishing a successful breastfeeding relationship is a total commitment in time and energy.

The hospital practice of weighing babies before and after feedings to determine how much milk they receive is both unnecessary and inaccurate. A simple statement from an inexperienced nurse such as ''He didn't gain any weight after that last feeding'' implies that he didn't get any milk. This may create just enough tension in an already apprehensive mother to trigger difficulties in a good breastfeeding relationship. Supplemental bottles in the nursery, either water or formula, interfere with the establishment of the supply and demand relationship as well as the timing principles previously discussed and therefore should be avoided. (See **Relief Bottles**, page 106 and **Potential Milk Allergy**, page 144 .) Not only are they unnecessary and confusing to the baby, but they also undermine the mother's morale by implying she hasn't enough milk to satisfy her baby.

A SUGGESTED TECHNIQUE FOR BREASTFEEDING

1. **Positioning Yourself.**
   Either sit up in bed with pillows behind your back, lie on your side in bed, or sit in a rocking chair with high arms. Pillows are a real must.

2. **Positioning Baby.**
   Undress your baby to promote skin to skin contact. Place a pillow on your lap and under the arm which will support your baby. Nestle your baby in your arms by letting his head rest in the bend of your arm, his back along your forearm, and his buttocks in your hand. His head should be straight, neither bent forward nor arched backward; his head not turned in relation to the rest of his body. His head (and body) should face your breast directly, as if an imaginary line were drawn from the center of your breast through the center of your nipple through the center of his mouth.

3. Manually express a few drops of milk and use this milk to moisten your nipple and areola.

4. Cup your breast with the other hand. Support your breast with your fingers beneath and your thumb above your areola.

5. Stimulate baby to open his mouth very wide. Tickle his lips with your milk-moistened nipple and as soon as his mouth is open wide, draw baby very close, centering your nipple and areola into his mouth. His tongue should be beneath your nipple; his lips should be relaxed and everted, not tight and pursed. Attempt to get a large part of your areola into baby's mouth. If you feel most of the pressure is painfully directed onto your nipple, pull his lower jaw and lip downward to open his mouth wider. If baby does not cooperate, break the suction and start again. It is important that baby learns how to suck the right way. Most babies learn to suck as a natural instinct. Some babies have to be taught.

As director of a university hospital newborn nursery, and as a pediatrician in several other hospital nurseries, I have had the opportunity to observe the influence of hospital breastfeeding policies on breastfeeding relationships. Mothers who practiced the above-mentioned principles to get the right start showed two outstanding differences. Their milk came in earlier, usually around the second or third day, as opposed to other mothers whose milk did not come until the fourth or fifth day. The incidence of a continued, successful breastfeeding relationship was much higher.

● **Getting Through the First Month—The Care and Feeding of the Mother**

The success or failure of the breastfeeding relationship is usually determined in the first month. Most nursing couples who can make it through the first month, usually settle down to a successful, long-term breastfeeding relationship. Despite what books and classes tell you, this first month will probably be the most exhausting, time-consuming and energy-draining period of your entire child-rearing experience. On the bright side, however, the investment you made in your breastfeeding relationship in the first month will pay life-long dividends to the health and happiness of your child. Establishing a successful breastfeeding relationship should be top priority, a total commitment in time and energy which supersedes all other familial and social obligations. Parenting is serious business and there simply aren't any shortcuts in the first month, the adjustment period.

Good nutrition is also essential. You will require an extra 600 calories per day of a balanced diet to meet your lactation demands. Each day you need at least 10 ounces of lean meat, fish or poultry; a serving of both fruit and vegetables; one egg; three to four servings of whole grain products; and at least one glass of milk (or its equivalent, such as cheese or yogurt. You don't have to drink milk to make milk). Vitamin and iron supplements may be prescribed by your physician. Imported beer which contains brewer's yeast is rich in Vitamin B and is a good nutrient source for lactation. Your nutritional requirements during lactation are very similar to the requirements during the latter months of pregnancy (see page 44).

Alcoholic beverages consumed in moderation (equivalent to two glasses of wine a day) will not harm your baby. I strongly discourage cigarette smoking during breastfeeding since nicotine may pass into your milk and to your baby. The effects of small amounts of nicotine on your baby are uncertain and it should be avoided. A newborn baby should not be exposed to the smoke from cigarettes, cigars or pipes. These fumes irritate his respiratory tract.

"All give and no take" may sound like good parenting but there is a limit to maternal reserves. Mothering of the breastfeeding mother by her husband, as well as supportive friends and relatives are essential. (See page 76 for tips on mothering the mother).

Fathers, make mothers feel like a queen by constantly rewarding her valuable and unique feminine role. Mothers, get as much rest as possible, although this is easier said than done. Attempt to master the art of cat-napping as soon as possible (use late pregnancy as an appropriate time to practice) because your sleep habits will become those of your infant's—short and frequent. If you have prepared yourself for the fact that a full night's sleep is a luxury rather than a right as a parent, then a change in sleep habits may not be such a shock.

Most parents who persevere in establishing good breastfeeding relationships during the first month sail relatively smoothly from then on. (For further discussion of the first month, see **The Adjustment Period**, page 73 .)

● **A Word on Relief Bottles**

It is customary in many hospital nurseries to give mothers a gift pack of formula with the subtle message "If you don't have enough milk or you want some relief, use formula in a bottle." I discourage the use of these bottles, especially for the first two months, for the following reasons:

1. At the very stage when a newborn is learning to develop an effective sucking technique, introduction of a rubber nipple and bottle may cause **nipple confusion** (see pages 99 , 117). Nipple confusion is less of a problem several months later when your infant's sucking mechanism is more mature.

2. Substituting a feeding with a relief bottle in the first few months may interfere with the harmonious supply and demand relationship and may throw the "timers" off. Engorgement often results from using relief bottles. If you must use a relief formula, empty your breasts by hand nursing (see page 101) when your breasts are full.

3. Even one bottle of formula may temporarily diminish the growth of normal intestinal bacteria and allow pathogenic bacteria to grow in the intestines. If you must leave a bottle for your baby, the bottle should contain human milk. (See **Storage of Milk**, page 120 .)

4. Formulas may introduce a potential allergen if your baby is allergic to non-human milk. The younger the infant, the greater the susceptibility of his immature intestines to potential allergens. Giving a cow's milk formula too early may result in more severe allergic reactions later on when cow's milk is introduced into your infant's diet.

5. Unless advised by your doctor for medical reasons, breastfeeding babies do not need extra water. They get enough water in your milk.

● **Scheduling the Breastfeeding Baby**

Very early in your nursing relationship, you will realize that the term ''schedule'' is a misconception popularized by baby book writers who have never breastfed. The only schedule your baby has is his own and the only two people who know how often and how much your baby should feed are you and your baby. One of the most beautiful and natural biological negotiations is a mother and her suckling baby working to get their supply and demand signals together. Listen to your baby's cues and don't clock-watch! Most babies will eventually learn to feed in a pattern that fits their psychological and biological needs.

Most mothers go through exhausting periods in the breastfeeding relationship when they would give anything for some sort of regular schedule. The following variables in the breastfeeding relationship may help you to understand the biological fact that breastfeeding babies do not schedule easily:

1. Your baby will suck as long and as frequently as his nutritional needs dictate. You may read that most babies obtain 90 per cent of their milk from a breast in the first five minutes. While this is often true, many babies need to suck longer at one breast to obtain sufficient milk, especially in the first few months. This may be due to the inefficiency of his sucking, or the fact that you may have a series of milk ejection reflexes rather than just one large milk ejection at the beginning of the feeding. In this case, your baby's own biological clock should be the only timer. (Some babies will nurse ten or fifteen minutes on the first breast before moving to the second breast; others will nurse a few minutes on the first breast, switch to the second for a few minutes and then back to the first (called **switch nursing**). The reason for this curious technique of switch nursing is very simple. When a baby begins sucking on the first breast, he initially gets the thinner foremilk. With continued sucking, a milk ejection reflex rewards him with a large volume of creamy, satisfying milk, which most babies obtain in the first three to four minutes of sucking. While your baby is sucking on the first breast, the second breast is leaking much of the foremilk. Rather than continuing to suckle the first breast for ten more minutes, the baby switches over to the second breast and immediately obtains pre-mixed, more satisfying hindmilk. Some babies soon learn that the second breast is best.

2. The fat content (the main appetite satisfier) in your milk changes during the day and throughout your months of nursing. Your baby may nurse more often when the fat content is lowest (e.g. late afternoon, early evening) in order to obtain sufficient nutrition.

3. Breast milk is more rapidly digested than formula and thus breastfed babies may feel hungry more often than formula-fed babies.

4. Babies have growth spurts during which they nurse more often and more vigorously in order to balance the supply and demand.

5. Babies often enjoy non-nutritive sucking and also periods of one-minute sucking, simply to obtain a little of the watery foremilk when they are thirsty but not hungry.

Your baby will automatically adjust the length and frequency of his feedings to obtain more calories when he is growing or more water when he is simply thirsty. He will also learn when to stop eating, a valuable lesson in appetite control. (See **Marathoning**, page 112 ; **Nursing Strike**, page 114 ; **Breastfeeding and Working Mothers**, page 119 .)

Overcoming Breastfeeding Problems

Virtually all breastfeeding problems occur because of inadequate preparation and a poor start to the relationship.

● **Milk Not Coming In**

This is the earliest of breastfeeding problems. As I make hospital rounds, it is disappointing to enter a new mother's room on the third postpartum day, only to find an unhappy and frustrated new mother saying, "My milk has not yet come in." What causes this and how can it be prevented?

During the first few days, breast milk normally consists of colostrum, small in quantity but rich in nutrition and protective immunity. By the third day, most mothers should feel their "milk coming in" and by the end of the first week, the sensation of the milk ejection reflex should be apparent.

A delay in milk production may be due to a medical complication at the time of birth, either in the mother or baby, which temporarily delays the bonding relationship and simply sets everything back a few days. If this occurs, it is necessary to prepare a mother for the fact that her milk may be late coming in, but that it will come in. Due to this unfortunate temporary disruption, she may have to work harder for the first week to establish the breastfeeding relationship.

In a well baby and a well mother, all too often the cause of "milk not coming in" is that someone is tampering with both baby's and mother's "timers." These "timers" are upset by not letting baby suck early enough, not rooming-in, not feeding on demand, and supplemental feeding of formula or water. Many times, upon hearing the complaint of "milk not coming in," I will seek out the nurses and ask, "Okay, confess, who has been slipping the baby extra food?" Often, well-meaning nurses not wishing to hear a baby cry, will feed the baby supplemental formula in the nursery. The formula temporarily satisfies his hunger so that by the time the schedule says baby should go to his mother, he is sleepy and not hungry. The baby will therefore not suck vigorously, the mother will not produce milk and the vicious cycle begins, often accompanied by anxiety and a feeling of inadequacy on the part of the mother, which further suppresses lactation. Early bonding, rooming-in and demand feedings, plus encouragement and support by the hospital staff, can prevent this problem.

● **Too Much Milk—Engorgement**

In addition to "not enough milk" there is the problem of too much milk, or **engorgement**, which is both a physical discomfort to mother and a frustration to baby. Engorgement in the first few weeks usually means that the basic principles of successful breastfeeding have been tampered with. Engorgement in the later months is usually due to some temporary upset in the baby's or family's routine that throws the "timer" out of balance (e.g. trips, too many demanding visitors whose presence leads to use of supplementary formula, and missed feedings). Engorgement is a very uncomfortable, vicious cycle. If your breasts are engorged, the nipple-areolar angle flattens so that your baby cannot suck on the areola (where the milk sinuses are found) but can only suck on a nubbin of your nipple (ouch). He gets less milk this way, but continued sucking stimulates milk production and engorgement increases. The increased milk production, but decreased milk drainage, causes the tension to rise within the lactiferous sinuses of your breasts. Your milk ejection reflex is suppressed and the milk stagnates further. You keep producing but not emptying. A basic principle of the human body is that fluid must be in a dynamic state (constantly moving) or infection of this stagnant fluid can result. Continued sucking on a non-producing nipple causes cracks which allow entry of bacteria into the breast. A breast infection called **mastitis** results. Painful breast enlargement and some swelling of the lymph glands under your arm may be the only result of engorgement. You may not necessarily develop mastitis. However, localized, painful, red, hot areas in your breasts, accompanied by fever and chills is often symptomatic of mastitis and medical attention should be sought before a breast abscess results.

Engorgement can usually be prevented by following the basic principles of successful breastfeeding:

1. Follow the tips for successful breastfeeding discussed on page 99 .

2. If your baby is not ready to nurse, but your breasts are uncomfortably full, manually express your milk into a bottle and freeze the excess milk for a time when it may be needed. (See **Technique of Manual Expression**, page 101 .)

3. If you wake during the night with uncomfortably full breasts, simply pick your baby up and put him to your breast to get some relief. This can usually be done without disturbing the baby.

4. Be sure your nursing bra is comfortably loose. A bra that is too tight may aggravate engorgement.

The primary goal in treating engorgement is to get the milk out. First, soften your breasts by manually expressing some milk (see previous section on hand expression) until your nipple protrudes enough for your infant to suck and for complete drainage. If plugged ducts are causing your engorgement, you may have to use more forceful manual expressions. **Above all, don't stop nursing!** Keep the milk flowing or infection will result. Hot or cold compresses may alleviate your pain and soften your breasts. Immersing the engorged breasts in comfortably hot water for ten minutes can facilitate emptying. Antibiotics are usually not necessary if your milk begins flowing well and mastitis has not yet occurred. Even if mastitis occurs, your baby's sucking, which starts the milk flowing again, is the main treatment for breast infection. Antibiotics are given to prevent the infection from worsening. If you have an infection, in addition to taking antibiotics, get plenty of rest and drink a lot of fluids.

One of the most common misconceptions regarding treatment of breast infections is that you should stop nursing and give the breasts a rest. This is certainly not correct and usually results in further stagnation of the milk, a worsening of the breast infection and premature weaning.

● **Sore Nipples**

Sore nipples sometimes occur during breastfeeding, especially if they become cracked. Following the principles of successful breastfeeding, especially nipple preparation prepartum, is a preventive measure. However, some degree of nipple soreness is to be expected during the first few days of breastfeeding. (Painful nipples around two to three weeks after delivery may be caused by a fungus infection. Your doctor should be consulted.)

At the first sign of soreness, break open a capsule of Vitamin E oil and massage it into and around your nipples. Later on, mild ointments such as lanolin (if you are not allergic to wool) may help, but use them sparingly. Expose your nipples to air and sunshine frequently. Applying ice may temporarily relieve the pain. Avoid soaps and other drying agents since these encourage cracking. Nurse your baby in different positions "around the nipple clock" thereby distributing the sucking pressure evenly around the nipple and areola. Getting more of the areola into the baby's mouth will relieve pressure on the nipple. To accomplish this, place your forefinger on baby's chin and pull your baby's jaw downward so as to open his mouth wider and evert his lower lip. This procedure should immediately relieve pressure on your nipples. Initially you may need another person to help you pull down your baby's jaw. You may also be able to take your hand off your breast to accomplish this.

Nursing less frequently does not help sore nipples since engorgement may result. A hungrier baby also nurses more intensely, which further aggravates the soreness. Nurse on the less painful nipple first and switch to the sore nipple after the milk ejection reflex occurs. Remember not to "pull" your baby off the nipple at the end of the nursing, but rather break the suction by inserting your fingers into the corners of his mouth and gently lifting his lips and gums off the nipple.

Inverted nipples (see page 100) that persist after baby's birth, despite nipple preparation, can be very frustrating. Continue preparation exercises. Manually erect and guide the nipple and areola into your baby's mouth. After prolonged sucking, your nipple should gradually evert itself. In my experience, nipple shields are of little value in the treatment of sore nipples, but a breast shield worn between, not during, nursing may help. (See page 101 .)

● **How to Control Your Weight While Breastfeeding**

Some mothers complain of difficulty losing weight while

breastfeeding despite the extra calories that are used during lactation. The principles of nutrition and weight control during lactation are very similar to those during pregnancy and adolescence. In order to provide for the nutritional needs of both you and your baby, you need a well-balanced diet. Most nursing mothers can eat around 2000 calories of nutritious foods per day and still control their weight. Avoid crash diets. These lead to nutritional deficiencies which may lessen your milk volume and reduce your stamina. Avoid junk foods which are high in calories and low in nutrition. Exercise is the safest and most effective way the lactating mother can control her weight. Exercise burns excess fat without compromising nutrition. This may be easier said than done since many nursing mothers lack the time and energy to increase their exercise. A practical exercise for nursing mothers is to take your baby with you for at least a half-hour walk each day. (For further nutritional advice see **Nutrition During Pregnancy**, page 43.)

● **Persistently Hungry Baby/Exhausted Mother— Marathoning**

"He wants to nurse all day and night—I can't seem to satisfy him and I am tired." The most important part of the preceding statement is "I am tired." Fatigue suppresses lactation and lessens your enjoyment of a new baby. The first question I will ask a new mother who is having breastfeeding problems is "Are you overly tired?" I know that as long as her maternal reserve has not been exhausted, she can cope with any problem, given a little time and guidance. If the answer is "Yes, I am exhausted" then she needs advice and support.

Perhaps an understanding of why babies marathon will enable you to be more accepting of this exhausting behavior. I believe that nature intended babies to marathon and this belief is supported by the evidence that human milk is digested more rapidly than formula and therefore breastfed babies need to be fed more frequently. Babies have "frequency days" when they want to nurse all the time. This is nature's supply and demand principle, working in response to a sudden growth spurt. These are natural signs from your baby which may tax your maternal reserve to the limit but will later reap a rich reward. Studies have shown that mothers who nurse frequently have a higher level of prolactin, the mothering hormone which is believed to enhance mothering qualities. Medically speaking, lactating breasts were designed to be drained not kept full. Mothers who nurse frequently usually experience less painful engorgement and fewer breast infections. In the first few weeks, it is good for babies to breastfeed around the clock. Afterwards, if your baby is thriving, it is not necessary to purposely awaken your baby during the night, but rather let him awaken you if he needs to be fed. In small and/or premature babies, and babies who are not gaining weight adequately, night feedings should be encouraged.

Advice in managing this problem is difficult to give. Much depends upon your priorities of parenting and your commitment to breastfeeding, but here are a few tips:

1. Don't feel your baby is not getting enough milk. This usually isn't true and this feeling alone may actually suppress your lactation. Signs that your baby is getting enough milk in the first few weeks are: frequent wet diapers (at least six to eight per day, two of which are bowel movements. This amount is meant as a guide only; it is not unusual for babies not to stool for a few days), weight gain (you can weigh your baby at the doctor's office), a generally happy baby, the baby has a vigorous suck and an audible swallowing of milk, and usually experiencing a milk ejection reflex during feeding. If your baby nurses very frequently, you may not always feel the same sensation of breast fullness as you do after a stretch of five or six hours without nursing.

2. Be sure your baby is getting mostly milk at each feeding and not mostly air. (See **Air Swallowing**, page 141 .) Also, remember that small, frequent feedings may be more in tune with your baby's appetite, albeit possibly more of a drain on your maternal reserves. Your baby may also simply love to suck, and gourmet that he is, may consider your breast his pacifier. If you have this type of feeding relationship, you might as well resign yourself to his pattern, put breastfeeding as your top priority at this time and do your best to relax during his feeding times.

3. Master the art of cat-napping. Sleep when your baby sleeps. This will require putting aside many of the seemingly important household chores. ''I don't get anything done'' is a common statement by mothers whose babies breastfeed frequently. You are getting done what really needs to be done — mothering.

4. Feed in a pleasant environment, turn on your favorite music, perhaps undress and lie down to increase skin-to-skin contact. He will eventually reward your perseverance by gradually lengthening his intervals between feedings. In my experience, fatigue is usually caused not so much by the baby's frequent feedings, but rather by the demands on your energy of his frequent feedings combined with those of pressing social and domestic obligations. If this is the case, the obvious answer is to transfer some of the energy required for your less important obligations to your baby. There will be plenty of time for these other things later on, but your baby is a baby now and won't be one for very long.

5. A common solution to this problem is the use of artificial fillers, such as a supplemental bottle or cereal given by Dad or a friend while you catch up on some sleep. This advice is considered heresy in the doctrine of successful breastfeeding and should be used only as the last resort. It usually does not work anyway. Filler food is a very tempting solution but if it is over-used, you will be tampering with your baby's supply and demand signals. It might actually trigger a chain of breastfeeding problems which may result in the end of your breastfeeding relationship. A sudden increased demand to nurse is often misinterpreted as a need for solid foods to satisfy him. This is usually not the case until the age of four to six months. Your baby is simply signalling that he needs more milk to meet the increased demands of a sudden growth spurt. If you accommodate his increased demand with more frequent breastfeedings, after a few days your supply will increase to meet his demand and the supply-demand relationship will be re-established. (See **When to Start Solid Foods**, page 129 .)

● **I Don't Have Enough Milk**

There may be brief periods during your nursing relationship when your breast milk decreases in quantity, usually as a result of some change in your environment, your nutrition, or the health of you or your baby. This is normally a very temporary frustration and easily corrected by reviewing your breastfeeding check list. (See **Tips For a Successful Breastfeeding Relationship**, page 99 .) This problem can usually be solved simply by getting more rest, learning to relax, drinking more fluids and nursing more frequently.

● **Nursing Strike**

Your baby may temporarily lose interest in nursing for a few days, but please don't immediately interpret this as his time for weaning. The cause of this temporary lack of interest in breastfeeding is usually either a physical upset such as a cold or teething, or some emotional upset such as a reaction to a recent change in his environment or your behavior. Give him extra love and security during this period and continue to offer your breasts (you may have to trick him, for example, during sleep) until the strike is over.

● **Breastfeeding the Sleepy Baby**

One of the most frustrating experiences for a new mother is breastfeeding a baby who likes to suck a little and sleep a little —the baby who after a few sucks, falls asleep before getting much milk. This is especially common in small and premature babies. To overcome this problem:

1. Undress your baby to increase skin to skin contact.

2. Manually express some milk immediately before feeding. This will soften your breasts and allow your little snoozer to get more of your areola into his mouth and thus get more milk more easily.

3. As your baby's sucking intensity and swallowing diminishes, a gentle prodding is in order, such as tickling his cheeks.

4. The "burp and switch" technique. If he refuses to resume effective sucking, take him off the first breast. Sit him upright, allowing the air in his stomach to rise and allowing him to burp. (See **Air Swallowing**, page 141.) As he awakens, switch him to the second breast. Repeat the procedure as he starts to fall asleep on the second breast (See **Switch Nursing**, page 107).

● **The Breastfeeding Baby Who Fails to Thrive**

The medical term for poor weight gain is **failure to thrive**. This discussion of failure to thrive is limited to the infant with no underlying illness which might cause him not to grow.

Failure to thrive in the first few weeks results from one of three basic problems: inadequate milk release, inadequate milk production or faulty sucking techniques. Poor weight gain in breastfed infants is usually due to inadequate release of milk rather than inadequate milk production, although the two are related. As we have previously discussed, when a baby begins suckling, he first receives the foremilk, which is like skim milk, a milk lower in fat and calorie content. With continued suckling, the letdown or milk ejection reflex should occur and your infant should receive the hindmilk, or whole milk, which is higher in fat, protein and calories. The failure of this milk ejection reflex and the consequent inadequate release of the hindmilk is the usual cause of failure to thrive in the breastfeeding infant. Babies who fail to thrive because they are not getting enough hindmilk do not appear sick. Their skin seems loose-fitting due to diminished fat and muscle growth and you are changing the usual six to eight wet diapers each day. The fact that his urine output seems normal but he is not gaining any weight means your baby is getting enough milk volume but not enough calories.

In my experience, the most common cause of early failure to thrive in a breastfeeding infant is that he did not get the proper start (see page 102), specifically resulting from the following situations: supplemental bottles were given, which led to nipple confusion; sedation given to the mother may have also sedated the baby and made him less eager to suck; the mother received improper advice and support during the early breastfeeding relationship while in the hospital; or there were postpartum adjustment problems (see page 74). Usually it is a combination of most of these problems which results in an inadequate breastfeeding relationship and consequently an inadequate milk ejection reflex. In order to determine if your milk ejection reflex is active, check for the following signs: Does your areola tense somewhat prior to feeding? Does your other breast begin to drip milk while your infant is suckling on one breast? If these signs are evident, chances are you are experiencing adequate milk ejection reflex even though you may not consciously feel your milk release. The next step is to check the list of factors that may inhibit your milk ejection reflex and milk production: improper diet, tension around the time of nursing, fatigue, lack of confidence that you can breastfeed, depression, smoking, caffeine or other drugs.

Once your infant's lack of weight gain is apparent, a vicious cycle begins. The less weight he gains, the less confidence you have. The feeling "I don't have enough milk" may trigger a chain of negative feelings which further inhibit your milk production. Let's break this vicious cycle and settle down to a comfortable nursing relationship by trying the following suggestions:

1. Improve your diet. (See page 105 .)

2. Obtain help to relieve yourself of fatigue-producing household chores.

3. Look at and stroke your baby during his feedings. The feedback your infant will give you will trigger the hormones necessary for your milk release.

4. Increase the frequency of feeding and approach each feeding with confidence. Although demand feeding is best for the baby who is gaining weight normally, you may try waking your baby during the day if he sleeps longer than four hours to encourage more frequent feedings. Taking your baby into bed with you at night will also encourage more frequent feedings during the night. Sleeping babies sometimes nurse very well. Mothers usually find the fatigue of night nursing less distressing than the worry about their baby's failure to gain weight.

5. Try **switch nursing** (see page 107). Use your baby's signals, not a clock, to switch to the other breast. As soon as the intensity of your baby's sucking begins to diminish and he pauses a little, renew his interest in sucking by switching immediately to the second breast. Then switch back to the first when his sucking signals dictate. Switch nursing seems to stimulate more of a mixture of foremilk and hindmilk and provides your infant with a larger volume of milk higher in calories, fat and proteins. This accounts for the old saying, ''The infant grows best at the second breast.''

6. Drugs which may interfere with lactation or baby's sucking ability are nicotine, caffeine, antihistamines, high doses of Vitamin B6 (pyridoxine), diuretics and oral contraceptives.

7. Oxytocin nasal spray, used either intra-nasally or sprayed into the back of the mouth, may improve milk ejection if the above measures are not successful. Consult your physician for advice on the use of this medication.

8. Faulty sucking techniques may also be a cause of failure to thrive in the breastfeeding infant. As we described on page 99 , proper sucking requires the baby to draw the nipple well into the mouth and compress the areola above the milk sinuses with his lips and jaws. Some babies engage in flutter sucking. They simply play with and lick the nipple but do not draw it far enough into the mouth and do not compress the milk sinuses around the areola with their lips and jaws. These babies get only the fore-milk, do not empty the breast well at each feeding and consequently do not grow well. In order to help your baby suck properly, experiment by holding him in various positions while he is sucking. Entice him onto your nipple by manually expressing a little milk. As he tastes the milk, make a longer nipple for him by grasping the areola of your breast between two fingers, or thumb and forefinger, and present the entire nipple-areolar area into his mouth. If he is not sucking on the areola, interrupt the feeding and begin again until he gets the idea. If your breasts are too full, it is difficult for your baby to grasp the areola. In this case, manually express some milk at the beginning of each feeding so that your baby is presented with a softer areola to grasp.

9. Unless advised by your doctor, avoid supplemental formulas as this usually increases nipple confusion, further interferes with the breastfeeding relationship and usually results in weaning. If supplemental formulas are medically indicated, use the Lact-Aid (available from your La Leche League). Lact-Aid is a small bag which contains formula and a tube leading from the bag to the nipple of your breast. The infant sucks on your breast and obtains both breast milk and supplemental formula. The supplemental formula provided by the Lact-Aid can then be discontinued as soon as your lactation and your baby's sucking techniques have improved.

Breastfeeding the baby who fails to thrive is primarily a matter of motivation. With the help of supportive physicians and your local La Leche League this temporary problem can be overcome.

Breastfeeding in Special Situations

● **Breastfeeding Your Premature and Hospitalized Infant**

A premature infant, particularly if he is sick and in a newborn intensive care unit, is a very heavy burden for parents. This is especially true if you have prepared yourself for a beautiful bonding relationship. The recent advances in newborn intensive care have alleviated this burden somewhat by increasing your chances of taking home a healthy baby from the hospital. This technology has also in some ways displaced mothering, and you may feel totally useless as your baby's care-giver. This feeling can eventually lead to negative feelings about your baby.

You should not be totally displaced as your infant's care-giver. This can be accomplished in two ways: by breastfeeding and touching. Even though you may not be able to hold your premature baby and he may not be strong enough to suck your breast, milk fed through a tube or eye dropper can still provide a bond which will be comforting to you and will provide valuable infection fighters and nutrients to your sick baby.

Premature babies need more proteins and calories for "catch-up" growth. It has recently been discovered that the milk of the mothers who deliver pre-term babies is higher in proteins and calories; another example of how the milk of a species adapts for the survival of the species.

Even otherwise healthy babies, who are only two or three weeks premature, may be slow feeders. They often suck weakly, tire quickly and fall asleep after only a few minutes of sucking. (See **Breastfeeding the Sleepy Baby**, page 115 .) Try to persevere. This frustrating feeding pattern will gradually improve as baby reaches term, i.e. a two-week premature baby will usually correct this problem by two weeks.

Premature babies should be fed more frequently for several reasons: Tiny babies have tiny tummies which fill more quickly. Premature babies tire more easily. Also, premature babies need more calories for catch-up growth. For this reason most premature babies should be fed every two hours. The sleep patterns of some prematures will not allow these frequent feedings. Whatever pattern gets the baby the most milk and you the most rest, is the preferred schedule. You may feel that you are constantly nursing. You are and your baby needs it.

Depending on the degree of his prematurity and illness, your baby will probably need supplementary formula as his prime nutrition source until he is mature enough to suck from your breast. By pumping your breast and having a strong desire to produce milk, you can provide food for your baby and keep your breast prepared for milk production until your baby is strong enough to suck. Human milk production by hand expression or with a pump is difficult for many mothers, but with medical assistance, La Leche League help, and a strong desire, you can do it.

In addition to breastfeeding, you can bond with your premature or sick baby by constant touching and stroking. In our university hospital nursery I encourage parents to sit beside their baby's incubator and to put their hands through specially designed ports so that they can gently stroke their baby's skin. As a result of this stroking, premature babies have fewer breathing disturbances. The contribution of the parent does indeed have a medical benefit. Parents who have been involved in the care of their premature or sick baby have fewer negative feelings towards, and fewer adjustment problems with, their baby later on. (See **Bonding Your Premature Baby**, page 49 and **Breastfeeding Twins**, page 477.)

● **Nursing Outside the Home**

Baby carriers (see page 420), nursing blouses or any loose top make nursing outside the home easier.

Certain cultures provide for carrying babies "in arms" constantly, a practice which would definitely have merit in our civilization. Public respect for a nursing couple should overwhelm any feeling of shyness or discomfort of nursing in public. You can be as discreet and private as you wish. "The public notices a screaming baby more than a nursing baby."

● **Working Mothers**

Whether you are working out of necessity or desire, breastfeeding is still to be encouraged, even though you and your baby may not always be within nursing distance of each other. The following tips on breastfeeding and working may help you keep your perspective as a mother even though you are working.

The choice of a babysitter who sincerely cares for your child's well-being is mandatory. (See **Tips on Choosing a**

Babysitter, page 190 .)

There will also naturally be some adjustment in your feeding routine. Feed your baby in the morning before you go to work, upon returning home, and then several times during the evening. Advise the babysitter not to feed him close to your time of arrival home so that a comfortable nursing relationship may begin immediately upon your return. Some babies actually choose to forego the bottle and wait for mother to return. If you work close to home, it may be possible to zip home during your lunch hour to breastfeed. Manually express your excess milk either at work or during nights and weekends. Store your milk either in bottles or in plastic bottle liners in the freezer (for two weeks), in the deep freeze (at 0° F if you plan to store it for many months), or in the refrigerator (if it will be used the next day). In this way, your baby can receive as much nourishment from your own milk as possible. Full-time mothering can resume on weekends when an increase in nursing frequency is to be expected, and actually should be encouraged, in order to keep your milk supply adequate. The ideal, of course, is to have the type of job which allows you to take your baby with you. I find that mothers who work and continue their breastfeeding relationship feel less anxious and guilty about leaving their baby. Both their baby and their work seem to profit. (See **Where's My Mommy?**, page 181 .)

Weaning

Early weaning is a custom in western society, yet I believe that it is an unfortunate break in the nurturing continuum. Weaning your baby should be a decision based upon your own parenting philosophies and the needs of your baby. I feel strongly that infant-led weaning is the best policy. When a mother asks me how many months she should nurse, I usually reply, ''There is no set number of years you should nurse your baby.''

In deciding this question, we may take a tip from nature. Nearly every species of mammal nurse their offspring until they triple their birth weight, which in humans is around one year of age. If your goal is to establish a comfortable maternal-infant bond, both nutritionally and emotionally, then infant-led weaning is the course to follow. Weaning may then occur any time between the ages of one and four years. Nursing toddlers are in my opinion, a beautiful sight. However, occasionally there may be raised eyebrows from poorly informed onlookers, whose negative feelings toward natural weaning betrays their lack of understanding of the toddler as a little person with big needs. For a toddler, breastfeeding is seldom the toddler's prime source of nutrition, but rather a snack or a consoling lift during periods of stress.

The story of babies who are weaned before their time often runs as follows: A baby is breastfed on demand for three or four months and is thriving well. Family life is smooth although mother is occasionally very tired. Baby is force-weaned at three months because of some factor which seems important at the time, such as a holiday. Within a month or two after weaning, the baby experiences illnesses such as diarrhea, colds or ear infections. Milk allergy is suspected and parenting the baby who was previously "such a well baby" becomes more stressful.

Parents who practice infant-led weaning seem to take their parenting commitment more seriously and the parent-child relationship operates at a higher level. This commitment also carries over to other aspects of child care.

● **Do's and Don'ts of Weaning**

The only "do" is to let your baby guide you about how and when he wants to wean. There are some definite "don'ts":

1. Don't wean by leaving your child abruptly. Except in special family circumstances, weaning by desertion is definitely to be frowned upon. It may be difficult enough for a baby to overcome separation from his mother without adding the stress of weaning.

2. Don't refuse your baby a nursing. Most mothers who practice infant-led weaning will automatically practice the "Don't offer, Don't refuse" advice advocated by the La Leche League.

3. Don't set up external standards for weaning. Do not try to wean your baby by a certain age or according to the expectations of others (e.g. Is that child still nursing?).

4. Don't worry that continued nursing will make your child too dependent. In my experience children who are weaned naturally, cling less.

The Non-Breastfeeding Approach to Infant Nutrition and Feeding

In the past five years, society has become nutrition-conscious. The principle of "I am what you feed me" has finally hit home to the modern day supermarket shopper. It is important to note that nutrition, or the lack of it, may have a profound effect on your child's physical and mental development as well as on his behavior, and may even affect his tendency to certain adult diseases so prevalent in our western culture.

What the RDA Really Means

We are constantly being advised what and how much to eat. Let's explore some of the scientific background and the rationale behind specific nutritional recommendations.

In the United States, two groups are continually studying infant nutritional needs—The Committee on Nutrition of the American Academy of Pediatrics and The Committee on Dietary Allowances of the Food and Nutrition Board of the National Research Council. These groups are composed of scientists working in the field of nutrition, who are motivated neither by profit nor popularity. Approximately every five years, they revise the **Recommended Dietary Allowances** (RDA). The RDAs are defined as "levels of intake of essential nutrients which, based on current knowledge, are considered to be adequate to meet nutritional needs of most healthy persons in the United States." Recommendations are made only after a certain dietary change has been investigated over a long period of time in a large group of infants. These groups emphasize that there are marked individual differences in nutritional requirements. To overcome the lack of knowledge about these differences, the RDAs exceed the needs of most individuals in order to be sure that the needs of nearly all individuals are satisfied. For most essential nutrients, if there is a wide margin of safety between excess and deficiency, the RDAs are usually considerably higher than the minimum requirements. If there is a narrow margin between deficiency and excess, the RDA may only be slightly higher than the minimal requirement. These safeguards are necessary because our knowledge of the exact requirements, deficiency levels, and toxicity levels, are not completely known for some nutrients.

How Formulas Are Made

The goal of the formula industry is to duplicate human milk composition as closely as possible. Although I recommend human milk as the primary source of infant nutrition, the commercially prepared infant formulas on today's shelves are both safe and effective sources of nutrition for most infants.

What do manufacturers put into their formulas? They first determine the basic recipe for all human nutrition—water, calories, proteins, fats, carbohydrates, vitamins and minerals. They next determine what the Recommended Dietary Allowances for all these ingredients are. They then determine what source in nature most closely resembles human milk. The answer is found by taking a step down our ancestral tree and investigating cow's milk. Cow's milk contains most of the nutrients necessary for infant nutrition, although not in quite the proper balance for humans. Certain vegetables such as soybeans are also a ready source of certain nutrients necessary for human nutrition. Formula manufacturers next take each of the basic nutritional elements and, using cow's milk and vegetable oil as basic building blocks, modify each of these basic ingredients to approximate as closely as possible the human milk recipe. Finally, by adding certain minerals and vitamins, an infant formula is created which, at least on paper, resembles very closely the composition of human milk. Commercial formulas have indeed closely approached the nutritional quality of human milk. However, the fats, carbohydrates, proteins and minerals of prepared formulas are not digested, absorbed and utilized quite as efficiently as those of human milk. The biological specificity of human milk (see page 94) is one of the basic stumbling blocks to preparing the ideal "humanized" infant formula.

Many earlier baby books mention recipes for preparing your own baby formula from evaporated milk, sugar, and water. These recipes are seldom used anymore and I do not recommend them. A mother is much better off spending her time on the feeding relationship than worrying about the mathematics of formula preparation.

Commercial formulas are currently available in three basic forms—powdered formula with directions on how much water to add; liquid concentrate to be mixed half-and-half with water; and ready-to-feed formulas which are ready to pour directly into a bottle. Your choice of formula is mainly a question of economics, powdered formulas being the least expensive, and ready-to-feed the most. One word of caution: Never mix the formula in greater strength than the directions state. Always add the specified amount of water. Adding too little water makes the formula too concentrated for your baby's immature gastrointestinal system and kidneys to handle, and may make him sick. Babies usually like their formula slightly warmed. Iron-fortified formulas should be used unless your physician advises otherwise.

Feeding: How Much?

How much formula should you feed your infant at any given age?

The RDA of infant formulas is based on a volume of formula per weight of your baby. The heavier the baby, the more formula he will require. In the more rapid period of his growth (the first six months), he will need a greater volume per weight ratio. Two basic principles govern how much you feed your infant—nutrition and desire. The following guideline on feeding volumes is meant to satisfy your infant's basic nutritional requirements. His individual desire may influence a change from these adjusted volumes. The following rule of thumb may be used for infants from birth to six months of age: 2-2 1/2 ounces of formula per pound per day (or 125-150 ml/kg per day). For example, if your baby weighs 10 pounds (4.5 kg) he may take around 20-25 ounces (560-700 ml) per day. This suggested volume will fulfill his requirements if formula represents his only source of nutrition. After six months, the daily volume of formula either remains the same until one year of age or gradually diminishes as the intake of solid food increases.

Scheduling the Bottle-Feeding Baby

How often should you feed your baby? There are two basic types of infant feeding "schedules." In **demand feeding,** an infant is fed every time his "little tummy desires." There is often no rhyme nor reason to his feeding pattern. In **schedule feeding,** an infant is fed at certain fixed times during the day, usually every three to four hours, and if he awakens during the night. Which pattern of feeding you choose depends on your individual principles of parenting, whether you are breastfeeding or bottle-feeding, as well as your domestic situation. Are you working outside the home and do you have responsibility for older children? Demand feeding caters to infant satisfaction; scheduling is for your convenience. These are challenging negotiations which you and your baby must settle during the first few months.

What is best for baby? Demand feeding is certainly more in keeping with the usual baby's behavior and satisfaction, since small frequent feedings are generally more comfortable than larger ones. Formula-fed babies are somewhat easier to schedule than breastfed babies because formula is digested more slowly. You may arrive at a compromise, or semi-demand type of schedule, which consists of one or two fixed feedings each day interspersed with demand feedings.

During the first few weeks, wake your baby for feeding if he sleeps longer than four to five hours during the day. Allowing baby to sleep longer than five hours between feedings during the day may result in a most exhausting "day-sleeper and night-

Feeding is a time of
special closeness.

feeder'' schedule. More frequent feedings during the day and bottles at 7:00 p.m. and 10:00 p.m. generally seems to be the most comfortable feeding schedule for most parents. This allows parents some free time in the later evening and the before-bed bottle may often lull baby into sleeping most of the night.

No baby wants to be fed on schedule, but I believe that the feeding relationship should be a comfortable one for parents too. If your baby's irregularity in feeding bothers you to the point that you sincerely do not enjoy the feeding relationship, then attempt to schedule his feedings by lengthening his feeding intervals. (See **Solid Foods** page 129 .)

Feeding time is more than just a time for nutrition. It is also a time of special closeness. The mutual giving previously discussed with respect to breastfeeding should also be enjoyed during bottle-feeding. Besides giving your infant the bottle, give him your eyes, your skin, your voice and your caresses. He will return to you more than just an empty bottle. The special warmth of skin-to-skin contact can be accomplished by wearing short sleeves and partially undressing yourself and your baby for feeding.

Fluorides

Fluoride is a naturally occurring mineral found in trace amounts in most foods, especially seafoods. Approximately ten million people in the United States live in areas where there is fluoride in the water at a concentration of approximately one part per million (1 ppm). Studies on these populations have shown two important facts—the incidence of dental caries is 50 per cent less than in the general population, and the rate of incidence of major diseases is the same as in the general population. Nature's own experiments on large numbers of people over many generations have attested to the value of fluoride as a safe and effective nutritional supplement for the prevention of tooth decay. Fluoride has been added to drinking water, and fluoride drops and tablets have been added to nutritional supplements for approximately thirty years. Fluoridation has been hailed as one of the three primary prevention measures of the century, along with water purification and vaccine immunizations.

How does fluoride work to prevent tooth decay? Fluoride is incorporated into developing enamel, rendering this enamel more resistant to attack from various acids. When should we begin the use of fluoride as a nutritional supplement? Calcification of the baby teeth begins before birth and is completed within the first year. Calcification of the permanent teeth begins at birth and is usually complete around ten years of age. Therefore, in areas where the fluoride content of drinking water is low (less than 0.3 ppm) we should begin using fluoride as a nutritional supplement in the early months of life and continue use until twelve years of age.

An excessive dose of fluoride can actually harm your child's teeth. Therefore, you should follow the advice of your pediatrician about using fluoride supplements. He will base his advice on his knowledge of the concentration of fluoride in your drinking water. Strictly adhere to the prescribed dosage. Many infants, especially those who are breastfed, do not drink much tap water during the first year of life. Commercial formulas are not manufactured with fluoridated water. If your infant is given ready-to-feed formula, a fluoride supplement may be prescribed for the first year. If a concentrated formula is used and then diluted with tap water, the need for a fluoride supplement will depend upon the fluoride content of your tap water. Whether breastfed infants should have fluoride supplements is still controversial. Human milk, like cow's milk, contains very little fluoride, irrespective of the fluoride content of the water. Some studies show that the frequency of dental caries in breastfed infants is identical to that of infants who are fed formula diluted with naturally fluoridated water. Studies in communities with fluoridated water supplies suggest that the fluoride obtained after the ages of six to eight months is sufficient to decrease the number of caries in the permanent teeth. The Committee on Nutrition of the American Academy of Pediatrics recommends that fluoride supplements be given to the breastfeeding infant at six months, in areas where the water is not adequately fluoridated.

Vitamin Supplements

Commercial infant formulas contain all the vitamins essential for infant growth. Remember, that in order to receive the daily recommended amount of vitamins, your infant has to take the entire can of formula each day. Since many babies do not consume this much every day, vitamin supplements are often recommended by pediatricians. In later infancy and childhood, the erratic diets of most children may cause pediatricians to recommend vitamin supplements containing A, D, C and often the B vitamins. Your pediatrician can best advise you whether vitamin supplements are necessary for your child. I do not believe in large doses, or mega doses, of vitamins such as Vitamin C and Vitamin E. They will be mentioned here only because they have received such widespread attention and have been so misused during the past five years. Nutritional and medical recommendations of a new medication or nutrient should be based on their proven effectiveness and their safety. Neither the effectiveness nor the safety of high doses of Vitamin C or Vitamin E has been proven, and therefore the excessive use of these vitamins is not currently recommended.

● **Vitamin Supplements for the Breastfed Infant**

Whether vitamin supplements are necessary for the infant who is breastfed exclusively is uncertain. Human milk contains adequate quantities of nearly all of the essential vitamins, although the Vitamin D content of human milk is lower than the RDA requirements. However, it does not seem possible that a milk which has been adapted for generations for survival of the species should be deficient in any nutrient. I suspect that although the quantity of Vitamin D may be low in human milk, its biological activity (the amount that is actually absorbed and utilized) may, in fact, be adequate to meet the infant's needs as long as the infant is exposed to sunlight. Vitamin D is derived from two sources—the exposure of the skin to sunlight (this converts compounds within the skin to Vitamin D), and the ingestion of Vitamin D from certain foods such as liver. If a mother's diet is suspected to be low in Vitamin D, or if you live in an area where exposure to sunlight is limited, especially during the winter months, Vitamin D supplements are recommended for the breastfeeding infant.

● **Iron Supplements**

Iron supplements in the form of iron-fortified formula or iron drops may be recommended by your doctor to prevent **anemia** or "low blood." Iron supplements are necessary for premature babies at least for the first few months. Formula feeding infants should receive iron-fortified formula. Some parents feel that added iron causes gastrointestinal upsets in their infants, although controlled studies comparing iron-fortified formulas and formulas with only a small amount of added iron showed no difference in the number of intestinal problems. Iron-rich foods (meat and iron-fortified cereal) may be offered to babies around the age of five or six months, according to your pediatrician's suggestion. Breastfeeding infants rarely need iron supplements during the first six months (see page 129 for discussion of iron in breast milk) but they should be given iron supplements or iron-rich foods thereafter. Iron supplements often give the stool a green color but this is of no significance. Sometimes iron drops may cause a temporary dark stain of the teeth. This can be avoided by brushing your child's teeth after the iron drops are given.

A Summary of Your Infant's Diet—Birth to Six Months

Planning your infant's diet from birth to six months is actually very simple, and this gives you the time to develop a good feeding relationship. If you are breastfeeding, simply breastfeed on demand (within reason). Solid foods or supplemental formulas are nutritionally unnecessary and should be avoided unless your baby's appetite and your breastfeeding relationship necessitate their use. Supplemental vitamins and fluoride may be prescribed by your physician.

If you are formula-feeding, offer your baby as much formula as he desires (usually around 2-2 1/2 ounces per pound per day) according to a mutually negotiated ''schedule.'' Solid foods are nutritionally unnecessary at this stage but may be added according to your baby's appetite and desire. Your doctor will advise you which formula to use and whether your baby needs vitamin, iron or fluoride supplements. (See Feeding Chart, page 141 .)

Feeding Your Infant from Six Months to One Year

Introducing Solid Foods

Infant feeding is basically a combination of nutrition, satisfaction and convenience. (The latter is not always possible.) For nutrition, your baby does not need solid foods before the age of about five or seven months, or even later if you are breastfeeding. There is no need to introduce solid foods until your baby cues you that he wants them. Since human milk contains very little iron, a common misconception exists that breastfed babies should receive solid foods containing iron early in infancy so that they won't become anemic. This could not be more incorrect. Babies who are breastfed rarely become anemic. Although human milk does contain a smaller quantity of iron than other foods, it is a biologically more active iron and is more completely absorbed. At least 50 per cent of the iron in human milk is absorbed from your infant's intestines, into the bloodstream, whereas only 4 per cent to 10 per cent of the iron in iron-fortified formulas and solid foods is absorbed. The uniqueness of breast milk iron (and other nutrients) is a relatively recent discovery which is still the object of very exciting research. This research is showing that feeding solids as well as breast milk may actually decrease the amount of iron absorbed from your milk.

It may be necessary to start formula-fed babies, especially those not receiving iron-fortified formulas, on solid foods containing iron around five or six months of age, when maternal iron given to your baby at birth begins to be depleted and the risk of anemia begins. If using iron-fortified formulas, it is nutritionally unnecessary to begin solid foods until your infant signals he wants them.

How will you know when your baby is ready for solids? The earliest signal is usually a change in his feeding pattern, showing that he is no longer satisfied with milk alone. He may show gradual disinterest in the bottle and take to solid foods readily. When a very young baby shows a sudden increased demand for milk and "wants to drink all the time," it is often misinterpreted as a need for solid foods. In this case, he actually needs more nutrition, which can be obtained from milk alone for the first five or six months.

A breastfeeding mother may find that she may have to nurse very frequently for a few days in order to increase her supply of milk to meet her infant's sudden increased demand. A bottle-feeding mother could do the same thing and increase the frequency of the formula feeding. Bottle-feeding mothers, however, seem to be more concerned with "too many bottles" and therefore interpret this increased demand as a signal for beginning solid foods. The baby is consequently started on solids rather than being given increased formula.

The use of solid foods as "fillers" to increase feeding intervals is a common but unwise feeding practice for breastfeeding or bottle-feeding infants under the ages of four to six months. The introduction of solids to some bottle-fed infants may prolong the interval between feedings, facilitate scheduling and therefore alleviate your exhaustion from too frequent feedings. However, early introduction of solid foods will interfere with a successful breastfeeding relationship with a baby who does not need solids. Your baby may also be signalling for something other than food, such as the need for more sucking or more cuddling. Try to appease him in ways other than feeding. (See **Obesity** for further discussion of this problem, page 150.)

Your baby's entire oral-facial anatomy is designed for sucking, not chewing. This intense sucking reflex usually lasts throughout the first year. Introduction of solid foods is easier when your baby has the maturity to handle the process of eating solids, such as sitting up with support, reaching out and touching the food, and "mouthing" a substance of thickened consistency. Babies begin to show readiness for this effort between four and six months, which is another reason for delaying the introduction of solid foods until this time. Another clue that your baby desires solids is if he thrusts his tongue forward if offered a little food on the top of his tongue, and then automatically pulls the tongue back into the mouth and swallows. Babies usually show this tongue-thrusting around six months.

Early introduction of solid foods also increases your baby's chance of food allergies later on. If there is a family history of food allergies, then certain solid foods should definitely not be introduced before six months or even a year (see **Food Allergies**, page 147). Do not mix solid food with formula in a bottle. This may cause choking and confuse the infant—should he chew or suck?

The how much and how often of formula feeding, together with the timing and introduction of new foods, is a combination of both the science and the art of infant feeding, and your individual principles of parenting. If both you and your baby are comfortable with your general feedings patterns, then you have negotiated successfully. If one of you is uncomfortable, then seek some help. Feeding a baby involves more than just physical nourishment and nutrition; both the parent and child should enjoy the feeding relationship. It is a time for closeness, touching and love. Your baby is learning how to trust that his needs will be met, and for a long time, milk and love are one and the same.

The following are suggestions about convenient timing for the introduction of solid foods, and the nutritional content of various baby foods. Remember, these are only suggestions and should be tailored to your baby's specific needs and desires.

● **Feed solids after your baby's bottle**
Milk is still the primary nutrition source during the first nine months. If you are breastfeeding, attempt to feed him solids between breastfeeding times. Solid foods may interfere with the absorption of the more valuable breast milk nutrients if both solids and breast milk are fed at the same time. Introduce new foods one at a time, allowing at least a week or two between new foods to see if the baby has an allergic reaction. If a definite allergic reaction occurs, do not attempt to feed this food again for at least six months, and then only a small amount. Choose the time of the day that is most convenient for you since a little mess is part of the feeding game. Mornings are usually the best time for offering solid foods to formula-fed infants because you have the

most time with your infant and usually do not need to worry about meals for the rest of the family. Breastfed infants should be offered solids when your milk supply is lowest, usually toward the end of the day. Start with about 1/4 teaspoon of a new food remembering that your initial goal is to introduce your baby to solids, not to fill him up.

● **Fruits**

Bananas are a good first food and may serve as a test to see if your baby is ready for solids. A very ripe mashed banana is usually a favorite food among babies because of its sweetness, smooth consistency and close resemblance to milk. Fruits contain as many calories per volume as milk but they are about 90 per cent carbohydrates and therefore are not a good source of balanced nutrition. For the young infant the prime benefit of fruits is that they mix well with most other foods and can often be used to increase the palatability of more nutritious but less tasty foods. For example, a baby may take a spoonful of cereal more readily if it is covered with bananas. In order to lessen the risk of fruit allergies, first introduce the fruits with lower citric acid content such as bananas, pears and apples and then the fruits of greater citric acid content, such as oranges and berries.

● **Don't drink your juice**

Drinking large volumes of fruit juice should be discouraged for several reasons. Undiluted fruit juice contains as many calories as the same volume of milk but is much less nutritious. Juice is also less nutritious than the fruit itself because it lacks the beneficial fruit pulp. It is also much less filling than milk and therefore infants can consume a much larger quantity without feeling full. I have noticed that the consumption of a large amount of fruit juice is one of the subtle causes of childhood obesity. I recommend diluting juice with an equal quantity of water, especially for the compulsive juice drinker. **Juice-bottle caries** (dental cavities) result when babies are given fruit juice in a bottle at nap time, or seem to always have a bottle of juice hanging from their mouths. The constant contact between the juice and rubber nipple and the baby's front teeth can result in early tooth decay. For this reason, dentists recommend that juice should not be given in a bottle but rather delayed until the baby can take juice from a cup.

● **Cereals**

Cereals are usually one of the first solid foods introduced because cereal is often used as a filler, something you may feel is necessary to lengthen your baby's interval between bottles and to encourage him to sleep through the night. This "filler fallacy" may be an unwise feeding pattern. Not only does it often not work, but it also may create problems in appetite control at an early age, thus contributing to eventual obesity (see **Obesity**, page 151).

I have always felt that babies are much more comfortable when fed small amounts frequently. Although in theory it may be best for baby to be given small, frequent feedings around the clock, an exhausted mother who is not enjoying her feeding relationship is of more concern than the use of food for filler. This is a question which you and your baby must resolve.

Cereals come in a variety of forms and are usually made with rice, barley, oatmeal, wheat, soybeans or a combination of these. Begin with rice or barley cereal, the least allergenic. Avoid beginning with mixed cereals in case your baby is allergic to one of the components. Isolation of the allergen then becomes difficult. Rice cereal is approximately 75 per cent carbohydrates and 7 per cent protein. Higher protein cereals, made primarily with soybeans, may contain as much as 35 per cent protein. Infant cereals make a good first solid because they are fortified with minerals such as calcium and phosphorus, B vitamins and iron. Begin with 1/4 tablespoon of rice cereal and mix it with formula or breast milk to the desired consistency. Remember, your purpose is to introduce your baby to cereal, not to empty the dish. Cereal alone is very bland and may be refused by your baby. You may then have to experiment by adding various fruits in various consistencies. Never force-feed your baby, since this will introduce a negative experience into his early solid feeding. If he cries, he doesn't want the food. When a baby is satisfied, he will turn his head away.

● **Meats**

Meats are approximately 55 per cent protein and 45 per cent fat, depending on the type of meat. Meats (primarily liver, beef, lamb and poultry) are excellent sources of iron. For infants not receiving iron-fortified formulas, meats are a prime source of iron. Avoid the use of so-called meat dinners, or meat mixtures. The protein and iron content in these mixtures is much lower than that in plain meat, and the starch content is much higher, thus defeating the purpose of giving meat.

● **Vegetables**

Vegetables are approximately 14 per cent protein, 6 per cent fat and 80 per cent carbohydrates. Usually the yellow vegetables, such as squash, are more easily taken in early infancy because of their taste and consistency. After six months, a raw carrot, which satisfies both the desire to grab and chew, can be used as a teething ring. In theory, vegetables are a much better source of nutrition than fruits and should be introduced earlier in infancy but because of their sweetness, fruits are usually better accepted by infants.

● **Egg yolks**

Egg yolks are approximately 21 per cent protein, 76 per cent fat and 3 per cent carbohydrates. They are a good source of protein. Although egg yolk is rich in iron, this iron may not be absorbed by the human intestines. An egg yolk every other day is sufficient and may be started any time after six months of age. Delay egg white until baby is a year old since egg white tends to be more allergenic than egg yolk. If your baby is generally allergic, or if you have a family history of allergies, delay both egg yolk and egg white until your baby is at least one year of age.

● **Dairy products**

It is wise to avoid cow's milk as a beverage until your infant is one year. Yogurt gives all the nutritional benefits of milk without the problems of lactose intolerance (See **Lactose Intolerance** page 145). Yogurt is made by adding a bacterial culture to milk. This culture ferments the milk and breaks down the lactose into simple sugars which are more easily absorbed.

The milk proteins are also modified in the culturing process and may be less allergenic. Cheese also has similar benefits. Most infants enjoy yogurt by around nine months.

Commercial desserts and puddings have no place in infant feedings.

Cow's Milk versus Formula

If you are formula-feeding, the main change in your baby's diet is a gradual decrease in formula around six months, and an increase in other foods as the prime source of your infant's nutrition. By one year of age most infants receive only 50 per cent of their daily calories from milk or formula. The basic decision at six months is whether to continue the formula you are using, to change formulas, or to switch to cow's milk.

Milk is the ideal food for each species (human milk for humans). Milk is not the ideal infant food when it crosses species lines (cow's milk for humans). The newer prepared formulas are much better suited to your infant's needs than cow's milk. Formulas are much closer to the composition of human milk and contain all the necessary vitamins. Most contain the additional iron supplements that are so very necessary at this age. Cow' milk is very low in iron. This, plus the iron loss from the minute amount of intestinal bleeding which may be caused by subtle milk allergy, may result in anemia (low iron level in blood) between nine months and one year of age. Cow's milk protein is allergenic to many babies in ways that may not be apparent to you. It does not seem wise to introduce a potentially allergenic milk at the same time that your baby's intestines are getting used to a variety of solid foods. The protein in formulas has been heat-treated to remove many of its allergenic properties. The difference in cost between milk supplemented with vitamins and iron, and vitamin- and iron-fortified formula is minimal, so it is both economically and nutritionally wise to stay with formula until one year of age. Perhaps thinking of formulas as "milk" will lessen the urge to switch to cow's milk. Early introduction of cow's milk and solid foods have erroneously been considered indices of a baby's maturity. Eating adult food is equated with growing up. Mothers love to say "Tommy is only six months old and he is already drinking the same milk we drink and eating all of our foods." What this mother is actually feeling is that her baby must be a very advanced, bright kid since he is eating more than her friend's baby.

When switching from formula to cow's milk at the age of one year, you must decide what type of cow's milk—whole, 2 per cent or skim. These three varieties of milk differ in fat content and therefore calorie content. In the first six months to one year many babies cannot absorb the high content of butterfat in whole milk. Also, whole milk has the same calorie content as commercial formula, and therefore offers no advantage to the calorie conscious. The "stamp out fat" propaganda of the 1970s has given rise to the increasing popularity of skim as a prime source of infant nutrition.

Pediatric nutritionists advise against the use of skim milk in the first year of life. It deprives the infant of a valuable source of energy and essential fatty acids, contains potential protein allergens, and it has a high salt and protein content which immature kidneys may not be able to handle.

A compromise is the use of 2 per cent milk which contains less butterfat and fewer calories than whole milk, but still provides the fat and fatty acids so necessary to a growing infant. In answer to this 2 per cent solution, formula manufacturers have introduced formulas which contain slightly less fat and fewer calories than the usual formulas used in the first six months. These seem to offer a reasonable alternative to an early introduction of cow's milk.

In summary, there is no nutritional rationale for introducing cow's milk before one year of age. When switching to cow's milk after one year of age, consider the following:

1. Do not use skim milk until your infant is at least two years of age.

2. If your baby is a compulsive milk drinker, overweight, or anemic, use 2 per cent milk.

3. If milk is not your baby's prime nutrition source, or if he is not overweight or anemic, use whole milk.

The Principle of Balanced Nutrition

How much milk and food should your baby receive during the period from six months to one year? To answer this question you should first understand the importance of proper distribution of calorie sources, called **balanced nutrition**. The calories your infant consumes should be distributed in the following amounts: 30 per cent to 45 per cent in fats, 35 per cent to 50 per cent in carbohydrate and 7 per cent to 15 per cent in protein. Your infant expends these calories in the following proportions: 50 per cent for basic metabolic needs, 30 per cent for energy expended during his activity, and 20 per cent for continued growth. (The percentage of calories needed for growth is greatest in the first few months [30 per cent] and gradually decreases to 5 per cent to 10 per cent toward one year of age.) Since a large portion of his calorie needs during the first year are for growth, it is during this period that nutritional deficiency may have the greatest effect.

A daily recommended volume of formula for an infant from six months to one year would be between 25 ounces and 32 ounces per day (710 ml to 909 ml), a volume which would fulfil approximately half the calorie needs of the average baby. Whether he should have more or less than this volume depends on his appetite and his consumption of nutritious solid foods. Between six months and one year of age your infant will gradually increase his intake of solid foods. By one year most infants receive about 50 per cent of their energy requirements from solids and the rest from formula or milk.

The next very important nutritional goal is to understand and practice balanced nutrition in the use of non-milk foods. Balanced nutrition means that non-milk sources of nutrition should complement the other sources of nutrition (human milk or formula) to provide the necessary amounts of fats, carbohydrates, proteins, minerals and vitamins. It only becomes important for you to consider balanced nutrition when non-milk food sources supply a significant share of calories and essential nutrients. For example, suppose your baby is one year old and consumes around 20 ounces of formula a day and a large amount of fruit juice, but refuses other foods. He might be receiving less than optimal amounts of protein, and probably less fatty acid, than required for normal growth. A nutritional deficiency exists. Suppose, however, he is consuming 40 ounces of formula a day and likes juice but simply refuses solid foods. If he is receiving a proper, iron-fortified formula, there is little likelihood of nutritional deficiency in this baby. He has simply chosen to retain milk as his primary source of nutrition. A third example is a one-year old baby who won't drink his milk, but consumes a variety of solid foods. If, for example, by the end of the day he has consumed 2 ounces to 3 ounces each of meat, vegetables, fruits, cereals and egg yolk, and 8 ounces to 10 ounces of milk, this baby receives balanced nutrition with a feeding pattern based predominantly on solid foods rather than milk. There is a wide variation in food preferences and nutrition requirements for babies, just as there is for adults. It is more important for you to understand the basic principles of nutrition rather than the mathematics.

Preparing Your Own Baby Food

The commercial baby food industry tries to achieve the economically impossible by keeping quality up and costs down. Additives are used to keep the food from spoiling and make it more palatable. However, parental pressure has prompted the baby food industry to eliminate monosodium glutamate, sugar, salt and various additives. Current labels emphasize more what the foods do **not** contain than their nutritional contents. Inflation of meat prices and vegetable prices has prompted baby food manufacturers to stretch these foods with starches and sugars, and to correct resultant blandness with flavor enhancing additives. Of exceptionally poor quality are the baby "vegetable and meat dinners," which are composed mainly of cereals, noodles and macaroni, and also contain refined sugars, starches and non-enriched grain. In my opinion, a steady diet of convenience foods has no place in infant nutrition.

It seems that the logical answer to this nutritional and economic dilemma is to prepare baby food at home. Making your own baby food from fresh lean meat and fresh seasonal vegetables and fruit is nutritionally superior to using commercially processed baby foods. To do this you will need a blender, ice cube trays with individual one ounce cube sections, small freezer

Making your own baby food is nutritionally superior to using commercially processed baby foods.

bags, and a pinch of ingenuity. Fresh fruits of all kinds can be puréed in your blender in any quantity. You can save time by preparing large amounts, freezing covered ice cube trays full of whatever is in season, and then storing the cubes in plastic bags. You simply thaw one of these frozen cubes and you have instant, nutritious baby food. Vegetables should be cooked by steaming rather than by boiling to preserve as many of their nutrients as possible. All kinds of meats can also be cooked, puréed and frozen in this manner. Liver is a specially good source of iron and protein. If the liver flavor is too strong or the texture too grainy for your baby, blend it with some cottage cheese. This makes a creamy pâté that may become one of his favorites.

Packaged infant cereals are convenient but they are of the "instant" variety, meaning they have been processed heavily and have little resemblance to whole grain cereals either in appearance, taste or nutritive value. Making your own baby cereal may be more time-consuming than making other foods but it is well worth the effort. You can pulverize grain (brown rice, wheat, soy flakes, etc.) in your blender and cook the grain powder with water for a few minutes to produce whole grain baby cereal. Add a little puréed fruit if you like. (Raw egg yolk can also be added to anything hot.)

Even teething biscuits and crackers can be prepared at home. Find recipes that contain whole grain flour and produce a nice, hard, no-crumble cookie. Teething can also be done on carrot sticks (try frozen ones), frozen bananas, or fruit juice popsicles.

Infants can drink the same fruit juices the rest of the family enjoys. Some dilution of the juice (whether it is freshly squeezed or canned) may be necessary, depending on your baby's taste. It is never necessary to add sugar, salt or any artificial preservative. Lemon juice can be used as a natural preservative.

Around nine months, finger foods become popular and may be more appropriate than puréed foods. Let your baby do as much for himself as your sense of tidiness can stand. Self-feeding is good for fine motor development and it is also more fun for your baby. He may balk if you spoon-feed him. Try to avoid letting mealtime become a battle of wills. Here are a few ideas for finger foods that are both appealing and safe for babies: pieces of peeled fruit, cubes of cheese (not processed), cooked carrot "wheels," vegetables with interesting shapes like peas and beans, tiny broccoli "trees," hard bread crusts, bits of cooked hamburger, flakes of tuna or cooked white fish (check for tiny bones) or chicken legs with a little meat still attached (also check for tiny bones).

Never offer soft drinks, candy, chocolate, cookies or cakes made with sugar or overly-sweetened with honey. Resist the urge to coax him to take "Just these last two bites to clean your plate." Never be resentful that he does not want any of the good food you took such trouble to prepare. The damage you do by forcing him to eat what he knows he does not need is much worse than a little wasted food.

Sometime in the second year of life your baby gets too busy to spend a lot of time sitting still to eat. After all, food is no longer a new experience after the process of eating has been mastered. This disinterest earns baby the title of Picky Eater. When this occurs, react wisely. Within the guidelines of nutrition, let baby eat what you know he enjoys. Let him have nourishing fin-

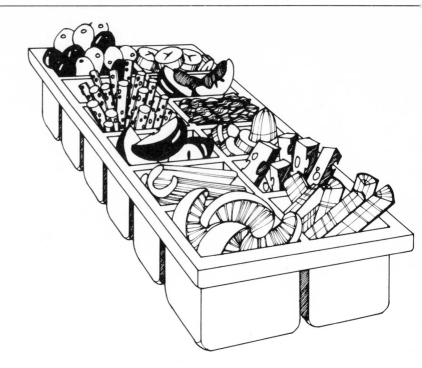

The toddler snack tray

ger foods that he can eat on the run. Present small amounts of food at a time rather than overwhelming him with a plateful. He can always ask for more. His desire to imitate will eventually urge him to join the family at the table. Avoid the temptation of giving your picky eater "junk food" in a desperate attempt to get him to eat something. Feeding a toddler is both an art and a science. How you present food may require ingenuity. For example, our two-year-old would not eat eggs. He loved to play with his little canoe in the bathtub. When my wife sliced up hard boiled eggs like little boats and marketed them as canoe eggs, he loved them. "Sitting still" and "eating three square meals a day" is an adult invention not in keeping with a toddler's busy day. Nibbling and snacking on the run is often the best way to ensure proper nutrition for your busy toddler. In our home, we have achieved some success in feeding toddlers by displaying an ice cube tray with various bits of colorful, nutritious favorites (marketed as a rainbow lunch) - carrot sticks, raisins, cheese cubes, whole wheat bread sticks, orange wedges, apple slices with peanut butter, etc. A busy toddler will often stop many times during his daily explorations to nibble.

INFANT FEEDING GUIDE • BIRTH TO ONE YEAR					
Human milk or iron-fortified formula (no cow's milk)					
	Birth	**6 Months**	**7 Months**	**8 Months**	**9-12 Months**
Solid Foods	Solid foods not necessary	Bananas Cereal Apple sauce Pears	Carrots Squash Mashed potatoes	Lamb Beef	Finger foods Egg yolk Yogurt Cottage cheese Introduce juice (by cup)

Feeding Problems

The feeding problems of the allergic baby, the colicky baby, the persistently hungry baby and the regurgitator have similar causes and, although they occur more often in formula-fed babies, the breastfed infant is by no means immune.

The Colicky Baby Colic is the most severe of all feeding problems. A colicky baby cries from intense physical discomfort, draws his legs up onto a tense, gas-filled abdomen, clenches his fists seemingly in anger at having this uncontrollable pain, and transfers this pain to his parents who feel equally helpless in determining the cause and alleviating the pain. "Colicky baby" is not synonymous with the "fussy baby," but many of the features do overlap. The basic difference is that colic is a physical problem, while fussiness is a problem of temperament. (See **Fussy Baby**, page 162 before reading further in this section.)

Although colic has many causes, the term is used here to refer to those babies who have physical discomfort resulting mainly from a feeding problem. Colic has three basic causes:
1. Excessive air swallowing and retention.
2. Milk allergy.
3. The pain-tension cycle in a hyper-excitable baby.

Swallowing and retention of air is the most common cause. Babies suck ravenously and therefore swallow enormous amounts of air, thus necessitating the ancient custom of "burping," "bubbling," or "winding" the baby. The ability to burp the baby has been equated with the feeding expertise of the infant caretaker. In pediatric hospitals, there is always at least one "feeding expert," a "grandmother-nurse" whose ability to get the most milk in and get the most wind out is widely respected.

Swallowed air can either settle on top of the food in the stomach and then be burped straight up and out with no discomfort, or it can settle beneath the food in the stomach and cause considerable pain, or regurgitation.

Regurgitation or "the spitter" problem is caused if the stomach is distended with milk and air beneath the milk (trapped bubble). The stomach contracts, the milk goes up, and the air goes down. The milk going up bothers the mother, and the air going down bothers the baby. The air winds its way through the intestines and stretches them, producing colicky pain. The crying, colicky infant draws his legs up on his abdomen. The movement is both an attempt to relax his abdomen and an instinctive attempt to pass the air through his rectum to relieve his discomfort. The regurgitated milk often carries with it some gastric acids which may "burn" the lining of the esophagus; this may be another source of pain.

Another problem occurs if air fills the stomach. The air gives the baby a false sense of fullness, whereupon he falls asleep without taking his needed amount of milk, apparently satisfied. The air soon passes and he awakens again, hungry for his next meal of milk and air. This is one of the most common causes for a **persistently hungry baby**, or the complaints that "he is never satisfied and wants to eat all the time" or "he falls asleep before he has taken much milk and wakes up in an hour, ready to eat again." (See **Marathoning**, page 112 .)

How to handle the air swallowing problem? Help your baby swallow less air by burping early and more often, especially if he is a ravenous eater or "gulper." You want to eliminate the air before it becomes trapped in the stomach. If you are bottle-feeding, be sure the nipple hole is large enough for the milk to pass freely through it. (The human nipple has many holes, allowing a free-flowing spurt of milk in response to baby's sucking, and a valve-like action which stops the spurt when he stops sucking.) If the rubber nipple holes are too small, he will suck more vigorously to obtain milk and consequently swallow more air.

As a rough guide, milk should drop at a rate of at least one drop per second from a full bottle held motionlessly upside down. If the nipple hole seems too small, take a small sewing needle and insert the eye end into a cork. Heat the needle end on a stove burner. When it is red hot, poke a hole in the nipple large enough to see through. Collapsible bottles (plastic bags which fit into a holder) may lessen air swallowing.

Another tip for managing air swallowing is to feed in the upright position, allowing gravity to hold the heavier milk down and to let the lighter air rise to the top of the stomach. You should also burp in the upright position, thus allowing the air to rise easily. Place a "bubble cloth" over your shoulder (a cloth diaper works well) and hold your baby upright over your shoulder, gently patting and stroking his back and walking around or rocking rhythmically. Jostling usually aggravates the situation.

If your baby does not burp and your maternal detective instincts diagnose the case of the trapped bubble (air trapped beneath the milk), then try shifting the position for burping. Lay him over your lap on his stomach or on his right side for a few minutes. This allows the trapped bubble to rise to the top of the stomach. Then hold him sitting securely upright, leaning forward against your hand, and allow him to burp. If your baby has none of the above feeding problems and is not a gassy baby (passing excessive gas through the rectum—a sign of failure to remove the air at the stomach end) then your feeding techniques are good.

Milk allergy can also be a cause of colic. Colic is less common in breastfed babies but, if it does occur, it may be due to an allergen in your milk. If you are formula-feeding, a change to a hypoallergenic formula may help and advice should be sought from your pediatrician. (See **Milk Allergy**, page 144 and **Breastfeeding**, page 145 .)

Much of the colicky tendency may be inherent in a baby's temperament and the pain-tension cycle becomes a contributing factor, causing colic to become a total family problem. (This is discussed in detail under **The Fussy Baby**, page 162 .)

● **Summary of the tips on the treatment of the colicky baby:**
1. Burp early and frequently.
2. Enlarge the nipple hole.
3. Feed and burp in an upright position.
4. Keep an upright position with gentle motion for 30 minutes after feeding.
5. Try a shift in burping position.
6. Hold securely and relaxed.
7. Feed in a quiet, dimly lit room.
8. Clear nasal passages —mouth breathing tends to aggravate air

swallowing.

9. Avoid sudden noises or startles.

10. Eliminate possibility of milk allergy by trying various formulas.

11. Seek medical advice and possibly intestinal relaxant medications.

12. Seek help from support groups for aid in breaking the mother-baby tension cycle.

Colic usually disappears between the ages of three and six months. By six months, babies are beginning to sit upright much of the time, their intestines are more mature, and they are better able to tolerate potential allergens.

Regurgitation

Regurgitation or "spitting up" is caused by excessive air retention, over-feeding, milk allergy or gastrointestinal reflux. Many babies spit up several times a day and the volume regurgitated always seems more than it actually is. At what point does spitting up become a medical concern? As a general guide, if your baby is gaining weight normally, then spitting up is more of a temporary nuisance than a prolonged medical problem. If your baby is not thriving, then a medical problem may exist. Treat regurgitation as follows:

1. Handle air retention and potential milk allergies as outlined in the section on colic.

2. Offer a smaller volume, with more frequent feedings.

3. For the condition of gastroesophageal reflux due to a temporary malfunction of stomach emptying, you may have to keep your baby upright most of the time and thicken his feedings as prescribed by a doctor. Regurgitation usually subsides by the age of six or eight months when baby sits upright.

Milk Allergy

Allergies to cow's milk, first described by Hippocrates in 400 B.C., affects approximately 1 infant in 15. The incidence of more subtle types of milk intolerance may be as high as 1 in 4. Symptoms produced by cow's milk intolerance are the following, in order of frequency: vomiting, diarrhea, abdominal pain, lower intestinal gas (bloating), eczema-like rash, and runny nose. Besides these more obvious symptoms, there may be subtle changes in your infant's or child's behavior in the form of irritability, hyperactivity, restlessness or fatigue. Milk allergy is often the underlying cause of the repeated colds and ear infections from which some children suffer.

For many years, the medical profession has been trying to

dethrone the sacred cow by promoting public awareness of the potential health problems attributed to the excessive use of cow's milk. In a 1974 exposé of the dairy industry, **Consumers' Report** seriously questioned the quality and safety of the milk they tested. The fact that cow's milk has continued to withstand the attacks of the medical profession and various consumer groups can be attributed to the efficiency of the industry's advertising (milk is marketed on an emotional level, tied in with mother-love) and the government lobbying of the American dairy industry.

Why is cow's milk so allergenic? The protein in cow's milk is species-specific, suited to the bovine intestines. Exposure of human intestines to bovine protein may cause minute gastrointestinal bleeding and result in anemia. These allergenic proteins may also be absorbed into your child's circulatory system, causing a rash, runny nose or wheezing.

Lactose intolerance is another problem with cow's milk which is more common than generally suspected. Lactose, the sugar in human and cow's milk, is normally digested by the intestinal enzyme lactase. Some infants, children and adults are deficient in this intestinal enzyme and cannot absorb lactose. Undigested lactose which accumulates in the large intestine results in diarrhea, gas (bloating) and abdominal pain. Most mammals become lactose intolerant after they are weaned, which leads researchers to believe that lactose intolerance is a normal process of maturity. Perhaps some children really do outgrow their need for milk.

Even the fats in cow's milk are not without their problems. The high percentage of saturated fats in cow's milk has led The American Heart Association to incriminate cow's milk for contributing to the high incidence of heart disease in our western, milk-drinking culture.

How can you lessen the chance of your child developing milk allergy? One obvious answer is to breastfeed your infant. The longer an infant is breastfed, the less likely is his chance of developing cow's milk allergy in later infancy or childhood. This is an extremely important safeguard if there is a strong history of allergies in your family.

A second preventive measure is to avoid early introduction of cow's milk and to either breastfeed or use humanized formulas for at least one year. The earlier that cow's milk is introduced to an infant's diet, the greater are his chances of later allergies. Although many of the humanized formulas have cow's milk protein as their protein base, the protein has been processed, thus lessening its allergenic properties. If there is a strong family history of allergies (and you are not breastfeeding), you should start your infant on a soybean or other hypoallergenic formula at birth and continue this for one year.

In defense of the infant or child who won't drink his milk, it is a medical fact that many infants and children who refuse milk are actually found to be allergic to it when medically tested. So, if your infant or child refuses to drink his milk, listen to him. He is trying to tell you something. Sophisticated medical tests are usually unnecessary to diagnose milk allergy. If you suspect your infant or child is allergic to milk, isolate a few symptoms, withhold milk and dairy products from his diet for at least three days and see if the symptoms disappear. Then challenge him again with milk and see if the symptoms soon reappear. If they do, repeat the process. If your child improves on the milk-free diet in two successive trials, then he is probably allergic to cow's milk.

Allergy to cow's milk protein is most severe in early infancy and often disappears or decreases by two to three years of age. Lactose intolerance, however, may persist throughout childhood and even adulthood. If milk allergy is suspected, your doctor may recommend feeding your infant a special formula which contains neither lactose nor milk proteins.

"But doctor, if he can't drink milk, where does he get his calcium?" is a common question that mothers of milk allergic babies ask. In the first place, calcium deficiency is rare. There is some calcium in most foods, especially in whole grains and vegetables. But since dairy products are still the prime source of calcium, try giving your child yogurt and most cheeses, all of which are tolerated by most milk allergic children because the lactose and proteins have been changed during processing. Yogurt seems to be a better food for children than cow's milk, since it offers the same nutrition without the problems (See Yogurt, page 134). Secondly, a look at nature may provide some insight about whether children really do need much milk after infancy. It is a medical fact that after infancy, many children gradually lose the intestinal enzyme lactase (the enzyme which is necessary for digesting the milk sugar, lactose), giving rise to medical speculation that perhaps the infant is not meant to drink milk after he is weaned from his mother's breast.

● **A note for breastfeeding mothers**

If your infant is experiencing any behavioral or intestinal symptoms such as colic or diarrhea, he may be allergic to the cow's milk in your diet. Cow's milk proteins do enter the mother's milk and may, therefore, be passed onto an allergic infant. If you suspect this, eliminate cow's milk from your diet and substitute yogurt and cheese.

Common Food Allergies

I am using the term "allergy" to mean any food which seems to cause your child some discomfort. Medically speaking, "food intolerance" is more correct than allergy. Food allergy is commonly called the great masquerader because, surprisingly, it causes a variety of symptoms in infants and children. The usual symptoms of food allergy are eczema-type rashes, especially on the face; puffy eyelids; chronic diarrhea; and a stuffy nose. Sometimes the symptoms of food allergy may be more subtle and may go undetected for a long time. These are called hidden food allergies and may show in the following ways: a pale, tired or droopy child; an irritable or hyperactive child (called behavioral intolerances); a child with headaches, abdominal pain or muscleaches; a child with recurrent respiratory infections. The most common food allergens are milk and dairy products, chocolate, eggs, sugar(cane sugar), citrus fruits, nuts, wheat products, corn, berries, food colorings and additives. If you suspect a food allergy in your child, immediately discontinue use of the offending food and its by-products for a period of one to three weeks. Then reintroduce it in small quantities after three weeks to see if the same reaction occurs. If it does, then this food should be put on the list of forbidden foods for at least two years. Surprisingly, the culprit in food allergy is often the food which the child craves. Food allergies are often temporary and after a couple of years your child may be able to tolerate a food to which he was previously intolerant.

If your child has any of the above symptoms or "just doesn't feel well" for no apparent reason and he has had a thorough medical exam showing no apparent cause for his unwell feeling, then you may have to do a bit of detective work to uncover a hidden food allergy. Do this with an "elimination diet"—the probable food allergens are eliminated one by one from your child's diet. New foods should be added one by one in gradually increasing amounts. Keep a careful record of your child's symptoms and forbidden foods. This strict type of elimination diet should be carried out only in consultation with your doctor.

How can you minimize the chance of food allergy in your

child? If there is a history of allergies in your family then your child is at high risk of also being allergic. The following preventive measures will lessen his chance of becoming an allergic child:

1. Breastfeed your infant for at least one year.

2. Delay introduction of solid foods for at least six months and then gradually begin with the less allergenic foods.

3. Avoid beginning with mixtures because if your infant is allergic to one of the components of the mixture, isolation of the offending allergen is very difficult.

4. Do not introduce the commonly allergenic foods until after one year of age.

During his first six months, your infant's intestines are immature and may allow certain foods to enter the blood stream. By "sensitizing" the child to this food, you predispose him to a later allergic reaction to it. This is the rationale for late introduction of solid foods in a potentially allergic child. (See **Milk Allergy**, page 144 for further discussion of feeding the potentially allergic child.)

How Food Types and Habits Affect Your Child's Behavior and Health

The Sugar Society   Cane sugar, the usual "table or refined" sugar, is so heavily processed that the few non-carbohydrate nutrients found in the natural state are removed. The resulting sugar is rapidly absorbed from the intestines, and reaches a high concentration in the blood. This triggers insulin release, which rapidly lowers blood sugar and stimulates eating again. A developing brain is very dependent on a steady blood sugar concentration as its prime energy source. Fluctuation in this energy source is accompanied by marked changes in behavior such as fainting, hyper-activity, aggression, irritability and depression. The ability to concentrate and learn is often compromised, and various bodily complaints such as headaches, visual disturbances, and abdominal pain may result.

Our sugar society has created a generation of sweet tooths. Our taste buds may be programmed from early infancy to desire the added artificial sweetness and we are hooked on this unhealthy habit which recent research suggests may even be linked to eventual obesity and heart disease. The association of sugar consumption and dental caries also constitutes a serious health problem.

That a sweet taste is a basic human pleasure is shown by the remarkable sweetness of breastmilk. Sweetness is also found in many natural foods such as fruit and honey. However, the natural sugars such as lactose of milk and fructose of honey have different patterns of absorption and utilization within the body and cause less marked swings in blood sugar concentration than the commercially processed cane sugar. Fruit and honey sugars also contain small amounts of additional nutrients (vitamins, minerals and traces of protein and fat), unlike nutrient-deficient refined sugar.

It is often difficult for a shopper to know how much sugar has been added to certain foods. Current label laws require contents to be listed in order of volume, so if sugar is placed first on the list of contents, the food is very high in sugar. This fact may be concealed, however, if manufacturers list sweeteners separately. Through breastfeeding and the use of natural fruit sugars, your infant's taste buds will not be programmed to crave the artificially added sweetness of junk foods later in childhood.

Food Additives How food additives may affect your child's behavior is discussed on page 293 .

Childhood Obesity

Ten to twenty per cent of our children are obese, and adult diseases related to obesity are reaching epidemic proportions.

What is an obese child? At what point should you worry that your child is becoming too fat? As a basic guide, if your child's weight is 10 per cent greater than it should be for sex, height and age, then he or she is overweight. If your child is 20 per cent over his ideal weight, he is fat, or obese. This is not always a reliable guide for determining whether or not your child is fat. Medically speaking, the amount of excess fat or ''flab'' is often considered a more important determinant of the degree of obesity than actual weight. Doctors call this **skin fold thickness**. They often measure various folds of flab throughout your child's body with calipers and use the changes in amount of ''true fat'' to monitor weight gain or loss. Strictly speaking, we are assuming that an obese child is overweight because of excess fat only, and not an excess of what is called lean body mass (muscle and bone).

How Children Become Fat—The Fat Cell Theory

Children normally grow because the size and number of cells in all their organs increase. Fat tissue, likewise, grows by an increase in fat cell size and fat cell number. During the first one to two years of life, considered to be the critical period for fat cell development, there is normally an increase in fat cell number. Another lesser spurt in fat cell number occurs in middle childhood (seven years) and again during adolescence. After growth is finished (adulthood), the number of fat cells probably remains constant and any increase or decrease in fat tissue results from a change in size of these cells.

If a child is over-nourished during infancy (the period of rapid increase in cell number), the excess calories produce an excess number of fat cells. The same is true of the fat cell growth spurt during middle childhood and adolescence. If an infant grows up with an excess number of fat cells, continued over-nutrition will cause these fat cells to increase in size. Obesity results, which simply means that there are more fat cells which get fatter in an obese child. Once the number of cells has been established, weight reduction occurs primarily by a decrease in fat cell size rather than by any appreciable change in fat cell number. Therefore, the infant with too many fat cells retains this tendency to obesity. He may have to consciously work to keep the excess number of fat cells from getting fatter, thus becoming a weight-watcher all his life.

Factors Contributing to Childhood Obesity

There are many reasons why children become fat and stay fat. Because individual differences play such an important role I will simply present some basic principles and concepts about obesity in childhood, and from these you may select factors which pertain to your child.

1. Do fat parents usually produce fat children? According to statistics, the answer is yes. Non-obese parents have a 7 per cent chance of having an obese adolescent. If one parent is obese, there is a 40 per cent chance, and if both parents are obese the probability may be as high as 80 per cent. There is controversy about whether inheritance or environment plays a greater role in obesity. Studies of adopted children show that these children tend to follow the body weight trends of their biological parents more than those of their adoptive parents. Therefore, some children are genetically more predisposed to obesity than others. Whether or to what extent they become obese depends on a variety of environmental factors.

2. Body type, determined largely by heredity, correlates closely with obesity. **Ectomorphs** (tall and lean)—the type who can eat everything and still not gain weight— accumulate much less adipose tissue and seldom become fat. Even in ectomorphs, excess calories may cause excess body fat but because of their lean-looking build they do not appear fat. Their food intake is also usually better related to their activity level. **Mesomorphs** (short and wide) have a greater tendency to obesity, carry excess fat much less attractively, and have more difficulty balancing their food intake with their activity level.

3. Weight control essentially requires a balance of calorie intake and calorie output. Children need calories to maintain their bodily functions (called basal metabolic requirements), to grow and to obtain fuel for exercise. Because children are growing, their caloric requirements increase with growth, whereas adult requirements stay the same and vary only with change of activity. If more calories are consumed than the child needs for growth and exercise, these excess calories are deposited as excess fat.

4. Appetite control means that the child consumes just the right amount of calories for his needs. His appetite adjusts to his changing needs, no excess calories are consumed and therefore no excess fat is stored. What causes appetite control and why some children can't control their ''appestat'' is not completely known but it is thought that early feeding habits may have a profound effect on appetite control.

Whether breastfed infants are less likely to become obese than formula-fed infants is a subject of controversy. One can pluck from the overstuffed medical literature any study which supports one's own bias. One factor about breast milk that compels me to believe that it contributes to appetite control is that breast milk changes to accommodate the needs of the infant, whereas formula does not. The fat content of breast milk changes during each feeding and also at different periods during the day. At the beginning of a nursing meal an infant sucks to get the milk flowing and obtains a large volume of foremilk (the early milk which is rich in protein and carbohydrate but low in calories). As the meal progresses, his efforts are rewarded with the richer hindmilk which contains more fat and more calories. The hindmilk may signal his ''appestat'' that he is full and he stops eating, having had both his sucking needs and his appetite completely satisfied.

In addition, some studies suggest that, as the infant grows, the fat content (and therefore the number of calories) of breast milk decreases. With increasing age infants need fewer calories per unit weight. It is only reasonable that a species-specific milk should change as calorie requirements change.

Mothers may sometimes mistakenly feel that their infant is hungry. When a thirsty, rather than hungry, baby is put to the breast he sucks in such a way that he receives the lower calorie milk that acts primarily as a thirst quencher. A bottle-fed baby does not have this advantage and receives a high calorie formula, regardless of whether he is hungry or merely thirsty.

5. Whether early introduction of solids contributes to eventual obesity is controversial, but the high rate of obesity in certain European countries which have advocated these feeding practices suggests that this practice may contribute to infant obesity.

6. Another infant feeding practice which may contribute to childhood obesity is the "clean plate syndrome." Early in childhood, especially between the ages of one and three years, mothers seem to assume that they, not their children, are responsible for their infants' intake. "He does not eat" is a common parental concern and a clean plate is often equated with effective mothering. Make nutritious food available, market it wisely, but let the responsibility for the volume of intake be your child's—he knows how much he should eat better than you. Your goal in infant and childhood feeding is not necessarily to fill him up, but to let your child learn to develop and exercise his internal appetite control signal.

7. The use of food as a reward or as a source of pleasure rather than as a source of nutrition may instill unwise food habits in a child who already risks becoming obese. I do not wish to shoot down a nice old custom like getting cookies at Grandmother's house, ("Nothin' says lovin' like somethin' from the oven") but some parental guidance is necessary in the "food for pleasure" practice.

8. The advertising media, especially TV, have contributed more to children's weight than to their brains. Studies have shown that the majority of children actually believe that commercials are true, especially when they see parents eating or drinking what the tube says they should. Children learn from commercials that eating is for fun or for when you are nervous, rather than primarily as a source of balanced nutrition.

9. Do fat children eat more than lean children? Most studies show that fat children do **not** eat more than lean children; some may even eat less. What is important, however, is that fat children normally exercise less than lean children. The child of normal weight achieves a balance between exercise and appetite. As he exercises less, he eats less and vice versa. The obese child, however, does not achieve this balance. As he exercises less, he does not eat proportionally less. So while it is true that fat children do not necessarily eat more food than lean children, they do eat more for a given amount of exercise than lean children. This is a very important basic point about childhood obesity. I believe that diminished exercise contributes more to childhood obesity than overeating.

Obese children become more involved in sedentary pastimes and even when they participate in team sports they are less active than their lean teammates. An interesting question is which came first, the inactivity or the obesity? Studies suggest that these children were initially less active. Infants with only moderate food intake but with a quiet, placid personality often become obese, whereas an infant with a very active temperament may not become fat even with a high calorie intake. Unfortunately, with time, a vicious cycle results. The less active a child is, the more chubby he becomes; the fatter he is, the less interested he is in physical activity.

10. Do fat infants become fat adults? If your infant is fat, he is likely to become a fat child; a fat child is likely to become a fat teenager and the majority of fat teenagers become fat adults. This unfortunate bit of reality supports the fat cell theory previously discussed and emphasizes the importance of controlling weight gain in infancy, the critical period which determines the likelihood of a life-long weight struggle.

Why Obesity is Harmful to the Child

Besides the adult diseases which may be related to being overweight, obesity definitely affects the psycho-social development of the child and adolescent. Our society does not love fat people. Our culture rewards leanness and penalizes fatness, particularly in women. Obese children often develop a poor self-image and low self-esteem. They are prone to social isolation and because they compete poorly in athletics, often choose more sedentary activities which further increase their weight. Obesity is not just a problem of the body but also of the mind, and the latter may actually become more significant.

Prevention of Obesity

How can you lessen the chances of your baby becoming obese?
1. Identify the high risk infant. (See page 150 .)
2. Breastfeed. (See page 151 .)
3. Use solid food wisely. Individualize your infant's non-milk sources of nutrition. Introduce solids when you sincerely feel he needs them, not according to the accepted norms of your neighborhood. Solids should be used for nutrition only, not as a filler to "hold him" through the night or to lengthen the interval between bottles. Not only does this unwise practice seldom work but it may also contribute to unhealthy patterns of appetite control. Encourage foods which are highly nutritious in relation to their calorie content. In other words, avoid foods high in calories but low in nutritive value. (See **Balanced Nutrition**, page 136 .) As we discussed on page 132 , the overuse of fruit juice may be a subtle cause of obesity. During the first two years you should be in complete control of what your infant eats, and he should be in control of how much he eats.
4. Encourage healthy eating behavior before unhealthy behavior becomes resistant to change. An ounce of prevention is easier than a pound of dieting. Channel the child into meaningful activities and skills to prevent boredom. A bored child risks developing unhealthy eating habits. The use of food as a substitute for meaningful personal relationships is an unwise practice (i.e. equating cookies with love). Discourage the child from eating alone or nibbling in front of the television set. Rid the house of junk food and provide low calorie snacks. Nibbling is healthy, providing the foods are nutritious. Encourage patterns such as eating smaller pieces and eating more slowly. Fast eaters tend to eat more.

The key to encouraging behavior which does not contribute to obesity in the older child and adolescent can be summed up in two words—involvement and success. Children and adolescents who involve themselves in teams, religious groups and extracurricular activities, and experience social and academic success, have a much lower chance of engaging in the less desirable behavior of over-eating.
5. A common concern that parents have is whether a medical problem is causing their child's obesity "Doctor, could it be her thyroid?" This is a realistic concern and is one of the reasons why any wise weight control program begins with a medical check. Generally, there is seldom any medical problem when your child seems generally well, and she is of at least normal height. Endocrine disorders causing obesity usually also cause

children to be short, whereas children who are obese, especially from over-nutrition, tend to be taller than average or at least average height. A short, fat child should always undergo a complete medical evaluation.

Management of Childhood and Adolescent Obesity—A Step-by-Step Approach

Obesity is an individual problem and needs a very individual program. A step-by-step approach in the management of childhood and adolescent obesity will be outlined. You should select those approaches which are applicable to your child's weight problem. It is interesting to note that by the end of adolescence, girls have about twice as much body fat as boys, and therefore girls are more predisposed to obesity during adolescence. Prior to adolescence, the difference in weight between girls and boys is not as marked. Because adolescent obesity is a more common problem in girls, I will use "she" in this section.

1. The first step is to determine how overweight your child is. By comparing your child's weight and height on a growth chart, your doctor can tell how many pounds she is over her ideal weight. For example, if your child is thirteen years old, of average height and weighs 120 pounds (the ideal weight on growth charts is 100 pounds), then she is 20 pounds overweight, and being 20 per cent overweight constitutes obesity. In addition to what the scales say, what may be more important is how fat she looks. Your doctor may measure the amount of excess fat (skin fold thickness in the upper arms, waist and back) with special calipers. Not only do skin fold measurements indicate whether extra weight is primarily extra fat, but they serve as a base for monitoring future gain or loss in body fat as your child's weight changes.

2. Why is your child overweight? Is it because she eats too much, exercises too little or a combination of both? What are her eating habits and her special cravings? Your doctor will also try to detect what her basic temperament is. Is she quiet and sedentary or is she a very active person? What is the family history of obesity and what are the current eating habits of both parents and other members of the family? Your doctor needs this valuable information in order to work out a behavior modification program.

3. Is your child strongly motivated to lose weight? Are you nagging her, or does she really want to lose weight? How does she feel when she looks at herself in the mirror? How does her weight affect her self-image? Self-motivation is the key to any successful weight control program.

4. Understanding the principle of **caloric values** of various foods and learning how to count calorie intake is very important in any successful weight control program. An intake of an excess of 3500 calories will be deposited as one pound of fat. A loss of one pound requires expending slightly more than 3500 calories of excess energy. Weight control means that the body uses the exact amount of calories consumed. The number of calories required will vary from day to day but if the ideal weight remains constant then there is good caloric balance. Excessive weight gain begins when the number of calories consumed are greater than the number utilized and the excess is deposited as fat. One important point is that only a slight excess in calories over a long period of time may still result in obesity. For example, an excess of 50 calories per day (equivalent to one chocolate chip cookie) could result in an extra five pounds per year. Another important principle is that of caloric deficit, which means that to lose one pound you either have to eat 3500 less calories or burn off an excess 3500 calories. Most effective weight control programs combine both of these methods.

5. Generally, the results of dietary control in adolescents are discouraging over the long run. Adolescents need much extra energy for their rapid growth spurt and unwise dietary restrictions may result in diminished growth in height. Besides being potentially unhealthy, crash diets which produce rapid weight loss usually do not last because the basic cause of the problem has not been treated. Adolescents are by nature hungry and it is very often not the volume of food that is the problem but the type of food.

6. A sensible approach to weight control is nutrition education. The most successful diets are built upon a person's food preferences (providing these are reasonably nutritious). After taking a careful dietary history, pick one piece of junk food (usually 100 calories worth, equivalent to two chocolate chip cookies). The cut-out-one-thing-a-day method is very successful. If your child does nothing else but cut out 100 calories from his present diet each day, he will lose 10 pounds in one year. Most children have only a slight excess in their calorie balance which they have had for a long time, and therefore only a slight reduction in calorie intake over a period of time may adequately control their weight.

For the very overweight child, a complete overhauling of the diet is necessary. In revamping the diet, try to retain in the new diet many of your child's preference foods (again, providing they are reasonably nutritious). Asking a person to continually eat what they don't like is doomed to failure. Changing eating habits which have been acquired over a long period of time takes strong motivation and patience. Both you and your child should be aware of the following food facts:

a) **Dairy Products.** The calorie content of dairy products is determined mostly by the fat content, because a gram of fat contains twice the number of calories as a gram of protein or carbohydrate. Choose dairy products that are low in fat, such as unsweetened, low-fat yogurt.

b) **Meat.** Like dairy products, the calorie content of meat depends upon the fat content. Lean meat is preferable for the dieter. Its relatively low water content makes a smaller volume of lean meat (and also cheese) a richer source of nutrients than the same volume of most other foods.

c) **Poultry.** Because of the lower fat content, poultry is lower in calories than meat and is preferable to meat (beef and pork) for the dieter. Removing the skin from poultry lowers the fat and calorie content. Depending on the type and its preparation, most fish is also preferable for the dieter.

d) **Vegetables** are a dieter's best friend because they are relatively high in nutritional value and low in calories. Lettuce is a free food, which means you can eat as much as you wish. Because of the very high water content, a lettuce and tomato salad is a good filler which does not have an excessive number of calories. Certain vegetables are more nutritious than others. For example, broccoli contains more protein per calorie than most other vegetables. Because of their high starch content (type of carbohydrate), corn, lima beans, and potatoes contain more calories than the same weight of other vegetables. Vegetable juice contains less than half the number of calories of fruit juice and provides twice the nutrition.

e) **Fruits and juices** are good sources of vitamins. Pure fresh fruit is nutritionally superior to the juice because the pulp content is preserved. Drinking an excessive amount of fruit juice may be a hidden source of obesity in young children because they can consume large quantities without getting full. Fruit juices have more calories and less nutritional value than milk and vegetable juices, but are certainly preferable to soft drinks as a thirst quencher.

f) **Cereals and grain products** can be a good source of nutrition but can also be high in calories, depending on how much sugar is added. Whole grain cereal is nutritionally superior to processed cereals.

g) **Oils** (salad dressing) are a no-no for the dieter. They contain nearly 100 per cent fat and consequently are high in calories (1 tablespoon of mayonnaise contains 100 calories which may be as many calories as the entire salad). Try low calorie dressings. Fried or breaded foods are naturally higher in calories because of the added fat content of the oils.

h) **Sugars and sweets** enjoy the prestigious title of junk food among the nutrition-conscious. Sweets that should be strictly avoided are the ''pure sugar'' type—table sugar, icing and frosting, candies, colas.

i) The preparation and processing of food have a great bearing on both the nutritional and caloric content. Generally, the more natural and non-processed the food is, the higher the nutritional value.

7. Exercise. Children often say ''I don't eat that much!'' Many obese children actually do not overeat and some remain obese even on a relatively low calorie diet. In this case, exercise is a safe answer to weight control, not further dietary restrictions. The two simple and successful methods of weight control in teenagers are to rid their diet of all junk food and to increase their exercise enough to use 500 calories per day. One hour of sustained exercise (e.g. running, swimming, walking fast) will use around 500 calories. Initially, a forced-exercise program may gradually improve your child's stamina and break the vicious cycle of inactivity. As your child begins to enjoy exercise more, she is likely to become more active.

8. Setting Goals. Children are by nature goal-oriented and often it helps to have a goal, e.g. a certain number of pounds to be lost over a certain period of time. How many pounds and how fast depends upon how motivated and how overweight your child is. A safe and realistic weight reduction is one pound per week until the ideal weight is reached. Remember that, ideally, weight reduction should remove excess fat tissue alone and should not deprive a growing body of nutrients necessary for growth. A gradual steady weight loss is not only the safest but the most likely to last because this method does not require a dramatic change in behavioral patterns but rather a slight modification. For example, cutting out the caloric equivalent of one cola and one cookie, plus walking half an hour each day would eliminate 500 calories per day and result in a one pound per week weight loss. I would not advise a more rapid weight loss than two pounds per week for the growing child, and even this should not be attempted without professional dietary counselling. (See **Weight Reduction in Sports Medicine**, page 398 .)

A realistic goal for the only slightly overweight child, especially the poorly motivated one, is the don't-lose-but-don't-gain-for-one-year method. With proper nutrition and increased exercise, your child will continue to grow and may even gain some weight, but over the year excess body fat will be lost, which is the primary goal.

9. Behavior modification is vital in the treatment of childhood obesity. If your child has been candid about her eating habits and all the particular behavior which may contribute to her obesity, then your doctor will be able to advise her on changing some of these weight gaining habits.

a) Examine the stimuli for eating. Does she give into eating when bored, while watching TV, because there is nothing else to do, or during emotional stress?

b) Is she satisfied with her social development, peer groups, teams, friends?

c) Is she satisfied with her academic achievements?

d) What is her degree of physical activity? Does she enjoy this activity? Is she an active player on a team or would she like to be? Are there enough physical activities at school?

e) Is there any emotional stress that contributes to her eating habits—conflict at home, relationships with parents or friends, school?

f) What are her basic eating patterns? Change the way her meals are served. Buffet dinners appeal to the compulsive eater. She will probably eat less if the family fills their plates in the kitchen and takes them to the table. Out of sight, out of mind. Use smaller plates. They trick the eater into thinking they are consuming more than they actually are. Cutting food into smaller pieces, eating it more slowly and using the old restaurant trick of filling up on a salad first (with low calorie dressing, of course) are habits your child should follow. Encourage the habit of eating only in one room, preferably the kitchen or dining room. This reduces the tendency to nibble in front of the TV or while talking on the phone.

The basic goal in behavior modification is to identify and change those factors which directly or indirectly contribute to obesity. A general principle of behavior modification is called **shaping**—behavioral changes proceed most effectively when we move gradually, each step moving closer to the final goal. A sudden, drastic change in behavior is usually more difficult and less effective than a gradual, continuous one. Group therapy may be more effective than individual counselling for teenagers' behavior modification. Most medical centers and children's hospitals have an adolescent medicine department or teen clinic.

Weight control pills, in my opinion, should not be used. Not only are they usually ineffective but they contribute to potential drug abuse, work against behavior modification and do not attack the basic problems of the obese person.

10. The school can play a very important role in childhood weight control. Courses on nutrition and weight control should be taught by a qualified instructor to students as young as eight years of age, before pre-adolescent and adolescent obesity stages. Even if poor dietary habits exist at home some of this nutritional counselling will sink into the child. School lunches should be monitored by the school nurse or nutritionist to see what is really in that brown bag. If the student's bag is full of junk food, this should be pointed out to the parents. The menu in most school cafeterias contributes little to the nutritional education of our youth. Soda and candy machines conveniently placed in student lounges reinforce the already unwise eating habits of the impulsive snacker. Generally speaking, all vending machines should either be prohibited from schools or, at least, their contents should be monitored. Athletic programs for girls should be founded. School girls as well as boys need outlets for physical energy but, until recently, schools failed to recognize that girls should have the same physical exercise opportunities as boys.

Parenting the Obese Adolescent

Most parents feel that their child's weight loss is their responsibility. This may be true for the infant and young child but not for the teenager. Your teenager's weight control is her responsibility, not yours. Your responsibility is to support her self-esteem, create a home atmosphere conducive to healthy eating habits and teach principles of good nutrition by your example. If you can practice the guides to prevention of childhood obesity which I suggested previously and if you can communicate well with your child in areas not relating to her weight, then you have fulfilled your responsibilities in parenting the obese adolescent. Parent-teenager conflicts, especially those between mother and daughter, often arise when there is excessive parental direction in a teenage weight control program. Leave the responsibility to your adolescent, the direction to her physician, and focus your parenting energies on the needs of your adolescent which are not directly related to her weight.

CHAPTER VI

COMMON CONCERNS OF BABY'S FIRST YEAR

Health Care for Your Baby

In North America, periodic and complete "well-baby" and "well-child" exams are performed by your physician at all stages of your child's development.

The purpose of these check-ups is to fully examine your child for early detection of any actual or potential abnormalities, to discuss various developmental and emotional changes at these various stages, to offer advice and consultation concerning your needs and problems during the years of parenting, and to provide treatment for any medical or developmental problems.

During these periodic office visits, your pediatrician also grows in his knowledge of you and your child. Seeing your child when he is well establishes an important reference point for a medical judgment when your child is ill. In most pediatric practices these periodic examinations are scheduled as follows: once a month for the first six months, and then at nine months, twelve months, fifteen months, eighteen months, two years, two and a half years, three years and once a year thereafter.

How to Get the Most Out of Your Visits to the Doctor

We have talked about the proper utilization of your pediatrician under **Choosing Your Pediatrician**, page 32 . Here are a few tips on how both you and your child can get the most out of your office visits. First of all, shortly before your appointment write a list of your problems and questions and memorize this list. Not only does this list provide you with a more meaningful office visit, but it also conveys to your doctor that you value these periodic exams. Secondly, I strongly advise that both parents attend these visits, especially in the first couple of months. There are certain topics that pediatricians like to discuss with fathers. In my practice, I do insist that the father attend the first office visit and, as a result, I find that many fathers seem much more involved in their baby's stages of development. This also conveys to the pediatrician a total family commitment to the baby

The Fussy Baby

Parenting the Fussy Baby

The fussy baby's impact upon family life is so great that he can absolutely destroy all the rewarding aspects of child rearing if he is not properly understood and handled. For this reason, the fussy baby problem cannot be discussed in cookbook fashion with absolute do's, don'ts and pat answers. We shall approach this problem in the three following phases:

1. understanding why babies cry and fuss,
2. understanding parents' reactions to fussing and finally,
3. suggestions about how to successfully cope with the whole fussy baby situation.

Why Babies Fuss

Fussing and crying are not synonymous. They differ in quality and quantity. Crying is your baby's signal of some basic need and very early in life your newborn will learn to blow his horn to communicate his needs. As you respond to his crying, and therefore to his needs, he learns more purposeful crying, resulting in his earliest form of language. This will persist until he can satisfy his own needs by walking and talking.

Your baby has different cries to signify different needs and he will demand of you an intuitive recognition of these signals. He has hunger cries, pain cries, attention-seeking cries and simple unsettling cries. For example, hunger cries usually begin loudly, are seemingly forced and stop easily when he is satisfied. They begin again in a louder more upset tone if his first attempt has not been promptly answered and are usually accompanied by sucking movements, lip-smacking and hand-to-mouth reflexes. By the end of the first month, you will get to know your baby' cries for various needs. The crying of the fussy baby is both confusing and frustrating because you usually do not know why he is crying or what he needs.

At what point do "normal crying" and "normal" cranky behavior become "fussy?" Let's define the "fussy baby" as one who has **prolonged** periods of seemingly purposeless crying which interferes with sleep, feeding and settling. He demands constant physical contact. He is discontented, unhappy and responds inconsistently to the usual modes of comforting. He is an extremely time-consuming, energy-draining, exhausting baby who often elicits negative feelings in his mother, puts a strain on his parents' marriage and produces anxiety and fatigue in the whole family, including himself. Let's explore some of the basic concepts of human behavior in order to understand basically why these babies fuss.

Human contentment or happiness is largely determined by the ability to adjust to change, to seek pleasurable experiences and to adapt to or modify unpleasant experiences. The smoother the continuum of change, the easier the adjustment. A contented person feels his world around him is right and he is right for the world. The world of the fetus in utero is a steadily changing, smooth continuum of experiences. In utero, your baby is in continuous motion and at a constant temperature. He is consistently lulled by the sounds of his mother; his needs are constantly and automatically met. The birthing environment and the early adjustment weeks and months provide a less secure, and certainly a more disordered, environment. I feel it is at this point that the "fussy" tendencies begin. His expectations of continuing life as before are shattered. The baby does not feel right. He is unable to adapt but he has an intense desire to be comfortable. This conflict between wanting comfort and not being able to achieve it results in fussiness, as if he were saying "I expect to feel good but I don't. I cannot help myself. You must help me by listening to what I tell you. Learn what makes me feel good and constantly give it to me until I make myself feel good."

Along with the inability to feel right, some babies fuss because they are unable to adapt to or block out unpleasant stimuli. Most babies are endowed with a **stimulus barrier**. For example, some babies will block out unpleasant noises by falling asleep. We call this process adaptability. In some babies, this stimulus barrier is more permeable than in others. These babies receive various labels—fussy baby, difficult baby, unsettled baby, challenging baby. These babies appeal to their parents to provide the stimulus barrier and security that they cannot provide for themselves. The fussy baby may also have a physical adjustment problem resulting in pain or discomfort, in which case he is usually termed a colicky baby. Colic is manifested by cries of discomfort, by drawing the legs up onto a distended abdomen and by passing much gas. The stools, despite much straining, are normal. Colic tends to occur at the same time daily. Between these episodes, your baby is completely well. Colic usually begins around two weeks of age, seldom lasts more than six months and is thought to be due to irritation of, or excessive pressure within, the intestines from excessive swallowing and retention of air, or from food allergies. (A detailed discussion of the colic problem is found in the section **Feeding Problems** page 141.) Parents seem more tolerant of colicky babies than fussy babies and seem to cope reasonably well when they have advice and support. When parents understand **why** their baby is crying and know that physical pain is the cause of his fussiness, it is handled with the usual sympathy and support that a parent shows for a child who is medically ill. However, the fussiness of a baby who cries for no identifiable reason is the most difficult to understand, and is therefore the most difficult to cope with.

Parents' Reactions to the Fussy Baby

The "easiness" of a baby is not a measure of your effectiveness as a mother. **Babies fuss primarily because of their own temperament not because of your mothering abilities.** A fussy baby can shake the confidence of a new mother. The less confident you become, the less you are able to comfort your baby's anxieties and the more inconsolable he becomes. This cycle often results in "escape" mothering rather than immersion mothering, an unfortunate break in the continuum of parenting. A fussy baby wants to feel right. Parents want to enjoy their baby but often don't. Both parents and baby are disappointed. The parents have recourse to outside help and counselling to help them adjust. The baby, however, has no recourse but his parents.

Fussiness is often in the eyes of the beholder. I keep a list of parents who have successfully coped with their fussy baby and often refer new parents who feel they have a fussy baby. After meeting with the parents on my list, the new parents often exclaim, "We don't have a fussy baby after all." Parents' expectations of what babies are like are often less than realistic. There are marked, inborn differences in temperament among babies, just as among mothers. This is the "for better or fo worse'' aspect of parenting which you must accept. You have a ''handful'' and he may remain a handful throughout childhood. Often when I am evaluating a hyperactive child, parents will volunteer that he has been a handful since birth. Later in childhood these children often tax the creativity and energies of teachers just as they do their parents. Take heart though, you probably have an above-average, intelligent, creative child who needs above-average, creative parenting.

''Should I let my baby cry?'' is one of the most common questions that pediatricians are asked. Probably more bad advice is given on this one short question than on any other topic in pediatrics. It is a question that no one can, or perhaps should, answer except the child's parents. Anybody who says ''Let your baby cry'' is placing adult value systems on a newborn baby, a judgment which is both presumptuous and unfair. Babies do not cry to annoy, to maliciously manipulate or to take advantage of their parents in an unfair way. They cry because they have a need. To ignore the cry is to ignore the need. A baby is not spoiled if he is picked up. He is more apt to be spoiled if he is not picked up.

Research on determinants of personality and eventual childhood behavior has shown that babies whose cries are respected and promptly attended to in the early newborn period have less tendency to become fussy babies for a prolonged period of time. As previously mentioned, trust in his environment is thought to be one of the prime determinants of an infant's eventual personality. A newborn whose signals are promptly attended to grows up trusting his environment and feels that the world is a pleasant place in which to be. The newborn whose cries fall on deaf ears grows up mistrusting his environment and his world and his personality may develop accordingly.

The newborn care policies which separate mothers and babies in our western culture probably make one of the main contributions to the fussy baby problem. Contrast these policies with those of other cultures where baby is born into the arms of his mother, is carried around with her while she is working, is fed on demand and sleeps skin-to-skin with the mother until he shows his signs of comfortable independence. Researchers have noted that babies born into these cultures fuss far less and seem more content.

Preventive Measures

''What can I do to help prevent my baby from becoming a fussy baby?'' This is a question mothers frequently ask, especially if they have previously had a fussy baby. Smoothing the transition from the intra-uterine to postnatal environment is the best way to minimize your chances of having a fussy baby. This is achieved by following the principles of successful parenting discussed in the previous chapters—Prepared Childbirth Classes, The Bonding Process, Breastfeeding Your Baby, Rooming-In in the Hospital, Preparing the Nest, Immersion Mothering. As you may have guessed, the underlying philosophy of these principles of successful parenting is a respect for the dignity of parenthood and the dignity of your newborn as a person. In my own practice, I have noticed that parents who practice the above principles are intuitively able to respond to their baby's cues and more effectively cope with a fussy baby.

A Step-by-Step Approach to Managing the Fussy Baby

The first step is to be absolutely sure that there are no physical causes for your baby's fussiness. This necessitates a thorough examination by your pediatrician. When making your appointment, mention to the nurse the magnitude of the problem and request an appointment that is convenient for both parents. Your doctor will need the following information: a detailed description of these fussy periods, how frequent they are; how long they last if there is any pattern to them; if they occur at any particular period of the day; how much these fussy periods seem to affect the general happiness of your baby; how much this fussiness bothers you as a mother, you as a father, and you as a couple and lastly, an answer to a question that I always ask parents "What do you think the cause of his fussiness is and what methods have you tried to handle it?" As your doctor examines your baby he is looking for any illnesses which will produce periodic pain such as chronic ear infection, eye irritation, throat infection, certain types of allergic or irritating rashes, severe constipation or hernia.

If your baby is apparently perfectly healthy and seems to have no apparent pressure or pain-producing illnesses that could account for his behavior, the doctor will then go to the next step of investigation: Is there a feeding or digestive problem? I usually suspect that the intestinal organs are the culprit when the fussiness is described as the colic-type previously discussed. Is he a hungry and chronically undersatisfied baby who is perhaps not getting enough to satisfy his desires? Most mothers have already eliminated this possibility by determining that extra food, either liquid or solid, does not seem to affect his fussiness. Is he allergic to his milk? Intestinal milk allergy must be high on your list of suspected causes. A change in formula may be prescribed by your doctor. If you are breastfeeding, then certainly he is not allergic to your milk but he may actually be allergic to some substance in your diet that enters your milk. To detect the offending allergen, an elimination diet may be prescribed for you. One by one, for a period of three days each, you eliminate the common allergens from your diet. These are dairy products, citrus fruits, gaseous vegetables (cabbage, onions, green pepper, broccoli), foods containing caffeine (coffee, tea, chocolates, cola), wheat products, artificial sweetener or coloring, medications that you or your baby are taking such as cold medications, vitamins or fluoride. If there is not a high suspicion that intestinal allergies are the culprit, it may be unwise to try an elimination diet because of the risk of producing a vitamin or nutritional deficiency in the mother or baby. This can further increase the fussiness of the baby and decrease the mother's tolerance.

Finally, is there some inhalant type of allergen around your home such as cigarette smoke, hairsprays, perfumes, certain cleaning products?

Unfortunately in most cases no apparent reason for your baby's fussiness is found. Consider the following "survival tips":

1. Motion and physical contact. The majority of fussy babies are calmed by two actions—motion and physical contact. The art of parenting the fussy baby determines what type of motion and physical contact he likes and needs, and how much you can give of yourself without exhausting your parental reserves. You have to experiment to find out your baby's response to different modes of touching and handling. He will probably prefer the intensity of bare skin-to-skin contact such as chest-to-chest. He may need almost constant stroking and patting. He may need the security of swaddling and firm holding. You will need to experiment to find which of the following positions he likes to be held: either bent over your shoulder, flat over your knee, directly in front of you with one hand on his back and the other hand on his bottom staring directly into his eyes while you sing to him and move rhythmically, or draped stomach-down over your arm, firmly clasping his diaper area, legs astraddle. After a while, you will develop your own "colic-carry." You may log many miles of walking, rocking, car-riding, floor-pacing, dancing, pram-pushing. Various types of baby carriers are ideal for this situation (see **Preparing the Nest** page 78). Within a few weeks or months, your baby will have told you what mode of transportation he likes best.

2. Relaxation. Consider whether you are having difficulty relaxing with your baby. Being held in tense arms may be very upsetting to a baby who is sensitive to these messages. This is called the "tense mother/tense baby" syndrome. Relax by taking a warm bath (with your baby if necessary) using the tension-release techniques which you learned in childbirth classes: having your husband give you a massage, getting outdoor exercise, taking the phone off the hook when you are relaxing, and using baby's sleep periods to do something just for yourself. Do what you want to do, not what you have to do.

3. Scheduling is usually a bad word in baby care but it may be an aid in caring for the fussy baby. Most babies do have their best time and their worst time of the day. Plan ahead for these periods and use his best time (the state of quiet alertness) for stimulating activity that will be enjoyable for him and provide learning experiences. Plan ahead for his worst times (usually at the end of the day or between 4:00 p.m. and 8:00 p.m.) by mustering up all the parenting devices that seem to calm him. See that this time of the day is free from unnecessary noises, interruptions or environmental stimuli that may actually overstimulate and produce startling feelings.

The Fussy Family

The next concept to understand in the management of a fussy baby is that this problem is a total family problem, not just the baby's problem. Babies usually have their more fussy periods between 4:00 p.m. and 8:00 p.m., just at the time when the family is usually all together and most family activity occurs. Picture the following family situation: Dad comes home after a very exhausting day at his office, opens the door to his castle and is greeted by his queen saying, "Take your fussy kid. I am tired and I am going to bed." Tired Dad then walks, rides and carries fussy kid until fussy kid happens to fall asleep, though probably not for long. Tired Mom and tired Dad then have a few moments respite from their fussy baby, but may often spend these few moments of peace fussing at each other about why they have a fussy kid.

The marital tension that a fussy baby produces can be alleviated somewhat by recognizing this problem early in the fussy period, confiding your feelings to each other and seeking medical help. Husbands need to be particularly supportive at this time. Tell yourselves that if you work together, you will all survive this fussy period, which does improve with time.

Support Groups

Seek help from supportive people and avoid the nonsupportive advice of the "let your baby cry" and "feed him more" philosophers. In fact, you reach a point in the management of all fussy babies when you need more support than advice. In your encounters with support groups, it is very important to verbalize your feelings. Tell them exactly what your feelings are. If you have a low acceptance level of your baby's crying and have reached the end of your rope, say so. Some very common feelings are "I hate my baby," "I feel I am being taken advantage of" and "I really dislike having to hold him so much but I know I must."

The type of support you will probably receive from these parents who have survived similar situations would be the following: "It's okay to have these feelings." "It's okay to hate your baby." "You will love him more than hate him." "You are not being taken advantage of." "You are not spoiling him. You are loving him and giving him what he needs." This is genuine supportive advice from caring parents who are letting you know that your feelings are normal, and that you are doing a good job of coping with a difficult situation that time and the principles of good parenting will correct.

Fussiness in Perspective

Crying is one of the most misunderstood childhood behaviors and, unfortunately, baby books and many of the sages of the century have contributed to the confusion about crying. From the moment of birth, your baby is encouraged to cry as a sign of health. In fact, he is even given "two points" (see **Apgar Scoring**, page 56) for crying lustily at birth. We now know that the state of quiet alertness is actually the healthiest state for a newborn. Many baby books by respected pediatricians state that it is normal for newborn babies to cry and fuss for two hours a day. This concept implies that newborn babies normally fuss for 25 per cent of their waking periods. If you think about it, if an older child or an adult exhibited disturbed behavior for 25 per cent of their waking periods we would consider them anything but normal. Here is a bit of ammunition for you to use in shooting down the "let your baby cry" philosophers. The cries of a newborn are largely of reflex origin and not a voluntary, cognitive emotion. A baby does not go through the thought process, "I am hungry, now I think I shall cry in order to get my way," or "I am lonesome, now let me think about it a minute to see how I can get picked up." **Reflex needs must be uncompromisingly and unconditionally parented, whereas the voluntary emotional expressions of later infancy are often negotiable.** (See

Feeding Problems, page 141 and **Sleep Problems**, page 170 .

Sleep Patterns and Problems in the First Year

Since one of the premises of this book is that you should enjoy your baby, both mother and baby must get enough sleep. An overly tired baby or mother is not a good situation. Fatigue dampens full enjoyment of anything. In previous chapters I have tried to convince you of the benefits of immersion mothering, which I admit may be one of the more exhausting methods o

The cries of a newborn are largely of reflex origin. A baby does not think, "I am hungry, now I think I shall cry in order to get my way." Reflex needs should be uncompromisingly and unconditionally met.

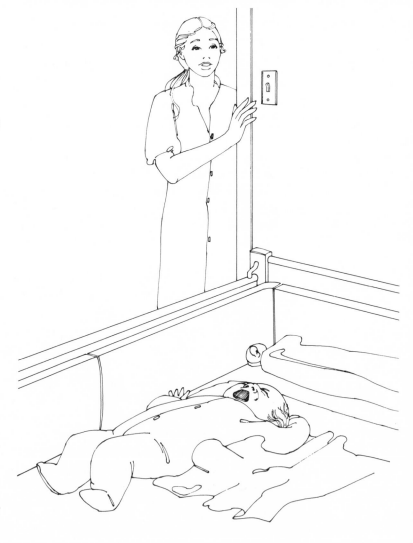

parenting. Therefore, I feel obliged to come up with some helpful ideas to get both you and your baby enough sleep.

The first point to appreciate is that your baby does not have an adult sleep pattern. His sleep patterns differ in quantity and quality from yours. There are two basic sleep states. **Active sleep** (also called REM, or rapid eye movement sleep) is characterized by rapid eye movements, frequent body movements and irregular respiration. **Quiet sleep** is characterized by a deeper sleep without eye or body movements. The quiet sleep state is a more mature state, meaning that the brain has complete control over stimuli that would provoke arousal from sleep. The ultimate in sleep-wake maturity is for a baby to spend the majority of his sleep time in quiet sleep and the majority of his wake time in the alert, attentive state.

In the first few months, your baby may sleep from fourteen to eighteen hours a day and his sleep patterns resemble his feeding patterns—small, frequent feedings and short, frequent naps. Initially, the newborn may sleep four hours at one stretch. Approximately 50 per cent of this time is active sleep and the other 50 per cent quiet sleep. By three months of age, the total number of hours your baby sleeps may change very little but the organization of his sleep patterns improves considerably. By three months, he is awake for longer stretches and his sleep periods are also fewer and longer. The amount of quiet sleep increases as his developing brain becomes capable of inhibiting arousal for extended periods. In later months, these sleep patterns reach adult patterns of approximately 80 per cent deep sleep and 20 per cent active sleep.

A baby's sleep pattern also reflects his basic temperament. Easy babies enjoy a larger percentage of deep sleep, and more difficult or active babies carry their waking personalities into their sleep and therefore have shorter periods of lighter sleep. This is a mismatch since more difficult babies should need more sleep, or at least their parents do. You will notice your baby's various sleep states—sometimes he is really "zonked" and motionless (deep sleep) but during his lighter sleep he is more susceptible to inner and outer stimuli, and he will whimper, grimace, smile and adjust positions. It is during this period of active sleep that disturbances occur.

The goal in parenting your baby to sleep is to minimize the influences which cause him to be aroused during these periods of active, light sleep. During the first few months, he is self aroused by very simple reflex needs such as hunger. If his hunger signal occurs during this light sleep phase he is certain to wake up. This is a basic need which has a right to be satisfied and this need to be satisfied takes priority over your need to sleep. As he grows older, his needs are not as much reflexive as cognitive. As his intellectual and sensory capacities develop, so does his dream capacity and therefore he may be awakened because of an inner fear. Again, his need to be consoled takes priority over your need to sleep. He may also awaken because he is reflecting upon a recently acquired skill which he chooses to exercise in the middle of the night. For example, he may want to play at 4:00 a.m. and depending upon how his requests are gratified, it may become a habit more than a need. (The basic difference between a habit and a need is that a habit is negotiable and a need is not.) In this case, your right to sleep takes priority over his habit. Some sort of negotiation takes place according to the temperament of your baby and your principles of parenting.

Most baby books pronounce that babies should be sleeping through the night by one to three months of age. This misconception is a carry-over from the days when the philosophy of child care was to train a baby to conveniently fit our preconceived ideas. Admittedly there are times when this works and may be advisable for a particular family situation. However, this philosophy usually works better for pets than for babies. In fact, most babies do not sleep through the night until three to six months of age, at which time the majority of babies do settle.

Research studies on sleep patterns in babies show that approximately 70 per cent of babies settle (meaning sleep without awakening from midnight to at least 5:00 a.m.) by three months, and 90 per cent settle by one year. There seems to be a tremendous variation in the age that babies settle. This depends on the baby's individual temperament and the age at which his brain matures into the previously mentioned adult sleep patterns. If you are blessed with a somnolent baby, consider it a luxury rather than a right.

Another unfortunate by-product of the ''Let's have babies conveniently'' philosophy is baby's sleep arrangements. There seems to be some urge to push babies out of parents' bedrooms into their own independent quarters. One very prominent and respected child psychology book states that sleeping in the parents' bed is bad for baby's mental health. These are clear examples of the popular misconceptions in baby care which neither common sense, scientific studies nor principles of good parenting supports. How and where you choose to place your baby's bed is a matter of your baby's individual temperament and your principles of parenting. I will not and should not try to impose my own personal beliefs upon you. I feel, however, that absolutely no psychological disturbance in your child (dependency, insecurity, sexual disturbances, etc.) can be attributed to sleeping close to the parents or even with the parents. The concept of the family bed is gaining increased acceptance. Humans are the only species whose offspring are evicted from the nest at so early an age. Many sleep disturbances are simply due to **separation anxiety**.

One of the common objections to the concept of the family bed is that if you let your baby come into your bed he may never want to leave. I do not think this objection is valid. If a baby is welcomed into the family bed early in infancy, both mother and baby enjoy this skin-to-skin contact, especially if you are breastfeeding. Most fathers gradually come to enjoy this family closeness. These children become so secure that they voluntarily leave the family bed between two and three years of age.

On the other hand, children who enter their parents' bed after infancy often do have difficulty weaning themselves from their parents' bed. These children are usually driven into the parents' bed by fears or insecurity. The parents do not welcome this intrusion. Older siblings do not usually accept this behavior and the child feels these negative vibrations. The result is that the family bed loses its effectiveness as a positive nurturing experience.

Some parents report that they do not sleep well with their baby in their bed, especially if he sleeps between them and, for example, rolls onto Daddy's side expecting to nurse. To avoid such problems, baby should sleep on the side of the bed between a guardrail and the mother.

Tips for Overcoming Sleep Problems

Let's determine how much of a problem really exists. If your baby resists going to bed and awakens frequently but does not seem overly tired during the day, and if you can get back to sleep easily and are not overly tired during the day, this is only a minor occupational hazard of parenting, not really a sleep problem. A sleep problem exists if your baby is overtired and this interferes with his behavior and the enjoyment of his developing stages during his waking hours, or if you are overly tired and do not fully enjoy immersion mothering (the motherhood-is-a-drag syndrome). If you have these feelings, then something must be done. Here are a few tips:

1. Some babies sleep too much during the day and therefore mix up their days and nights. The signal that this may be occurring is when you find yourself saying, "He just doesn't seem tired at night." Try adjusting his nap period. Lengthen the morning nap and shorten the afternoon nap. Babies who sleep longer stretches than four to five hours during the day will often awaken at night.

2. If there is some pressing social reason for getting your baby to bed at a certain time, push back his usual nap time to earlier in the morning and earlier in the afternoon, make his afternoon nap shorter and provide him with some entertaining (but not overly-stimulating) activity to keep him awake during the late afternoon.

3. An ideal schedule if you have evening plans and want baby to be asleep is to get your baby to sleep following his early evening feeding. He may sleep until 11:00 p.m., awaken then for another feeding and thereafter sleep through the night.

4. Babies who won't accept this intrusion into their sleep patterns are the "p.m. fussers," babies who have their most active energy-releasing (and draining) period in the late afternoon and early evening. This type of baby often has a basic need for something during this period and these needs should be respected (see **The Fussy Baby**, page 162).

If your baby's problem is not wanting to go to bed rather than staying asleep, and you know he is tired (yawning, droopy eyelids, "He doesn't know when to give up") try the following:

1. Have a quiet hour before bedtime. Instead of sensory-stimulating activities such as "bouncy-bouncy" or "upsy-downsy," try soothing activities such as lying on Dad's chest listening to his heart beat and his breathing movements, listening to soothing music, carrying him around using a rhythmic rocking motion or even taking him for a car ride.

2. "Mother" him to sleep—a breast or a bottle plus a rocking chair is usually a winning combination.

3. An older child such as a toddler usually looks forward to the bedtime ritual of reading a book, taking a bath, putting on his pyjamas, saying "night-night" to everyone, playing a bedtime record or singing a lullaby.

4. Your toddler may love to be parented to sleep, with you lying in his bed with him until he is asleep (or you are asleep). Babies who fall asleep in their parent's arms usually settle more easily than when they are put to bed awake.

What about the baby who goes to sleep reasonably well but wakes several times during the night and won't go back to sleep?

1. Try to soundproof his sleeping area. Oil the squeaks in his crib or cradle, put rubber coasters under the bedposts or put a rug under his bed and on the surrounding floor. Minimize any subtle, irritating noises that may arouse him. Be sure he is well-fed, has a dry diaper, a clear nose, and adequate warmth and humidity.

2. Clothe him in the attire in which he settles best. Some babies like loose garments which do not stifle their activity when they awaken and resettle. Others like the security of being firmly swaddled.

3. Babies who have difficulty sleeping through the night are best fed just before you go bed so that both of you retire around the same time. Again, aim for the 7:00 p.m. and 11:00 p.m. "ideal schedule" if he will cooperate. You may want to try an added "filler" of solid foods such as cereal in a desperate attempt to prolong his nighttime sleeping hours, but this usually does not work. The use of fillers to keep baby sleeping is a common practice but I feel it is unwise and may contribute to problems in appetite control and obesity in later childhood.

4. Many babies awaken during the light sleep phase, fuss for a few minutes, squirm and toss, and then settle themselves back to sleep, having found a comfortable position. If your intuition tells you this is what he is doing, don't break any speed records rushing to settle him. Allow him some time and space to resettle himself. If he is not settling well after a short time and seems to be revving up to a point where he is obviously not going to sleep without some outside help, try a firm, secure "laying on of the hands" on his head or back, just enough to convey your presence and relieve his separation anxieties. He may settle in his bed without being picked up. If he still won't settle and you feel that he really has a need for "3:00 a.m. mothering," pick him up and mother him quietly, without excessive sensory stimulation (lights off), and then promptly return him to his bed.

What if you have tried all the above but you and your baby have still not negotiated a full night's sleep? Then he is probably telling you that he does not like to sleep alone and does not like his crib. You may try a simple mattress surrounded with pillows on the floor next to your bed, or move his crib adjacent to your bed with the bar closest to you down so that he sleeps in his own crib but has closer contact with you. Medical research is being conducted on the brain wave patterns of mothers and babies during sleep. Perhaps someday medical research will confirm that the brain waves of mothers have a beneficial effect on their babies if they sleep close to each other.

You may want your child to sleep in your bed. If the quantity and quality of sleep for the whole family improves following this "now we are three" solution, then you have found the right answer. Only you can make this decision.

What about sedatives to help your baby sleep? Both physicians and parents generally do not like giving sleep medications to babies and I share this reluctance. However, a mild sedative might be advisable for one or two nights only, just enough to break the "tired baby-tired Mom cycle" and allow you a much deserved, and needed, prolonged sleep period. If your sleep deprivation is compromising your daytime immersion mothering, then consult your baby's doctor about the temporary use of a mild sedative for your baby.

Common Skin Rashes of Early Infancy

Normal Baby "Marks"

Nearly all newborns have smooth, reddish-pink, dot-like marks which are most prominent on the nape of the neck, on the forehead between the eyes, and on the upper eyelids. These are more correctly called **nevi** and are not, strictly speaking, rashes. They are areas of skin where the blood vessels are prominent and simply show through your baby's skin. They are normal. As your baby grows and accumulates thicker skin, these areas become less prominent and usually disappear by one year of age. Grandmothers have humorously referred to these marks as "stork bites" and some mothers of babies with prominent forehead nevi have used these as signals of stress or strain—"His red lights go on when he is angry or having a bowel movement." Chalk up another one for mother's observational powers.

Most babies have tiny, whitish, pinhead-sized bumps called **milia** which are most prominent on the skin of the nose. They are caused by plugging of the skin pores. With gentle washing, these disappear within a few weeks.

Non-Caucasian babies often have bluish areas on the skin of the lower back. These normal spots are often confused with bruises. They also disappear with time.

In the newborn period, your baby may have a pimply, oily facial rash which resembles acne. This is due to distended oil glands and retained secretions. Like teenage acne, it is caused by increased hormonal levels (from prenatal life). This rash disappears with normal facial hygiene and gentle washing with a mild soap. A similar acne-like and crusty rash may be present behind the ears and on the scalp. This is called **seborrhea** and in addition to normal skin hygiene, you may need to use a prescription cream.

Birthmarks

A common type of birthmark is a red, raised area of the skin often referred to as a strawberry. This strawberry-like area is called a **hemangioma.** These may grow larger before they become smaller and may become a source of cosmetic concern. Don't worry, these nearly always disappear within several years. When you see the strawberry turning grey, it is beginning to disappear.

Cradle Cap

Cradle cap is a flaky appearance of the skin of the scalp often resembling dandruff and, if mild, seldom needs any more treatment than gentle washing. Occasionally this cradle cap may become crusty, oily, and plaque-like, and may persist for months if not properly attended to. If your baby's cradle cap progresses to this crusty stage, massage vegetable oil into the crusty area, especially on his soft spot, and then gently remove the softened scales with a fine-toothed comb. Wash off the excess oil. If the cradle cap continues to reappear, especially in thick crusts, a prescription cream and a tar shampoo may be prescribed by your physician. Acne-like and seborrhea-type rashes seem to be worse during the wintertime and are aggravated by the low relative humidity and dry air caused by central heating. If you find your baby's skin consistently dry and flaky, a cool mist humidifier in the bedroom should help.

Prickly Heat

Prickly heat is a tiny, clear, pimple-like rash with a red base. It appears in areas of the skin where there is excessive heat and moisture retention such as behind the ears, in neck folds, and in areas of the trunk covered by excessively tight-fitting clothing. It should be treated by gentle washing in cool water, and by dressing your baby in lighter weight, loose-fitting clothing. A simple solution is bathing with baking soda. Add one teaspoon of baking soda to a cup of water to make a solution that is both soothing and cooling. (See page 81 for a discussion of general skin care and the use of powders and oils.)

Diaper Rash

Diaper rash is a fact of civilized, bottom-covering baby life. Diapers were invented to protect the environment from baby's excrement, and his skin rebels at losing its freedom of exposure. Since diaper rashes are caused by chemical irritations, moisture retention and mechanical rubbing, prevention should be aimed at these three areas.

Urine is not by nature a chemical irritant, but if it is allowed to sit in the diaper against the skin, bacteria react with the urine to form ammonia. This is a chemical irritant to the skin and accounts for the pungent odor of wet diapers. The following are suggestions for preventing and treating diaper rash:

1. Quick changing of a wet diaper is the first step. If diaper rash is a persistent problem, several changes during the night will help.

2. Wash your baby's diaper area with plain water or mild soap, rinse well, and blot dry. Too much soap or excessive rubbing irritates already sensitive skin. Your nose should detect the clean smell of an ammonia-free bottom.

3. Avoid tight-fitting diapers and rubber pants which retain moisture and prevent the skin from breathing. Rubber pants are social pants to be reserved for occasions where "being a baby" may not be socially acceptable. Use rubber pads instead of rubber pants to protect bedding.

4. If disposable diapers are used, be sure to fold the edge of the diaper down so that the polyethylene lining does not touch and irritate the skin.

5. Expose your baby's diaper area to air and sunshine as much as possible.

6. Protective creams and pastes are usually not necessary or advisable on non-irritated skin. Diaper rash should be treated early, before the skin barrier is broken down and becomes infected. Once the first stage of skin irritation appears (reddening), apply a barrier cream such as zinc oxide and follow the above steps carefully. Babies are more prone to diaper rashes if they have an intestinal infection, diarrhea or are teething. Barrier creams should be used under these circumstances.

7. Avoid cornstarch on the diaper area. This encourages the growth of fungi. If the diaper rash persists and the reddened area becomes raised, rough, or pustular, then a fungal or bacterial infection may be present and, in addition to carrying out the above measures, a prescription medication may be required.

Sniffles—Baby's Early "Colds"

Babies are nose breathers and depend upon clear nasal passages for noiseless, comfortable breathing. In the first few months, babies' nasal passages are easily clogged with lint from blankets and clothing, dust, irritating milk residue and his own secretions. Proper care of these sniffles begins with a good "nose blow." Since your baby is too young to effectively blow his own nose you must help him. Prepare some "nose drops" with a pinch of salt in a glass of water (no more than 1/4 teaspoon to 8 ounces of water) and with a plastic dropper squirt a few drops into each of his nostrils. These drops often loosen the secretions and stimulate him to sneeze or cough, his own protective mechanisms for clearing his breathing passages. Next, take a rubber bulb syringe, a nasal aspirator (available at any drug store) and gently suck out the loosened secretions. He will probably protest loudly. A humidifier or cool mist vaporizer during the winter months may counteract drying of the nasal passage caused by central heating.

Around his second or third month, your baby may cough and gurgle and you may feel a "rattle" in his chest. His nose is clear and the secretions are too far back to get at with the aspirator. This "two-month cold" is not strictly speaking a cold since no infection is usually present. It usually results instead from retained saliva secretions which your baby has not yet learned to handle and swallow. The rattle you hear and feel in his chest is from the noise and vibration produced by the air passing through these obstructive secretions in the back of his throat and is not really "in his chest." No medication is necessary. He will not choke on these secretions and with time he will learn to effectively handle the nuisance of all these secretions in the back of his mouth. Saliva noises usually lessen when the baby falls asleep because babies produce less saliva when they sleep. Environmental irritants, especially cigarette smoke, can irritate your baby's breathing passages. In fact, children whose parents smoke have more colds. (Infectious colds are discussed on page 342 .)

Thrush

Thrush is a common fungus infection of the mouth which consists of cottage-cheese-like white patches on the inner cheeks, the tongue and the roof of the mouth. It seldom causes your baby much of a problem and is easily treated by prescription drops. Occasionally, this yeast infection may be transferred to the mother's nipples, causing a yeast infection of the breasts. It may also be transferred to your baby's diaper area, causing a fungus-type diaper rash.

Discharging Eyes

Most infants begin tearing by three weeks of age. Normally, the tears should drain from the nasal corner of his eyes into the nose via passages called tear ducts. The nasal end of these ducts is covered with a thin membrane which usually breaks open shortly after birth, allowing tears to drain into the nose. In many babies, one or both of these membranes fail to open, resulting in excessive accumulation of tears in the blocked eye. A yellow discharge from the eye indicates an infection within the region of the tear duct. Treatment consists of gently massaging the tear duct in the nasal corner of the eye for a few seconds, six times a day, plus appropriate antibiotic eye drops. Massaging the tear ducts exerts pressure on the fluid within the ducts, which may break open the membrane and allow proper drainage. If you notice excessive tearing, mention this to your doctor during your baby's check-up and he will instruct you in tear duct massage and medication. Blocked tear ducts, properly treated, usually open up by six months of age.

Pacifiers

Does my baby need a pacifier? Some babies have a tremendous need to suck and seem to enjoy more sucking than feeding alone provides. If your baby does seem to settle and appear more comfortable when offered a pacifier, then certainly respect his wishes. Pacifiers are a stop-gap measure which should be used only when mother absolutely cannot give herself and baby needs to suck. If you are breastfeeding, pacifiers should be avoided during the first few weeks because they may cause nipple confusion. (See **Nipple Confusion**, pages 99, 106, 117.)

Where's My Mommy?

The Effects of Mother-Infant Separation

One of the inevitable dilemmas of mothering is separation from your baby, either by choice or necessity. The wide variation in individual family situations makes this a very difficult subject to write about. How long and how often to leave your baby depends upon your priorities of parenting and your family situation. A few general considerations may assist you in making your decision. As long as you consider both yourself and your baby's needs and you feel comfortable with your decision, then you have probably made the right choice. Most importantly, do not feel guilty—it is a very unhealthy emotion that can be harmful to your parenting abilities. If you are feeling guilty you need to explore your situation to find the cause of the guilt.

We have already discussed the importance of mother-infant attachment in the newborn period, a process called **bonding** (page 47) through which your baby is uniquely sensitive to your touch, smell, voice, eyes, and breast, and rewards you with a reaction of his own which further reinforces your mothering instinct. Both infant and mother seem to have biological radar systems which are attuned to each other. There is a growing body of scientific research which shows that both mother and infant benefit from being close to each other. Yes, we are finally proving what the common sense of species survival has known all along.

Can you carry this attachment too far? Isn't separation a normal maturing process for the baby? Is my immersion mothering fostering an unhealthy dependence? Caring mothers have asked these questions many times. The question is not so much one of dependency but one of trust. Your baby cannot trust you too much. In fact, babies who are the product of immersion mothering seem very dependent upon their mothers for the first two or three years. These infants usually become secure in their own self-esteem and their environment and actually become less dependent children later on. Possessiveness should not be confused with immersion mothering. Possessiveness is restrictive, non-constructive, and prevents a child from doing what he needs to do because of some need you have. In the first year of life, tiny babies do not have the resources to parent themselves through their own anxiety periods and I feel that absolutely no good can come from "not making them so dependent."

Babies have specific needs. Besides their obvious need for food and physical comforts which can be provided by a sincere, substitute care-giver, babies need eye-to-eye contact, skin-to-skin contact and mind-to-mind contact, all of which a mother provides best. If you are breastfeeding, separation from your baby also deprives him of your milk. Even if your breastmilk is left with the babysitter, the feeding relationship is just not the same when a bottle is given by a sitter.

Why is substitute care-giving second best? The substitute mother may not be able to pick up on the baby's cues and sense what he needs. She does not enjoy the same feedback appreciation from your baby, which would further increase her mothering of him. (See page 96 for discussion of the hormonal stimulation of the mother instinct.)

In addition to these needs, babies also have their stress periods which cannot be scheduled for weekends or after working hours. Only you can effectively parent your baby through these stress periods because only you can be perfectly attuned to his needs. It is difficult to schedule mothering. You may be lucky enough to time your absences during his nap time or sleeping time, or he may not experience apparent stress periods while you are away. Most babies, however, do have some unexpected need periods and stress periods each day. Being away from him during these times deprives him of his most valuable support resource and also deprives you of a chance to further cement your friendship. Babies learn resignation easily. They learn to accept unfulfilled needs, but at the price of lowered self-esteem and trust in their environment.

Children are spontaneous, and parenting means being available when a children's spontaneous activities occur. Infant and child development is a series of actions and responses. The infant performs an action (e.g. makes a sound) and a tuned-in mother responds to the infant's accomplishment by showing delight. An infant quickly learns to expect certain responses to his actions. If he does not receive his anticipated reward he becomes confused and stops producing. The feedback an infant receives for a developmental accomplishment is one of the most meaningful ways of stimulating infant development. (See section on speech development, page 219 for an example of mother's unique role.)

The vicious cycle of non-attachment is a very subtle problem that creeps into the lives of certain mothers and babies. A woman who is primarily career-oriented or who lacks confidence in her mothering abilities may have difficulty really getting into mothering. Although she sincerely loves her child, her conflicting feelings about immersion mothering result in increasing the use of substitute care-givers. As a result of the loss of constant feedback from his mother, the infant does not reward the mother with his own feedback which should further stimulate her mothering. This is especially true if there is a mismatch of temperaments between mother and baby. As a result, the baby and mother subtly drift further apart, the mother to her own career and the baby to substitute care-giving. Periodic attempts to get back into mothering are unsuccessful because the continuum of action/response has been interrupted.

As the child grows older there may often be no readily identifiable effects of this non-attachment. However, the older child sees less clearly defined mother-father roles since both have careers. Studies have shown that daughters of career-outside-the-home mothers tend to place more emphasis on non-mothering careers and the cycle continues into the next generation.

An alternative to part-time mothering is immersion mothering, of being consistently available and attuned to the needs of your baby. Your baby, in turn, rewards your efforts with his feedback, which further stimulates your mothering and a full-time mother-infant relationship develops. During the first years of life, the primary need of an infant is to trust his environment, a trust which depends upon a secure attachment to his mother as the primary care-giver. This process is called **imprinting**. An infant who trusts his primary care-giver is relieved of many of the anxieties of parenting himself through the early developmental stages. He can therefore devote more of his energies to the developmental skills. Consider the analogy that many adults are not as productive in their professional life if they are unhappy in their personal life. Likewise, a baby's "professional life" (his developmental skills) may not reach its full potential if he is insecure in his maternal attachment. The concept of immersion mothering, being available and attuned to the needs of your baby, is in my opinion the absolute best for your baby. Whether this concept of mothering is best for your family situation can be answered only by you.

A common question mothers of young babies often ask is, "What is the effect on my baby if my husband and I go away for a much needed relief weekend?" Babies will often show grief reaction signs at temporary separations—refusal to eat, crying, sleep disturbances and mood changes. Parents often relate that when they return from such a holiday their babies will often give them the cold shoulder. Pediatricians are often put on the spot when asked such questions. We are caught between what seems to be best for parents and best for baby. Since the baby is too young to be consulted, I will represent my little client and offer the following opinion: If your baby does not adjust easily to substitute care-givers, avoid extended absences (more than a few hours) from your baby until he reaches the age at which he can understand the temporary nature of separation (usually around three years). In reality, it is impossible to put a time limit on how long you may leave your baby. This depends on a variety of individual factors such as how separation-sensitive he is, how comfortable he is with your substitute care-giver, how important the reason is for leaving your baby.

An alternative solution to this "relief from baby" feeling (with which I am in complete sympathy) is to take your baby with you on your holiday. On the surface, this may sound like you are defeating the purpose of getting away, but in fact it is primarily the change that offers relief, not just getting away from your baby. (See **Father Feelings**, page 85, and **Family Recreation**, page 311.)

Working Mothers

All mothers are working mothers. In this section, I mean mothers working outside the home. Nearly all baby books state flatly that full-time mothering is the ideal and I feel the same. However, financial constraints and the attractions of the market place have put a strain on modern mothers, and this stand of "stay at home and take care of your child" is just not that simple. This discussion will center around two main changes which I feel must occur in order to keep the dilemma of the working mother in perspective. Society must place a higher value on the unique contribution and dignity of the profession of the full-time mother and the working society must become more flexible in order to accommodate the mother who wishes a dual career.

The working mother is nothing new. In past generations mothers worked, but they worked around the home. Their working and mothering were integrated. Women were culturally prepared for motherhood and men were prepared for the work force. Industrialization, urbanization and the current educational system have changed these traditional roles and women now have many options. The educational system prepared girls and boys to ''be something'' and for girls that something is not motherhood. Career counsellors and women's magazines have marketed the idea that it is difficult to derive satisfaction from mothering alone. Baby books (including my own) and child care experts extol the virtues of motherhood as the supreme career. The government is taking away more and more money from the middle income families so that economic constraints now weigh heavily upon many mothers. Today's woman is caught in a dilemma between what her instincts tell her (be a mother) and the many attractions outside the home. If she chooses both she is made to feel guilty and is accused of not doing either well. If she chooses a career outside the home she is made to feel guilty for not being an effective mother, and if she chooses full-time mothering she is constantly reminded that she is ''just a housewife and mother.'' The answer to this dilemma is that society must be flexible enough to accommodate whichever role a woman chooses for herself.

The first step is to increase recognition of the value of full-time mothering as a career. High schools and colleges could add seminars on ''mothering'' to their career-planning courses. Child-study courses could be added to the curriculum and the science of imprinting could be stressed to the scientifically oriented. The concept that mothering is a mindless profession consisting of changing dirty diapers and wiping runny noses could be overcome by emphasizing the mind-to-mind relationship that is unique to the mother-infant attachment.

Too often a person's worth is measured in tangible assets. The full-time mother does not get a paycheck or a profit-sharing plan. However, the imprinting of her mothering efforts on her child and the child's resulting imprint on society are immeasurable contributions.

Another innovation which would benefit the contemporary working mother would be for the working world to offer a mother who chooses to work outside the home, a flexible work schedule—a flexibility which will allow her to keep mothering as a primary career. Women now have a major impact on the total labor force. In 1979, approximately 40 million women in the United States worked outside the home. The greatest increase in the number of working women has been in the group consisting of mothers of young children. I find this trend somewhat of a paradox. At the same time as there is an increasing recognition of the importance of mother-infant attachment, young mothers are entering the work force in increasing numbers. Child-bearing women should not be forced into making a choice, rather they should be given the opportunity to do both. The woman who wants to work but is forced by culture to mother, or the woman who wants to mother but is forced by economics to work, will be an unhappy person. Her child will not be as happy or reared as well because the mother has not been allowed to follow her own desires.

Here are some alternative working arrangements for you to consider:

1. Part-time work. The greatest change in the work market in the past decade is in the trend toward part-time work, or mini-shifts. Industrial studies have shown an overall benefit from this trend, mainly in increased efficiency and productivity and a greater worker supply. Part-time work is good for those mothers who simply want to ''get out of the house.'' If economics is the main factor, part-time work rarely results in a good pay cheque. You spend your earnings on carfare and lunches without receiving any of the benefits of the full-time employee.

2. Flextime (part-time work with flexible hours). This recent innovation is a boon to the working mother. Pilot studies in Europe and the United States have been very successful. With this method, you work a set number of hours but you choose which hours you work. This flexibility allows the working mother to adjust her time to her child, to be at home when he is sick or has a special need. These jobs are still hard to find. Be innovative and contact companies you would be interested in working for, suggesting flextime to them.

3. Flextime jobs in your own home. Do a careful search of the needs in your community. You may be surprised at the variety of work you can do in your own home, at your own pace. To illustrate the ingenuity of the contemporary mother, I know a computer technician who does her work on a portable home computer which is tied into the main office. This mother can ''go to the office'' without leaving her nest. Working at home requires discipline since you won't have the incentive of an office routine. Establish business hours so your friends won't be tempted to call you just to chat. Convert a spare room into an office. You might even want to open up a small business, perhaps with a friend. Another popular part-time job is babysitting in your own home. (See **Babysitting Arrangements**, page 190 .)

4. Shared Jobs. This type of work arrangement requires cooperation between two women, each sharing the work of one full-time job. It requires a mutual agreement between two caring mothers who will each be flexible enough to ''cover'' for the other when their children have special needs (I will work if your child is sick and vice versa).

5. Consider going back to school to develop additional job skills. Make sure you have a quiet place and enough time to study. If you have been out of school for a while, take one or two courses to start with. Going back to school will lay a solid foundation for the future. It is also compatible with parenting since you can choose your hours.

Other considerations for the working mother:

1. Father Involvement—Shared Child Care. The working mother bears the conflict of a dual career. She is expected by society and her family to be a full-time mother, and that's double-time without extra pay. This family situation demands some role-sharing by the father. If you are lucky enough to enjoy flexible schedules, the father is the obvious substitute care-giver.

Also, there is nothing in the biological composition of women that says only women can do housework. Husbands of working mothers must take a greater share in running the household. Perhaps the only fringe benefit to children of these alternative working arrangements is increased father involvement in child-rearing. In fact, studies show that fathers who work the experimental four-day week spend a major portion of their increased leisure time with their children. It is often difficult for husbands to fully appreciate the deeply ambivalent feelings which plague today's mother, especially if she has or previously had a career outside the home. A woman completes a college degree, enters the world of work, achieves recognition for her accomplishments and achieves a real sense of personal worth. For some women, to leave this completely and become a full-time mother may be difficult. It is vitally important for husbands to recognize that this drastic career change may not be easy. A caring and involved husband can help the full-time mother derive as deep, if not a deeper, feeling of personal worth from mothering as she derived from her previous career. (See **Father Feelings**, page 86 and page 87 for involvement suggestions.)

2. Breastfeeding and the working mother. Many mothers automatically consider breastfeeding and working incompatible. Breastfeeding, however, may be even more important for the working mother, for the following reasons: Breastfeeding alleviates some of the guilt stemming from leaving your baby since he gets your own milk (albeit from a bottle) when you are not there. Breastfeeding provides a unique mother-infant attachment that a babysitter cannot give your child and adds an element of consistency to care-giving. Flexible work schedules can be arranged to accommodate breastfeeding. If your employer objects to this intrusion into your work, obtain a doctor's note that you should breastfeed your baby. It is noteworthy that, in recent test cases in the United States, the courts have upheld the mothers' right to breastfeed babies while on the job. Employers, courts and unions do not like the image that they are against mothering. (For tips on successful breastfeeding while you are working, see page 119.)

3. Bargain with employers. Successful working arrangements for contemporary mothering require a combination of your ingenuity in marketing your skills and the flexibility of employers in accommodating the working mother. Industrial studies show that part-time and flextime working mothers are very efficient and employers get more for their money. Employers are becoming increasingly aware of the unique contribution of the working mother. In a world where worker productivity is becoming an industrial concern, you are in a good position to bargain with your employer by pointing out how valuable you can be.

4. "Must" you work? Apart from professional reasons, many mothers work to ease the financial constraints of a world in which prices are increasing faster than take-home wages. Before deciding definitely that you must work to earn extra money, consider the following: Although your paycheck may seem a sizeable addition to the family income, how much do you really have left by the time you subtract the cost of a change in tax status, transportation, clothing for work, meals at work, convenience foods, babysitting expenses, maintenance help at home and more medical bills (babies in daycare centers do have more colds). You may be surprised how much you are worth in dollars and cents just to stay at home. Next, could you borrow the money for a couple of years and arrange to repay when you return to work? Grandparents may be a willing source of funds. This would be their best investment in their grandchildren's future. Another possibility is to temporarily change your standard of living. Do you really need a second car, a yearly vacation, improvements to the house? This decision requires a mature sacrifice by couples who understand the priorities of parenting.

5. To some women who have previously pursued an active career outside the home, staying at home is what they have difficulty adjusting to, not only the change of career. Home to a tiny baby means where the mother is. If staying inside the house bothers you, go out and take your baby with you. You may be surprised how portable your infant is.

Who's Mothering Your Baby?

If you decide to work outside your home, you must answer the important question of who will mother your baby while you are gone. The demand for quality substitute mothering is far greater than the supply and you may be greatly disappointed when you begin to seek quality care for your baby. You will soon realize that the modern day English nanny, Mary Poppins or the governess from the "Sound of Music" will not be easy to find. If you have a full-time job, your baby may be cared for by a substitute mother for more than 50 per cent of his waking hours. Let's now discuss some of the possible effects of the non-nurturing environment of some daycare centers upon your child.

In her book, **Every Child's Birthright: In Defense of Mothering**, Selma Fraiberg gives a splendid account of the daycare center dilemma, a viewpoint I strongly share. She calls the effects of a succession of anonymous babysitters **"diseases of non-attachment,"** or the incapacity of a child to form human love bonds. The period of infancy is the critical period for the establishment of these bonds. A child who is passed through a succession of anonymous babysitters may have difficulty forming these love bonds in infancy and may therefore have varying degrees of difficulty forming them in later childhood. Also, a child who does not have a strong love-attachment with his parents may have equal difficulty forming a secure love-attachment to a babysitter, even if she is a consistent and caring one. The child who does not learn to love may have great difficulty in controlling his impulses, and this absence of human attachment is often reflected in aggressive and impulsive behavior.

Another daycare disease is the absence of feedback stim
ulation so vital to infant development. When a baby exercises
newly acquired developmental skill the mother acknowledge
that skill and the baby in turn continues to exercise the skill i
anticipation of the mother's response. If no one responds to thi
skill (because there are ten other babies who also want someon
to respond to them) he soon loses his motivation for exercisin
his skills.

Babysitters

With these considerations in mind, let's explore some of th
alternatives for caring for your child.

Because of the importance of forming human love
attachments in the first two years, try to keep the same babysitte
for a long period of time rather than hiring a succession of differ
ent sitters, all of whom remain anonymous to your child. If you
child is a toddler it is often preferable for him to be cared for i
his own home, which he knows and in which he is secure
Because this one-to-one sitter relationship in your own hom
may not be economically feasible, other child care alternative
may be necessary. An increasingly popular source of extr
income is to look after several children in one's own home. Yo
may be fortunate enough to find a caring friend who is doin
this. If the other children are of a similar age this may turn out t
be a learning experience for your child, a sort of extended pla
group.

You may try the shared babysitter arrangement in which
group of three to four working mothers with similar values abou
child rearing jointly hire a sitter to come to one of their homes
This arrangement has economic advantages over the one-to-on
relationship and also allows you to have more control of wha
you get from your sitter.

Parent cooperative babysitting is another alternative. I
this arrangement four or five mothers arrange to care for eacl
other's children one day a week. I feel that small groups of chil
dren of similar ages (three or four children at the infant and tod
dler age is a manageable number) in the home environment witl
a caring and consistent babysitter is a preferable arrangement to
commercial daycare center.

● **Tips on using part-time babysitters in your home**

Present a familiar face to your baby. During the first few year
your baby will experience periods in which he is unusually sensi
tive to strangers. This is not the time to introduce a strang
babysitter so try to stick with the reliable faces to which he ha

become accustomed. One of the most frightening experiences for a young infant is to awaken to the sight of an unfamiliar face.

I believe that grandmothers often make the best babysitters. What they lack in mobility for chasing or playing with a busy toddler, they often make up in their genuine love for your child.

Convey to your babysitters that you consider the job of babysitting a serious business. Also convey to them the particular needs that your baby is likely to exhibit while you are gone, and give instructions on how they are to handle certain behaviors. I don't like the term babysitter. It is static and unfeeling. Babysitters are substitute mothers. Point out to your babysitter how you wish your child to be mothered during your absence. A baby's separation anxiety can be lessened if the substitute caregiver responds to the baby's cues in a familiar way. Your mother substitute should have the phone number where you can be reached, the number of a closely available friend and also that of your pediatrician.

Daycare Centers

I have mixed feelings about the value of government supported daycare centers. The tax dollar would be better spent subsidizing the mother to allow her to take care of her own child rather than subsidizing a strange facility to care for a child so that the mother can work for another facility. It is time the government realized the economic and cultural value of the professional mother.

Parents often worry about what infectious diseases their child may catch by attending daycare centers. It is true that infants in daycare centers contract more colds and diarrhea, probably because the working mother is obliged to leave her slightly ill child at the daycare center. However, I do not worry much about what the child may get at the daycare center. I worry more about what the child doesn't get.

Another incurable disease of modern daycare is that it is now big business. Big business has a way of manipulating legislation to perpetuate its own interests. In answer to the cry ''We need more daycare centers'' the government spends more money, taxes are increased to cover subsidies to these daycare centers, more women of middle and lower income families are forced to work to meet the increasing cost of living resulting from higher taxation, and consequently more daycare centers are needed.

Another unfortunate reality of daycare is that you get what you pay for. There are professional daycare centers staffed by adequately paid personnel, educated in childhood cognitive development. These high quality centers provide an enriched environment for children whose mothers wish to pursue a career outside the home. However, these are expensive and beyond the means of most working mothers.

Like many businesses, daycare centers try to keep overhead down. However, the child who is the primary consumer has no say in the quality of the product he receives. In most daycare centers it is impossible to give effective daycare at an affordable cost. It is interesting that in European countries where a government subsidy is given to mothers for daycare, most mothers choose not to spend this subsidy on commercial daycare centers but rather to seek alternative home care for their child. Yes, the daycare disease also has its medicare. Government regulations cover facilities and staff to child ratios. But how do you legislate child-caring?

How do children reared in daycare centers compare to home-reared children?'' The only way the daycare scientist could study this question is to rear a child by immersion mothering for a few years and then "rewind the tape" and mother the same child all over again using part-time mothering and the daycare center. Obviously this is impossible.

To be fair, there are some excellent daycare centers affiliated with hospitals or universities, or tied in with the Montessori school system. These centers are staffed by interested, caring persons who have a basic knowledge of the needs and cognitive development of children. The goal of these daycare centers is to supplement home care, not replace it. Strengthening the family unit is the major priority of their program. The fee for these daycare centers is based on a sliding-scale according to a family's individual income. Unfortunately, the supply of these "super centers" is far less than the demand and at present there seems to be no easy cure for the daycare disease.

Tips on Selecting a Daycare Center

If the daycare center is the only economically realistic child care alternative for your family situation, the following tips will help you select a quality daycare center:

1. Visit the prospective daycare center and draw your own conclusions about whether the needs of your child will be adequately met in the particular environment.

2. What is the ratio of care-givers to children? One care-giver can usually care for the needs of no more than six children (or four infants).

3. What are the credentials of the staff? Is the staff genuinely sensitive to individual needs? What do the care-givers do when a tiny baby cries? What are their methods of "disciplining a toddler?" Does the staff have special training in cognitive development and stimulation of a child at various stages? And most of all, are the staff nurturing-type people, genuinely interested in children? Does the staff welcome suggestions from parents regarding the special needs of their children?

4. Is the philosophy of the center to strengthen the family unit, supplement home care rather than replace it, and to respect the child as an individual?

5. Are the facilities clean? Is the equipment safe and appropriate for various age groups? Unfortunately, the same economic constraints that compel mothers to work also prevent some daycare centers from hiring the quantity and quality of staff and equipment necessary to provide a quality facility.

6. A child over two years of age will get more for your money if you enroll him in a full day preschool such as a Montessori preschool. In this type of program, he receives both educational and custodial care. (See **Preschools**, page 281.)

What qualities do you look for in an infant care-giver? Besides carefully examining the overall qualities of the daycare center, examine the qualities of the care-giver who will be caring for your child. Watch her in action. Is she sensitive to the child as a person? Does she enjoy eye-to-eye contact with the child? Does she touch the child often? Does she talk to the child often and in a way that shows she really cares what the infant feels? Language (visual, tactile, and vocal) is a powerful communication tool that conveys caring. Does she have a working knowledge of the usual developmental milestones and infant stimulation at various ages? Is she flexible? Is she able to adapt to the ever-changing moods of some toddlers? Does she have a genuine sense of humor, which is a must in order for any care-giver to be able to cope with toddlers? Watch how the children relate to the care-giver. If a child has that certain sparkle in his eye as he relates to his care-giver then you can be sure that the child is comfortable with her. Infants and children are the best critics of their own care.

CHAPTER VII

PARENTING YOUR CHILD THROUGH DEVELOPMENTAL STAGES

The First Two Years of Life

The Meaning of Development, Intelligence, Personality and Temperament

The purpose of this section on child development is not to see how your child compares with the "usual" child at a given age or to answer the question "Is my child developing normally?" This comparison to "norms" approach is best left in the hands of your doctor. You should enjoy your child's development. What is his individual pattern of development? What are his personality traits? Devise your own methods of stimulation according to your perceptions in parenting. Be aware of your infant's cues and how to pick up on them to stimulate and enjoy his individual patterns of development.

Before embarking on our voyage through child development from birth through adolescence, you should understand a few basic concepts. Your child's behavior is, simply, what he does, and for ease of discussion a child's behavior is grouped into five areas: gross motor behavior, or postural relations and movement; fine motor behavior, or the way he uses his hands and eyes; adaptive behavior, his organization of input to solve certain problems or attain certain goals; language behavior, both receptive (understanding) and expressive (any audible or visible method of communication, which not only includes speech but the entire domain of body language); and personal-social behavior, or his adaptation to the social culture in which he lives.

In most infants, development in these five areas of child behavior follows an orderly pattern according to your child' chronological age. Child development charts indicate that at given age most children will have a certain skill. For example most children are able to sit between six and seven months o age. Remember that these figures are averages and there is wide range of normal variations among children. Progression i more important than timing; thus it is not so important that you infant sit at six months and walk at twelve months. What is mor important is that each month his behavorial skills progress i comparison with the previous month. He will be slower than th chart in some areas and ahead of the chart in others. Progress i all five areas of his behavior must be considered before making judgment about his development. In this section, only the majo and more interesting features of development will be discussed Many developmental features, especially in the first year, ar interesting curiosities but they may have little relevance to you child's development or eventual intelligence. Since your child outward behavior is often a manifestation of his inner feeling our approach to development will consider his feelings as well a his actions.

"Intelligence" and "personality" are the amalgamatio of all five areas of behavior. These are influenced by the input his senses, environmental influences and his handling of life experiences. How much influence can you have on your child eventual personality and intelligence?

Over the decades, psychologists such as Piaget, Gess and Burton White have been theorizing upon the "nature versu nurture" concept — does super parenting produce a super kid To what degree your child's temperament and intelligence determined by heredity, and to what degree by environment ar parenting, will probably never be completely known. Despite th great volume of psychological studies on the determinants of pe sonality and intelligence, we are back to the drawing board common sense and parental intuition.

Psychologists seem to agree upon one basic concep Your child has a **maximum intelligence potential** which genetically, not environmentally determined. How close comes to reaching this maximum potential depends upon th richness of his environment and his parents' input.

In addition to the concept of maximum intelligen potential, your child has genetically determined personality trai or temperaments (activity level, adaptability, intensity, attentio span, positive or negative moods, etc). These congenital temperaments are described in detail in **Temperament and Behavior Disorders in Children** by Drs. Chess and Thomas. In simple terms, we often describe a child's temperament with words like high strung, sensitive, an easy child, a challenging baby. Although your child's basic temperaments are genetically determined, they can be modified positively or negatively by parental influence into what we may term a child's **personality**. For simplicity, we will use the term personality to mean the final form which the basic temperaments take, having been modified over the years by experiences and parental nurturing.

If I were to ask parents about the one thing they wish for their child, most would reply "I want him to be happy." This is right on the mark! Let's coin a term called **the happiness factor** and suppose each child has a certain maximum level of this at each stage of his development. Happiness, as used here, implies that your child reaches his maximum intelligence potential, undergoes some positive modification of his basic temperaments and lives in an environment which allows his innate talents to flourish. It also implies success (all parents seem to want their children to succeed) but this success is on his terms, not yours. It implies as well that the child's self-esteem is healthy. Remember, the happiness factor is the end result and the bottom line of child-rearing. It is this happiness factor that I strongly feel you, as parents, can influence for better or for worse in your child. **A child's self-esteem is not genetic.** Nurturing has a profound effect on a child's concept of himself.

Birth to Six Weeks—Visual Language

A one-week-old newborn's motor, sensory and reflex capabilities are described in detail in the section **The Amazing Newborn**, page 65. The rest of the first month seems to be spent simply getting adjusted to his new environment. This period is characterized primarily by irregularity in sleep and breathing patterns and feeding times. Muscle movements seem uncertain and purposeless. The newborn, however, does more than just eat and sleep. He is drinking in all the sights, sounds, smells and touches of this person he is getting to know as Mother. The newborn's periods of quiet alertness depict concentration that is surely worth noting and respecting. Realizing the depth there is in this little person adds immensely to your appreciation of your amazing newborn.

No great strides in motor development are made during this first month. It seems as if he is simply trying to sort out and

197

organize all of his equipment before attempting to use it. His head control is just strong enough to clear his nose from the bed if he has to. Most waking needs are met by feeding and touching. His eyes, mouth and skin are his primary sources of information and feedback. Since most of his six or eight waking hours will be spent feeding, a good feeding relationship is the primary parental goal at this age. Mothers who enjoy their feeding times really enjoy their newborn baby. The first month is a period for security and organization rather than one for stimulation and achievement.

Between four and six weeks the first really interesting change occurs, the development of sustained eye-to-eye contact. Before this time, a newborn can briefly attend to stripes, pat-

Birth to six weeks

terns, reds and yellows, and the human face. A newborn's developing vision is like the focus of a camera. His vision is monocular. At the monocular stage, his eyes work independently and he sees two images. Gradually these images merge into one and he focuses clearly, especially within a distance of twelve inches. Around the age of four to six weeks, your baby may stare intently at your face or a bright object. He may even make an attempt to trace its movement if it moves slowly. As you stare at him, he will have a definite binocular regard for your different facial expressions and reward you with his own. His smiles and alert visual expression convey to you that he likes what he sees. His eyes seem to love seeing another set of eyes. Give him yours. This stage is the beginning of one of the most meaningful modes of human communication—visual language.

Six Weeks to Three Months— Visually Directed Behavior

The period from six weeks to three months is one of the most interesting stages of infancy. We may briefly describe the transition as one from "sleeper" to "looker" to "doer." The primary change during this stage is **visually directed behavior**. As with all stages of development, signs of intent precede ability. During the first few weeks, your baby could see well, but his vision was clear only within twelve inches and binocular focusing was temporary at best. In this new stage, he achieves sustained binocular vision, or the ability to focus on interesting objects like a human face. His vision is best at a distance of within three feet. This is his social debut—his coming out. His real communication with the outside world begins. Sustained social smiling is his first show of genuine emotion, a magnificent change to behold—the sober six-week-old becomes the sociable three-month-old. The more he sees, the more he wants to see. This visual ability is the major key which opens the world for him to explore.

The first discovery by our visually directed explorer are his own body parts, and his first conquest are his hands. A wise choice, little one—hands will be your first tools for most of your life's accomplishments. In the previous stage, most of his actions were reflex in origin. In this stage, the transition from "looker" to "doer" is the first manifestation of your baby's intelligence. He seems more in control of his actions as they become obviously purposeful. He sees his hands clearly, attends to them for a comfortable period of time and seems to be thinking "These are mine. They are always there right in front of me. They are interesting. And sometimes they hit together. Did I do that?" He clasps his hands together in front of him (mutual fingering), mar-

Six weeks to three
months

vels at the sensation of how these two body parts complemen
each other and then like all explorers, after he has found on
treasure, he wants more. He uses his newly discovered eye-han

team to swipe at objects dangled before his eyes. He continues to swipe at them until one day he conquers the objects by grasping them, although he is able to hold them only momentarily at this stage. He has discovered the pleasures of his mouth so "Why not get my hands and my mouth together?" Finger sucking results, often shortly following a pleasant feeding experience, as if he is trying to reproduce this pleasant sucking sensation with his own equipment.

To take full advantage of his newly acquired visual skills, he learns to move his head from side to side a full 180°, visually tracking anything in sight. When lying on his tummy, not wishing to miss out on the visual delights above him, he lifts his head to a 90° vertical position, and by three months he can finally hold his head higher than his bottom. During the first few weeks, most babies seem to hold their head to the right most of the time. I suspect the reason is that babies are usually held in the mother's left arm (nearer her heartbeat) and the mother is usually positioned to the right of the baby, causing him to voluntarily turn to the right most of the time. By alternating "head" and "foot" in his crib and providing more interesting objects to his left side, you can balance this rightward head-turning tendency. By three months of age, this rightward head-turning tendency diminishes, as he develops his desire to track objects for a full 180°.

At this stage, the strength of his leg muscles greatly increases. By age three months, baby can momentarily sustain his weight while held in the standing position—a feat which delights him, no end. Standing does not cause bowed legs.

How do these recently acquired skills affect his behavior? Babies at this stage are bright, alert, responsive and gregarious. They sleep less and cry less, probably because there are more exciting things to do with their waking hours. They usually smile at everyone. I find babies at this stage very easy to examine. Just a very intense stare into their eyes seems to mesmerize them into complete trust and enjoyment of the examiner.

What can you do to stimulate your baby? Since his favorite source of stimulation is your face, make use of it often. Stare at him, smile at him, use different facial expressions of delight and amazement. The feedback you receive will be amazing as babies begin to mimic at this stage. Since visually directed behavior is the hallmark of this stage, his "toys" should be so directed. Crib devices are stimulating and fun. Mirrors and mobiles are the M&Ms of the crib world. Mobiles should now be constructed not only to be gazed at, but also swatted at. Safety mirrors (metal rather than glass) should be placed about eight inches from your baby, allowing him to flirt with his self-image. Cut-outs which emphasize colored patterns and stripes will draw his attention. Babies don't like lying in their cribs for prolonged periods. Therefore your crib devices should be moved to other areas of the house where your baby can sit and gaze at them.

Three to Six Months — Reach Out and Touch Someone

The three- to six-month-old perceives different shapes and textures. He grasps with both hands and attempts to find the most direct route from hand to mouth. His mouth, like his hand, is an organ of touch. His lips and tongue process objects, just as his fingers do, and add information about the quality of the object plucked from his infant world. The advertising slogan "reach out, reach out and touch someone" aptly depicts the three- to six-month-old infant. He will touch your face, grab and play with your hair, pull Daddy's beard and pull at your glasses and your clothes. Objects that are not within easy reaching distance are of little interest to him as if he is thinking "If I can't get them into my hands, why bother with them?" All shapes and sizes—rings, rattles, blocks and balls—delight his newly acquired perception of shapes and textures.

The three-month-old may be distracted very easily during feedings. He may suck a little and look a little. If the surrounding visual delights overwhelm his desire to nurse, you should nurse in a quiet, less stimulating room of your home for a couple of periods during the day.

A four-month-old is the typical, beautiful, picture-book baby—lying in push-up position, chubby, rounded, smooth, bright and alert, smiling and very photogenic. His activity shifts into high gear. He awakens early in the morning to a world of living color, eager to practice his newly acquired skills.

Many of the feeding and adjustment problems of the first three months have been managed. He seems to enjoy himself more and you enjoy him more. Laughter, giggling, babbling of vowel sounds, his response to tickles and teases all complement his emerging sociability.

Foot and torso movements also become part of his motor repertory. Kicking motions are constant and enjoyable. By placing the soles of his feet against his cribside or against your hand he can "push off," thus discovering his first method of self-propulsion. Turning over is amazing to him the first time he does it and he continues to delight in this new skill. You may notice that his elbows and knees crackle when you play with

Three to six months

him. This crackling is due to the lax bone support of his rubber-like ligaments; it is normal. Don't worry about these joint noises; your baby is designed to be handled.

During his first six months, your infant constantly rewards you with the excitement of change, one of the most exciting of all human attributes. His eye color, usually blue at birth, is most often permanently established by six months. His newborn baby hair is usually gone by this stage and is gradually replaced by his permanent hair, which also undergoes a change in color. Drooling signals the onset of teething. This "drippy

stage'' produces some unusual sounds and behavior in you
baby, often leading to some concerns about health. This mouth
ful of saliva results in a postnasal drip, especially while you
baby is lying on his back. It also produces a hacking cough as th
saliva ''goes down the wrong way,'' causing you to feel that h
has caught a ''cold.'' As he learns to cope with his abundan
saliva this cold will disappear. In addition to producing th
postnasal drip, the saliva drools out of his mouth and soaks hi
sheets, producing a **drool rash**, an irritation around his mout
and cheeks. His breathing sounds may temporarily take on
gurgling quality as the air and the saliva compete with each othe
in his throat. His very efficient cough and swallowing mecha
nism will cope with this. Sucking on fingers and anything else h
can get into his mouth is frequent at this stage. As many as fou
hours a day can be spent in this extra-nutritional sucking, a pleas
urable experience for him as well as one which soothes hi
swollen gums.

● **Play and Stimulation**

The three- to six-month stage begins your baby's real playtime
Mirrors (fully encased stainless steel instead of glass, of course
are still a favorite, and mirror talk is fun. Mobiles and cradle
gyms are still popular. They are most beneficial just after a nap
or upon waking in the morning, when you may not always b
ready for him and would like him to entertain himself. Mos
babies at this stage do not enjoy spending a great part of thei
waking hours in their crib. They want to be where the action is
Babies love to be surrounded by other children, and some babie
actually prefer other children's faces to adults'—excep
mother's, as hers will always be his favorite.

By six months of age your infant can be propped up in
sitting position in his highchair to take his place at the famil
table. Feeding periods become fun but messy. Balls, rattles
cubes, toys that dangle, toys that feel pleasant and are brightl
colored (red and yellow are the favorites) are used with grea
gusto. A fun game at three months of age, which encourage
hand-eye coordination and visual development, is to dangle
ring (3 to 4 inches in diameter) on a string and slowly move th
dangling ring from side to side within baby's reach. This encour
ages him to track the ring visually and grasp a moving objec
Babies love to be held in front of you and play with your face an
hair. Babies at this stage also smile unprompted at an approach
ing face. Baby's smile, in turn, elicits a reaction from the perso
and, if this reaction is appropriate, it will be rewarded with a big

ger smile from the baby. This is the beginning of social dialogue—a baby learns he can elicit certain responses from other people. Your gestures are rewarded. His coos and chuckles of the previous stage progress into laughter, squeals and the heavy breathing of intense excitement during play. He will alternate his desires for playing with some "thing" and some "body."

Swings are a valuable mother substitute when there is a pressing household obligation and your baby needs relaxing. Bounce chairs and jumpers may give your baby an entertaining feeling of self-propulsion at this stage. Jumpers should not be used before a baby is four months of age or until you notice that his head does not wobble when he bounces.

Six to nine months

**Six Months to
Nine Months—
Sitting and
Playing**

By age six months your baby will probably have mastered the primary developmental skill of the first half-year—visually directed reaching. The next six months is spent acquiring two other basic skills: **manipulation**, or what he can do with various objects once he has them; and **locomotion**, how he can get to various objects of interest under his own power.

Each stage of development involves one primary skill, the mastery of which triggers a long series of accomplishments. In this stage, sitting is the prime skill. The ability to sit without assistance, usually mastered around seven months, opens a wide, new world around him. He sees his environment straight on, certainly a more realistic perspective than the one he gets looking at his world lying on his back. Give baby a lot of practice, surrounding him with a circle of pillows to cushion his falls if you can't be sitting next to him constantly. The upright position opens new ways for him to use the objects he learned to reach for and grasp during his first six months. He can pick up toys in front of him and transfer them from hand to hand. He can bang objects on various surfaces, producing different sounds with different bangs and objects. He can throw them, watch them, hear them land in various places and he can drop the objects from his highchair and attract his audience into a "pick it up" game. Because of his desire to pick everything up, careful surveillance of what he picks up and puts into his mouth is necessary. He is no longer content with simply reaching and grasping a toy but now wants to "make something happen" with it (e.g. a jack-in-the-box, "I press down, lid pops up."). This concept of cause and effect is a forerunner of memory skill.

Picture your seven-month-old sitting in the middle of the room a few feet from various toys beyond his reach. His intense curiosity and desire to reach his toys, coupled with his increasingly strong arm, chest and leg muscles, seem to plant the idea in his mind "I have the capability to reach my toys, now how do I get them?" The problem-solving locomotion is another milestone in his emerging intelligence. The principle that intent precedes capability in the development stages is shown perfectly in the pre-walking stage of the eight- or nine-month-old infant. His locomotive style is as individual as his personality. The first manifestation of locomotion is a series of arm, leg and torso movements which are usually uncoordinated but reflect his knowledge that these are his wheels and he simply has to learn how to roll on them. These antics may begin as bouncing on his bottom, waving his arms and lurching forward on his hands in the direction of the object. He may initially worm his way across the floor by creeping on his tummy, using his legs for propulsion and his arms to steer. He may scoot on his bottom, propelled along by one leg and one arm, and finally, he may graduate to a full crawl with tummy off the ground and legs and elbows bent.

The style of locomotion is not as important as the intent. No two babies go from point A to point B in the same style at the same age. It would be a fascinating "race" to line up ten babies of eight or nine months of age in sitting position, ten feet from a tempting toy and let them go. The variation in scoots, creeps and crawls would be astonishing but the results would be similar. You will find it fascinating to watch your baby "rev up his engines" in the early locomotive stage. He will usually sit there for a few minutes bouncing up and down on his bottom, whirling his arms and legs and finally, when his engines have reached a certain momentum, lurch forward in relentless pursuit of his desired prey. In his creeping and crawling he may often resemble a crab, moving backwards, sideways and forward until he determines in which direction he really wants to go. Your baby may take some hard knocks in his drive to master crawling. Belly flops and falling backwards are to be expected.

During this stage he will use his developing leg and arm strength to pull himself up to the standing position, using any hand grip within his reach. He will cruise merrily along the sides of his crib or sofa or whatever arm-level object can steady his teetering torso during his journey.

Nine-month-old babies are perpetual motion. Dressing may become a wrestling match and feeding a wild target practice for you.

Your baby may like to drink from a cup at this age. Assistance will be necessary because he has no concept of water level in a cup. Finger foods become popular. "Cheerios" are fascinating and may often be used as an attention-holder while the rest of the family has a peaceful meal. Mealtimes should not be a struggle for either of you. He won't starve if he does not consume all the food you would like him to. He may exhibit a determination to feed himself and fail miserably but it is the attempt of the skill that is important at this stage, not its mastery. Teeth (see page 233 for teething tips), usually the two lower central incisors, may cause him to bite your nipple toward the end of a feeding, a very uncomfortable feeding practice. This may be quickly overcome by a firm reprimand and by removing your nipple when it is likely that he has finished eating and is now playfully nipping. Sometimes he may bite if he has drifted off to sleep and will stop if you rouse him for a moment.

The smooth, always good-humored personality of the preceding stages may not always carry into the six- to nine-month stage. Your baby may become more discriminating in his reactions to anyone outside his immediate family. This stranger discrimination does not occur in all babies at this age. Abrupt mood swings are common and must be respected. Teething pain and sleep disruption may contribute to the occasional unpleasant behavior at this age. Older siblings sometimes exert a calming effect on an upset six- to nine-month-old, as only a child can help a child in certain circumstances. So, if the going gets rough, call in the reserves of your other children to entertain and play with baby.

● **Play and Parenting**

Since locomotion is your baby's forte at this age, simply provide space for him to roam and objects for your little hunter to hunt. Set him in the middle of the floor, surround him with a few scattered household objects and away he'll go. Self-entertainment lasts longer at this stage than at any preceding one. A sudden change in his activity level during play is usually a signal that he is either tired or hungry. Sophisticated toys are unnecessary at this age and should be left for grandparents and friends to buy. Pots and pans, wooden spoons, blocks and balls can make up his first basic toy collection. With these toys he can bang, throw, put in and take out. Babies love to crinkle paper at this age. The various debris that will appear throughout your previously tidy house over the next couple of years serves as a constant reminder of his presence. "Make things happen" toys such as busy-boxes and light switches become a favorite. "Shake-shake" toys enable him to make various sounds. Infants between six and nine months increasingly appreciate sounds, such as background music. His attention to language is just beginning. You can introduce your baby to language at this age by talking simply and clearly to him during your care of him. Talk about what you are doing, for example, diapering, feeding, bathing. In this way he associates words with objects and actions. (See page 219 for further discussion of language development.) Parents are still his favorite source of stimulation. "Hide and seek," "peek-a-boo" games, "arms up so big" and "wave bye-bye" expressions are popular and stimulating at this age.

● **Walkers**

I have mixed feelings about the benefits and safety of walkers.

The great popularity of walkers makes one feel a comment is necessary. Walkers do satisfy a baby's exploring tendency and leg muscle activity but I also feel that a walker may provide your baby with a physical capability with which he is not yet mentally able to cope. Also, I wonder if walkers lessen a baby's motivation to crawl and to move completely under his own power. In my practice I have seen many accidents attributed to walkers. Like all such devices, they should be used under constant supervision, or in places where potentially dangerous items have been removed. (See **Walkers and Safety**, page 426.)

- **Playpens**

A playpen is a contradiction in terms. Play to a baby over six months usually means freedom to roam. Playpens do not provide this freedom. Most babies become bored in them in short order. At best, they may be used as a temporary play area where baby can be safely put if he must be left unattended for a few minutes. (See **Playpen Safety**, page 426.)

- **Shoes**

Walking usually brings about a trip to your friendly neighborhood shoe salesman. When your baby begins standing and walking, his feet and ankles hardly seem ready for weight-bearing. His feet may appear very flat because of the abundant fat pads in the area of the arch. As he grows, his fat pad becomes less apparent and a fully developed arch can usually be seen by four to five years. The rubber-like ligaments supporting the knees and ankles cause his knees to turn in and his ankles to turn out. The appearance of this knock-kneed, weak-ankled, flat-footed little toddler may inspire you to want to correct all these apparent deformities with an expensive pair of shoes. At this stage shoes usually serve no orthopedic value in your child's foot development. For the majority of toddlers the shoes they were born with, their bare feet, are the best shoes for muscle development. Certainly wait until your infant has been walking for several months before confusing him with shoes. If shoes are necessary for warmth and protection, they should be easy to put on and take off, and should have a very flexible, non-skid sole. (For further discussion of shoes and infant foot development, see **Orthopedics**, page 386.)

Nine to Twelve Months—The Pre-Walker

This period is highlighted by refined crawling, cruising and standing — all forerunners to the art of walking. Your baby's creeping and crawling efforts of the previous stage are refined into a rhythmic hands-and-knees crawling. He crawls to a piece

Nine to twelve months

of furniture, pulls himself up to a standing position and realize
that he can stand under his own power. Standing triggers another
means of locomotion called cruising, whereby your infant side
steps along furniture, using his legs for locomotion and the furni
ture for balance. Once he discovers his leg power, his next desire
is to refine this leg power into unassisted locomotion. He learn
he can hold onto furniture or onto a parent's hand with one hand
lift one foot up and down, and then put one foot in front of the
other. The transition from walking with assistance to standing
alone and walking alone is a matter of muscular balance.

Climbing stairs and other things delights his sense o
achievement. Climbing satisfies his need for locomotion
achievement and exploration without the need for the balanc
required in walking. If he learns to crawl up the stairs, teach him

to back down safely.

● **Play and Stimulation**

Small object play is a favorite at this age. He loves to point and poke. Thumb and forefinger grasp is refined, enabling him to further enjoy "pick it up and put it in" games. Container-type playthings satisfy his emerging "what's inside" curiosity. Kitchen utensils, pots and pans, balls, mixing bowls and spoons are still the old reliables. Gesture games ("so big," "pat-a-cake," "wave bye-bye") become even more popular at this stage. "Peek-a-boo" and "hide the object" games are not only fun but provide a valuable learning experience, because now your baby has the intelligence to know that objects which are beyond his perception exist. Enticing him to remove obstacles to find a desired object contributes to the formation of a fundamental intellectual function—problem solving. One of my favorite games and also one of our children's at this stage was the "where's baby?" game. Place a cloth over your baby's head and then exclaim, "Where's Heather?" Your baby will then pull the cloth from over her head and you both laugh at the pleasant surprise. "Daddy on the floor" is an enticing target for the crawler. Babies love to crawl all over Daddy, "flying" and then "landing" on Daddy's chest. At this age many babies begin associating Dad with play and Mom with care, and vocal attempts toward the concept of "Mama" and "Dada" may begin.

Twelve to Eighteen Months— Parenting the Toddler

This stage presents the major turning point in your child's developmental and educational life. The roles of both parent and infant take on a new meaning. Before twelve months, given reasonably effective parenting, most infants achieve the usual developmental milestones without difficulty, according to their innate program. Excluding speech development, there is little evidence that increased parental stimulation can accelerate a child's motor development during the first nine months. When your baby sits, crawls, turns over or transfers objects is mostly due to his inner programming and not due to outside stimuli. The primary goal of parenting during the early stages is to establish a secure love attachment between infant and parent. It is in this endeavor that parental input reaps a rich harvest.

At twelve months your parenting takes on a wider perspective. Your parental input from now on will have a profound effect on how closely your infant achieves his maximum developmental and intelligence potential. Besides continuing to build a strong love attachment with your baby, your parenting role widens to that of advisor, educator, and authority figure and your energy is naturally expected to increase to meet the demands of these new roles. Mothers seem to have nearly boundless energy reserves to cope with the increasing demands of this age and I sincerely admire all of you for this ability.

Although mothers can usually sense their infant's personality right from birth, from one to two years of age a child's individual personality traits really begin to blossom. Parents are usually quite adaptable to the developing personality of their child. Children, in turn, are beautifully resilient. They are able to bounce back from life's many little setbacks and emerge from these experiences a bit wiser. The combination of adaptability in parents and resiliency in children is a winning combination which enables you to enjoy parenting the toddler.

Just as this period is a turning point for parents, it is also a turning point for your child—the period of development of language and locomotion. The average age for walking is from twelve to fourteen months (the usual range is from nine to sixteen

Twelve to eighteen months

TIMMY, THAT'S NOT SAFE.
LET'S PLAY WITH YOUR TURTLE.

months). Let me preface this section by stating that earlier walking is of absolutely no advantage to either parent or child. Early walkers have an insatiable curiosity and drive for locomotion, fall more often and have more accidents than more calculating babies who do not walk until they are sure they can do it well. In his previous stage, your infant began learning the concept of balance. The transition from sitting to standing with assistance, to cruising, to standing alone requires an increasing facility for balancing. Your baby may begin walking stiff-legged, with feet out-turned in a wide-based gait, and arms out-stretched for balance. Eventually you will notice that the gait narrows, the feet turn inward and the arms drop from the imaginary balance beam. When these signs appear, you know your little staggerer has mastered walking and is ready to roam the house at will, satisfying his curiosity to explore. He will lead you on a merry chase to protect him from the dangerous objects in his environment and to protect your treasured and previously tidy house from his assault. Climbing stairs (and other things) delights him and gives him a sense of achievement but is naturally a source of worry to you. The combination of his intense curiosity and his new-found locomotive abilities opens new avenues of parent-child communication which we will now discuss. The main points I wish to convey concern normal or usual toddler behavior and how you can both cope with and enrich his behavior during this stage.

● **Declaration of Independence Stage**

The period from twelve to eighteen months is often called the "declaration of independence" stage. However, the desire for independence is greater than the capability. This results in another characteristic feature of this age—ambivalence. His desire to explore is even more intense now because he has his "own wheels" to move from place to place. Sometimes he wishes to be independent of his parents in locomotion and problem-solving and sometimes he doesn't. At times he may cling as he did when he was little, giving you the clue that he feels threatened by his new powers. He probably wants limits compatible with his capabilities, and help with problems that over-tax his short attention span. Enter mother's two new roles, advisor-educator and authority figure. Your toddler needs your support while he works out his anxieties created by his internal ambivalence. Your newly appointed roles necessitate simply being available for refuelling his needs. To be effective you must be available to take advantage of the first great educational opportunity of your first year of parenting—to help solve the problem when he approaches you. When a child begins to use another person as a resource for a problem he cannot solve by himself, he has learned a vital educational skill. Notice I have not yet used the magic word which all parents eagerly await for in every baby book—discipline. I am building up to the concept of discipline which will be covered in a subsequent section. Suffice to say here that if you build a solid foundation of parent child love attachment and assume the role of an effective advisor-educator at this stage, then you have laid the foundation for your role as an effective authority figure.

The second year is often presented in very negative terms such as the Terrible Twos, Negativism and "I'll be glad when this stage is over." Any self-respecting toddler would certainly disagree with all these unkind words and feel he is simply misunderstood. The media has done children a disservice and if all toddlers were to act in the way they are portrayed there would be many an only child. Let's approach this stage as one of the most exciting and meaningful (albeit exhausting) stages of development.

Your toddler really is not a negative little person. He is positive. He knows absolutely what he wants and is determined to get it at all costs. The "no-no's" come from his outside world. Perhaps it should be called the negative stage of parenting.

A basic feature of infant development is that the acquisition of a new skill compels the child to master that skill, using it to achieve other skills. Until his ability to walk develops, your infant is a passive observer of the world around him, dependent upon other people for pleasure and stimulation. Walking opens a new world for him and gives him an insatiable appetite to conduct his independent research of the world around him. He has boundless energy, driven on by the urge to explore and uncover new secrets previously denied him. Doors are to be opened, drawers pulled out, buttons pushed, knobs turned and objects taken apart. He is a going concern from dawn until dusk, stopping briefly to refuel on love and food, only to jump down again and continue his relentless pursuits. He succumbs to an occasional nap and does not yield to the enemy of sleep without a fight. His previous hunger for food and bodily pleasure are transferred into an insatiable appetite for the excitement of the world.

• Setting Limits

Our little navigator does not chart his course carefully. His explorations are directed more by impulse and trial and error than by calculation. He needs some aids to navigation, some out-of bounds signs. This is where the parents' role of setting limits comes in. The role of authority figure increases and the inevitable conflict of wills begins. Toddlers are basically directed by impulse, searching for a sense of direction initially beyond their own capability. The dilemma of parenting a toddler is to arrive at a proper balance, to exert just the right amount of restraint and guidance without hampering your toddler's desire to learn. Too much restraint may actually prolong the "negativistic" stage. Don't regard this stage as a permanent threat to your parental powers. Rather, it is a passing developmental stage in which his exhausting behavior is normal and necessary for him to advance to the next stage, having learned a reasonable degree of self-control without loss of self-esteem.

Toddlers are not willfully destructive or disobedient. They simply do not yet have the automatic control system to govern their intense impulses. As Selma Fraiberg states beautifully in her book **The Magic Years**, "Toddlers exhibit a declaration of independence but they have no intention of unseating the government." Her classic description of normal behavior of toddlers is, in my opinion, the most beautiful and accurate ever written, and I encourage you to read this section of her book.

Parents' role as educator of their child and designer of his environment peaks in the second year. "How and what do I teach my child?" is a usual parental concern at this age. Provide exposure to outside information, his objective world, people, situations or enriched environment. Meaningful enrichment is not measured by the number of toys on his shelf and the number of child-rearing books on your bookshelf, but rather by simply being available on an "as needed basis." You are still the pivotal point in his widening universe. Watch your toddler in his daily rounds through the house, periodically checking on your whereabouts as if he is thinking that "it is comforting to know that my consultant is on stand-by should a problem arise."

Choose toys appropriate for his stage of development. The best judgment is based on your ingenuity and intuition about your child's temperament and likes rather than by toy manufacturers. Play is to a child what education is to an adult; it is the means by which he learns about his world. Imitation is a toddler's textbook. When your toddler wants to play "Mommy's little helper," appreciate that it is attempting the task which is a learning experience, not the finished product.

Appreciate the concept of **gradualism**. Your infant must process information at his own comfortable rate. Excessive and inappropriate stimuli may plug up the "processor," resulting in temper tantrums. Good education is good timing, because of the so-called sensitive periods during which a child is particularly receptive to certain stimuli. In his later years, formal education is not mood-dependent. He must learn given subjects at given times, whether he wants to or not. Education at the toddler's age is very mood-dependent because learning at this stage is by choice. If he is not in the mood to sit alone with you and read a book, then he will not be receptive to the potential learning in this activity and you might as well let him choose his activity. If he brings you a book and you are available to read with him, he will be receptive. (Tips on teaching your child are discussed in **Giving Your Child an Educational Advantage at Home**, page 227 .)

Eighteen Months to Two Years

Toward the end of the second year, your toddler's behavior is directed less by impulse, and trial and error, and more by thinking and calculation. Throughout the second year your infant has learned primarily by experience (e.g. a stool is for climbing on and sitting on, the cupboard is where the cookies are). Sometime in the latter half of the second year, a toddler learns to take two pieces of information which he has learned by experience and attempts to put them together to form an idea. For example, he might think "If a stool will make me higher and the cookies are in the cupboard, if I pull the stool in front of the cupboard, I can climb up and get the cookies."

Between the ages of eighteen months and two years, language is the prime developmental milestone which triggers a whole series of achievements. By this time he has words for objects, words for actions and is developing words for feelings and desires. By putting these three language facilities together, your toddler can accomplish many feats. Objects have names and he can recreate the objects in his mind when he hears or thinks of the name of the object. He is developing the concept of "I" and by the response of his care-givers to his long stream of "I wanna's," he learns to manipulate his adult world to meet his desires. Language allows a child to better control his impulses. Language stimulates more desirable behavior since the child can now show his feelings with words rather than by acting out. (For a more detailed discussion on language development, see the subsequent section, page 219 .)

In this stage, the toddler is a great imitator. Putting on Mommy's lipstick, walking in Mommy's shoes and carrying Mommy's purse or Daddy's briefcase are favorites. The combi-

Eighteen months to
two years

nation of learning by imitation and the emerging concept of ''I'' results in the ''I do it myself'' phase. He brushes his own teeth, feeds himself, unscrews lids, dresses himself, washes hands, goes to the refrigerator for food and drink. Since imitation is one of the prime learning stimuli for toddlers, you can capitalize on his desire to imitate and ''do it myself'' by demonstrating certain tasks to him slowly and deliberately.

By age two the toddler's walking is refined into a rhythmic arm-swing gait. Running, jumping, walking backwards, pivoting and stair-walking are added to his repertoire of locomotion. Fine motor advances are shown most graphically in his progression from large, crude scribbling to simple line-drawing and circle drawing.

● Hunger Strike — ''Baby Won't Eat''

''My baby won't eat'' is a common complaint at this age. A brief discussion of what is the normal eating behavior of a busy toddler might assure you that your infant won't starve. First of all, you have been accustomed to him eating a lot the first year. During the first year he eats a lot because he grows a lot; he triples his birth weight by one year. However, from one to two years, his rate of growth decelerates. Because his rate of growth is less, he requires fewer calories.

Three meals a day is an adult invention. Toddlers are too busy to sit for three, long periods each day and would rather stop their busy explorations for an occasional brief refuelling before continuing their relentless pursuit of more interesting activity. Toddlers are by nature picky eaters, and actually small frequent feedings are probably the healthiest way to eat anyway. He may eat well one day and ''eat nothing'' the next; he likes fresh vegetables one day and refuses them the next. This patternless eating is usual, and if you average his food intake over a week or month, you might be surprised to learn that his diet is more balanced than you thought. The average one- or two-year-old's daily nutritonal needs are met by: one pint of milk (if he tolerates it), 2 ounces each of meat and vegetables, a slice of cheese, 2 ounces of fruit, one egg and appropriate vitamin supplements. Respect his likes as long as they are nutritious. Avoid the junk food and junk juice trap in your desperation to feed him something.

If your toddler is continually dawdling, messy, and is becoming increasingly unwelcome at the family table, here are a few tips. Remember toddlers love to imitate and they love ''all by myself'' things. Capitalize on these desires by getting him hi own little dish and utensils. Set his dinnerware at his highchair and when he sees everyone sitting at the table eating he will most likely want to join you and want to imitate your eating, at his own pace. Offer him small portions and let him imitate how you eat. This is much easier on both of you than using force. Leave nutritious snacks lying within his reach so that he can eat when he is hungry and when he wants to. His own little table and chair in the kitchen is a winner for enticing him to his own "dining room."

As I previously discussed in the section on **Feeding**, mothers are the tastemakers of the next generation. Try to program your toddler against junk food so that by the time he reaches school age, when you no longer have complete control over what he eats, he will have healthy eating habits. (See page 140 for toddler snack suggestions.)

● **Toddler Play and Stimulation**

The most meaningful games and stimulation at this age are discussed in detail in the section on Language Development. At this stage, toddlers enjoy taking part in games, listening to records, and carrying things around the house. The "Mommy's little helper" desire peaks at this age and because of the emerging facility for language, the toddler's "helping" actually becomes more interesting. Play groups of three to four toddlers may contribute to a child's incipient sense of sociability. Although at this stage most toddlers are engaged primarily in parallel play, there is a certain body language that goes on among children of similar ages, with each having a different way of expressing himself. Besides offering mothers some needed relief at this stage, play groups also offer a mother the chance to observe her child in action with other children.

● **How Your Child Learns Language**

Language is the one developmental milestone that parental stimulation can affect profoundly. How a baby learns language is a fascinating phenomenon which encompasses not only the sounds he produces but the relation between his senses and many aspects of his environment. I shall use the term "language" not only to mean the sounds your baby produces (speech) but also his body language, how he moves in response to your sounds and how you move in response to his.

Although a newborn does not speak in the usual sense, there is a type of mother-infant language that begins in the newborn period. It is called **entrainment**. Film analysis of a mother and her newborn shows that the baby moves in a rhythm synchronous with his mother's voice rhythm, similar to an adult nodding his head in tune with a speaker. Mother's perception of the rhythmic feedback of her newborn's gestures and facial expressions in turn stimulates her to continue her communication. The resulting "dance" enjoyed between mother and baby is the first demonstration of a baby's body language. The results of this first communication appear throughout the months and years. Studies have shown that mothers who bonded with their babies at birth and continued the practice of immersion mothering, spoke to their babies more, used a more meaningful type of dialogue (more questions, more cue words, more adjectives, fewer commands and more concrete words). Drs. Klaus and Kennell studied the babies of these mothers and found they achieved higher language scores. So it does seem that the quality of mothering can affect language development in your child.

The effect of immersion mothering on the infant's language development is a beautiful example of the mutual feedback infants and mothers enjoy. An infant rewards his mother by certain body language (eye contact, body movement and babbling sound). The mother's "mothering" is stimulated by her baby's body language and she is encouraged to further stimulate him. The baby senses this delight in his language and is motivated to increase his own language. This mother-infant dialogue continues throughout infancy as the prime stimulus for language development.

Mothers do not have to read a book on how to teach their babies to talk or resort to a "method" to stimulate their infants to be early talkers. If you practice the immersion mothering (and fathering) which I have repeatedly advocated in this book, you will naturally be an effective speech teacher for your baby. Mothers have a unique pitch in voice inflection which babies pick up very early. Your infant will mimic these intonations. He will respond differently to mother's higher pitched voice than dad's lower pitched voice. Mothers who are really into mothering seem to talk naturally to their infants about what they are doing (e.g. changing the diaper, washing the face) in very simple words; a "mother talk" that babies understand. Mothers and babies have their own communication network.

Although babies vary tremendously in the timing of speech development, there are certain similarities we shall now discuss. Baby's first speech sounds begin in the newborn period as separate cries for different needs and he adapts these cries according to the response he gets. The earliest non-crying speech sounds are throaty noises. Around three months, the increased production of saliva prompts the baby to play with sounds, gurgling, sputtering and bubble blowing. Babbling long strings of vowels (ba, ba, ba, ba) begins at this time along with "cooing" and squeals of "ah" and "eh." Around four or five months of age, during the stage of visually directed behavior, certain tuned-in persons can engage a baby in a "stimulating conversation" in which the baby waves his arms and legs, claps hands, breathes heavily in great excitement, and his squeals and smiles seem to mesh into his first attempt at laughter. Around four to five months, babies begin singing ("ou-ee") at objects which they can now hold for a longer period, and may utter sounds of protest when their favorite objects are taken from them.

You and your baby may enjoy frequent **nursing conversations** when your baby makes noises of satisfaction. Babies begin using noises to get attention at this age. Around seven or eight months, babies begin forming a sound for mother although the actual words, "Mama" and "Dada," may not come until a few months later. By nine months to a year, most babies will respond to their own name. Around nine or ten months, babies have usually chosen one household word, such as "cat," although they often say only one part of the word ("ta" for cat).

Gesture games (Bye-Bye, So-Big, Pick Me Up, Pat-a-Cake) are a favorite pastime around ten months. Around this time babies connect names and objects such as ball, block, baby. Once they make this connection they will respond to simple requests: "Close the door," "Pick up the ball." "No-no," meaning stop, is usually understood by ten to eleven months.

From twelve to eighteen months, exciting changes in language development occur. Your toddler's language progresses from **receptive language** (understanding words) to **expressive language** (saying words), although children will continue to understand more than they say for the next several years. He first learns words by imitation. He hears the sound and attempts to parrot it. If this sound is accompanied by action, gestures or objects, he next learns that these actions and objects have names. The formation of certain sounds such as "th" and "l" result in a variety of mouth contortions, tongue-clicks and jargon of various degrees of intelligibility. This jargon should be neither imitated nor corrected but allowed to evolve into correct sounds by repeatedly hearing the correct sounds from his parents. Once your child masters the art of sounds heard, objects seen and sound imitation, his language has a snowball effect which pro-

duces a vocabulary of around fifty words by twenty-four months.
After the toddler has a basic repertoire of about a dozen words
he keenly practices these words by repetition according to how
much he is encouraged. Your toddler's initial speech repertoire
will be mostly simple nouns like car. He then picks up on ges
tures associated with these sounds and adds action words such as
"go bye-bye" to his vocabulary. His next advance is to connect
these isolated words to create meaningful phrases so his efforts
resemble a budget telegram, for example, "bye-bye car." He
associates bye-bye with leaving the house (which he learns from
your gestures when you depart) and "car" as the moving object
which transports him from one world to another. Now, let's ana
lyze what he really has learned by his "bye-bye car" phrase.
First, he has learned to put the two words together to form a con
cept, and secondly he has learned how to use this concept to
express a wish. " **I** want to **go** bye-bye in the **car**" is what he is
really saying. This language gives him the sociability to express
an "I" desire; secondly, it affords him a tool to use his adult
companions as resources to help him get his desire. Outside of
crying to indicate needs in early infancy, this is the first major
step towards using social intelligence to control his environment.
He takes great delight in this achievement and, according to his
audiences' responses, this may trigger a long chain of "
wanna. . ." He learns that with language he is no longer a
passive individual but now has the word power to use the adult
world around him for his satisfaction.

His language gives more meaning to his mental images
which allow him to magically create a favorite character in a
mental drama. For example, "Mama" is a mental image of a
wonderful person who does nice things for him. He can magic
ally recreate her when he needs her. Sleep mumbling is consid
ered an expression of the mental images he is recreating when he
takes his world to bed with him. The combination of language
and mental images paves the way for magical thinking, fantasies
and fears which creep in usually between two and three years.

Between eighteen months and two years the words for
objects, the words for actions, and the words for feelings, all
seem to come together, resulting in a further snowballing of lan
guage development.

Language makes child-rearing a bit easier. The interac
tion between mother and child is enhanced when a child learns to
express himself. Language allows a child to be more in control of
his impulses. For example, when he attempts to touch a hot stove

and mother says "no-no," ("no-no," meaning stop,) it can be mentally grasped by a child of one year of age. (Using the word "stop" rather than "no" is really preferable.) From the age of eighteen months to two years, mother's constant gestures and repetition of, "Stop, the stove is hot. It will hurt you," finally sink in. The concept of hot and hurt are word-associated ideas that check his impulse to touch and also educate his emerging cause and effect intelligence. We will discuss more about the use of words and impulse-checking in the section on discipline.

● **How To Enrich Your Child's Language Development**

I wish to preface the following list of language enrichment tips by emphasizing that mothers have a natural intuition about their children's language development. The "method" you use will naturally flow from you as part of effective mothering.

1. Picture books. Before, or around one year of age, begin looking at picture books together. After pointing to the picture and repeating the name of the object, your child will develop his word-object association. As your child advances, select increasingly stimulating books, appropriate to his stage of speech development. Next, stimulate his recall of the names by pointing to an object and saying "What's this?" Show him the whole page of assorted objects and ask "Where is the ball?"

2. Expansion. Expand a word into an idea. For example, if a child asks "What's that?" and points to a bird you answer "That's a bird," and you add "and birds fly in the sky." You have not only answered his question and he has gained a word for the object "bird," but you have also given him a word-associated idea that "birds fly in the sky." Continued repetition of this saying will stimulate the child's next thought as "bird...fly...sky." Babies seldom speak in full sentences until the latter half of the second year but rather use **cue words** within each sentence. Instead of saying "I want to go bye-bye in the car" the child will simply say "bye-bye car." You may expand on these cue words by asking, "Do you want to go bye-bye in the car?" In addition to expansion, **model** the words for the child, i.e. provide the appropriate words or phrase for your child with the expectation that he will repeat the word after you. Expansion, modelling, and picking up on cue words are particularly important for the child with lazy speech habits who gets his way by pointing all the time. For example, a child who points at the cookie jar and says "Uh ookie" or simply points to the jar and says nothing, should be motivated with modelling the right word ("cookie") and expansion ("Tell Mommy 'I want a cookie'.''). A child whose expressive speech continues to lag behind his receptive speech simply needs a little more motivation to speak.

3. Imitation. Infants learn speech by imitating the speech of their care-givers. Don't use too much "baby talk." Talk to your infant in the language you want him to learn.

4. Word games and action songs. These make language learning fun. Babies love to play games about their own body parts and will learn quickly what their toes are after they have played "This Little Piggy" several times. Rhythm games which employ counting and finger play such as "One, two, buckle my shoe..." will hold the toddler's interest. Action songs such as "Pop, Goes The Weasel" are particularly helpful for encouraging gestures and cue words. For example, if you repeat "Pop Goes The Weasel" several times and jump up and down, when he hears the word "pop" he will take this cue word, utter a semblance of "weasel" and jump up by himself.

5. Questions. Toddlers seem to enjoy the inflection of your voice when you ask a question. Questions imply that you welcome a response of some kind and he will usually oblige. Toddlers respond to questions and commands.

6. Correcting toddlers' speech. Remember the main goal of toddler language is to communicate an idea, not a word. It is important for some babies to babble a while and experiment with their own sounds without outside attempts to refine them. These toddlers are simply storing their language information for a sudden rush of intelligible words and phrases around two years. Much of a toddler's speech may be unintelligible under the age of two. This is normal. Use the above-mentioned concepts of modelling and expansion to give him guidance. If you sense your child is having trouble with certain sounds, make a special effort to repeat these sounds frequently yourself and capitalize on your child's desire to imitate. Correct by repetition, not by embarrassment.

7. Feedback. Between two and three years of age, a child's greatest speech achievement is the ability to express feelings in words. By sensing what he is feeling, and feeding your perceived feelings back to him in words, you can enrich this ability (e.g. "You seem angry, tell Mommy why.").

8. Eye-to-eye contact. This is very important. I find that looking very intently into a child's eyes during an examination has a calming effect on a suspicious child. If you can maintain eye contact with a child, you can maintain his attention. Eyes have unique language all their own, and you want your child to be comfortable speaking into another person's eyes. The ability to be comfortable with eye-to-eye contact is a language enrichment exercise which will benefit your child the rest of his life.

9. Keep your speech simple. Use too much disconnected chatter and your child will tune you out. Speak slowly in simple sentences and pause frequently to give your child time to reflect on the message.

10. Choices. Give your child frequent choices. For example, "do you want an apple or an orange?" This not only obliges him to reply but also stimulates a thought process of decision-making.

11. Respond to his cues. A basic stimulus for all developmental achievement is the response the child receives for his efforts. If your child is pleased with the response a certain bit of language produces, he will be encouraged to practice his cues. Some children have an endless number of "What's that?" questions. If they receive answers they like, plus an expanded answer as a bonus, they will be more comfortable in using the adult world as a source of information.

Speech and Hearing Checklist

The main reason for a delay in a child's speech development is a hearing impairment. Because of the wide variation in the rate of speech development among normal children, it is often difficult for parents to tell if their child's speech delay is abnormal or if he is simply a "late talker." In "late talkers," the understanding of words and phrases (receptive language) progresses normally but their expressive speech is late. If you suspect that your child does not understand or respond to words according to the following progression, his hearing may be impaired. The following is a simple guide about when to be concerned about your child's hearing and speech development.

Three to six months. Does your infant react to your voice even when he cannot see you? Babies should normally attend to their mother's voice and turn their heads in the direction of sound at this age.

Seven to ten months. At this age, babbling should normally increase. Does he seem to respond to gestures more than to voice? Babies with normal vision have a magnificent capability to understand sign language and may be responding more to your gestures than to your voice.

Twelve to fifteen months. Does he respond to his own name? Can he point to his favorite toys? Can he point to a few body parts?

Eighteen months to two years. Does he respond to simple requests "Bring me the ball," "Go get your shoes?" Does he enjoy being read to and will he point out certain pictures when you say the names of the pictures?

Two to two and a half years. Does he show interest in the sound of TV commercials? Is he beginning to put two-word sentences together, e.g. "Bye-bye car?"

Two and a half to three years. Does he sing a few simple songs or notes and seem to enjoy them? A child with good hearing enjoys sounds which bring him pleasure. Hearing impairment is one of the subtle causes of an unhappy child. Does he respond when you call him from another room? A three-year old should be able to locate the source of the sound from a distance.

Three to four years. Does he speak in four to five word sentences? Can he carry out a sequence of two simple directions, e.g. "Go find Bobby and tell him dinner is ready"? Does he tune the TV or radio unusually loud? (For further discussion on hearing impairment, see **Hearing**, page 225.)

● **The Quiet Child**

Some children are quiet because of their temperament and family culture. People of certain cultures are verbally reserved. People of some other cultures seem to talk loudly, with grand gestures. Children tend to follow the language habits of their family. If you are a quiet family and your child is quiet, this may be his normal behavior and should be respected.

● **Stuttering (Stammering)**

Around the third year, many children show periodic hesitation and syllable repetition which we call stuttering. This pattern of speech is more accurately termed a "normal dysfluency," and is a normal part of learning to talk. An important point to remember is that stuttering is more in the ear of the parents that the mouth of the child. A child may not consider himself a stutterer until someone calls his attention to it. A normal dysfluency becomes stuttering when a child becomes aware that he isn't speaking correctly and his dysfluency is further intensified by outside communicative pressures.

What can you do for a stuttering child? First of all, realize that parents alone cannot improve their child's speech. Speech development must come primarily from within the child. Parents can only create an environment of security, boost his self-esteem and engage in language exercises which he enjoys and performs well. For example, encourage your child to tell a story which you and he know he is comfortable with. If you sense that your child is particularly tense in a certain situation and begins to stutter, devote your energies to making him more at ease and his stuttering will naturally subside. Don't attempt to 'correct' his stuttering by saying "slow down," as this will only reinforce that talking is difficult, increase his fear of speaking and draw attention to his speech. It is vitally important that a child **enjoy** speaking and not regard speaking as an unreasonably difficult task. Do not interrupt your child as he is expressing himself. Allow him your full eye-level attention so that he is not afraid of being interrupted. 'Correct' by example. Your child must hear good speech if he is to become a good speaker. Use relatively simple adult language and speak at a slower rate. Increase the complexity and the rate of speaking as he becomes more fluent.

Most children do not become consistently fluent until eight years of age. However, regardless of his age, if your child exhibits fear of speaking because he is unable to speak comfortably or because other children make fun of him, a speech therapist should be consulted. If you notice a gradual improvement in your child's speech fluency and he seems increasingly more comfortable when speaking, then there is no cause for concern.

How to Give Your Child an Educational Advantage at Home

The period from birth to three years of age sees the most rapid development of your child's brain. How you parent your child during these formative years has a profound effect on his later formal education. An infant's desire and capacity for learning is first manifested in the newborn period by his state of quiet alertness, a state in which he is most receptive to outside stimuli. An extension of this state of quiet alertness is the tremendous power of concentration infants and young children have. The ability of the young child to learn several languages simultaneously and without confusion, a feat which is much more difficult for an adult, demonstrates a child's great capacity for learning.

● **The Educational Continuum**

A young child's developing brain has an immense capacity for learning and he has an insatiable desire to fill this capacity. A child who is learning to his fullest potential at his own comfortable pace feels more valuable as a person. As a result of these feelings he desires to learn more and the cycle continues. His world becomes increasingly interesting to him, and he becomes more interesting to himself and to others. The fulfilled child becomes accustomed to the joy of learning and the good feeling

it gives him. A child with this headstart begins his formal educa
tion with a positive attitude toward learning. Intuitive paren
will pick up on their child's cues, will learn from their child ho
he wants to learn and how to feed his learning. The result of th
continuum is that you raise your child's educational life to
higher level.

What happens to the child who is a product of a le:
stimulating environment? If a child's curiosity is not satisfied, h
becomes less curious. If he is not presented with challenges, h
becomes less motivated. If he has no model to imitate, he
without direction. The result of this break in the natural educa
tional continuum is that the child's desire to learn operates at
lower level. When he enters kindergarten or first grade he is sue
denly overwhelmed with the information of whichever educatic
system is popular at that time. Because he has not developed
joy of learning in his earlier years when interest and curiosi
were at their peak, he may rebel and become less interested :
learning. A dull and wasted child is an unhappy child.

The message I wish to convey to you in this section is th
home education does not mean saturating your child with info
mation. It means creating an environment which allows his ind
vidual desires and talents to flourish at his own individual pac
the result being increased self-esteem.

Parents are their child's prime teachers. Parents are n
required to fit their child into a system. The school should n
replace the home but should rather be an extension of it. Th
home lays the foundation for attitudes, values and motivatio
Without this strong home foundation, a child's school educatic
is less effective.

● **Steps in Giving Your Child an Educational Advantage**

1. The earliest ''education'' you can practice are the concepts
immersion mothering and involved fathering as advocated in th
previous chapters. As a result of these practices, an infant trus
his environment and feels right. This feeling provides the bas
for learning. An unhappy or disturbed child cannot learn to h
full potential. Maria Montessori stated that ''education shou
start as early as the birth of a child.''

2. Parents are educational models for their children. The your
child learns from your actions, the older child from your attitud
and values. Example remains the best teacher at all ages. Yo
child wants to imitate and it is up to parents to give him som
thing valuable to imitate.

3. Enriching your child's language development (see page 2:

for tips on language enrichment) is one of the earliest contributions parents can make to their child's education. A child with enriched language ability develops an early capability to manipulate his environment and therefore learns more from it.

4. A developing child wants a sense of order. A young child's developing brain is searching for organization. A sense of order in his environment complements this need and makes learning more enjoyable. The following are specific suggestions on how to provide order in your child's environment:

a) Use low shelves instead of toy boxes. I learned this lesson with our first child. When Jimmy was three years old I felt that a father should be building things with his child and so we built him a beautiful big red toy box. This box served as a convenient catch-all to keep his many toys in one place but had little teaching value in encouraging his sense of order. Low shelves with one-foot-square compartments, each containing one or two valued toys, are much better than a pile of toys in a box. Too many toys may confuse a child. Picture a child standing before a shelf displaying appropriate toys for his age. He surveys his limited world of toys and chooses one he is interested in at that particular time. If they are in a pile, the one on top is usually selected. Rotate toys frequently to keep his interest high.

b) Child-sized furniture and his own table and chairs allow your child to be comfortable sitting for a longer period of time, thus encouraging task completion and concentration.

c) Eye-level wooden pegs, where he can hang his own clothing, encourages a sense of responsibility for his own belongings. If room tidiness is important to you, begin with the simple aids like shelves and pegs, and increase your requirements with your child's advancing age. An orderly environment complements the child's orderly mind.

5. The concept of "expansion" as an aid to learning. A child best learns what he is interested in. The value of home education is that a parent can usually sense what their child is interested in at a given time. Short periods of spontaneous learning are often more meaningful than large blocks of time. A frequent scene is one of a two- or three-year-old bringing a somewhat tattered book to his parents and asking them to "read a story." The child is interested and receptive at this moment. A parent who is available and interested can expand this child-initiated opportunity into a richly rewarding learning experience. For example, instead of simply reading the words of the book and pointing to the pictures in the book, associate these words and pictures with objects in the real world (for example, point to a tree in the book and to the trees in your yard in order to expand on the concept of tree). Expansion not only requires concentration by your child but also by the parent. A child senses when the parent is not completely tuned into the here and now. Even though you are there physically, your mind may be somewhere else; your child can really sense this. When a child is in the mood for a learning experience, such as reading a book, he often has tremendous powers of concentration and demands equal concentration from you (See page 229 for further discussion of the concepts of expansion and language development.)

6. Repetition is a learning tool at all ages but especially so for the young child. On several occasions when reading a familiar story to my three-year-old, I would inadvertently leave out an important word and he would immediately call my attention to it.

7. Music. Infants and young children have a fascination for music and researchers have shown that some babies attend more to classical music than children's songs. Perhaps it is the variety of pitch and mathematical order in classical music that interest children. I have noticed that early exposure to music and the parental stimulus of piano lessons brought out a talent in one of our children. This increased his self-esteem which, in turn, made him want to learn more music; the educational continuum was on its way.

8. Art. A large blank coloring pad, a variety of crayons, and a little parental guidance is one of the most meaningful, early home educational devices. Fine motor movement, learning patterns and shapes, and a sense of creativity are all enhanced through this simple exercise.

9. Nature. A beautiful exercise is to walk with your child through your garden, forest or on a beach, talking about and exploring all the beauties of nature. Nature teaches because it is real and in motion. Picture books are static fantasy. I suspect that a young child's absorbent mind is often confused by too much picture book fantasy. I am watching my daughter explore our garden. She sees different colors, feels different textures of grass and leaves and sand, uses thumb and forefinger to pick a flower, pours sand into and out of a container, sees tiny bugs and insects (children are fascinated with smallness and minute detail), feels the wind and sun on her face, watches the bird fly from tree to tree, hears the sound of the birds, the wind in the trees, and the ocean. Simple walks through the garden with an attentive parent as a nature guide is a rewarding educational experience for the curious child.

10. Give choices. The ability to make wise decisions is fundamental to the development of the child as a thinking person. As soon as your child has command of receptive language (usually by age two years), give him frequent choices, e.g. which shirt to wear, which book to read. With increasing age, increase the complexity of the choice. The child of two to three is emerging from the trial and error stage and moving on to one of more calculated reasoning. Decision-making encourages this development.

11. Make idle time meaningful. Much time with your child is spent simply waiting (e.g. doctor's office) and this precious time should not be wasted. This is a good time to switch on your parent-child communication network. Bring along "mother's bag of tricks," filled with such prizes as scribbling pads, magic slates, hand puppets, picture books. Keep a mental log of word games. A young child's attention span is short and you may have to switch channels frequently to maintain interest. Some particularly challenging and intelligent children will demand increasingly challenging games to hold their attention. As one very intuitive mother of a bright child once told me, "Sometimes I am mentally exhausted, she keeps upping the ante." Educational activities during otherwise idle time have a fringe benefit—they keep the child out of mischief.

12. Use community resources. Make use of the educational resources in your community such as zoos, museums, fire stations, factories. Field trips to community resources are very popular in school. Parents can use these educational resources also.

13. The carry-over principle. It is vitally important for your child to experience success in some field of learning. If he succeeds in one task, his self-esteem will be boosted and this feeling will carry over into other fields of learning. Identify what your child is interested in and good at, create an environment which allows his interests and talents to flourish and this carry-over may have a snowball effect on his learning at all ages of the educational continuum. (See carry-over principle in **Learning Disabilities**, page 308.) Appropriate methods of play and stimulation for given ages and stages, which give your child an educational advantage, are discussed throughout this chapter.

Your Child's Teeth

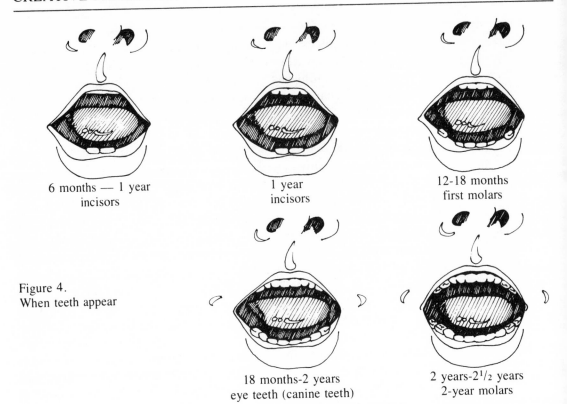

6 months — 1 year
incisors

1 year
incisors

12-18 months
first molars

Figure 4.
When teeth appear

18 months-2 years
eye teeth (canine teeth)

2 years-2¹/₂ years
2-year molars

When Teeth Appear

Your baby is born with a full set of teeth, although you don't see them because they are still up in his jaw. Around the age of four months, many babies begin to drool profusely in preparation for teething. There are three types of teeth:

1. Incisors, the sharp chisel-like front teeth which are used for cutting foods.

2. Cuspids, the pointed teeth at the corners of the mouth which are used for tearing and holding foods.

3. Molars, the square teeth with round projections (cusps), located at the back of the gums and used for grinding foods.

The timing and sequence of teething is extremely variable and the following is only a guide. Your child will begin losing his primary teeth (baby teeth) around six or seven years of age. Your child sheds his primary teeth in the same sequence as they appeared, usually losing three or four teeth per year until around twelve years of age when all the primary teeth have been shed.

The thirty-two permanent teeth (adult teeth) begin to appear around six to seven years of age. At this time the "six year molars," which are usually your child's first permanent teeth, erupt. (See Figure 4.)

**Teething
—Doctor, Could
It Be His Teeth?**

The teeth are blamed for a wide variety of ills that beset the growing infant, some justified and some imaginary. If an infant shows unusual behavior, such as night-waking, the teeth are a ready scapegoat. Parents seem to accept disruptive behavior in their infant better and respond to it more sympathetically if there is a ''cause'' for this behavior. You may find that your doctor is wisely reluctant to blame the teeth for fear of missing a more serious medical cause. If you think of teething as an irritation of the upper end of the grastrointestinal tract, it may be easier for you to understand how your baby feels.

The most common discomforts that seem associated with teething are drooling, with a resulting ''drool rash'' on your baby's cheeks, increased finger-sucking and gum-rubbing, diminished appetite, wakefulness, irritability, slight fever, and loose stools with a consequent diaper rash. Teething may be confused with a cold. When the ''drool'' collects in the back of his throat, your baby may cough and there may be a raspy sound to his breathing. A runny nose or watery eyes, especially if the discharge is thick and yellow, should **not** be attributed to teething. If these signs are associated with increased irritability, your baby may have an ear infection. The four molars and first cuspids which appear between the ages of twelve and eighteen months are the most likely to cause trouble. If several teeth are erupting at the same time, babies are often extremely uncomfortable.

Treatment of teething discomfort is aimed at controlling the fever and pain with aspirin or acetaminophen (see page 339), alleviating the local discomfort with a cool teether (frozen banana, cool spoon, raw carrots, ice) or massaging the gums with your finger. In my experience, topical anesthetics applied to the sore gums are usually ineffective.

**Caring For Your
Baby's Teeth**

Why care for your child's primary teeth since they're going to fall out anyway? You may consider your infant's primary teeth as foundation teeth on which the health and location of the permanent teeth depend. The primary teeth save the proper space into which the permanent teeth grow. They also influence the proper development of the jaw and facial bones. Therefore, premature loss of the primary teeth, especially the molars, through decay or injury may permanently affect your child's jaw and tooth development. The following suggestions will help you care for your baby's teeth:

1. Dental care for your baby begins at birth. Breastfeeding contributes to proper jaw alignment because of the different pressures exerted on the jawbones during suckling. Breastfed infants have fewer cavities because of the nature of the milk and the natural rinsing action during breastfeeding.

2. Begin fluoride supplements early in infancy (as discussed in detail on page 126), and follow your dentist's or pediatrician's advice on the use of fluoride for your infant.

3. Beware of a condition called **nursing-bottle teeth**. As soon as your baby's teeth come in, avoid giving milk, formula, or juice in a bottle at nap time or while falling asleep. When your baby falls asleep, he produces much less saliva. Because of this the milk, fruit juice, or formula in the mouth is neither digested nor washed away, but remains on the teeth. Bacteria in the mouth changes the sugar into decay-producing acids and the protective enamel is eroded. The teeth become brittle, resulting in premature loss of the primary teeth and a long series of dental problems. If your infant must fall asleep with a bottle in his mouth, give him water instead of milk or juice. Nursing-bottle decay does not occur in breastfeeding babies because the milk flows more toward the back of the mouth, and when the infant stops sucking the breast nipple contracts and milk automatically stops flowing. Milk and juice may continue to flow through an artificial nipple even when an infant stops sucking. It is wise to discourage juice drinking from a bottle anyway, and I recommend you delay giving juice until your baby can take it from a cup.

HOW TO CARE FOR A CHILD'S TEETH
• Breastfeed
• Avoid bottles while sleeping
• Give juice from a cup, not a bottle
• Begin fluoride supplement early
• Discourage prolonged thumb sucking
• Avoid junk food
• Proper brushing and flossing
• Dental check-up and cleaning every 6 months

4. Thumb sucking seldom displaces the front teeth unless your child continues this habit beyond two and a half years and exerts heavy and prolonged pressure on his front teeth (see **Thumb Sucking**, page 270). Pacifiers dipped in honey or other sweeteners can cause tooth decay and this practice should be discouraged.

5. Dental hygiene. Tooth decay is first caused by the formation of **plaque**, which is an invisible sticky film that is constantly forming on the teeth and contains harmful bacteria. The bacteria in the plaque acts on the sugar in the food and forms a decay-producing acid, which is held against the teeth by the plaque. Because tooth decay is caused by plaque and sugar, the aim of dental hygiene is to keep the plaque from forming by frequent brushing, especially after meals, and by avoiding sugar, especially prolonged contact of sugar on the teeth, which occurs with prolonged sucking on lollipops and hard candy chips which lodge upon and between the teeth.

It is wise to take your child to the dentist around two years of age, even earlier if your pediatrician suggests it. Proper brushing and flossing techniques will be demonstrated by your dentist or the dental hygienist.

Teaching Your Child to Brush

How do you get your infant to brush his teeth? Begin brushing your infant's teeth as soon as he will cooperate. Around eighteen months, you can capitalize on two natural urges —"just like Mommy" and "all by myself." While you are brushing your teeth, encourage your toddler to watch. When he shows the desire to brush, give him his own toothbrush and holder and some brushing guidance. Place a mirror on the bathroom wall at his own level. It is usually better to wait until your baby shows some interest in brushing his teeth. Forced toothbrushing in a reluctant child may create a negative attitude to dental hygiene. The frequency of brushing and how you brush is more important than how long you brush your infant's teeth. Children's toothbrushes should have soft bristles and should be replaced frequently. A brush with bent bristles will not clean properly. Although I encourage you to teach your child to brush his own teeth, most children under the age of four years cannot, in fact, clean their own teeth effectively. Better hygiene is achieved if you brush your child's teeth for him and show him the right way. If brushing is difficult, the following method is useful to clean the teeth of an infant. Place your infant on your lap face up with his feet pointing away from you. Using a 2'' x 2'' piece of gauze

wrapped around your forefinger, vigorously wipe his teeth an
gums. Let your finger be his toothbrush. Some dentists recom
mend that you clean your baby's gums even before his teet
erupt.

Iron drops may cause a temporary dark stain on you
baby's teeth. This can be minimized by administering the drop
further back on his tongue, rinsing his mouth with water after
wards, and brushing frequently.

Dental Accidents

Dental accidents can be minimized by using mouth protector
during all contact sports. If a tooth is knocked out, wrap it in
wet cloth or put it in water. Do not clean it as this may injure th
roots. Take your child and the tooth to the dentist, within thirt
minutes if possible. A re-implanted tooth may function for sev
eral years.

A hard blow to your child's tooth may push the tooth ou
of alignment or may injure the tooth pulp and cause the tooth t
turn black. A **displaced tooth** (either forward or backward
should be re-positioned by your dentist within three hours
before swelling of the underlying tissues makes re-positionin
difficult. If the displaced tooth interferes with your child's bite
then dental attention may be required to avoid further injury t
the displaced tooth. Injured teeth are often sensitive to hot an
cold, and your child should also refrain from biting on any har
food for a few days until the tooth is stabilized. If you are uncer
tain whether immediate attention to a dental injury is needed, ca
your pediatrician or dentist.

Basic Principles of Effective Discipline

We are accustomed to thinking of discipline in the negativ
sense, as punishment or restriction. We shall, however, discus
discipline as a positive concept in which the motive of the paren
in each disciplinary act is a teaching one; consequently, each ac
provides a learning experience for your child.

I consider a disciplined child an infant who **trusts** h
environment and is secure in his love-attachment with his care
giving parents; a happy child who radiates both self-control an
self-esteem in his desire for parental approval, in an environmen
of mutual respect; a child who, upon graduating from each stag
of development, emerges a better person for the problems he ha

solved and the parental input he has received and, upon final graduation from his home education, he emerges a happy, feeling person, confident about the intellectual potential he has achieved, at peace with himself and society, with his actions directed by his conscience. In this chapter, we will discuss all of the above components of your child's development as a disciplined person.

Perhaps no subject in parenting has been written about more, but practiced less, than effective discipline. Why has the concept of discipline changed so much during the past forty years? Discipline is like nutrition. There are different requirements for different stages of development. Although children's nutritional requirements have always been basically the same, we have learned more about these requirements, and we can now feed our children more intelligently. The same applies to discipline. Children have always needed discipline but our knowledge of their requirements is continually changing and, I hope, improving. Also, the child of today is not the same as the child of twenty or forty years ago. Children today are being raised in an educated, deep-feeling, pressurized, relatively affluent and intensely exciting society. Children today have many more choices of direction in an increasingly complex society. Our principles and practices of discipline have, by necessity, become more complex, or perhaps more mature.

Is there really a basic difference between today's child and the children of several generations ago? A child is a child and why shouldn't the same principles of discipline hold true now that held true before? I strongly believe that certain principles of discipline, which we will later discuss, will always be necessary and will not, or should not, change. It is our approach to these principles that must change. For example, authoritarianism (dictatorship without explanation) was the basis of child discipline for centuries. "I am your parent, therefore I expect your unconditional submission to my teachings." This was similar to the law of the sea "I am not always right but I am always Captain."

In the 1950s, this doctrine of authoritarianism gave way to the doctrine of **permissiveness** or the complete lifting of all control systems. The child was his own authority. I suggest to you that permissiveness was, and ever shall be, a total disaster—to the child in particular, and to the society in general. Why? Because this doctrine violates a basic principle of human nature —that respect for authority is fundamental to harmonious living.

In the 1970s, we saw the pendulum of discipline settle in the center. Parents developed a philosophy of discipline which added fairness to the doctrine of authoritarianism and took irresponsibility from the doctrine of permissiveness. They arrived at an approach to discipline based upon the foundation of mutual respect for the feelings and rights of both the child and parents.

What really has changed in the past ten years? I feel that one basic principle underlies the changing philosophy of discipline—an increased awareness of the child as a feeling person. A prime example is the dramatic change in birthing environments over the past ten years. Prior to 1970, there was little concern for the feelings of a newborn baby during childbirth. The philosophy of "Respect for the Dignity of the Newborn," which has so improved our child-birthing practices, is also being carried into the homes and schools and is improving our child-rearing practices. Effective discipline can be achieved by following the basic theme of this book—understanding increases effectiveness. If you thoroughly understand certain basic principles of discipline, both from your viewpoint and that of your child, you will be comfortable about the practice of discipline, and will therefore be more effective.

Discipline Begins at Birth

Around the time of their baby's eighteen-month check-up, many parents will ask "Can we discuss something about discipline now? Isn't this the age I should start disciplining my child?" I often reply "You started disciplining your infant at the moment of birth." Your first "disciplinary action" was to develop the **concept of continuum parenting** described on page 13. The continuum child is at a low risk for eventual discipline problems. In the newborn period, bonding, rooming-in, and breastfeeding form the triad of trust, the foundation of effective discipline. This is followed by immersion mothering and involved fathering. Babies who are the product of these practices during the first three years simply feel right. They are secure in their feelings about themselves and their environment. Discipline is a feeling within the parents that prompts them to convey to the child what behavior is expected of him. It is a feeling within the child that prompts him to please his parents and to perceive which behavior makes him feel right. It is this mutual feeling that, I think, underlies the whole concept of effective discipline. If a mother and baby are really tuned into each other, the love between them naturally leads to a desire to please each other.

Immersion mothers have a way of conveying expected behavior to their child. They have more realistic expectations of their child's behavior and seem more perceptive about the feelings which prompt certain behavior. The child, in turn, feels sensitive to what behavior is expected of him and this leads to his desire to please his parents. This is a beautiful level of parenting to be on, and if you have reached it, you have laid the foundation for effective discipline.

Most parents equate discipline with obedience. To a certain extent this is true, but to some children obedience means submission of their will to that of their parents. Submission of one's will to another can be a fundamental human problem at any age. The continuum child seems to perceive obedience not as a submission, implying a weakness, but as a natural behavior which makes him feel right if he obeys and not feel right if he does not obey. Since these babies are used to feeling right, they want to continue feeling right throughout childhood and so are easier to discipline.

This concept of discipline is especially important in parenting the so-called difficult baby or challenging baby. A baby who is a handful in infancy has a greater chance of being a handful in later childhood, when he is often called a strong-willed child. These children are at high risk for discipline problems. Even in homes where a secure parent-child love attachment exists, some children are just more difficult to discipline than others, mainly because of their individual temperaments, not your parenting practices. This type of child is endowed with very strong needs. A challenging baby presents a real nurturing dilemma to parents, especially if he is your first baby. Parents consciously or unconsciously try to escape from a difficult baby to protect their own sanity, and I can understand this. Easy babies are simply more enjoyable to nurture. The more difficult baby, however, may actually be the one who needs more nurturing, the one who needs immersion rather than escape mothering. A difficult baby and non-nurturing parents is a combination which creates a high risk for eventual discipline problems. Adoption of the concept of continuum parenting lowers this risk.

Respect for Authority

One of the main concerns our "older generation" has about the younger generation is its apparent lack of respect for authority. To some extent this is a justified concern. Let's analyze some of the reasons why this has occurred and what we can do about it.

Respect for authority is fundamental to harmonious living. However, I do not feel that respect for their authority is an unconditional right of parents—it must be earned. Obedience is owed to the parents, not respect. Respect for parental authority implies love and trust, and because of this love, there is a natural desire to please. It is imperative that a child respect his parents because a child's respect for his parents provides the basis for his attitude toward the adult world in general, and any authority figures in particular. If you have a child who does not respect reasonable authority, then a real problem exists.

Our first method of earning the respect of our children is to practice the concept of continuum parenting. To a continuum baby, respect and obedience are the same. With increasing age and maturity comes a natural and increasing reluctance to accept unexplained authority, especially in our current educational atmosphere in which creativity is so strongly encouraged. This fact of life in today's maturing child places an increased responsibility upon parents to mature along with the child and to have enough respect for his feelings to provide explanations for your actions. If you have a secure love-attachment with your child and offer explanations which also consider his rights and feelings then you will earn the respect of your child. Children want and need limits. They also want to respect authority. The age of the "benevolent dictator" is over and as your child increases in wisdom and age, he deserves a larger voice in the family government.

Respect Your Child

Respect the **feelings** of your child. This concept will serve as the basis for understanding and dealing with undesirable behavior. The methods of discipline which I encourage in this book all consider the rights and feelings of your child as he matures through each stage of development. If a disciplinary action is necessary because of misbehavior, consider your child's feelings resulting from his misbehavior, and also the effect on his feelings and self-esteem resulting from your disciplinary action. Any form of effective discipline must consider the self-esteem of the child. You cannot control his feelings, only his actions. Point out the errors of his ways not the errors of his personality.

Encourage his expression of both positive and negative feelings and appreciate that if he cannot express his feelings with words, he will do so with undesirable deeds. These negative feelings may be like a blow-off valve for inner anxiety. If he cannot express negative feelings as a child, he may not be able to express them as an adult. The expression of negative feelings in your child (e.g. "I don't like you, Mommy") should not be construed as disrespect for authority, but rather as a positive sign that your child is comfortable enough in his relationship with you to be able to express negative feelings to you. This is especially true for the older child and adolescent, whom we will discuss later.

What happens to the child and the parents who did not lay the foundation during the first year of life? Entering the second year of life, the child naturally enters the stage of wanting independence, but he wants independence with guidance. He gets into trouble and he won't listen. The parent then resorts to methods and books and parent-effectiveness courses. The result of this approach is that discipline becomes a science, a list of actions and reactions, "If he does this, I should do that." The child is then made to fit into a system of discipline. Once this unfortunate stage has been reached, you are no longer guiding, and the child feels this. You are playing the difficult game of catch-up or, in other words, "My child is doing this. Now what do I do?" **It is very hard to guide from behind.** This is what I would like you, as caring parents, to avoid. Once discipline leaves the realm of intuition and feeling and becomes a science, then it is likely that your methods will be shallow and ineffective.

● **Trust Yourself!**

Parents, trust and believe in yourselves as effective teachers of your child. If your methods of discipline are based on a genuine love of your child, respect for his feelings and a realistic expectation of his behavior at each stage of development, then whatever methods you are using are the right methods for you and your child. It is beyond the scope of this book to discuss every disciplinary situation, so I have chosen to discuss certain basic principles for effective discipline. Once you understand these principles, you become your own best advisor.

Mothers are the most effective teachers because they have a built-in radar system for their child's body language. They intuitively know how to get into their child's mind and understand his feelings. Fathers often tend to take a more logical, less intuitive approach. I feel that, as long as both the mother's and father's methods of discipline are based on the aforementioned principles, they will tend to complement each other and their child will profit.

Disciplining your child also involves a certain amount of

parental self-discipline. As your expectations of him increase, so his expectations of you increase, and there will be a need to alter your methods as he passes through each developmental stage. Discipline problems usually appear at the transition between developmental stages when your child passes from the usual balance into imbalance, so characteristic of graduating from one stage to another. A thorough understanding of what your child is going through at a given stage, and effective discipline during that stage, results in the prevention of problems that may occur in the subsequent stage.

How to Encourage Desirable Behavior

Misbehavior is a relative term, similar to the "evil is in the eye of the beholder" principle. A certain act may be considered misbehavior according to your interpretation of "correct" behavior. In order to fully understand the term "misbehavior," you need to understand the wide variation in behavior of children at different stages of development, how certain acts are necessary for your child's adjustment to a particular stage and the inner forces which propel him from one stage of development to the next. In addition to a general knowledge of child behavior, you should acquire a thorough knowledge of your child's particular behavior pattern. What are his likes and dislikes? What are his strong points and weaknesses? What are his personality traits which you particularly like? Which are those that you feel need some modification for his own good, not necessarily to conform with your desire? Every stage of a child's development has both desirable and undesirable features because of the natural conflicts so characteristic of each child at each stage of development. Your child's development and temperament is unique, so do not always compare him to his peers or insist that he always conform to your expectations.

Encouraging desirable behavior is a preventive medicine for discipline problems. The following list suggests ways to encourage desirable behavior in your child:

1. The older infant and younger child progress from impulsive trial and error behavior to more calculated, reasoning behavior. The latter ensures physical and emotional satisfaction and avoids pain and anxiety. Your child has an intense need to belong. Early in life, your child develops the capacity to manipulate his adult environment. Between the ages of four and six years, he develops a concept of how he may reach the status of belonging and of what roles he may play in the family. It is this concept that determines his behavior.

A common piece of advice frequently offered is "Simply ignore it. He'll grow out of it. It is just a stage." In order to solve the problem of what behavior should be attended to and what behavior you should ignore in your child, ask yourself the following questions: Is his behavior hurting himself or hurting others? Is he damaging property? Is he getting on your nerves or those of others to the extent that the rights which adults also have are being violated? These types of behavior in your child do need attending to and correcting. On the other hand, if your child's behavior is simply a nuisance to you and does not harm him or others, then perhaps you should grin and bear it.

2. Young children are constantly bombarding us with "Why this?" and "Why that?" Perhaps we may take a tip from them and also ask "Why." Why does a child misbehave? Is he trying to simply get attention? Is he engaging in a kind of power struggle? Is he trying to fit into a group and has not found his role? Is he tired, bored, hungry or sick? Often if we approach our child's behavior with "Why is he doing this?" rather than "What is he doing?" it will help us understand the feelings behind his behavior and enable us to take effective steps to channel it.

3. If you sense the onset of a certain undesirable behavior the technique of distraction often works. Guide him into a more acceptable kind of activity or act before you are forced to react.

4. Another positive way to encourage desirable behavior is to create a **child-considered environment**. This is much easier and much healthier than issuing constant "no-no's." Respect your child's curiosity and consider his size-related needs. By removing potentially harmful objects and installing child-size furniture, you will help your child to feel that this is his home too.

5. Be tolerant in situations in which your child is pushed beyond his capabilities. For example, during long car rides it is unrealistic to expect ideal behavior in young children. It is also unrealistic to expect a young toddler to walk down the aisle in a supermarket and not touch anything.

6. Next, take a firm stand. Children are uncomfortable with uncertainty. Make sure your child has a clear idea about what is expected of him. For example, "We are going to Grandma's and I expect you to be careful around her furniture." Notice the phrase "I expect you." This conveys to your child that you really expect good behavior. If you say "Don't touch Grandma's things" he will feel that you expect him to misbehave and he probably will.

7. Use the principle of **positive reinforcement**. Reward your child for good behavior. If your child likes what he gains as a result of good behavior he will be inclined to repeat this behavior. Let's discuss some ways to encourage cooperation in your child. Appreciate that your child sincerely wants to please. He craves your approval and dislikes the inner anxieties produced by continued undesirable behavior. Because your child is basically motivated toward desirable behavior, it is up to the parents to pick up on this motivation and "Catch him in the act of being good." Praise him and make him feel important, no matter how insignificant his accomplishments may seem. Use affirmative words in your general vocabulary.

Love rewards are suitable for the younger child. These consist of hugs and praises, and a very pleasant tone of voice when a desirable behavior is encountered. A **thing reward** is suitable for the older child when the concept of gift-giving can be fully appreciated by him. Rewards should be given immediately after the desired behavior, given entirely on your own terms, not always anticipated or expected by your child, and often reserved for especially desirable behavior. You must be careful of what I call the "dog biscuit principle." Your objective is not (as in animal training) to give a biscuit every time the requested act is performed because you may find that he does not perform the act unless he gets the biscuit. If this occurs, it means he has lost the internal motivation for effective discipline. Discipline is teaching not training. The basic concept you wish your children to learn from the reward system is simply that their life in general can be much smoother and much happier if their behavior is desirable. It is this concept that will carry through into their social, educational and employment life.

Two additional concepts are extremely important in encouraging desirable behavior, especially in the older child. One is the concept of the **privilege responsibility ratio.** Older children, growing up in an affluent society, receive increasing privileges at increasing ages. Unless we parallel these increasing privileges with increasing responsibilities, we are depriving our youth of a realistic preparation for the adult world. It is what they have from within that dictates their happiness as adults, and it is the sense of responsibility they will thank you for later, not affluent privileges.

The other is the concept of example, both from parents and the usual hero figures with whom children identify. The picture of self-discipline you convey can be one of the most profound ways of really getting through to your older child and adolescent. The old saying "Do as I say and not as I do" really does not hit home with any child.

**Alternatives to
Punishment**

● **Understand Your Child's Position**

Remember that when dealing with your child's undesirable behavior you should also consider his feelings. Nothing frustrates a child more than feeling his parents don't understand his position. An effective way to appreciate your child's feelings during any disciplinary action is called **the feedback technique.** This technique requires carefully listening to what your child is saying or attempting to say, formulating in your own mind what your child is trying to express, and feeding back to him the feelings that he has just expressed to you. This technique is even beneficial at the toddler stage. The toddler may not be able to express his feelings verbally but he is able to understand your verbal expression of his feelings. For example, "You are angry and that is why you broke the toy. I understand." This technique is equally effective with the older child and adolescent who do not like to listen to your opinions of their behavior until they feel that you truly understand how they feel.

The clock is one of the greatest obstacles to child-rearing. How often have you heard "Come along, Johnny. It's time to go." Johnny is reluctant to obey. He is really involved in his own activity and is being asked to give it up willingly, to obey a clock which has no meaning to him. As an alternative, consider whether the other priority which the clock says you must meet is really so important that it must take priority over your child's activity. If it really does, then announce your intention to leave ahead of time so your child can prepare emotionally. For example tell him "three more games" or "in five more minutes."

● **Time-Out Method**

This method often proves successful for what I call the three non-negotiable behaviors of your child—endangering himself or hurting another, willfully damaging property or becoming an unacceptable nuisance. For example, two of your children are fighting and the fighting seems to be getting out of control. You step in and firmly state, "Go to your rooms immediately and think about what you are doing to each other. You may come out when you can control your behavior." You have achieved your desired goal in disrupting the fight and you have used your action not as a punishment but as a right of a parent to stop an activity potentially harmful to them. You did not say, "Stop the fighting" but rather simply stated emphatically that they go to their rooms. You have not acted like a judge but rather as a referee in a game that was not being played by the rules. You have also given them time to reflect upon their behavior and to, you hope, draw their own conclusions about the wisdom of fighting in general and with their siblings in particular. Also, you have not placed limit on when they can return from their rooms but rather have given them a choice to return when their behavior is under control. In this way everybody wins and everybody learns.

Another example, using the age-old problem of fighting over toys, uses a timer to employ the time-out method. When the children are having trouble sharing, you announce that for five or ten minutes Johnny gets the toy. When the bell rings it's time for Johnny to give it to Tommy to have for the same amount of time (the older the children, the longer you can ask them to wait). When the timer goes off again, it's back to Johnny who, by now probably doesn't want it anymore. In one family who uses this timer idea, the older sibling runs to her mother saying "Mom set the timer. Suzy won't share."

An extension of the time-out method involves **physical restraint.** It is used in emergency situations when you have no time to employ psychology. You have to act immediately because the child is out of control. For example, when a child is about to inflict bodily injury on himself or another, you may have to grab him firmly and hold him securely while you are explaining "You are angry and have lost control of yourself and I have to hold you until you feel better because I love you and do not want you to hurt yourself . . ." When his body relaxes and he has regained some control, continue with the time-out method to give him time to reflect on the feelings that caused him to lose control and, perhaps, how badly he felt after he lost control. You have exercised your authority and achieved your desired end of stopping his undesirable behavior, but you have done so in manner that becomes a learning experience for your child and increases his respect for you as an effective and caring authority figure.

● **Logical Consequences**

The principle of logical consequences is a disciplinary technique which simply means that a person in authority makes a request or rule only after it is discussed with the child. The consequences of disobeying are clearly stated to the child. If he chooses to disobey, he automatically also chooses the consequences. This principle is better explained by using an example from my family in which we utilized the three following techniques of discipline for the older children: **the family council, negotiating and mutual problem-solving, and logical consequences.**

Our family problem was getting our four children ready

for school in the morning, without an exhausting hassle in time for the car pool driver. First, a family council was called and the mutual problems of the adults and children were stated. The children were asked why they had difficulty finishing their breakfast in time for the car pool and were asked to come up with suggestions about how to make the morning rush hour less hectic for everyone including themselves. Mother stated that her problem was feeding four late and disorganized children in the morning and she too offered suggestions. The solutions offered were that lunches were to be partially prepared and clothes were to be laid out the evening before. Mother would have breakfast ready at a certain time and the dishes were to be cleared off the table also by a certain time. Anyone who was late for breakfast and was not ready when the car pool driver arrived simply took a very long walk to school. This point was not negotiable. Everyone agreed this was a fair solution to the problem and, after a few long walks to school, there was a much smoother morning rush hour around our house.

The logical consequences approach differs from traditional punishment in several ways. First, this is real life. Any society must have rules of social order as well as consequences for breaking these rules. Sports utilize logical consequences. For example, a football team plays according to the rules to which all players agree beforehand.

The rules are made in the interest of safety and enjoyment and if a rule is broken, the logical consequence of a penalty is accepted. A child should have a choice in his behavior too. If he chooses misbehavior, he logically chooses the consequences but he made this decision himself and, therefore, it has effective teaching value. He also has to cope with the undesirable feelings which result from choosing the undesirable consequence. The ability to cope with these feelings can also be a learning experience. This method results in your child appreciating one of the basic points about life which you are striving to teach through "discipline": Life is smoothier and happier when behavior is desirable.

The principles of the family council, mutual problem-solving and negotiating, and logical consequences, all illustrated in the above example, are based upon two very important requirements for effective discipline of the older child and adolescent: rapport and mutual respect for the rights of parents and children. I have found it very helpful to frequently ask myself how good my rapport is with each of my children, and to search for little signs that will give clues to the strong and weak point of our communication. These clues may come in simple ways like the way your child looks at you, his tone of voice when h speaks with you, his way of asking you for help and his ability to relax and have fun with you.

Punishment as a Discipline Technique

What about the child who still defies your authority, even thoug you have considered his feelings and attempted explanations? I this case, punishment, the old stand-by of disciplinary tech niques, may be employed. Let's analyze potential effects of th technique of punishment on your child's overall discipline There are three goals of a disciplinary action:

1. To promote desirable behavior.

2. To stop undesirable behavior.

3. To leave a learning experience within your child.

Punishment alone fulfills only one of these goals—i stops misbehavior and is usually very effective for the moment But the power of punishment eventually breaks down for the fol lowing reasons: punishment alone is discipline from without; i temporarily curbs an undesirable act but usually provides no teaching and does not encourage genuine motivation from within. At best you will achieve an internal motivation similar to the effect of the electric fence on cattle. They learn to keep away from the fence in order to avoid the punishment of the shock Punishment stops action but may ignore the feelings which prompted these actions. To certain children who are very inse cure in their environment and about their love relationship with their parents, the negative attention of punishment may be bette than no attention at all. Continued punishment may actually motivate the child to avoid the punisher, and your parent-child relationship may be severely compromised. Punishment also loses its effectiveness as a child grows older. This is understand able for as a child matures in age, his concept of self also matures, and being forced to submit to the will of another natu rally becomes more humiliating.

As a practical father of four, I can say that there certainly are times when punishment is necessary but, as my wife and learned more about discipline with each successive child, we found ourselves using the technique of punishment less and less Firm punishment is justified when you have tried all the othe techniques and your child is in danger of hurting himself o another, of damaging property, or if he defies reasonable paren tal authority and is old enough to realize he is doing so.

If you use punishment as a discipline technique, use it wisely and fairly. It should be given at the time of misbehavior. A child should not be told "Wait until your father gets home and then you'll get it." The punishment should be short-lived, followed immediately by an explanation of why he is being punished and accompanied by some act of love on your part. Remember your goals are to teach, to prevent a repetition of undesirable behavior and to increase respect for you as an authority figure. Withdrawal of privileges (e.g. television) is probably the most common punishment. As easy as this electronic pacifier is to switch on to keep children quiet, it is just as easy to switch off as punishment. The TV is a ready weapon for discipline, but usually there is no relation to the misbehavior so it is not really an effective punishment. An example of an effective punishment which both teaches and fits the misbehavior is the following: Your three-year-old child has repeatedly been told not to ride his tricycle out into the street and the reason has been clearly presented to him. You may add, "I expect you to stay in the driveway and if you do not, the tricycle will be put away in the garage." You have conveyed to your child what behavior is expected of him, and why, and the punishment (which relates to the misbehavior) if he chooses to disobey.

There is one privilege that should never be withdrawn as punishment and that is your child's allowance. Allowances are given as a teaching aid to develop a sense of economic responsibility and its withdrawal as a punishment defeats the purpose for which it was given. Using money as a lever could develop a very undesirable pattern of behavior for your child to model. Older children may be allowed to participate in determining an appropriate punishment for them (see **Logical Consequences**, page 246). In this way, you exert parental authority fairly by respecting their self-esteem and you, in turn, will gain their respect as a fair but firm authority figure.

If you have particularly strong-willed children it is often tempting to over-use punishment. These children are often difficult babies, even in early infancy, and mothers will often mention, "He has always been a handful." Around two years of age, he receives the designation of "a strong-willed child." This type of child is endowed with very strong needs and has an intense curiosity which must be satisfied at all costs. His mind is already made up and he does not allow himself to be confused with facts. If it is any consolation, these babies are often of above-average intelligence and often have sense enough not to bite the hand that feeds them, especially if they sincerely feel that the hand love them. These little entrepreneurs of childhood may be the forerun ners of very productive adults, providing their parents use a their ingenuity to arrive at a method of discipline which respect the intense will of the child and also allows them to keep thei cool while doing so. Strong-willed children are often above average children who need above-average parenting.

Since a strong-willed child may defy most of the usu principles of discipline, here are a few guidelines to help you b comfortable with your own methods:

1. Acceptance of certain undesirable traits in another person is necessary prerequisite for any harmonious relationship betwee two people. Parenting a strong-willed child implies a strong leve of acceptance.

2. Develop a plan of your own that you are comfortable with. you find yourself saying "This isn't me and the plan is not work ing," then drop it. Any method that loves, teaches and works i the right method for you.

3. Convey your love often and sincerely.

4. Avoid the previously mentioned dilemma of escape mother ing, page 239.

5. Above all, compromise. His self-esteem needs protecting Chalk up the small things and let him win the battles of mino significance. Save your energy and disciplinary ingenuity for hi major behavioral disturbances.

6. Avoid confrontation of wills. Think ahead and try not to plac yourself in a position where you are butting two stubborn head together; neither can win.

7. Be firm. A strong-willed child is not comfortable with wishy washy parents. Be sure he has a clear understanding of wha behavior is expected of him.

What is the effect of continual punishment? A chil whose behavior is motivated by fear of punishment is often eas ily, but deceptively, controlled. His behavior is submissive an compliant but may lack spontaneity and self-confidence. He ma be the picture of a docile child but inwardly he is anxious. Thi child sooner or later rebels and when parental controls are lifted he is left floundering in a highly complex world without his ow controls.

Spanking

To spank or not to spank? That is the question which for year has produced emotional and controversial books, magazine arti cles and television programs. It has even become a politica question. Some day there may be a law against spanking. There is less spanking now than there was ten years ago simply because of the great respect today's parents have for the dignity of the feelings of the child. If you are waiting for a dictum "Spank" or "Don't spank," you are reading the wrong book. Absolute do's and don'ts simply do not, or at least should not, exist in "disciplinology." The only dogmatic statement I will offer to you is that I believe it is an injustice to do bodily harm to a child. A slap on the bottom may be justified in a particular child in a particular circumstance (e.g. defying reasonable authority) and by a particular parent. The decision about the wisdom of such actions belongs to the discretion of the parent not to a third party disciplinarian far removed from the reality of your family.

Spanking is, however, at the bottom of the list of effective discipline techniques. It is a deterrent, not a teacher. Spanking as a regular means of behavior control is doomed to failure. You can temporarily control the child's behavior but you cannot control his feelings and this is where spanking fails. Spanking humiliates the dignity of the child, may alienate the "spanker" and the "spankee," encourages retaliation and plants the seed of violence in the child. Spanking contributes very little to the formation of his conscience. When children feel they have paid for a crime through corporal punishment, they no longer feel guilty about their actions. We will discuss later how properly channelled guilt feelings are necessary for building an effective conscience. (See page 252 .)

If you spank, spank wisely, spank seldom, and never spank in anger. Don't be afraid to express and explain your negative feelings to your child. Children must learn that adults have tempers too and he should know the feelings which prompted your spanking. Your explanation of your feelings conveys that you respect his self-esteem enough to offer him an explanation. "Reflex spanking" may be called for in certain life-threatening situations (e.g. running across the street) in order to reinforce a certain prohibition. If you have a secure love attachment with your child, spanking will probably not damage it, but it certainly won't contribute to it either.

Excessive spanking or "beating" is a major cause of child abuse in the next generation. Children whose behavior was controlled by spanking have a tendency to use this discipline technique on their children. It is awesome that so many adults can remember so vividly their spankings as a child. What a misfortune to the dignity of childhood and parenthood when otherwise beautiful childhood memories are colored by the vivid recollection of spankings. If you find yourself spanking more and harder, then there is a fundamental breakdown in your parent-child relationship. You are setting the stage for child abuse, and professional guidance should be obtained.

For those who feel that "to spare the rod is to spoil the child," let me say a word about this rod. In his book, **How To Really Love Your Child**, Dr. Ross Campbell points out that the "biblical rod" was really a shepherd's staff which was used to firmly, but kindly, guide the sheep. Instead of spanking, let me suggest that loving guidance be the rod of today's discipline.

The Formation of a Conscience

Many of the methods of encouraging desirable behavior previously discussed were directed at external control methods. These outside influences are not enough and are primarily used for the younger child. Our ultimate goal is to encourage desirable behavior in your child from within. His own inner voice should direct his behavior.

We may define conscience as the inner voice of reason which dictates a child's behavior. He may not always listen to his conscience but it is always there. The first concept you should appreciate is that an effective conscience is learned; it is not inborn in any child. Because it is learned, it follows that your parental teaching, or discipline, in the formative childhood years will have a profound effect on your child's conscience. Encouraging desirable behavior from within has lasting effects. By tracing a hypothetical case from birth to adolescence, let's now discuss what you as parents can do to contribute to the formation of an effective conscience in your child.

During the first eighteen months, you and your infant cement a secure love-attachment. From eighteen months to two and a half years, his intense curiosity to explore is combined with an insecurity about his own capabilities. This prompts you to set **desired limits,** desired by both your infant and you. You organize a child-considered environment which takes into account his inner feelings and his intense need to explore, but which also protects him and his environment from harm. "No" and "Don't touch," having been repeated often enough, finally start to sink in, mostly by reflex, but also with some reasoning. Your child is secure in the limits you have set because he is secure in his love relationship with you.

With increasing language comes increasing discipline. There is a gradual decrease in your use of negatives. **Authority**

with explanation begins, which achieves the two-fold purpose of preventing undesirable behavior and also initiates the process of forming a conscience. Your child is still secure in his respect for your authority because he is first secure in his love for you.

When your child is somewhere between four and six years of age, your previous methods of effective discipline, together with your methods of positive reinforcement of his desirable behavior and negative reinforcement of undesirable behavior have, you hope, developed into the very basic concept in his mind that "My life is much smoother and therefore I am much happier when my behavior is desirable." The roots of his conscience have been laid and nurtured and the fruits begin to appear between ages four and six. He now has a sort of inner policeman which begins to direct behavior from within.

When your child begins school, he spends the major part of his day away from you, but because of the roots you planted, he subconsciously "takes his parents with him." He is now the prime dictator of his behavior but the imprint you have made upon him during his formative years now becomes part of him. There is continued parental influence as well as influences from such sources as teachers, peers and the church. All these influences contribute to the continued development of his conscience from school age to adulthood. A secure love-attachment with his parents and respect for parental authority is necessary during the formative years. They lay the foundation for a continued love-attachment and respect for authority during his school years. If he does not respect parental authority, he will have difficulty respecting any authority.

During the years from age six to age twelve, another basic human feeling comes into play which further contributes to your child's developing conscience—the feeling of guilt. Many of the teachings on child psychology and child discipline state that guilt feelings in a child are a "no-no," and that we should do everything in our power to avoid making a child feel guilty. I do not share these opinions. I feel that experiencing immediate guilt feelings (caused by misbehavior) is a necessary part of the development of both self-control and conscience. It also serves as an added constraint on impulsive behavior and aids the development of an effective conscience in later childhood and adulthood. Feelings of guilt for committing morally wrong acts are healthy, especially in the older child and adolescent.

The familiar statement "Criticize the act, not the child" is certainly true but it has little value in teaching responsibility. For example, if a child spills his milk you don't say, "You bad boy . . ." instead you say, "You spilled your milk because you were not being careful. Please get a towel and wipe it up." It is devastating to a child to hear a parent yell in a loud, angry voice and to see a contorted, angry expression on a face that is expected to be familiar and trustworthy. The child shrivels up inside trying to block it out and hide, so any possible disciplinary effects are lost. This also produces a harmful, inflated guilt that is a very heavy burden indeed for a child (or anyone). If this happens, you must ask forgiveness.

Feeling a sense of responsibility for an action is fundamental to the development of an effective conscience. Also, if a child feels badly, then this feeling is a learning experience for him. He does not want or like this feeling, and it is his dislike of this feeling which contributes toward avoiding repetition of this act. A child really wants to **feel right.** Experiencing negative feelings and developing the ability to cope with them is a positive learning experience which your child should be allowed to have. Guilt becomes unhealthy if it is allowed to become a lasting attitude in the child. I do believe that terms like bad boy serve no useful disciplinary purpose and are destructive to self-esteem. It is the inability to cope with negative feelings that causes a personality problem, not the negative feelings themselves.

When your child reaches adolescence, he may challenge both the value systems which have been taught to him, as well as those dictated by his own conscience. Consider this normal, healthy adolescent behavior. I usually consider this the finishing touch to the development of a person's conscience prior to reaching adulthood. As your child matures through childhood to adolescence and adulthood, your methods of discipline must also mature. Discipline based upon mutual respect is most necessary at this age. **Parental example** contributes more to adolescent discipline than heavy lecturing. Challenging traditional values and the apparent temporary disruption of conscience-oriented behavior is normal for adolescents, even for those who have a strong love attachment to their parents and who feel respect for parental authority. They eventually return to their original value systems which were laid down in the pre-adolescent years, and they emerge from the turbulent adolescent years disciplined and conscience-directed adults, ready to impart a similar type of discipline to their own children.

Now, let's leave the continuum of discipline and resume our voyage through child development.

Two to Three Years

Characteristics of this Stage

This stage is characterized by three interesting features, an awareness of self, mastery of language and the beginning of social peer relationships. A two-year-old is indeed a beautiful person, not at all characteristic of the label Terrible Two's.

The facility for expressive language which begins to develop in the previous stage mushrooms in the two-year-old. It is this improving language skill that enables the child to become a truly social person. Jargon gradually gives way to complete, intelligible sentences. His ability to speak in increasingly complex sentences enables him to hold the attention of adult audiences and his peers. To be able to carry on a meaningful dialogue with your own child is a richly rewarding experience.

The facility for expressive language enables the two-year-old to verbalize his feelings and demands. He shows less tendency to act out his anxieties by deeds because he is able to do so by words. Language further secures the ability to manipulate his adult environment and adds "bigness" to his concept of self. If the previous stage of limit-setting and outside control has been successful, the two-year-old begins to show some inner control of his own. He becomes more certain of his limits because he has had a year to sort them out. Although stubbornness occasionally rears its head, there is generally less negativism on both sides. He becomes less clinging and obstinate and you become less restraining. The two-year-old has conquered his home environment. He has explored every nook and cranny of his room and has conducted his independent research on every object within his broadening reach. As he feels more comfortable in his home environment and secure in the control of his own body, his behavior becomes less impulsive and he becomes more of a thinker. He considers alternatives before acting. He becomes increasingly aware of cause and effect relationships. His emerging mental world is very egocentric. He sees things entirely from his own point of view and how he can use the outside world to suit his own needs.

Two-year-olds are very affectionate. This is really a hugs and kisses stage. I would have to regard the show of affection as one of the highlights of this age. It is a beautiful "father feeling" to be met at the door by a little child with open arms who demands "Pick me up."

Creativity emerges during this stage. The skills of

stacking, scribbling, finger-painting and working with clay ar
refined. Your little architect takes great pride in his creativ
accomplishments and is eager to show them to you. Talk abou
his accomplishments and discuss the details of his creations. Th
two-year-old becomes an increasingly willing listener, especiall
regarding his own creations. One of his favorite activities i
doing things with you. As you do something together, talk abou
what you are doing.

Children at this age show an innate appreciation fo
order. Parents should respect this by providing appropriat
shelves and space for the child's belongings. A young child i
gradually trying to sort out all the clutter in the busy worl
around him. An orderly play room with his own eye level shelve
helps to unclutter his world. (See **Order**, page 229.)

In addition to order, two- to three-year-olds enjoy routine
and customs. They are most receptive to learning manners an
courtesy.

A child who is secure in his love attachment with his par
ents and is comfortable both in his exploratory mastery of hi
home environment and in his expressive language, is a child wh
is secure enough to seek relationships with his peers. Remem
bering our principle that undesirable behavior often appears a
the beginning of a new developmental milestone, you may notic
certain extremes of behavior, from shyness and withdrawal t
overt aggression, as he attempts to handle the anxieties of tryin
to fit in comfortably with his peer group. Parental guidance an
support and the "law of the jungle" will get him over this hur
dle. Usually by three years of age, your child will have gon
through enough gives and takes to get his social act together. Hi
developing memory allows him to file away his learning experi
ences for future reference. A combination of language, memory
introspective thought and anxieties results in the fears and fanta
sies so common at this age. A child often learns to handle hi
fears through fantasies and this magical thinking should b
respected.

**Toilet
Teaching—A
Child-Led
Approach**

During the past ten years, the changes in toilet training practice
reflect the general changes in child-rearing practices which w
have previously discussed. In this section let's discuss toile
training using a child-considered approach based primarily upo
a respect for the bodily functions of your child. These function
develop according to your child's developmental timetable
Since the timing for toilet training is different for every child, th

following guidelines are meant only as a basis for you to construct your program of toilet training, according to your child's temperament and abilities.

● **Parents' Attitude**

The first step is to ask yourself what your attitude is toward toilet training your child. Do you regard this feat as your accomplishment? Do you view toilet training as a duty of good mothering, to be mastered by a magical age which is set by your social group or outside pressures? If you have these feelings, let me suggest an alternative approach. Let's consider toilet training as a developmental skill which your child will learn when he is ready. Your guidance begins when he is ready and continues at a pace directed by him. The terms "toilet teaching" and "toilet learning" imply that there is less pressure from without and more respect for his feelings from within.

As opposed to the child-considered approach, the pressurized early toilet training approach is potentially harmful to your child. In countries where the practice of early and parent-led toilet training is followed, children are indeed "trained" earlier but relapses are more frequent and later problems of bed-wetting and constipation are more common. Therefore, the question is not "When should I begin toilet training?" but rather "When is my child ready for toilet learning?"

● **When Is He Ready?**

Watch for your toddler's signals that he is ready. Around eighteen months (fifteen months to two years) your infant may become aware that excrement is coming out of his body. He becomes increasingly aware of his genitalia, and his neuromuscular sensations are mature enough that he has begun sensing he "is going," "has gone" or "is about to go."

Basically, he is ready when he is interested. Watch for such signs of interest as investigating his or her body equipment, investigating the toilet as if thinking "What is it for?", watching Mommy and Daddy and brothers and sisters, making some imitative gestures such as squatting, and showing Mommy and Daddy what he has made. When these signs appear, he is ready and probably also willing. At this stage of development, toddlers normally exhibit two strong desires: **imitation** and **identity searching**. These "just like Mommy and Daddy" and "all by myself" urges can be capitalized upon to lead to a successful infant-led toilet learning. He must be in a state receptive to learning. Toddlers also normally have periods of extreme stubbornness or negativity in which they may resist any attempt to learn a

new skill, and this temporary phase should be respected. This
one of the reasons why it is difficult to toilet teach a toddler whe
a new sibling arrives, and also why regressions in a previous
taught two-year-old should be expected with the arrival of a ne
baby. If you catch your child in an imitative, interested a
receptive mood, he should be a willing pupil.

● His Own Place to Go

The next step is to give him his own place to go. His own pot
chair or plastic toilet is much better than expecting him to subm
himself to the adult toilet. How comfortable and willing wou
you be to perform on a toilet five times the size of your prese
one? Respect his size by giving him an appropriate facility. Pla
his potty next to yours to capitalize on his desire to imitate a
wait until he voluntarily approaches his chair and sits on it. H
may do so with his clothing on or make some overtures to be di
robed, also "just like Mommy." The main point is to beg
teaching by imitation. Watching Mommy and Daddy and brot
ers and sisters will motivate your infant to "do it, all k
myself." Once this internal motivation is apparent, he should l
receptive to a little guidance toward refining his techniques.

● What to Call It

Teach him words for his actions. As a general principle the ab
ity to verbalize actions makes developing any skill less stressf
and more successful. This is a good opportunity to develop
realistic approach to genitalia and bladder and bowel function
It is amazing how many different words are used for peni
vagina, urination and defecation. Call it like it is. Otherwise yo
infant may pick up vibrations that you are uneasy about the
parts of the anatomy. Penis, vagina or vulva are usual
pronounceable or at least understandable at this age. Urinatic
and defecation are beyond him. It is better to use simple on
syllable words which contain a lot of vowels such as go pee or g
potty. When he is old enough to understand urinate and bow
movement, then use these terms. By having words to expre
actions, he can begin to associate an urge to pee, how to pee a
a place to pee. Verbalizing makes toilet learning easier. This
another reason for delaying toilet teaching until your child h
reasonable receptive and expressive verbal ability.

● Be Attuned to His Signals

After he has learned how to go, where to go and what to call
the next step is to recognize his signals for when he is about
go. Mothers are usually so attuned to their infant's mannerisn
that they know when his production is on its way. Signs such

grunting, squatting, a change in facial expressions, or a sudden lull in activity usually signal that he is ready to have a bowel movement. When you recognize that he is about to go, give him a helpful "Go potty." You should go to where his potty chair is and encourage him to follow. This is more effective than carrying him to his toilet and reinforces the "all by myself" principle. Sooner or later, the repetition of this verbal suggestion from you will sink in and he will associate the urge to go, with the "go potty" and do it all by himself.

If your child seems to have a bowel movement around the same time each day, you may suggest to him that he sit on his potty around this set time. There is a physiological aid for bowel training called the **gastrocolic reflex**. When the stomach is full, the colon is stimulated to empty. This is why some infants may be taught to have a bowel movement right after breakfast each morning. This after-breakfast bowel movement is very effective in preventing constipation in the infant and especially in the older child. Remember, many children normally have a bowel movement every two or three days. If your child is obviously resistant to the bowel scheduling, don't insist. A child can probably produce urine any time he wishes but a bowel movement can only be produced when the stool is ready to be evacuated and signals for evacuation are present.

Do not teach your child to "hold on to" his urine. Teach him to quickly respond to his urge to go. Holding on to urine too long may increase the chance of urinary tract infections, especially in girls (See **Urinary Tract Infections**, page 382 .)

● **"Big Boy Pants"**

After daytime dryness has been successful for a few months he may graduate to **training pants**, which further encourages "all by myself." Expect a few accidents when his signals get crossed. This is a normal phase in learning a new skill. Your attitude towards these accidents is very important as an infant can pick up on a mother's anxieties about bowel and bladder functions. He may react to your negative attitudes about the problems of constipation, bedwetting and actually use his toileting or lack of it as a weapon against you. Older children are often simply so preoccupied with the activity of play that they miss their bladder or bowel signals. A suggestion which may accelerate bladder and bowel awareness is to let your child go without diapers or pants when it is practical.

Praise his successes and minimize his failures. There is no place for punishment in toilet teaching. You wouldn't repri-

mand an infant for tripping while he was learning to walk. Litt
boys take great delight in urinating standing up "just li
Daddy" and equal delight in spraying the environs of the toil
with his newly found ability. Teach him to wipe up his litt
messes. This is not a punishment but rather encourages him
take responsibility for his actions. A little guidance in targ
practice may be in order for boys. Later in the toilet teachir
stage when your infant will want to "wipe myself," instruct li
tle girls to wipe from the vagina to the rectum to lessen the poss
bility of urinary tract infections from the bacteria in their stool

In my experience, infant-led toilet teaching usual
begins between eighteen months and two years and is successf
by the age of two and a half or three years. Girls are more readi
trained and trained earlier than boys by a few months. The fir
child usually achieves complete control slightly later than subs
quent children. If the child-considered approach is used, yc
may find bowel and bladder control comes simultaneously. Th
varies among children, however, and it is unimportant whic
comes first.

Bedwetting

Let us approach bedwetting not as a medical problem or illnes
but as a family nuisance, secondary to a developmental delay
the maturity of one of your child's bodily functions such as bla
der control.

● **At What Age Should You Be Concerned About
Bedwetting?**

There is widespread variation in the age at which children rema
dry throughout the night. By age three years, the majority
children are dry at night and by age six years, 85 per cent to 9
per cent of children enjoy nighttime dryness. Pediatricians us
ally consider bedwetting after the age of six years as cause f
concern, an age at which 8 per cent of girls and 10 per cent to
per cent of boys still wet their beds. This decreases to 1 per ce
or 2 per cent at age fifteen years. There is no magic age at whic
you should be concerned that your child is still wetting his bed.
depends primarily upon when your child is concerned. Althoug
bedwetting may be considered as simply a developmental dela
in some children, it should not always be ignored. Most childr
sincerely want to learn how to control their bodily functions a
want some guidance from their parents and physician
achieving bladder control.

● **How Your Child Achieves Bladder Control**

In early infancy, bladder emptying occurs mostly by a refl

which we will term the **bladder emptying reflex**. This means that when the bladder reaches a certain fullness and the bladder muscle has stretched to a certain point, these muscles automatically contract to empty the bladder. Sometime between eighteen months and two and a half years most children have an awareness of bladder fullness, the first step in bladder control. Next, the child becomes aware that he can consciously inhibit the bladder emptying reflex and hold on to his urine. As a result of his efforts, his functional bladder capacity increases. The bladder emptying reflex gradually weakens with increasing age and conscious inhibition, and daytime bladder control is achieved. Nighttime control occurs when the bladder capacity increases and the bladder emptying reflex becomes so weak that it is overcome by unconscious inhibition of urination. Delay in bladder control can occur if there is a delay in awareness of bladder fullness, a small functional capacity or a prolonged activity of the bladder emptying reflex. These components of "bladder maturity" occur at different ages in different children.

• Why Does Your Child Wet His Bed?

In support of the theory that bedwetting is a developmental delay in maturity, consider the following. Many of a child's developmental milestones (for example, when he begins puberty) are hereditary and there is often a hereditary connection in bedwetting. If both parents were bedwetters, the child has a 70 per cent chance of being a bedwetter. If only one parent was a bedwetter, the child will have a 40 per cent chance of following his parent's nocturnal habit.

Parents will often attribute their children's bedwetting to deep sleep. While this may be true of some children, EEG (electroencephalogram) studies on bedwetters have not confirmed that these children are generally deep sleepers. In some children bedwetting is actually considered to be a **sleep disorder**— the loss of bladder control occurs as a child passes from one sleep stage to another.

Children who wet their bed sometimes have functionally smaller bladders and void more frequently. This, in addition to the hereditary basis and the fact that, given time, the majority of children achieve bladder control, all suggest that a delay in bladder control (bedwetting) is simply a developmental lag in acquiring mastery of a bodily skill. There are late walkers, late talkers, and late dry-nighters. This group of children comprise the majority of bedwetters and will be helped more by understanding and guidance than by medical treatment.

• Psychological Causes of Bedwetting

There are many theories, mostly speculative, none proven, that bedwetting is caused by psychological problems. It is possibl that bedwetters are more prone to psychological disturbance: but this is only a general correlation and does not mean that you child has a psychological problem. In fact, some physicians wh manage a lot of bedwetters feel that there are no more psycholog ical disturbances among bedwetters than among the general pop ulation. Like the gastrointestinal tract, the bladder control of young children is affected by emotional stress, thus prompti many children to wet the bed during periods of stress. If you child has previously been dry but suddenly begins wetting h bed, suspect that the contributing factor might be a recent emo tional disturbance, but only after your doctor has eliminated a urinary tract infection as the cause of the bedwetting.

• Effect of Toilet Teaching Methods Upon Bedwetting

Parent-forced toilet training is associated with a much highe incidence of prolonged bedwetting than the child-considere approach of toilet teaching which I advocate. It is a well-know educational principle that forced training of any skill in a studer who is not receptive to learning and who does not yet have th maturity for that skill will lead to failure. Dr. T. Berry Brazelton in a study of over one thousand children who were toilet taugh by the child-oriented approach (similar to the method advocate in this book), reports that nearly all of the children were dry b age five years.

Is there something wrong with my child's plumbing

In a very small number of children (approximately 3 per cent) there is an anatomical problem in the genitourinary tract whic may contribute to bedwetting. Clues that an anatomical abnor mality or repeated urinary tract infections may be causing you child's bedwetting are poor bladder control in the daytime, and sudden recurrence of bedwetting after a long period in whic your child has been previously dry. Since these two features ar also common to bedwetters who have psychological problems parents must be careful not to always attribute bedwetting to psy chological disturbances. Seek medical attention if these two fac tors are present. In most children, there is no apparent anatom ical or psychological cause for bedwetting and, by five or si years of age, the problem is becoming not only an increasing nu sance for the family but is becoming more of a concern for th child.

• Parenting the Bedwetter

Rather than discuss how to stop bedwetting, let's discuss the topic on a more positive basis—how to encourage nighttime bladder control. The most helpful way to prevent a bedwetting problem is to use the child-oriented approach to toilet learning. In this method, toilet learning is considered just another developmental stage which your child will master at his own rate, with a little well-timed and child-considered parental guidance. At least a three-month period of successful daytime bladder control is necessary before nighttime control can be expected. Daytime control is mastered when your child learns to coordinate and control his abdominal, bladder and pelvic muscles; learns to sense the urge to urinate when the bladder is full; to hold on to his urine until he can make it to the potty; and to stop the stream at will should untimely urination begin. When the bladder is full, the signal to hold on is conscious during the day. At night, we are asking the child to subconsciously hold on to his urine when his bladder is full. This may be asking a lot of the sleeping child. Nighttime bladder control simply means that the child's subconscious desire to hold on overcomes the reflex of a full bladder to let go. A healthy and successful conscious daytime bladder control makes the subconscious nighttime control much more effective.

What about the child who has already survived daytime toilet teaching, is six years old and still wets his bed? We cannot go back and toilet teach him all over again. The following suggestions are guidelines on parenting your child through a dry night.

The first step in achieving nighttime bladder control is to examine your attitudes to your child's bedwetting. It is important for parents to understand the many factors which contribute to a child's bedwetting, that there is usually no one cause nor one treatment for this problem. Can you accept this problem as a temporary developmental delay, a nuisance which must be understood, support it and parent it as you did his other developmental stages? Not only are those positive attitudes necessary for parents, but it is necessary to convey this positive reinforcement to your child. Avoid giving mixed messages. Don't tell your child you are not angry that he wet the bed but at the same time complain about washing the sheets. Above all, avoid parent-child struggles for compliance. Pressure and disgust only prolong bedwetting. I do feel, however, that he should help with the laundry and stripping his own bed. This is not a punishment, but simply ensures that he help take some responsibility for this fam-

ily inconvenience. To simplify laundry, use a large rubbe
backed flannel pad on top of his regular sheet.

The next step is to examine your child's attitude towar
his bedwetting. Does he understand the principles of bladd
control and does he understand that there are individual diffe
ences in the rate of maturation of bladder control? Does he kno
that his bedwetting does not mean that he is still a baby and
different from all other children? Children do not want to w
their bed. They dislike waking up in a wet, odorous bed as muc
as you dislike the nuisance of washing sheets. They are alread
painfully aware of the social stigma of bedwetting and do n
need negative feedback. You might explain, "You are a big bc
now, but your bladder has not yet grown up and we need to wo
on this problem together to try to keep you dry at night." A.
him if there are certain fears or dreams that he has at night or
he is bothered by some disturbing situation in his environment.
is very important for the child to mature and succeed in oth
areas of his development in order not to feel that he is a "baby
everything." Do not let his bedwetting interfere with his norm
social development. He should still be encouraged to go to sur
mer camp or stay overnight at a friend's house. You should act
ally encourage the latter since this is one of the stronge
motivating forces for him to be dry. Since many mothers ha
experienced bedwetting in their own child at some time, tl
mother of your child's friend should certainly understand tl
problem and be equally supportive. Taking his own rubber pa
and sleeping bag may relieve some of his embarrassment. It
very important that your child take the primary responsibility f
his own nighttime bladder control. You and his doctors will l
his support resources, but bladder control is part of his own boc
and he must learn to master its function as he does his other bo
ily functions. Self-responsibility plus outside positive reinforc
ment are the keys to parenting your child through dry nights.

● **The Role of Your Child's Pediatrician**

Your child's doctor can assist you and your child in attainir
nighttime bladder control in several ways.

1. He may discuss toilet teaching with you during your infant
fifteen to eighteen-month check-up.

2. A pediatrician may teach you and your child about the mech
nisms of bladder control and bedwetting in general. Understan
ing a problem usually increases a person's acceptance of it. I
may show your child simple diagrams, such as how the "dougl
nut muscle" opens and closes to help him hold on to his urine.

3. The pediatrician may work out a positive reward system to encourage nighttime dryness. The positive reward system is based upon increasing your child's desire to be dry and to make this desire so strong that, in the subconscious state, it overcomes the reflex desire to empty his bladder. Parents and child should devise a reward system which is meaningful to the child. This could be gold stars on a calendar for every dry night or a penny in a box for every dry night. Instant daily rewards are more effective in children than delayed rewards such as, "If you are dry for three months, I'll get you a new bicycle." A system which I have successfully used is to have the child himself call me at the end of each week and tell me how many dry nights he has had. We then briefly talk about his successes or failures and continued encouragement is given. Doctor-child personal dialogue conveys to the child that he is primarily responsible for his bladder control and that the doctor, whom most children want to please, is his understanding support person.

4. Your doctor may also recommend **bladder exercises** to increase bladder capacity and neuromuscular control and awareness during the day which hopefully will carry over into the night. These include:

a) **Progressive urine withholding.** This method involves encouraging the child to drink large amounts of fluid and to voluntarily hold his urine for increasingly longer times, even though he has the urge to void. Theoretically, as his bladder capacity increases (measured by how much urine he voids), he is able to control his urination and also becomes aware when his bladder is full.

b) **Stop and go.** The child is advised to start and stop his stream several times during urination. This gives the child an awareness that he can actually control his bladder if he wants to. These bladder exercises are most effective for the child who has difficulty controlling his urination during the day. The merits and safety of these bladder conditioning exercises are questioned by some urologists because of the possibility of producing urinary tract infections. I share this concern. These exercises should not be done without the advice of your doctor.

c) **Fluid restriction** after supper is one of the oldest recommended practices for decreasing urine volume in the bladder. This may be a bit uncomfortable to a normally thirsty child and I have never been impressed that this practice helps a great deal, but it may be worth a try. Foods and drinks which contain caffeine (cola and chocolate) should be avoided since they increase urination. Encourage your child to empty his bladder completely before going to bed. Little boys, tired and in a hurry, often dribble a little and off they go. Use the triple voiding technique of encouraging your child to ''grunt and get it all out'' by voiding three times. You may try to awaken your child (called the ''shake and wake'' method) to void before your retire. If you do this, be sure to waken him enough so that he can empty his bladder. Otherwise this inconvenience serves no purpose.

5. Bladder conditioning devices. Pad-and-buzzer devices are basically, sheets of metal foil which lie under your child's sheet. When urine hits the foil an alarm sounds and awakens your child, you hope, as he is about to let it all go and he arises to complete his urination on the nearby toilet. These devices are inexpensive, safe and far more effective than either psychotherapy or drugs. Relapses are common after the device is discontinued and a second course may be necessary to achieve permanent success. Children usually accept this device well because it is their own device for their own problem. Discuss the use of these devices with your doctor.

6. Medication. Certain medications given a half hour before bedtime may be effective in controlling bedwetting. These medications are believed to help bladder muscle control and affect the state of sleep. They are most effective when bedwetting is due primarily to a disturbance in sleep rhythms. Medications are seldom prescribed to children under the age of six years, because bedwetting has been arbitrarily defined as ''normal'' in a child under six. I feel medication should be used when all other methods have been sincerely tried and have failed, and when your physician decides that the psychological disturbance to the child and family resulting from prolonged bedwetting outweighs the potential side-effects of medication. Relapses into the habit of bedwetting are common after the medication is stopped.

Parenting the child who wets his bed requires loving guidance. It should be based upon an understanding of bladder control as well as an awareness of the effects of the problem on your child's self-esteem. To what degree you employ any or all of these suggested methods for bladder control depends upon the severity of the problem and the attitudes of you and your child toward bedwetting.

Temper Tantrums   Temper tantrums are not abnormal. They do not mean that your child is basically emotionally disturbed or has received ineffective mothering. They should not always be considered misbehavior. Let's take our usual approach to dealing with behavior by first understanding why your child has these tantrums.

I feel there are two basic inner feelings which prompt most temper tantrums. A child has an intense curiosity and desire to perform an act but very often the desire is greater than the capability. This leads to intense frustration which is released in a healthy, outward tantrum. Secondly, newly found power and desire for "bigness" propel him toward a certain act and suddenly someone from above, especially someone he loves, descends upon him with a "no." Acceptance of an outside force contrary to his strong will is very difficult. It is a conflict he cannot handle without a fight. He wants to be big but reality tells him how small he is; he is angry but does not yet have the language to express his anger, so he does so through his actions. He does not yet have the ability to handle emotions with reason, so he chooses to cope with his inner emotions by a display of outward emotions, which we term "tantrums." This outward show of emotions such as anger and frustration is also a newly found ability which he should be allowed to express and learn from.

The most frightening temper tantrums are breath-holding spells. During the rage of a tantrum a child may hold his breath, turn blue, become limp and may even faint. In some children, the breath-holding episode may resemble a convulsion and become even more alarming to the already worried parents. Fortunately, most children who hold their breath do resume normal breathing just as they are on the brink of passing out. Even those children who faint quickly resume normal breathing before harming themselves. Try to intervene just before the child loses control. These episodes usually stop when the child is old enough to express his anger verbally.

Temper tantrums become a problem for both the parent and the child. How should you handle temper tantrums? First, realize that you can't handle them you can only respect them. They reflect your child's emotions which he has to handle. Your role is to support him. Too much interference deprives him of his power and a release of inner tension whereas not enough support leaves him to cope all by himself without the reserves to do so effectively. This can be an exhausting and frightening experience for both the child and the parent. Again, the "ignore it" advice is poor advice. Ignoring any behavior problem in your child deprives your child of a valuable support resource and deprives parents of an opportunity to improve their rapport with their child. Simply being available during a tantrum will give your child a needed crutch. Temper tantrums bring out the best i intuitive mothering. If your child is losing control and needs hel to regain control, often a few soothing words or a little help (I' untie the knot and you put on the shoe) may put him back on th road to recovery. If he has chosen an impossible task, distrac him or channel him into a more easily achievable play direction Keep your arms extended and your attitude accepting. Occasion ally a very strong-willed child will lose complete control of him self during a tantrum. It often helps to simply hold him firmly bt lovingly and explain, "You are angry and you have lost contro I am holding you because I love you." You may find that after minute of struggling to free himself he relaxes in your arms, as to thank you for rescuing him.

Temper tantrums in public places are embarrassing and is often difficult to consider a child's feelings first. Your fir thought is more likely to be, "What will people think of me as mother?" You may solve this dilemma by removing him t another room where he can have his tantrum in private but sta with him for support. Tantrums often occur when we impos unrealistic expectations on a child. To expect a curious toddler t be the model of obedience in a supermarket where he is sur rounded with a smorgasbord of tempting delights may be askin too much. Children who are overly tired are especially prone t mood changes and temper tantrums. **Low blood sugar** ma cause temper tantrums to occur long after the last meal or ju before the next meal is due. Fatigue and hunger explain wh many temper tantrums occur in the late morning and late afte noon. Some tantrums occur when the child senses that his mothe is not tuned into him. The child resorts to a tantrum in order t break through to her.

Fortunately, toddlers have a magnificent resilience fc recovering from temper tantrums. They usually do not sulk fc long periods of time and the properly supported temper tantru usually wears off quickly in the child (but may leave paren exhausted). How long will these tantrums last? Fortunately, ten per tantrums are self-limiting for several reasons. Your chi does not like these feelings and as soon as he has developed lar guage to express his emotions you will find this bizarre behavic subsides.

Biting and Scratching

Biting and scratching are two of the several undesirable but nc necessarily abnormal behaviors of the toddler. Why do childre bite? There are about as many theories about biting as there a teeth. Biting usually occurs between the ages of eighteen months and two and a half years in a pre-verbal child, and lessens when the child can effectively communicate his feelings with language. Because his mouth and his hands are his first tools of communication, biting and hitting are to him forms of communication. However, he soon learns this is undesirable behavior by others' negative reactions.

What should you do about your child's biting? First, try to determine why your child bites, and the circumstances in which he bites. Then give him support. When your child has a strong emotion to express and does not have the vocabulary to express it, help him. You may try the previously mentioned feedback technique (see page 245), whereby you try to determine what feeling your child is trying to express and feed this back to him in your own words. When approaching any undesirable behavior in your child I would recommend that you first consider the feeling and the cause behind the action, rather than the action itself.

Biting attracts attention very quickly and if a child wants to be the instant target of attention then biting is a sure thing. Disciplinary action fulfills the craving in some children for attention and reinforces their undesirable behavior. In these cases the "ignore it" advice may be applicable. In general, however, ignoring undesirable behavior is an unwise approach.

Biting is very hard on mothers. The mother of the biter is both disturbed and embarrassed; the mother of the bitee is naturally upset that her child has been hurt, and negative feelings between mothers may result. A good way to handle this is to discuss beforehand that your child is a biter, that you are concerned, and that the child needs supervision. When a child bites remove him from the play group with appropriate admonitions such as "Biting hurts and it is wrong to hurt." Above all, don't bite him back. You are a mature person and biting is an immature, undesirable act. It serves absolutely no disciplinary purpose.

Biters should always be supervised in groups. If a child consistently hurts another child by biting and scratching, it is often wise to separate the children. This isolation will teach the biter a valuable social lesson.

Often, biting occurs when a child is tired or in close quarters with another child and a play conflict arises. If, by experience, you can detect the usual circumstances which prompt your child to bite, then attempt to act before these circumstances are allowed to arise. When your child's verbal skills improve and his emotions can be better expressed by language, biting usuall subsides. Biting in the child over three years of age with goo verbal skills is more concerning and professional guidance should be obtained.

Thumb Sucking

In early infancy, sucking on fingers and thumbs satisfies mor than an infant's need for sucking. It soothes sore gums durin, teething and helps the infant derive pleasure from his body parts As the sucking need diminishes toward the end of the first year some infants retain thumb or finger sucking as a normal metho of using their body parts to obtain pleasure or relaxation Between one and two years, infants find ways of handling thei anxieties and insecurities by holding on to some object such as blanket, cuddly dolls or animals and by using their own securit object—the always available thumb. Even the child of four o five may occasionally seek consolation in his thumb during peri ods of stress. Early infancy is a period of beautiful security an sucking is one of the symbols of this secure phase. It seems bot normal and healthy that the older infant and young child ma occasionally return to the comforts of thumb sucking to handl insecurity.

Thumb sucking bothers adults more than infants. Parent should not always interpret thumb sucking as a sign of parenta failure and think, "Why should my child be insecure enough t need a crutch like his thumb?" Some babies need to suck mor than others and will continue it well into childhood. I feel that for many children, the ability to use their body parts for self gratification is a sign of strength rather than weakness.

But what about his teeth? Thumb sucking may normall persist until your child is between two and a half and three year of age and usually causes no orthodontic problems. Beyond thi age, however, persistent thumb sucking, especially at night, wit a large amount of negative pressure in the mouth and pulling o the front teeth, can result in protrusion of the upper front teet and pushing back of the lower front teeth, resulting in an over bite. If your pediatrician or dentist advises you to discourag thumb sucking because of developing orthodontic problems then explain to your child that he should stop sucking his thumb not because thumb sucking itself is bad but because he is makin his teeth crooked. If a child is old enough to be harming his teet by thumb sucking, he is usually old enough to understand thi reasoning.

How to prevent this persistent thumb sucking? First o

all, in the great majority of infants and children, thumb sucking does not cause orthodontic problems and does not fall into the category of a childhood disease that must be prevented. Persistent thumb sucking is unusual among babies who are breastfed on demand with infant-led weaning, and among babies who are the products of immersion mothering policies previously advocated in this book. If your child is a persistent thumb sucker, don't try mittens, restraints or foul-tasting paints on the thumb. Talk to your child. Help him to verbalize his feelings during what may be a stressful time. A change in your attitude may put the situation in its proper perspective. Try giving him a soft toy to cuddle at night. Instead of immediately thinking, ''I wonder what is this child's underlying insecurity?'' you may have a more positive thought such as, ''Isn't it beautiful that the child is using his own resources to handle some need?''

Fears and Imaginations

During the first year, an infant's main fear is that his needs will not be met. If an infant is held when he needs holding, comforted when he is crying, gentled when he is anxious and fed when he is hungry, he becomes a trusting person. If an infant's needs are not consistently met, he becomes a fearful person. I feel that babies possess the capability of resignation. A baby whose needs are inconsistently and unpredictably met resigns himself to a lower level of expected care. Although this resignation may be a protective mechanism against continued fear of his needs not being met, this protection may be at some expense to his self-esteem.

Fear of separation from mother reaches its high point during the second year. When mother is out of sight, she is gone. The infant has not yet developed the capability to reason that she will be back. Preventive medicine for your infant's fears during the first two years is immersion mothering and simply being available. The result is that a three-year-old is secure enough in his own self-worth and in his parental attachment to be better able to cope with the fantasies and imaginations of the next couple of years.

Around two years of age, a child begins to detach himself somewhat from the protective shield of mother. Locomotion, language and an insatiable curiosity prompt him to investigate his environment. He discovers many new things but does not yet have the capability to evaluate their meaning or their safety (e.g. the fear of the dark, animals, swimming pools, loud noises, vacuum cleaners, upsetting faces, insects). Exposure to a variety of the new items without the ability to evaluate them is a set-up for

271

fears at this age. Fear of unknown objects and situations is usual. Don't waste energy trying to convince your two-year-old that certain feared objects won't hurt him (e.g. the vacuum cleaner, which to him is a noisy monster that eats things). The simplest way to parent the two-year-old through the common household fears is simply not to expose him to these objects without your presence until he has the capability to evaluate these fearsome objects himself, which usually occurs around three or four years of age. Leave the light on in or near his bedroom and his bedroom door open if he is afraid of the dark. Play with a feared thing yourself and he will soon learn (on his own terms) that it is not a fear object. Have fun in the swimming pool and your child will eventually wish to join you. Some young children use mothers as an extension of themselves in overcoming fears. You are the test pilot. If it is safe for you, then it must be safe for him. Respect your child's fears as a natural reaction to his exposure to the world of the unknown.

As if the real world were not scary enough, the ability to form mental images between two and three years of age opens the world of magical thinking with its consequent fears and fantasies. A two- or three-year-old is able to mentally recreate objects, animals and faces which he is exposed to in real life. His mental images may be even more scary than the real thing. A small animal may be as big as a dinosaur in a child's mind. Disturbing objects seen during the day may reappear in fantasy form at night, resulting in the sleep disturbances so common in the two- to four-year-old child. Parenting your child through these fears requires a combination of understanding why he has these fears, of avoiding unnecessary exposure to feared objects and situations beyond his ability, and of helping him to understand the world around him.

Sibling Rivalry

● **When a New Baby Arrives**

Sibling rivalry is normal social behavior in a growing family. In order to appreciate why this behavior occurs, let's look at it from the older child's viewpoint. There is usually not a problem when the child is over three because he is no longer totally dependent upon his home for attention. By this time he is, or at least should be, secure in his role in the family, secure in his love relationship with his parents and beginning to seek stimulations outside the home, such as nursery school or peers. When a new baby arrives, a three-year-old can cope better than a younger child. He is not as threatened. He is old enough to be reasoned with and

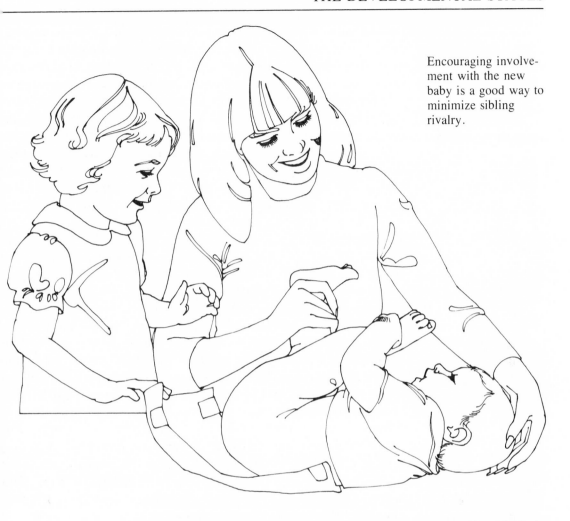

Encouraging involvement with the new baby is a good way to minimize sibling rivalry.

involved in the new baby's care. He can now verbalize his feelings (e.g. "I hate that baby"), whereas the younger child can show his feelings only by actions.

The problem of undesirable behavior toward a new baby occurs more often in a child under three. The toddler has spent his entire past year searching for his identity and for his role in the family. He is mastering the art of manipulating his adult environment to fulfill his desires. He has accomplished his "all by myself" tasks such as toilet learning. But just as he almost has it made, along comes an intruder who complicates his secure world. It is thus understandable that he must defend his position. It is how he chooses to defend his empire that may present problems for parents.

Your displaced toddler may show hostility and aggression

toward the new baby. His behavior may be particularly undesirable when visitors or grandparents shower their attention upon the new arrival. It is also very common for him to regress to his babyhood and want to be a baby too. Your once successful toilet teaching seems forgotten and wet pants again appear. Your toddler may resort to the bottle or want to breastfeed. This so-called tandem nursing is actually a beautiful relationship and should definitely not be discouraged. When our fourth baby arrived, our then two and a half-year-old briefly resumed nursing, quickly became tired of this and then went around sucking on two bottles for a few weeks. These regressions are temporary and should be handled with an accepting, loving attitude.

- **Parental Goals**

Two important parental goals when dealing with sibling rivalry are coping with the undesirable behavior in the older sibling and teaching the older sibling to cope with his feelings about the younger sibling. Please remember, as I stated in the section on discipline, that you cannot control your children's feelings toward each other but you can influence their actions. Prepare your child early for the new addition to the family. When the bulge becomes obvious, show him pictures of "baby in Mommy's uterus" and pictures of him when he was a baby. Let him feel the baby's kicks and market this whole affair as fun. When you go to the hospital it is usually better to explain your apparent abandonment to him in very simple terms. A young child is more interested in hearing what will happen to him rather than where you are going or that you will return with a baby. Tell him that grandma will take care of him, do something special, give him his supper, read him stories and put him to bed. Say you will see him tomorrow (three-year-olds have usually mastered the concept of tomorrow) and then arrange for him to be brought to the hospital to see you. It is usually better to let him remain in his home and have a sitter or grandparent take care of him there. Leave a special toy for him each day. Phone him several times a day from the hospital and encourage visits from your child while you are in the hospital. If a bedroom shuffle is needed to make room for the new sibling, do this long before the baby arrives or he may feel exiled from his home.

- **Involvement**

Involvement is the next key. Let him change the baby's diaper, dress baby, bathe baby. Teach him gentleness and throw out an occasional phrase like, "Just like Mommy did with you when you were a baby." Involvement with the new baby is a good way to prevent the usual attention-getting antics of a displaced older sibling.

Make him feel important too. When visitors come to make a fuss over the new baby, point out things your older child has done and include him in the festivities. A wise gift-bearing visitor will also bring a gift for the older child. Father involvement is often the key to preventing undesirable behavior in the older child. If fathers take time to provide some special attention to the older child, then what attention he has apparently lost from Mom has been compensated for from Dad. The "something special time,"as we call it in our family, is especially helpful in a large family. As the family size increases, each child strives for a sense of identity and of belonging within the family. Fathers, if you can take some time out every few days to do something special with each of your children individually, these meaningful moments will give them a feeling of individual worth, improve your rapport and help satisfy each child's bid for equal time.

Encourage your child to express his negative feelings verbally and he may not express them in deeds. If he says "I hate that baby," don't say "No you don't." To deny his feelings is to deny his right to feel emotions. Pursue his thoughts with him.

Encourage the older child to eventually assume the role of teacher of the younger child. This technique will profit both of them. The older child feels a sense of bigness and may begin to feel that it is fun to be older and wiser. Your older child also serves as a real source of developmental stimulation. Babies seem to respond more, and for longer periods of time, to the face and language sounds of children than they do to the faces and sounds of adults. Using your child as a teaching model encourages desirable behavior towards his younger sibling.

• Rivalry Among Older Children

As children become older, they need to learn to cope with their feelings about their brothers and sisters. I would advise you to let older children work the feelings out in their own way, as long as the struggle doesn't get out of hand. A natural parental urge to defend the younger child exists but it is often difficult to determine who is the instigator in a conflict. It is not always the older child.

• The Continuum of Apology

An important part of learning to live with others, which you want your children to understand, is the ability to set things right after one or both parties have been wronged either accidentally or on purpose. A child needs to understand that he has hurt another either physically or mentally, and that this requires an apology. A simple statement like "I'm sorry Bobby," in a sincere tone of voice, accompanied by a touch on the shoulder or a handshake begins the healing process. The one receiving the apology must make his gesture of forgiving. The words "That's all right Jimmy" complete the healing process. Apology and forgiveness will be easier to teach your children if you act as an example. If you are accustomed to sincerely saying "I'm sorry" when you have made a mistake, your lessons will not go unheeded.

● **The Middle Child**

The middle child is really caught in the middle. The older child naturally has more responsibilities and privileges, the younger child gets more attention because younger children usually require more care. The middle child may therefore feel, "Where do I fit in?" Some children are more prone to shaky self-esteem than others because of individual temperaments. If your middle child shows signs of poor self image, the following suggestions may help:

1. Take inventory of your child's self image at each stage of development. Is he happy, involved and experiencing success or is he excessively moody and bored?

2. Beware of complacency. Because children usually are resilient and adaptable, a middle child may give the outward sign that he has got it all together, but he is inwardly dissatisfied with himself. Does he play "so well by himself" because he wants to or because he is forced to?

3. Have special time for each child. Unfortunately, it is a fact of family life that time with your children does not operate on a supply and demand basis. Parents seldom spend enough time with each child, especially in large families. Both mothers and fathers should increase the one-to-one special time with the middle child.

4. Encourage the activities in which your child experiences success.

Regardless of his place in the family, a child should never feel that he is number two.

Child Spacing

Having children is an individual family decision which involves so many variables that no one can answer this question for you. I think you should have children when you want to. The decision should not be founded on psychological principles, although there is some theoretical advantage to spacing children three years apart. We have discussed why sibling rivalry is less when children are spaced three years apart. I feel, however, that sibling rivalry is an over-rated problem and should not be a major consideration.

We may take a tip from nature, where you find natural child spacing through prolonged breastfeeding. Breastfeeding is a very effective, but not a 100 per cent foolproof method of contraception and is only effective if one breastfeeds often and completely. In some cultures where babies are breastfed exclusively for three or four years there is a natural child spacing of five years.

One consideration when thinking about "child spacing" is that having children too close together deprives them of their identity and is too exhausting to the mother. On the other hand, the constant companionship of a close-in-age sibling provides a rewarding (albeit occasionally competitive) camaraderie. Again, this is a personal decision which can only be answered within an individual family.

Three to Six Years—The Preschooler

By the time your child is three years of age, you and he have together built what we may call the fundamental person. By this, I mean that your child has graduated from each stage of development a better person for the skills he has acquired, the problems he has solved, the emotions he has felt and expressed, and the love-attachments he has made. By age three he is aware of his total self—what he feels, what he can do, what he is comfortable doing, what he cannot yet do. He has defined his role in the family and by age three he has mastered using his parents as support resources. The combination of the parental guidance we have discussed in previous chapters and your child's own basic temperament and intelligence potential produces, by age three, a child who has acquired the motor, language, adaptive and social skills which make up the fundamental person.

A child who has fulfilled his potential in acquiring these skills enters the three- to six-year stage needing primarily to refine the basic skills learned in the first three years. A child who is deficient in any or all of these basic skills by age three must expend energy learning or re-learning these skills; he is always playing catch-up. I do not believe that a child's personality is totally determined by age three but it is certainly well on its way and the ability to change a behavior trait becomes increasingl, difficult with age. The years between ages three and six, th so-called Golden Age, are usually smoother on both parents an child. The refinement of acquired skills usually produces les anxiety than the struggles necessary for their acquisition durin; the first three years.

The Three-Year Old—He's Got it All Together

When you "get your act together," you feel good about yourse and I think this is what generally makes the three-year-old stage smooth period of development. Tantrums and other behaviora anxieties of the two-year-old were simply a manifestation of hi struggles to get himself together. By age three he has mastere three major abilities—motor, language, and calculated, rathe

Three to six years

than impulsive, behavior. It is upon this foundation that our three-year-old builds his next developments.

In the area of motor development, a three-year-old has usually developed the concept of laterality and directionality. He throws and catches, he runs, turns and pivots with confidence. His walking assumes an adult-like gait. Climbing is still a favorite sport and jumping off greater heights is a typical three-year-old challenge. He becomes aware of how much physical abuse his developing muscles and bones can comfortably handle and begins to learn to protect himself from injury.

The development of his fine motor ability allows him to become more domesticated. He feeds himself with less of a mess, brushes his teeth, washes and dries his hands, cleans up after himself, dresses himself and begins learning the task of managing the buttons and bows on his apparel. Three-year-olds usually retain their desire for a pleasant bedtime ritual but begin to treat themselves and their parents to an uninterrupted night's sleep, which is also usually accompanied by the luxury of bladder control.

Your three-year-old has a language repertoire complete enough to effectively communicate his desires and feelings. He understands you and feels you understand him. This language facility results in less tantrum-like behavior, since he is able to express his negative feelings with words rather than actions. His behavior becomes less impulsive and more directed. It seems that his abilities have finally caught up with his desires.

Mastering language adds the finishing touch to the love-attachment feeling your child has for you and begins the social rapport stage between parent and child. Your child is simply fun to talk with, to take walks with and to play word-games with. At this stage, your child may assume the role of a close friend, a pal who is just fun to be around.

Children of ages three and four thrive on new experiences that seem arranged just for them. My four-year-old calls this ''something special,'' a desired or surprise activity for which he is singled out. This ''something special'' becomes increasingly important as the number of children in your family increases.

In **peer relationships** the law of the jungle prevails. Three-year-olds show a desire to refine their social attitudes and varying degrees of social readiness. He desires peer play groups of varying sizes. He exhibits the usual phases of hitting, shoving and anger which many children must experience in order to learn what is socially acceptable behavior within any given peer group. Demanding, possessive, aggressive and withdrawn behaviors are all realistic expectations of this stage. A little loving guidance from parents should be offered but it is usually the law of the jungle that is the most effective behavior director in the peer group.

Toy squabbles are to be expected since possession means ownership at this age. If sharing is a major play problem with your child ask other children to bring a few of their own toys when they come to visit. Capitalize on a natural desire of children to play with another child's toys. As he grabs another toy, another child will grab his toy. He will learn to give a toy to get a toy and, again, the law of the jungle will prevail. Eventually the pride of ownership in his own toys will be refined to the point that he will share possessions with his peers. (See **Time Out Method Of Sharing**, page 245.)

Gender identity becomes apparent during this stage, and distinct behavioral differences between the sexes appear. Generally speaking, boys are more aggressive and engage in more active play than girls of the same age. How much of this early gender difference is genetic and how much is acquired poses an interesting question. I feel that both genetic and cultural influences play an important part in this early gender identity. Girl infants are gentled more than boy infants. Parents are more likely to "rough house" with boys and engage in more quiet "nesting" activity with girls, such as reading and playing house and dolls. These parental play instincts are probably healthy and consequently I certainly will not offer any opinion against their merit. Your child may question you about sex. Sexuality education is discussed in detail on pages 325-329.

Masturbation is common in the three- to six-year-old child and is a natural consequence of exploring his entire body. As your child learns more about his body, he also learns which body parts have different sensations. Genital play is a source of self-gratification. This is not abnormal and seldom indicates that there are any underlying emotional disturbances. Masturbation may also be included in the long list of body actions that the child uses to relieve stress. Thumb sucking and penis-pulling satisfy the same need in the child, but the latter is certainly more disturbing and embarrassing to parents. Although excessive masturbation in some children may indicate a deprivation of tactile stimulation in their environment, in the majority of cases this practice should not be taken as a reflection of ineffective parenting or an emotional need.

Certain masturbation practices in little girls such as mounting objects and rubbing their genitalia against these objects can lead to urinary tract infections and should definitely be discouraged. If a child's masturbatory activity should be discouraged for medical reasons, it is important not to convey to the child that it is wrong to use their body for self-gratification. Use a more subtle approach such as distraction, or channelling the child into other play activities which provide tactile stimulation. A four- to six-year-old is usually able to understand how the abuse of certain body parts can lead to medical problems. Be careful to avoid statements such as, "If you keep that up it will make you sick." Such statements may have a lasting, detrimental effect on a child's sexual development. Children often take a simple fact and distort the information to create fears and fantasies about their genitalia. Put the onus on the doctor by saying, for example, "Remember what Doctor Smith said about pressing too hard on your vagina."

Preschools —How to Select One

An important parental decision at this stage of development concerns preschools. Why? When? Where? The basis of our discussion on preschools will again follow the theme of this book—respect your child as a feeling person.

How do you determine when your child needs a preschool? By the age of three, most children show a strong desire for companionship as well as a desire to refine the skills they have thus far acquired. Preschools serve both these desires. Whether your child's needs during this stage can be met more effectively at home or at a preschool depends primarily upon your child and the general family situation. Therefore, the decision must be made by you. There are a few points you can consider when deciding.

Mother is still the most effective teacher. Preschool education begins at home, and an outside facility should add to and complement the home education, not be a substitute for it. You may, therefore, initially wish to send your child only a few hours each week and let him extend his time at preschool at his own pace.

The preschool should be an extension of the home and, therefore, the facility you select should have the same child-rearing values and priorities as you. Ask advice about various preschools in your area from other parents who share your principles of child-rearing. Parents sharing the same values of child-rearing have been responsible for the "co-op preschools" (parents take turns staffing the school). What the co-op lacks in consistency and organization, it often makes up for in parental interest.

Visit the preschool for a preview. The four major aspects you should consider are the teachers, the equipment, the curriculum and the child interaction.

Call ahead to find out the best time to visit. Surprise visits have mixed benefits. For a variety of reasons it may not be a truly representative day, or the director and particular teacher may not be available if you arrive unannounced. Take your child along. You will get different vibrations from your child at various schools. Mothers are especially intuitive about their child's positive or negative feelings.

Discuss the general philosophies of the school with the director and observe the specific qualities of the teacher who will be working most closely with your child. How does she handle apparent misbehavior? Does the child get the needed support when he is apparently failing an effort? Is the approach to discipline basically child-considered? Are the groups small (maximum of ten children per teacher)? Are the children really enjoying themselves and interacting? Are they smiling? Are they interested? Do the children's creations decorate the walls? No matter how crude a child's creations may be, are they praised and respected? Are the snacks nutritious? (I believe that all preschoolers should have mid-morning and mid-afternoon snacks because of children's tendency to low blood sugar following prolonged activity.) Is there alternating active and quiet play, so necessary for this age? Examine the outside play equipment. Is it safe and well-planned? For example, climbing equipment is generally safer and more instructive than swings. In addition to checking the climbing equipment, which teaches gross motor development, examine the arts and crafts equipment used for fine motor development. Are children taught that everything has a place? This encourages a sense of order. Are they encouraged to "mess a bit" in something such as finger painting? If you are big on "preparedness for school" then you will want to examine the preschool's methods of reading and writing preparation, their "cognitive stimulation" activities.

If the school does not seem suited to your child, shop around. There are many other factors, such as cost and distance from home, which may also affect your decision.

Three-year-olds have some separation anxieties, so initially accompany your child into the school and remain with him as long as your intuition tells you it is necessary. It is not unusual for your child to periodically not want to go to school. Three- and four-year-olds have ambivalent feelings about the pressure to educate them. Play these periods by ear. If your child is constantly unhappy in a particular school, take him out. Sometimes, whether or not he is ready for a preschool is a question which can only be answered by your child.

Daycare centers versus preschool? Your primary need may be daycare, particularly if you work outside the home, but at this stage your child needs more than just babysitting. Preschools which are designed to stimulate and educate naturally provide "daycare." You get much more for your money (and so does your child) by enrolling your child in a good preschool rather than depositing him in a daycare center. (See **Daycare**, page 191 .)

Montessori Schools

In the early 1900s, Maria Montessori, an Italian physician, founded what were then called "children's houses." I consider her manner of education as a philosophy of child development and a plan for guiding this development. Her philosophy of educating a young child is based upon the following considerations:

1. Self-education. Dr. Montessori believed that a growing child has "sensitive periods," stages in which certain types of learning are easiest for the developing brain to acquire. For example, the sensitive period for order is from two to three years of age, for writing from three and a half to four, for numbers and reading from four to five years. The Montessori philosophy of preschool education is based on an understanding of these sensitive periods. The impulse to learn must come from within the child. A child educates himself if he is given the proper environment in which to succeed.

2. Individualized education. A child's individual interests and capabilities are respected. He learns at his own pace and is encouraged to succeed with a minimum of frustration. Each step of learning is a preparation for the subsequent step.

3. Age and stage-appropriate learning materials are used, which capture a child's attention and hold his concentration. These include various cylinders, blocks, colors, cards and sound instruments, all designed to enhance a child's sensory, motor and intellectual skills. One example of a Montessori school learning aid are sand paper letters (letters of the alphabet cut out of sand paper). A child sees the letter, feels the letter and then is encouraged to trace the letter in sand or on a piece of paper. Sight, touch, memory and motor abilities are enriched by this one simple exercise.

4. The classroom environment is quiet yet busy. A child is free to choose his activity and materials. He is encouraged to "get into things" and there are no admonitions such as "No-no" and "Don't touch." Freedom of movement around the classroom is encouraged yet there is freedom with direction. Furniture, shelves and floor mats are child-size. Everything has its place. A sense of order prevails and the child has easy access to all the activities.

5. The term "directress" is used instead of "teacher" because she directs the child to teach himself, a subtle but very important distinction.

The Montessori philosophy seems to reflect the real meaning of education (to lead, to draw out). The Montessori environment is designed to lead, not to push, although a child is encouraged to persevere in completing a task. A child learns how to learn in a Montessori school. Work and play are synonymous and learning is a joy to the absorbent mind of the young child. A child seems to intuitively realize that the environment has been prepared just for him. He respects this, consequently his behavior is more desirable, boredom is rare and self-discipline prevails.

● **How to Get the Most Out of Your Montessori School**

The guidelines for selecting a Montessori school are the same as those mentioned for selecting any preschool. If you are uncertain whether the Montessori school philosophy is suitable for your child, let your child be the judge. Place him in the Montessori school of your choice. If he thrives well in this environment then it is for him. In order that you and your child get the most benefit from the Montessori philosophy, attend the school regularly and observe your child's progress. Most Montessori schools have observation rooms with one-way mirrors, allowing you to observe your child in action.

Also, request periodic conferences with your child's teacher and inquire about his strengths and weaknesses and how you may continue some of the child's most pleasant school experiences in your home.

Children's TV Guide

The question about how much television a child should watch invariably arises at this stage. Television is a fact of modern electronic technicolor family life and it is here to stay. Probably no other recent invention has had a greater effect on society in general and family life in particular.

The purpose of television is twofold; to teach and to relax. I believe television can be a valuable teaching aid for your child, if used wisely. A child can tour the world with his eyes, without leaving the living room.

Children also deserve to relax and be passively entertained a bit, just like adults. The old argument "What did children do before television?" is irrelevant because prior to the invention of television children did not have as many educational pressures upon them and, therefore, perhaps they did not need an occasional therapeutic escape. Let's examine the effects of television upon your child:

1. Watching television is a passive event. At the very stage of development when your child wants to do things with his mind and body in order to learn and have fun, he learns that he can simply push a button and achieve instant gratification, without using either mind or body. Indiscriminate television-watching can be detrimental to the developing child.

2. Television affects family values. Television is an unwelcome family member. It imposes questionable values upon your child, who lacks the wisdom necessary to judge values foreign to his family's teaching. Preschool and school-age children are susceptible to "hero identification." Television allows heroes of questionable repute to enter your living room.

3. Children do not distinguish between learning and entertainment. They learn from everything they see. Television violence fosters detrimental behavior and poor values. Violence depicted on television has long been implicated as a cause of aggressive behavior in children. Violent television programs do not relax children. They create anxiety rather than leave your child with a good feeling. Parental pressure has succeeded in reducing television violence somewhat but as violence decreases, sex on television increases. Children are being presented with unhealthy male-female stereotypes. At the very time home and school are teaching children healthy male and female roles, television exploits both sexes. It teaches children that a man's show of muscle and the shape of a woman's body are what makes a person "big" and that mutual exploitation is the desired route. Children under age five years are usually unable to completely distinguish reality from fantasy. Too much fantasy is not the balanced diet needed to prepare the child for the real world.

4. Television fosters poor physical and dental health. Statistics

claim that the average child hears 23,000 commercials yearl
and watches twenty-five hours of television weekly. (This i
probably more time than the ''average child'' spend
communicating with his parents.) Over one half of these com
mercials advertise foods of questionable nutritional value. No
only does television foster unhealthy eating habits in our youn
consumers, but television also encourages the ''take a pill an
feel better'' philosophy. The doctrine of materialism adds fuel t
this sugar-coated, pill-taking, sedentary television life. Childre
are constantly told that what they drive, drink, wear, smoke an
eat really counts. Studies have shown that children under te
years of age actually believe most of these commercials. Televi
sion has a hypnotic effect on many children, and the degree t
which these commercials, television violence and poor huma
values penetrate a child's unselective mind is frightening. Tha
commercial messages really do sink into a child's mind is evi
dent by how often young children, even three-year-olds, wil
walk around singing a television slogan. In 1974, Canadian tele
vision stations, both public and private, stopped commercial
aimed directly at children.

5. ''Will television hurt my child's eyes?'' is a common questio
parents ask. The American Optometric Association recommend
that to avoid eyestrain a child should not sit too close to the screen
A distance of at least five times the width of the picture tube (six t
eight feet) is advised. Turning on a lamp near the televisio
decreases eyestrain caused by the contrasts of watching televisio
in a dark room. Also, avoid placing the TV where the sunlight ca
cause glare on the screen.

The following guidelines may turn a potential liability int
an asset for both family and child:

1. Parents should screen the program for content and try to judg
the potential effects on their child, just as parents do whe
selecting a book.

The programs should be age-specific (suited to you
child's age group) and should have a positive influence on you
child. (Programs from the Children's Television Workshop ar
commercial-free, age-specific and learning-directed.) Discus
with your children your reasons for screening television in gen
eral, and certain programs in particular. Convey to them that yo
have their best interests in mind. If your child is hooked on televi
sion you have to help him select alternative activities such as read
ing or family games to ''wean him from the tube.''

2. Watch television as a family. Without parental guidance, the television can be very disruptive to family unity. If part of the program you have selected turns out to be contrary to your family values, turn a potentially negative learning experience into a positive one by discussing the values. For example, ''How do you feel about those two men fighting and hurting each other? Could they have settled their disagreement in another way?'' A commercial break is a good time for a discussion on the program content. It is also a time for a little anti-commercial campaign of your own. If the message of the commercial is contrary to your family values or your good sense of nutrition point out to your child how misleading these messages are. In this way the child is being educated to make judgments about the many messages with which various media will bombard him throughout his life.

3. Television is a plug-in babysitter which, I admit, is a boon to large families on rainy days. This use, however, defeats your pre-screened program approach. An alternative is the electronic television game. The television screen becomes an electronic ping-pong table. At least with these devices children are ''in to it'' instead of ''it into them.'' Video cassettes, if used wisely, can also be a great asset. You can choose what your children watch and market it as ''something special.''

4. The content of the programs your children watch on television is more important than the actual length of time they watch. However, as a rough guide, television viewing, especially by preschoolers, should be limited to no more than one hour a day. In our home, watching television is ''a special event.'' Teach the wise use of television when your child is young, before he becomes addicted to television, which is a difficult habit to kick.

5. Look for organizations and books which encourage the wise use of television. Join ACT (Action for Children's Television), a nation-wide citizen's organization whose aims are to decommercialize and improve the quality of television. ACT's address is 46 Austin Street, Newtonville, Mass. 02160, 617-527-7870. Membership in ACT includes a subscription to their magazine **RE:ACT**, which will keep you up to date on the problems and pleasures of children's television, and includes a critique of various television shows which can be helpful to parents who are selecting their children's television programs. ACT's specific goals are the following: to persuade broadcasters and advertisers to provide diversified quality programs for children; to eliminate racial and sexual stereotypes in children's programs; to encourage the development and enforcement of appropriate guidelines relating to the media; to educate parents and others involved with children about the importance of television's effects on children; to stimulate research, experimentation and evaluation in children's television. ACT also sponsors **A Family Guide To Children's Television**, by Evelyn Kaye (New York, Pantheon Books, 1977). Also available from ACT is a book called **Promise and Performance: ACT's Guide To TV Programming For Children With Special Needs**, (Cambridge, Mass., Ballinger Publishing Company, 1977). This book features programming for mentally retarded and perceptually handicapped children, a long-neglected audience.

The Teacher's Guide To Television and Prime Time School TV provides study guides for the PTS-TV educational programs and is available from Prime Time School TV, 120-S LaSalle Street, Chicago, Illinois 60603. Another booklet, **Watching Television With Your Children**, published by the ABC Television Network, is available at ABC affiliated stations.

Organizations listed above represent only a few of many whose motive is to change television into a positive, creative force in the lives of our children.

Parenting the Hyperactive Child

The hyperactive child, like the fussy baby, is one of the most difficult problems parents, other children and pediatricians face. Their impact upon family life is so great that, if not properly handled, hyperactive children can destroy all the joys of childrearing. This type of child may often show a hint of what is to come shortly after birth when he is labelled a fussy baby, a difficult baby or a colicky baby. He startles easily, settles poorly. His incessant demands exhaust everyone around him and his piercing cries can be only temporarily and inconsistently appeased. He requires constant gentling. This baby is in constant motion and so are his parents, who spend most of the first year walking, rocking, floor-pacing, riding and stroking their baby.

When the "fusser" becomes a toddler, locomotion adds fuel to his fire, and the normal impulsive behavior of this age group is compounded. While the usual toddler shows gradual direction and organization of his impulsive behavior toward the end of the second year, the hyperactive child shows increasing disorganization and a decreasing ability to handle this disorganization. His frustration level increases and so does the emotional expression of his inner turmoil. Toward the end of the second year, the normal parental feelings that "I'll be glad when this stage is over" give way to the realization that this stage is no over, nor is it passing, and perhaps the child does indeed have a problem which requires professional guidance.

Hyperactivity may not be considered a major problem in some children until they begin preschool. I feel the main reason for this is that the home environment is less restricting, less demanding. There is a wider latitude in acceptable behavior within a child's world at home. He is more comfortable in the familiar physical environment of his house, his parents are the only authority figures he has learned to manipulate to his own satisfaction and his peer play groups are usually small. School imposes many demands to which he does not adapt easily. There is a narrower latitude of acceptable behavior, authority figures vary, and the play groups are larger and less tolerant of socially unacceptable behavior.

A hyperactive child's school behavior is usually impulsive, disorganized, and seemingly poorly directed. During periods of quiet activity, his attention span is short and he is easily distracted. His warm-up period for any new task is usually long. He speeds from task to task but neither finishes nor enjoys any of them. The hyperactive child is inattentive, restless and fidgety. Parents and teachers have difficulty satisfying the hyperactive child. As he becomes aware of his inadequacies at school, he becomes increasingly disruptive during classroom activities and excessively demanding of teachers. He begins to tax the teacher's reserve as he has taxed his parents' reserves. In situations of active play (e.g. the playground) in which a high level of motor activity is expected and appropriate, his hyperactivity may not be a problem to him, but his impulsiveness is.

Both his preschool learning and his social maturity suffer. At the very age when he wants and needs peer acceptance, his group rejects his unconventional behavior and, he feels, rejects him. He retaliates with more socially unacceptable behavior and a vicious cycle begins. His frustration tolerance becomes as low as his self-esteem and his already compromised personality further disintegrates. In the end, the hyperactive child becomes an unhappy child.

The hyperactive child syndrome is characterized by its variability from child to child, and when and why it occurs within an individual child. It is the quality of motor activity that distinguishes these children from normally active children, not the quantity of motor activity. This is especially true of the older hyperactive child.

The cause of this behavioral disorder is not known. Only

in about 5 per cent of these children is any brain disorder detecta ble. Therefore, it is usually considered a personality behavioral problem rather than a neurological deficit. Because the wide spectrum of disorders associated with this problem such as learning disabilities or neurological deficits, many term exist to describe the condition. Minimal brain dysfunction hyperactive child syndrome and organic personality syndrom are a few. The newest term, **attention deficit disorder wit hyperactivity,** is a good one since it focuses on the essenti problem (an inability to concentrate). This problem of selectiv attention may or may not be accompanied by appare hyperactivity. The condition is relatively common, occurring an estimated 3 per cent of children, ten times more often males. A familial pattern seems to exist, although this is difficu to accurately determine. But some parents do volunte "According to his grandmother, he's just like his Dad was."

Successful parenting of the hyperactive child requir early recognition of the babies who are at high risk of becomir hyperactive children and an understanding of the importance instituting early treatment and preventive measures. In rece years there has been a growing realization that parents make t best behavior therapists for their children. Parents who mana with the fussy baby and trying toddler, instinctively use t **principle of competing behavior** (e.g. gentling of the fus baby, see page 167). If you have successfully parented your w through the fussy baby period, you have a greater chance of su cessfully parenting your hyperactive child.

Hyperactive infants need immersion mothering rath than escape mothering. We have previously discussed the pare tal dilemma that easy babies are simply more enjoyable to nu ture and that parents may either consciously or unconscious escape from more difficult babies. There is also an occasion mismatch of temperaments—an energy-draining baby and mother with a low tolerance level. If you find that your parent reserves are weakening, and most parents of hyperactive childr find this at some time, talk about your feelings with your pedi trician. It is not unusual, nor unhealthy, for a parent to confe "I don't like him. I am not enjoying being a parent. I look fc ward to being away from him. Our marriage is also suffering Talking about your feelings helps to put them in perspective.

Your children cannot, or at least do not, often verbali their feelings so easily but when you dig into their feelings abo themselves the hyperactive child is usually very unhappy. If h hyperactivity is compromising the joy of parenting and interfering with his intellectual, social and personality development, then he indeed has a problem which needs professional guidance. Truly hyperactive children do not usually "grow out of it" but rather "grow into" more serious social problems in adolescence and adulthood.

There are some guidelines to follow to parent the hyperactive child. First, your pediatrician will outline a treatment plan in which he will counsel parents and child, speak to the school and often seek the assistance of child psychologists for additional medical advice. This is a team approach. Parents, teachers and medical professionals play a role and your pediatrician or any capable counsellor acts as the focal point of the treatment regimen. So that parents will not have to ask "What do we do now?" a plan is very important. This plan will consist basically of a behavioral modification program, and possibly medication. The methods of behavioral modification will be custom-tailored to your family situation and your child. Many of these methods are described in **Discipline** page 236 . The counsellor (your pediatrician or the medical professional designated by him) will counsel you, your child and his teachers and will make specific recommendations which will periodically be modified according to the child's progress.

● **Behavior Modification**

Behavior modification techniques used to help the hyperactive child are geared to the problems of each child, but there are certain general principles that apply to most of these children. The first step is to find exactly what undesirable behavior is to be modified:

1. Disruptive behavior: non-compliance, inappropriate noises or physical aggression.

2. Attentive behavior: short attention span.

3. Motor behavior: fidgety, continuously "out of seat."

4. Poor academic performance: usually a "completion of work" problem.

Most hyperactive children show a combination of all of the above, but one behavior may stand out as most in need of modifying.

The second goal of behavior modification is to teach the hyperactive child what is called **appropriate situation control**. Much of the behavior of the hyperactive child is not inherently bad or disturbing. His behavior is, however, inappropriate and disruptive in certain situations (e.g. in a classroom). To most

children, a chair is something to sit on. To the hyperactive chi
a chair is an object to stand on or lie under. While situatio
appropriate behavior may be natural for some children, it mu
be learned by the hyperactive child. Learning situatio
appropriate behavior for the hyperactive child is ultimately
question of motivation. The principle of positive reinforceme
which we described in the section on discipline (page 243)
used in behavior modification to encourage situation-appropria
behavior. The child is rewarded for appropriate behavior and n
rewarded for inappropriate behavior.

Behavior modification therapy also requires an analys
of all the possible environmental factors which may inadve
ently reinforce various behaviors. Hyperactive children tend
be expert manipulators of their environment. As a result, parer
and teachers may be subconsciously reinforcing inappropria
behavior with too much special attention.

Most effective behavior modification programs for t
hyperactive child must include some behavior modification
the parents. Hyperactive children are often developmental
immature for their age and may need parenting appropriate tc
younger child. Parents' expectations should be at a level suited
their child's developmental age, rather than his actual age.

Generally speaking, parenting the hyperactive chi
requires counselling tailored to the child and the entire family s
uation. These children are often of above-average intelligen
and therefore need above-average parenting and learning expe
ences. Part of the treatment plan is to discuss these concepts wi
your child's teacher, since associated problems are usually pre
ent at school.

Hyperactive children are also sometimes treated wi
medication. Medications usually prescribed are stimular
which, in a hyperactive child, work to stimulate that part of t
brain which decreases the tendency to being easily distracte
thus ensuring more purposeful behavior. These medications a
both safe and effective for carefully selected children.

Because parents are often reluctant to use medication f
behavioral modification of their child, I would like to allevia
some of these understandable concerns. As in the case of .
medications you should consider the consequences of not usi
them. Is it fair to your child to withhold the benefit of a prov
medication which may enable him to be a happier person? It
similar to giving him a medication that may enable him to
physically healthier. Also, children who do respond to the

medications do so immediately. Time is important to a developing child who can ill afford several years of unproductive behavior. Medication is an adjunct to behavioral modification, seemingly setting his "behaviorstat" to a point at which he is more receptive to behavioral modification and learning. In fact, for many hyperactive children, behavioral modification therapy is ineffective without medication.

There are also several controversial modes of treating the hyperactive child. As with many medical illnesses, desperate parents accept unproven modes of therapy. Because you love your child you are susceptible to the "cycle of confusion." You go from specialist to specialist searching for anything which might help. Your desperation, however, often makes it difficult to evaluate whether a treatment is working. At the time of writing, the following treatments of the hyperactive child are controversial:

1. It has been suggested that certain food additives (artificial coloring, flavoring, and preservatives) may cause hyperactivity in children and their removal from the diet may alleviate this behavior. Experiments have yielded conflicting results. The most controlled studies seem to indicate that large doses of artificial food colorings do decrease learning performance and adversely affect the behavior of hyperactive children, but may not affect learning or behavior in children who are not already hyperactive. Whether your individual child is vulnerable to the behavioral effects of food additives must be answered on an objective trial basis. The effects of high sugar diets and "junk food" are not controversial. Sugar does adversely effect behavior in many children and therefore should be avoided especially by the hyperactive child. Food allergies (especially milk) can adversely affect a child's behavior and an elimination diet may be necessary (see **Food Allergies** page 147).

2. Orthomollecular medicine (the use of mega-vitamins, trace elements and dietary manipulations) is a controversial concept in the treatment of the hyperactive child. There are no studies demonstrating either the safety or the effectiveness of this approach. I suspect this concept has become popular because this "medicine" can be "prescribed" without a license to prescribe.

ying

The emergence of the concepts of truth and falsehood is part of the moral development in the two- to five-year-old child. There are four types of "lying" which at this age are natural and not at all alarming. Actually lying is often too strong a word for the storytelling children engage in. Let's view "lying" from child's level and respond accordingly.

There is the "get me off the hook" lying. Either a chil denies something altogether (no matter how obvious) or h names a scapegoat to protect himself from punishment. In case of obvious incrimination, you can help your child get to the trut by avoiding questions which will invite a falsehood and which h will see as a trap. For instance, don't say, "Did you break th plate?" Rather say "I guess this plate got broken because yo were being careless." You want the child to learn there is n need to lie.

The second type of lying in children five years of age ar older is the deliberate lying calculated to get someone else i trouble. When this is discovered (and mothers have an uncann sense of knowing when their child is not telling the truth) conve to the child that you will consistently and firmly disapprove this behavior and that he will suffer logical consequences (se **Logical Consequences**, page 246).

Thirdly, a child learns to lie because he feels that the par ents don't want to hear the truth. He learns very quickly to cove up his true feelings with falsehoods if you contradict or corre him when he expresses negative feelings (e.g., your child say "I hate my brother" and you respond "No you don't."). Th lesson soon becomes clear that the truth hurts and lying smoother. Parents should listen to all feelings. The child has right to feel, be it bitter or sweet, and needs the freedom express both.

Finally, wishful thinking, or fantasy lying, is designed impress and thereby gain status in the eyes of the listener. This so of conversation goes on all day between four- and five-year-old Fantasy thinking is normal behavior in an imaginative child an should not always be discouraged. If the listener is an adult, he ca help the child differentiate between wishes and reality. It is ver important to respond in a way that shows you understand th meaning of the story rather than simply deny what the child says put him down. For instance, rather than prove the lie when yo hear, "We went to Disneyland yesterday for my birthday," yo can say, "You wish you went to Disneyland. You wish you had a that fun. But what did you really do for your birthday?"

Stealing

Taking what does not belong to you is a working definition of th term stealing. Like lying, stealing is an "adult" term which too strong to use in all cases at all ages. Toys that turn up in th pockets of a three- or four-year-old after a visit to a friend's house, or candy found clutched in a sticky fist after a journey through the supermarket needs to be dealt with, but in a way that contributes constructively to the development of a child's sense of property. Possession means ownership to a young child and gradually in the early school years he learns the difference between mine and yours.

Approach any act of stealing with a desire to understand the meaning of the object to the child and the meaning of the impulses that accompanied the act of stealing. If a child feels deprived of sufficient possessions he may try to set the balance right by taking what he feels he needs to make him feel right.

Stealing may also be used to get even with a friend who has done something to deserve an attack, since young children see objects as an extension of the person. Stealing which occurs inside the family may indicate that the guilty party feels he is getting short-changed in comparison with his siblings. Sometimes stealing has nothing to do with a desire for what was taken but is, instead, a way to get a thrill (usually in the older child) or a way to get caught and punished to ease guilt feelings stemming from a totally unrelated act. Lastly, some children may be having deep problems with their sense of self-worth and may steal as a way of asking for help.

The example of the clutched candy can be dealt with very calmly and firmly while still allowing the child to retain his dignity. "The candy belongs to the store. We'll have to take it back." In other instances (e.g. money taken from your purse) you must first be sure the child is guilty. If you are certain that he is guilty don't ask him if he is, thus possibly compounding his act of stealing with the act of lying. Tell your child that you know he took the money, that you disapprove of his actions but that you want to know what feelings prompted this action. Your child may not know why he took the money. Your goal is to open some type of dialogue which encourages a child to analyze his feelings and to realize the wrongness of his act. As with any undesirable behavior, parents should try to understand why their child is stealing. It could be that he simply wants money and feels that stealing is the only way to get it. Providing an allowance, or the opportunity to do some odd jobs whereby he can earn money, often solves the money-stealing problem.

To punish for stealing, the logical consequences method (see page 246) is usually the most effective. Letting your child know that his action disappoints you also contributes to his pun-

ishment. The logical consequences method conveys to your chil
that he is responsible for his actions. In situations of deeper con
cern or when your child seems in over his head, consultatio
with your doctor may be necessary.

Six to Eleven Years—Middle Childhood

The child from age six to age eleven enjoys a certain personalit
equilibrium. By this age he is secure in his position within th
family, he has developed some social attitudes and has acquire
some preliminary educational skills at home or in preschoo
Middle childhood marks the beginning of a child's more form
education and a refinement of his social attitudes. Although th
family remains the center of his world, he reaches out fc
social relationships and peer acceptance and may spend th
greater part of his day in pursuits outside the home.

In order to enrich his self-esteem and emerging persona
ity your child has two special needs at this stage, the need fc
social relationships and peer acceptance, and school succes
Let's discuss how you can influence those needs.

**Peer Acceptance
—Parenting the
Shy Child**

"How can I help my child win friends and influence people?"
"Should I get involved with his friendships?" are questions pa
ents frequently ask at this stage. Generally, you should allo
your child to build his own social relationships at his own con
fortable pace and you should not interfere. This approach is co
rect for the child who has a good self-image, makes friends ea
ily and seems to have it all together at this stage. If your chilc
however, is a very sensitive individual with a fragile self-esteer
who is having difficulty fitting in, then I feel that it is wise fc
parents to become somewhat involved in his social environmen
Failure to parent your child through his social problems ma
deprive him of a valuable support system. It will also depriv
you of a chance to convey to your child that his parents are, an
always will be, his best friends.

If your practices have been oriented toward supportin
your child's self-esteem and fostering a secure parent-child rel
tionship during the first six years, then your six-year-old has
good foundation on which to build his social relationships.
your child does not feel good about himself it is difficult for hin
to feel good about others, and if he does not have the secure lov

Six to eleven years

attachment at home, he will have difficulty developing attachments toward others outside the home.

● **Social Aids**

1. Your child needs success at this stage. Create an environment in which your child's strong points are allowed to flourish. Is he good at a certain sport or certain musical instruments? Identify these talents and encourage them. Every child needs to be good at something. Success certainly contributes more to self-esteem than failure.

2. What are your child's interests? Reading, building, sports? Encourage his interests. You may wish your child to have certain interests which you feel are healthy for him. He must be allowed to pursue his particular interests (providing, of course, they

involve basically desirable behavior). After he masters his inter
ests, his self-confidence may be such that he can go on to the
interest which you feel he should have. (See **Carry-Over Princi
ple**, page 308.)

3. Welcome his friends into your home. Your child's home i
his castle too, the place where he is most secure and confident
where he can use this security to his social advantage, especiall
if he is a shy or withdrawn child. Your child is more likely to be
a successful player if the game is played in his park. If your chil
succeeds at home, he is more likely to also succeed away from
home. Encourage your child to invite a friend to spend the nigh
at his home, thereby encouraging one-to-one social interaction in
a secure environment.

4. Encourage friendships with children who have compatibl
temperaments. For example, a child with a domineering person
ality will contribute little to the self-esteem of a shy child.

5. Should you try to influence your child's choice of friends
This is a very common dilemma for parents of a child over six
Certain children show certain undesirable behavior at this stage
(lying, stealing, cheating, damaging property) and parents fea
this will rub off on their child, but the "children's legal system"
and the "law of the jungle" can provide valuable learning expe
riences for your developing child. Part of your child's socia
development at this stage involves forming a consciousness o
right and wrong. I believe that parents should encourage friend
ships with children from families with values similar to thei
own. With parental guidance, your child will learn to cope wit
the undesirable behavior of his peers without feeling he has to
join them. Guiding your child rather than sheltering him is
more realistic and lasting approach.

The Child Who Fails to Learn— Learning Disabilities	School entry is an important milestone for your child and succes in school, or lack of it, can have a profound effect on your child.

● **The System or the Child?**
It is important for parents to determine whether the disability i
within the child or within the system. The term "disability" is
relative term. We have set up a system of education in which th
great majority of children are expected to perform at a certai
level at a certain age, and we have based school entry upo
chronological age rather than mental maturity. As many as 1
per cent of grade school children may have varying degrees o
difficulty learning all subjects according to the methods of learr
ing the system uses. In other words, those who learn within th

system have "learning abilities" and those children who do not learn within the system have "learning disabilities."

Many children have to make a unique adjustment before starting their formal education. Before school entry, your child's growth and development is directed by reasonable freedom of choice. He naturally strives toward goals which reward him with a feeling of success and he avoids less achievable goals. For example, if the child knows he lacks the talent for a particular sport he simply tries a sport more comfortable to him, thereby undertaking more realistic goals and protecting his self-esteem. When he enters school, he has to adjust for the first time to a system which tells him what "sports" he must play and also how he must play them. The educational system requires him to perform in all subjects at a given level. He cannot choose to participate in one subject and not in another. The adjustment to the loss of freedom of choice for six hours a day, five days a week is, in itself, a learning milestone. Most children make this adjustment easily, but some children are understandably not so adaptable.

• A Step-by-Step Approach to the Child Who Fails to Learn

The following is a suggested step-by-step approach to determine why your child is failing to learn and what to do about it. This approach is outlined on page 300.

Step 1. Medical evaluation. I find the main question parents ask when coping with a child who has learning problems is, "Where do we go now?" Parents and child are often left to flounder in a sea of uncertainty about their child's educational course. Consult your pediatrician. His aim is to treat the complete child.

The evaluation of learning problems is time-consuming and it is unwise and unproductive to throw the question at your physician during a visit for another problem, "By the way, Johnny is doing poorly in school." Most physicians set aside time at the end of office hours for such problems. When phoning to make your appointment, mention the nature of the appointment to the receptionist and she will schedule appropriate time. Often it is best to speak directly with the doctor and he will tell you what information he needs to know. Before your doctor sees your child, it often helps to provide him with your concise, personal, written assessment of your child's school problem and a concise letter from your child's primary teacher describing her assessment of his problem. (In some cases, your doctor may wish to speak directly with your child's teacher by phone.) Spe-

STEPS IN EVALUATING A CHILD WHO FAILS TO LEARN

HISTORY FROM: PARENTS, TEACHERS, CHILD

NEURODEVELOPMENTAL ASSESSMENT
signs of mental delay
signs of developmental delay
signs of minimal brain dysfunction

SENSE PERCEPTION
does he see normally
does he hear normally

STEP # 1

Child's
Doctor

EMOTIONAL PROBLEMS
with parents
marital discord
sibling relationships
behavior problems

INSUFFICIENT EXPOSURE
moves, changing schools,
absenteeism, sickness, phobias

DISABILITY OF EDUCATIONAL SYSTEM
mismatch of child and system
lack of classroom discipline
no individualized program

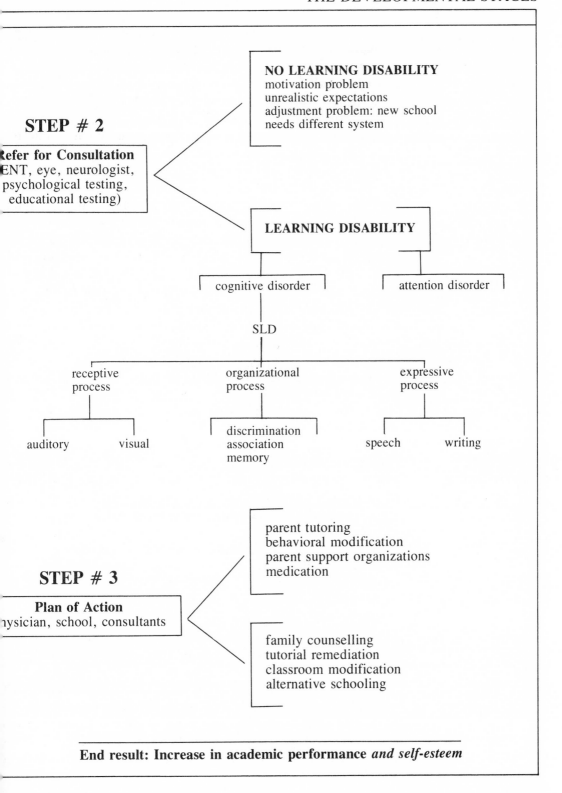

STEP # 2

Refer for Consultation
(ENT, eye, neurologist,
psychological testing,
educational testing)

NO LEARNING DISABILITY
motivation problem
unrealistic expectations
adjustment problem: new school
needs different system

LEARNING DISABILITY

cognitive disorder

attention disorder

SLD

receptive
process

organizational
process

expressive
process

auditory   visual

discrimination
association
memory

speech   writing

STEP # 3

Plan of Action
physician, school, consultants

parent tutoring
behavioral modification
parent support organizations
medication

family counselling
tutorial remediation
classroom modification
alternative schooling

End result: Increase in academic performance *and self-esteem*

301

cifically, your doctor will want to know what the school performance problem seems to be, how much the learning problem affects the emotional development of the child and how much it concerns both the teacher and parents. It is important for your doctor to have this information before he begins his assessment.

Your doctor will look for the answers to a number of questions. Is there a medical problem preventing your child from learning? Is there a deficiency in sensory perception? Does he see and hear normally? Vision and hearing tests are performed to eliminate these causes. Is his neuro-development normal for his age? Are there signs of mental or motor delay? Are there minor neurological signs called **minimal brain dysfunction**? It must be pointed out here that there are certain neurological differences found between children who have and don't have learning problems. This is why every piece of the puzzle in the assessment of a learning problem must be considered in the context of the total child. Otherwise, there is a tendency to make unwarranted cause and effect conclusions. Your physician will also evaluate your child's fine motor skills, gross motor skills and hand-eye coordination and will try to make two judgments. Are there any signs of neuro-developmental delay? Do these delays affect your child's learning potential?

After his assessment of your child's neurological health, your physician will examine the relationship between the family and child. Is there marital discord? Are there problems with sibling relationships? Are there underlying behavioral problems which may prevent your child from learning? Is your child generally happy in the three areas of importance at this age—home, school and peer relationships. Are there emotional problems which may interfere with his learning or result from his learning problem? It is often difficult to determine whether emotional problems are the cause of or the effect of the lack of school success.

Next, is there a problem of exposure? Has he missed a lot of school because of sickness, vacations, phobias? Has there been a recent move, a change of schools, or is it simply a temporary adjustment problem which is affecting his emotional and school performance?

Is the disability within the child or within the educational system? Does the school "fit" the child? Is the classroom too noisy and undisciplined? Is he in a so-called "open" system when he should be in a more structured system? Having observed children who are not doing well in school, I am sympathetic to their difficulty in learning in a noisy, over-crowded classroom with over-worked teachers. Do the parents and teacher have unrealistic expectations of their child's ability to learn to his full potential in his school environment? Often a learning disability is alleviated by correcting this mismatch between the school and child, and by providing a more individualized program of teaching in a more structured and disciplined educational environment.

Step 2. Refer to other specialists for consultation. After eliminating the above primary causes of learning problems, your physician and teacher may think that a true learning disability exists and initiate a thorough evaluation called **testing**. The educational and psychological evaluation of a child with a potential learning disability is beyond the expertise of most general pediatricians. Therefore, your doctor will refer your child to a variety of consultants to obtain their opinions regarding the child's learning problems. These consultants may be medical sub-specialists such as ophthalmologists for vision testing, ear specialists for hearing evaluation and neurologists for neurological assessment. Also, your physician or school will refer your child for psychological and educational testing. These evaluations are done by psychologists specially trained in administering and interpreting these various tests. Since many parents show some understandable anxiety about having their children go through a barrage of tests, I will briefly describe the nature of these tests and discuss their importance.

● **What Do Intelligence Tests Really Mean?**

There is a widespread difference in opinion as to what the term "intelligence" really means. For ease of discussion, we will consider intelligence as the ability to learn. An intelligence quotient (IQ) is a relative term. It is a score which indicates your child's ability compared to the ability of other children of the same age to reason on an abstract level, to solve problems, to understand the meaning of words and, incidentally, to take intelligence tests.

The IQ is computed as follows:

$$\frac{\text{Mental age of your child (test results)}}{\text{Your child's actual age}} \times 100 = IQ$$

For example, if your child is ten years of age but his scores are comparable to those of a twelve-year-old his IQ is 120. A word of caution is needed about giving your child a number for his "smartness." Intelligence is not a static quality. Intelligence should not be thought of as something a child has, but rather something which he develops. Heredity may play the most important role in determining a child's maximum potential intelligence, but how close he comes to achieving this potential is determined by his nurturing and the effect of a variety of life experiences upon him. Growth of intelligence is similar to growth in height. How tall you will be (your maximum height) is determined primarily by heredity. How close you come to achieving this maximum height depends upon a variety of influences such as your general health, and nutrition.

The belief that a child's IQ does not change is wrong. Studies have shown that a child's IQ may be increased significantly by increasing his happiness factor and by enriching his environment. Children with behavioral problems have shown increased IQ (judged by IQ tests) when their behavior problems were alleviated and no longer adversely affected their ability to learn. Whether an IQ test measures the intelligence of your child is questionable. The important point is that the standardized IQ test actually measures the skills necessary for adequate performance in the school system. The main purpose of these tests is to serve as a reference point for a child's ability to learn compared to his actual learning.

The most popular intelligence test is the WISC-R (Wechsler Intelligence Scale for Children - Revised). This test is composed of verbal sub-tests and performance sub-tests. The verbal sub-tests reflect a child's alertness, memory, awareness of surroundings, comparisons, concrete and abstract thinking, simple arithmetic and vocabulary, and general reasoning ability. The performance sub-tests take the basic abilities which the child exhibited in the verbal testing and require him to use those abilities to perform tasks such as arranging pictures in their correct order, completing the missing parts of a picture, putting pieces of a puzzle together and generally using hand-eye coordination and non-impulsive thinking.

What beneficial information does this IQ testing give us? First, it eliminates the possibility that a child is mentally retarded and therefore confirms that he has at least an average intelligence with which to learn. Second, it gives an idea of the potential level of achievement that can be expected by your child. Third, wide discrepancy (25 points) between verbal and performance IQ test results suggests that a problem (learning disability) of attention or of processing information exists. This finding may prompt the psychologist to administer additional sub-tests to detect where the information processing problem lies (i.e. what is the specific learning disability [SLD] which prevents your child from reading, writing or spelling). The more specifically the learning disability can be defined, the better the chance for correction.

The next step is to administer **educational tests**. Achievement tests are administered to determine if, indeed, a learning problem really exists. An achievement test tells how much your child has learned in comparison to other children of his age. If the IQ test shows he is of average intelligence and his achievement tests show average achievement, then certainly no learning disability exists. This testing combination also appeases the unrealistic expectations of parents and teachers that a child could be doing better. If the achievement test results are far below the IQ test results, then a learning disability may indeed exist. The final step is an additional series of educational tests to determine just what in your child's learning process is the specific learning disability.

In order for you to understand what these educational tests are designed to detect, let's briefly summarize what faculties your child needs in order to learn in the typical school system (assuming both home and school environment are conducive to learning).

1. Visual-motor ability is when fingers and eyes work together to copy letters. Letters in the English language are basically constructed from a line (—, |) and a semi-circle ($\subset$, $\supset$), e.g., b and d. Children will commonly reverse such letters as "b" and "d," e.g. dab for bad. Reversals are not necessarily abnormal nor always indicative of a learning disability.

2. Visual memory is the ability to remember and recall letters and words after seeing them, in the order seen, in a left to right orientation.

3. Visual discrimination is the ability to recognize how one word differs from a similar word, e.g. pin, pun, pen.

4. Auditory-memory-sequencing is the ability to accurately repeat the words spoken in the sequence presented. Your child must learn to associate a particular sound with a sequence of letters. This requires the recall of some patterns and their organization in sequential language.

The various educational tests to determine specific learning disabilities (SLD) are designed to detect problems in the visual and the auditory processing of information.

In addition to the information processing skills described above, there are certain behavioral prerequisites to learning. First, the child must be able to sit still and selectively attend to stimuli. Attention disorders frequently accompany a SLD and further contribute to the learning problem. Secondly, he must show some impulse control, be able to accept limits and cope with occasional frustration and failure. Problems with these abilities should have been attended to prior to school entry. (See **Attention Deficit Disorders**, page 290.)

Learning problems associated with visual and auditory faculties, and attention abilities are reflected in a child's reading which is why a reading disability (i.e. dyslexia, from the Greek "I can't read") is often the first sign of a learning disability. Because reading is necessary for learning many other subjects, most attention is usually given to a child's ability to read in school.

All this testing should provide answers to the following questions: Does a learning problem exist? If a learning problem does exist is it due to a learning disability? If a learning disability exists, is it due to an attention disorder (he is not receiving the information) or is it due to a cognitive disorder (he is not processing the information correctly)? If a processing disorder exists, what is the specific "crossed-wire" in the system, i.e. the specific learning disability?

Step 3. Plan of action. After the medical sub-specialty testing and the psychological and educational testing is complete, your physician will review the test results and the specific recommendations made by the sub-specialists. He will be looking at the following:

1. Does your child have all the normal tools to learn or is he a child who is just not motivated to work to his full intellectual potential?

2. Is there a mismatch between child and school? Should an alternative educational method be considered, or should some attempts be made to modify his classroom situation in order to minimize distractions?

3. Is there an underlying emotional problem which is preventing him from exercising his educational potential?

4. Is there, indeed, a learning disability which is either an attention disorder or a specific learning disability?

Often the school problems are a combination of many of the above factors. Your pediatrician will then discuss these results with you and will try to correlate the various test results and suggestions into a plan of action to combat your child's learning problem. You should understand that no learning disability can be diagnosed from a single test result. What is important are results of the various test results taken in the context of the complete child. I must emphasize this point. It is important to consider all the factors involved in your child's learning, as outlined on page 300, because, for the majority of children, there is no one single reason why they do not learn. All too often the learning disability label is given to a child without either adequate explanation or evaluation. If a SLD is suspected, your doctor will suggest that your child's learning requirements could better be met by an individual program which provides him alternative methods of learning. It is best if these alternatives can be worked out in his present school system with assistance from the teacher, school psychologist and any other educational professional who may have special tutoring expertise in the field of learning disabilities. Often your child's self-esteem suffers as a result of a learning disability. This results in emotional problems which further hinder learning and a vicious cycle begins. Your pediatrician will also counsel you and your child on understanding and managing these secondary emotional problems. If an attention disorder is at the root of the learning problem, your physician may suggest medication, behavior modification or both. (See **The Hyperactive Child**, page 288.)

The aim of evaluating a child with a learning problem is not to bestow a diagnostic label, but rather to arrive at an individualized program of education which will both improve your child's academic performance and increase his self-esteem.

● **Parenting the Child with Learning Disabilities**

Because of the widespread publicity about learning disabilities, parents often ask if there is any way they can prevent their child from developing a learning disability. If your child has a specific learning disability (problem with information processing) then this problem is an inherent one which you cannot prevent. You can only modify the potential problems that result. Parents can make two basic contributions to their learning-disabled child. They can alleviate the emotional problems stemming from lack of school success and they can be sensitive to signs of trouble. Early detection and modification of learning problems in the preschool years is the best solution. (See related sections **Selecting** a **Preschool**, page 281, and **Parenting the Hyperactive Child**, page 288.)

With the trend toward preschool attendance growing, many potential learning problems can be spotted and remedial programs started prior to grade school entry. If, during the preschool years, you suspect that either a behavioral problem or a learning problem exists, then the choice of grade school becomes an important parental decision. Select a school to suit your child. Preschool entry should occur when your child is mentally, not chronologically mature for this step. This requires two things from parents: realistic expectations of your child's behavioral and learning potential and time and energy spent on school selection. For example, if your child has a basic problem with concentration and attention, then sending him to a so-called progressive or open system school may be unwise. He may adjust better to the more traditional, structured method of schooling.

What would happen if you didn't pay much attention to your child's poor school performance? Wouldn't he simply grow out of it? No, he probably will not grow out of it. He will more likely grow into a more serious problem. Persistent and untreated school failure deprives your child of a feeling of success and weakens his self-esteem. In order to protect his self-esteem and to obtain a feeling of success and peer recognition, he may direct his energies toward alternative, undesirable activities. The risk of juvenile delinquency increases.

● **The Carry-Over Principle**

The following are some specific suggestions on helping your child with his learning problems. First, your child must succeed in something. By encouraging activities at which he succeeds, you can give him the opportunity to build his self-esteem. By encouraging success in one skill he increases his self-esteem generally. This may carry over to result in an improvement in his learning problem. For example, if he is good in a certain sport, craft or school subject, then honest praise and encouragement of his strong points is as important as attention to his weak points.

Should you become involved in your child's tutoring? It is generally recommended that teaching be left to the teachers and parenting be left to the parents. Unless a learning disability exists which requires very specialized tutoring, I feel parents can and should become involved in the child's tutoring. Teachers have two qualities, competence and concern. What a parent may lack in competence (specialized methods of teaching a SLD child) he or she makes up for in concern and intuition. An alternative tutoring method is for a parent, preferably a mother, to receive some tutorial education to enable her to understand and to assist her child with his SLD. Although some educators may disagree with the parental tutoring concept, I feel that in no aspect of child rearing or child educating can science totally replace the parent. A word of caution is necessary if you are to become involved in your child's tutoring. You should not allow your entire parent-child relationship to be consumed by your child's learning problem. **Focus more attention on how he feels rather than on how he learns.** Focusing too much of your parental energy on your child's school problem may be counter-productive. It is necessary to continue pursuing the enjoyable activities of family life not directly related to your child's learning problem.

School Phobia
School phobia is referred to in medical circles as the "great imitator" because it is one of the most frequent medical examples of a child presenting a physical complaint which, in fact, stems from an emotional cause. School phobia results in poor school attendance and is caused by an inappropriate anxiety about leaving home, a fear of attending school or both. Your child will seldom admit that he is afraid to leave home or to attend school. He is more likely to say he has to stay home because he feels sick.

Suspect that school phobia is the cause of your child's pains when your child's physical complaints are vague. He has abdominal pains ("My stomach hurts"), nausea, vomiting, poor appetite, headaches, tiredness, weakness, occasional pallor, insomnia the night before school, chest pains, a sore throat or a dry, single cough during the day (children with respiratory infections usually cough more at night, tend to cough in a succession of five or more coughs and cough up some mucus). Some parents claim their child feels hot, but when they take their child's temperature it is normal.

These symptoms appear on school days, usually Sunday night or Monday morning, and disappear during weekends and holidays. The back-to-school month of September is the most common time for school phobia.

You may suspect that school phobia is the cause of your child's pain but, for the benefit of your child, your child's physician should make the diagnosis, not you. If the problem is indeed school phobia, your child's physician will be struck by one particular feature. Your child's symptoms are out of proportion to any objective physical findings. In addition to a complete physical examination, your doctor may wish to perform a few simple laboratory tests. If the physical exam and laboratory tests are normal then your suspicion of school phobia is supported.

● **Parenting the Child with School Phobia**

With the help of your child's doctor, your goal is to find a method of getting your child to school while still respecting his feelings. Separation-from-home anxiety is usually more of a problem than fear of school, so let's focus on why your child is afraid to leave home. It is quite usual and normal for a child to experience temporary separation-from-home anxiety when he first begins school, but normally this anxiety gives way to a feeling of comfortable independence.

When beginning your efforts at parenting your child back to school consider the following: Is your parent-child relationship fostering an over-dependency on home? Are you fostering a home dependency by consciously or unconsciously conveying to your child that you do not want him to be separated from you? An old psychology axiom summarizes the problem: "A child cannot be expected to tolerate separation from his parents if the parents cannot tolerate separation from the child." I do not feel that a strong dependency is always wrong or should be corrected, since it may simply be a manifestation of a secure and healthy parent-child relationship. However, a secure parent-child relationship should ideally enable the child to be more secure in his away-from-home relationships, which are very important for the personal and social development of a school-aged child. Examine your parent-child relationship. Is there any reason why your child should have an exaggerated fear of leaving you? Does he feel some harm may come to you or to his home when he is away? Don't confront your child with "Why are you afraid to go to school?" because you are likely to get nowhere. Instead, ask him "Why do you want to stay home?" This approach respects his feelings and he may eventually volunteer the reason for his separation-from-home anxiety. An example of this anxiety is a nine-year-old patient of mine who was refusing to attend school because there were many recent divorces in his class. He was afraid to leave home for fear his parents would divorce.

Next, attempt to find out if there is any threatening situation at school. Is he not experiencing success socially or academically? A discussion of the problem with the teacher may help to uncover these problems. A temporary school phobia is common after a child misses school for a prolonged period. This may be due to embarrassment at having missed school and having to justify his school absence to his peers, or a fear of being unable to catch up on missed work.

Your child's doctor can assist you in parenting your child back to school. He will perform a complete medical examination, giving your child a complete bill of health, and proclaiming that your child does not have an illness that should keep him out of school. He will then insist that you and your child return to school immediately. Sometimes, when your child insists that he is sick just before school time, tell him you are going to take him to the doctor and the doctor will decide whether he is well enough to go to school. Avoid focusing on your child's bodily complaints since this may simply reinforce his anxiety about his various aches and pains. Your child's doctor will also assist you in counselling your child and supporting his feelings. The aim of this counselling is to convey to your child the message that ''School attendance is not negotiable, but my parents and doctor will help me overcome my fear of leaving home or attending school.'' By getting your child back to school you break the vicious cycle of increased dependence on home which fosters more fear of school. This allows the healthy desire for school and social success to overcome his separation-from-home anxiety. To insist that he return to school without also attempting to respect his anxieties and determine the cause of his fears deprives your child of valuable parental and medical support resources.

Family Recreation Family recreation should be given top priority in the continuum of child-rearing. Family recreation allows both parents and children to see each other as sources of fun. Parents are often so caught up in the science of child-rearing that they overlook the pleasure of simply enjoying their children. Children often see parents as providers, educators and disciplinarians, not as sources of enjoyment.

Family recreation provides a time when family life is not disrupted by the extraneous social and economic pressures which require parents to spend so much time away from their child. This allows the focused attention so necessary to the developing child. This beautiful, fun time with your child allows you to really appreciate what a child can do with his senses, his motor coordination, and his feelings. It is a time to discover your child. One of the true joys of parenting is the spontaneous humor that occurs when parents and child are simply having fun together.

● **Family trips.**

There is, among all parents, a sincere feeling that ''We need to get away from our children'' or ''We need to be with each other.'' As a father of a large, demanding family I sympathize with the desire for these relief holidays. I would like, however, to propose an alternative— **family holidays**. What most parents really need is to get away from the many social, economic and job-related pressures, not their children. We have discovered that our children add a touch of reality to the vacation and make the whole trip much more meaningful. This is particularly important for fathers who can seldom afford the luxury of family time with no competing outside pressures.

Children need time off too, especially during the pressure-filled years of middle childhood and early adolescence. We have noted an improved school performance and general elevation in mood in our older children after returning from a family holiday.

Middle Childhood "Blues"

A very common phenomenon which occurs in children between seven and eleven years of age are vague one- or two-week periods during which they just seem down. Parents will call their pediatrician saying the child seems tired, not completely happy, perhaps not completely well. They are not sure what the problem is but there is a problem. Because the symptoms are so vague, parents are not even certain they should be concerned. The pediatrician examines the child and can find no physical problem.

To understand what causes these periods in your child, reflect upon your own life. There are periods when you seem uncertain of your direction in life, of your competence as a parent, your job, your social life or your marriage. You sit back and reassess what you have or have not accomplished.

I feel that these blue periods in childhood are similar to the ones in adulthood. There is pressure on your child to produce—school pressure, peer pressure and parental pressure. In addition to external pressures, a child begins to assess himself at this age: Who am I? Where am I going? What do my parents and friends think of me? The combination of uncertainty of his direction and, perhaps, dissatisfaction with himself dampens his motivation and outward show of energy. He slows down awhile to refuel. He seems sad and tired, a touch depressed. Childhood depression is one of the most commonly overlooked childhood problems. Parents are concerned because the child is supposed to be happy and active, not sad and tired.

Middle childhood blues may appear at a time of marital, financial or business stress which causes parents to be preoccupied with their problems. Children at this stage are particularly sensitive to the stressful vibrations within the family.

There are often associated vague physical complaints such as a single, dry cough, headaches, muscles aches or abdominal pains. If these periods occur in the pre-adolescent years of ten to eleven, the many body changes which are occurring may themselves cause fatigue.

This is a good time to take inventory of your parent-child relationship. What does your child need at this time? He needs reassurance about his worth, his abilities and his place in the family. If there are many children in the family, your child's blues may signal a need for more individual attention, a time for introducing a few special ''just for you'' outings. It may also be a good time for a family vacation. Parenting your child through these reassessment periods can be a great aid toward preparing for parent-child communication during the coming adolescent years.

Adolescence

Adolescence begins around eleven years of age and ends with the beginning of adult responsibilities, usually in the early twenties. The term ''adolescence'' refers to the physical and emotional changes which occur from the onset of the rapid growth phase to the end of physical growth. The age at which these changes occur is extremely variable from person to person. ''Onset of puberty'' is the period in which the body's sexual characteristics begin to appear.

Adolescence

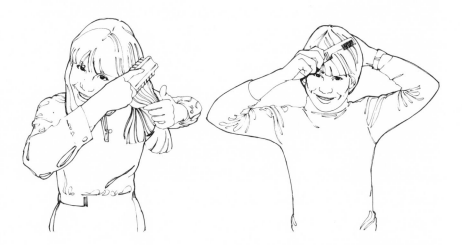

**Adolescent
Sexuality**

I wish to use the term sexuality to mean not only the physical changes that occur in the adolescent but also the feelings which are associated with these changes. The sum total of the physical changes and emotional adjustment to these changes culminate in what we may call the sexual person.

**Physical Changes
in the Adolescent
Girl**

The earliest physical change in girls is the budding of the breast glands. When these glands enlarge they feel like tiny lumps which may be slightly uncomfortable and tender to touch. It is important for you or your physician to prepare your daughter for these changes. (It is interesting to note that boys also have a few lumps of breast tissue when they begin puberty. These lumps may also be tender and parental explanation is necessary.) Breast enlargement is extremely variable and may begin as early as eight years of age. Usually around twelve or thirteen years of age nipple pigmentation and rapid breast enlargement begin.

The appearance of pubic hair heralds the onset of **menarche** (the beginning of menstruation), which begins usually within a year after the pubic hair appears. It is usual for a persistent, clear vaginal discharge to begin several months before menarche. There is a wide range in the age that menstruation begins (ten to sixteen and one half years). The average age of menarche is twelve and one half years. It is vitally important to explain menstruation to your daughter before her first period. It is usual for the first menstrual year to be very irregular. Ovulation usually occurs one to two years after menarche, at which time your daughter is fertile. Cramps or abdominal pains occurring mid-way between periods may signal that ovulation has begun. Besides the sequence of breast enlargement, menarche and ovulation, other bodily changes occur in the adolescent female. Her pelvis widens. There are increased fat deposits on her buttocks, breasts and hips, giving the female contour. There is a growth of axillary (underarm) hair and some girls even have the nuisance of a slight increase in facial hair.

Your daughter's growth spurt usually begins before menarche. Her rate of growth changes from the 1-3/4 inches to 2 inches per year of middle childhood, to the rate of 3 inches per year during the next two years, with most girls reaching their adult height by fifteen years. Girls begin their adolescent growth spurt and reach their adult height approximately two years earlier than boys.

The skin changes of puberty seem to mirror the intense hormonal changes, as if the excess hormones were coming out of the skin. Oily skin, pimples and blackheads (teenage acne) are a common result. An interesting fact of adolescent female life is that both the onset and the sequence of puberty (breast development-menarche-ovulation) are now occurring at an earlier age.

Physical Changes in the Adolescent Boy

The onset of puberty in a boy is not as obvious or sudden as in girls because there is no one easily identifiable change such as menarche. Increasing size and sensitivity of the testes is usually the first sign of male puberty. Pubic hair increases, followed by axillary and facial hair. The growth spurt in boys begins two years later than girls but continues two or three years after, until around eighteen years when adult height is usually reached. Deepening of the voice and elongation of the penis usually coincides with the height spurt. Nocturnal ejaculation ("wet dreams") usually begins one year after the height spurt begins and signals the beginning of male fertility. As girls should be prepared for menarche, boys should be prepared that noctural ejaculation is a normal occurrence in a developing male. Boys also show a temporary increase in breast tissue (small, tender lumps beneath the nipple) as well as a temporary increase in fat deposit.

Obesity tends to cause some embarrassing changes in adolescent males. Obese boys may accumulate excess fat on their breasts and also in their pubic area. This pad of pubic fat may encircle the penis and partially hide the penis, making it appear small. The combination of large breasts and small penis is embarrassing in our male locker room society.

While the female develops bodily contours by increased fat deposits, the male loses body fat and increases muscle mass during adolescence, giving him the male contours that are as important to the build-conscious male as fat contours are to the female.

Delayed Adolescence

"Why am I smaller than my friends?" is a real concern among adolescents who are not maturing as fast as many of their peers. When your child says "smaller" he or she usually means not only in height but also in sexual development. Teenagers are aware of and sensitive to the size and appearance of their sexual characteristics. Excluding an endocrine abnormality as the cause, most of these children are called "familial short stature with delayed adolescence," which simply means that the internal genetic factor that stimulates the adolescent growth spurt to begin is, for unknown reasons, delayed.

The adolescent late bloomer may be very concerned that she does not yet need a bra and has not yet had her menarche, or that he does not have a hairy face and deep voice and everything is shorter than his friends. Reassuring the delayed developer is a joint venture to be undertaken by parents and physician. It is vitally important that an adolescent develop his sexual identity regardless of his physical endowments. If a girl, for example, feels good about herself as a female she will feel confident in a group but, if not, she will have difficulty relating to both sexes. The adolescent's physician will reassure her that there is nothing wrong with her, and you, as parents, can contribute reassuring information such as, "I was the last one in my class to get my period. Don't worry, your time will come soon," or "It took your Dad a while to grow and around fourteen he suddenly got taller very fast."

Emotional Development of the Adolescent Sexual Person

One of the earliest drives an adolescent experiences is an enormous surge of inner energy. This is due not only to sexual drives, but also to an overall increase in body energy, probably a product of increased hormones.

Adolescents are active and initially this increased activity may appear to have no definite direction. Parents who try to contain this human dynamo usually end up exhausted. The first developmental challenge that the early adolescent experiences is how to adapt to these physical changes and channel these inner energies in a meaningful direction. Initially, the body energies may be released in aggressive behavior and the sexual energies released by masturbation and ejaculation. Sexual fantasizing is usual, especially among girls. (It is common for an adolescent to imagine what he can do long before he realizes what he really wants to do.)

Maturity implies defining these actions with feelings. The initial sexual drive of a purely physical nature begins to be tempered by feelings toward the opposite sex. The adolescent reflects upon how he feels about himself, how others feel about him and how he feels about others. Boys remain more action-oriented, pursuing sports and physical activities whereas girls tend to become more feeling-oriented.

The initial move to relate with the opposite sex is likely to be clumsy, indirect and motivated mainly by physical attraction. Telephone flirtation begins early because this means of communication avoids the face-to-face contact which the adolescent does not yet feel ready to handle. When feelings toward the opposite sex are added to the physical attraction, the adolescent is one step closer to a mature relationship. In the male, a quality of tenderness is added to his physical drive and in the female, reality replaces her romantic fantasizing. The result is that for the first time in adolescence, another person becomes as important as the adolescent himself.

Peer Relationships

Coincident with pulling away from his parents and seeking an independent existence, the adolescent desperately needs peer relationships. Peer acceptance and belonging to a group is one of the most intense adolescent needs. An adolescent must first learn to relate to persons of his own sex before he is confident in handling himself with members of the opposite sex. If a girl feels good about herself as a female person, has a strong sexual identity with other girls and is confident in her female relationships, she is likely to be more confident in the company of boys.

The Need for Self-Identity

Throughout adolescence your teenager is constantly striving for an identity: what he really is, what he wants to be, what his friends think of him, what his parents think of him, what the world is all about and where he is going. He strives to determine what he expects for himself and what society expects from him. Adolescents resent being stereotyped and rightly so. There is no such thing as the typical teenager. There are certain steps and goals necessary to the evolution from childhood to adulthood. However, the steps that adolescents may take and the methods they choose to achieve these goals are extremely variable. Your adolescent may take several routes of trial and error; each one will enable him to get closer to an awareness of himself.

The following are some common behaviors that adolescents exhibit during their quest for maturity.

1. Adolescents are prone to narcissism. Your teenager may have grandiose ideas and imagine himself bigger than he really is. During this stage, he is prone to experiment with daring adventures and increasing risks (e.g. driving recklessly). Both success and failure, complemented by proper parental support, help the adolescent to learn what his abilities and weaknesses are.

2. Erratic thinking and feelings are common (e.g. "I love Bob, I hate Bob, I hate all boys, I love Bob." "I have all the answers, my parents don't have all the answers, nobody knows anything, and the world is the pits.") Around this time, adolescents begin to realize that their parents are no longer omnipotent beings. While this is healthy, it can also produce anxiety. Idealization is transferred to friends, movie stars and sports heroes.

3. With the development of abstract and idealistic thinking, you adolescent may challenge traditional value systems, including those you have worked so hard to teach. This simply means that he is searching for which parts of his world are worthwhile and have meaning for him because he really believes in them, no because someone else advocates them.

Later Adolescence

Toward the end of adolescence, behavior becomes less turbulent By this time, adolescents have usually developed a secure iden tity and a relatively stable personality. The late adolescent i more able to control his impulses, delay gratification and assum a responsibility to himself and to society. Most boys and girl have defined their relationships toward the opposite sex. Th ability to comfortably handle genuine feelings toward the oppo site sex may be one of the most positive influences towar achievement of an adolescent's ultimate goal—maturity.

Parenting Your Adolescent

Successful parenting of the adolescent necessitates a balanc between respecting your adolescent's quest for self-identity an still offering parental guidance when you feel he needs it or pref erably when he feels he needs it.

Parents need to prepare for adolescence in what I call th "warm-up period." This suggestion is based on the principl that the best way to prevent undesirable behavior is to encourag desirable and meaningful behavior. Toward the end of middl childhood (nine to ten years), just as you are enjoying the relativ equilibrium of middle childhood, realize that potential troubl lies ahead and take preventive steps. This is a time to take a com plete inventory of your parent-child relationship and your chil as a total person. Ask yourself the following questions:

1. How effective is my communication with my child? If it i not good, improve rapport now. The adolescent period is th most difficult stage in which to begin parent-chil communication.

2. How good is my child's self-image and what can I do now t help him increase his self-esteem? A child who enters adoles cence with a positive self-image is likely to have less adolescer turmoil.

3. What are his current interests, involvements and attachments The adolescent needs involvements and attachments—better it b in meaningful activities and groups. In the pre-adolescent period encourage involvement in a skill or sport in which he is bot interested and capable and which is likely to continue through adolescence. Studies have shown that adolescents who are strongly involved in church and/or school activities are less likely to seek out undesirable activities.

When your child reaches adolescence, effective parent-teenager communication is very important. Teenagers often go through stages in which they communicate very superficially with parents. Teenagers clam up, and parents feel left out. They press the teenager to open up and he increases their frustrations by becoming more aloof. Respect the fact that teenagers are often very private people, not because they are deliberately trying to disturb you, but because the privacy stage is just another symptom of their need for independence.

To improve your parent-teenager communication:

1. Be available on a one-to-one basis. Time with each parent gives your adolescent the opportunity to open up and communicate when his defenses are down. An example of this is what I call the DDD method (Daddy-Daughter Date). Fathers, an occasional night out with your daughter is a very effective setting for father-daughter communication. The sexual identity of an adolescent girl can be much improved by what she feels is her image in her father's eyes.

2. Tell your teenager you understand a dilemma that he may be facing, and in your own words, tell him that you are very willing to act as a support resource. You have opened up your door to him; whether he choses to enter is his own decision. Pressing for communication is doomed to failure.

3. Convey your love to your adolescent as if he were still a child. Physically, he may be an adolescent but emotionally he may still be a child. Touching, eye-to-eye contact, kind words and individual attention are just as necessary for the adolescent as they are for the child. If your adolescent feels your guidance is based on love for him, he will respect your discipline, whether or not he agrees with it.

How effective your parent-child communication is during adolescence is a measure of your relationship prior to adolescence. Instant intimacy with an adolescent is rarely possible. Adolescent-parent communication is the result of the many steps of continuum parenting.

Concerns of adolescence

● **Dating**

When adolescents should begin to date is a common dilemma facing parents. There is no definite answer. It depends upon your parenting philosophy and the maturity of your adolescent.

It does not seem to make sense to arbitrarily state an age at which your adolescent may date, e.g. "You may not go out on a date until you are sixteen." Let me suggest some alternatives.

1. Encourage boy-girl activities at a younger age. Encourage chaperoned mixed parties before the mutual attraction between sexes is mostly physical. It is important for boys and girls to learn to enjoy each other's company on a non-physical, non sexual basis first.

2. Encourage mixed outings, e.g. church youth groups, school clubs, backyard dances. These group activities give the adolescent the opportunity to relate to both sexes in the "comfort in numbers" setting.

3. In a family recreation activity encourage your adolescent to bring his friends along—male and female.

4. Evaluate the circumstances of each date before giving your permission. Ask who they are going with, where they are going and when they will be home.

The art of communicating with a dating teenage daughter or son is to convey that you require your adolescent to manifest certain level of responsibility before he or she may date, you trust your adolescent's judgment to behave as a responsible person, you expect your adolescent to trust your judgment about whether he or she may go on a certain date. You are not being an old-fashioned parent if you say no. You are simply being caring and involved parent.

Parents are usually more concerned when their teenage daughter is asked out on a date by an older boy and she seeks their permission. Since girls mature earlier than boys, they may want to date sooner and with older boys. First, be sure she really wants to go. If you sense that your daughter is not ready for this involvement but is being pushed into early dating by her peers or older boys, then say no. Your daughter can simply relate to her friends that her parents said no. Your daughter is then off the hook and you are a welcome scapegoat.

● **Acne**

Acne is one of the physical nuisances of adolescence and reflects the influence of increased hormones on the oils of the skin. The culprit which causes the unwelcome "zits" is the **sebaceous gland**, tiny glands which are attached to the root of the hair, especially in the face and back. These glands produce an oily substance, **sebum**, which lubricates the hair. The hormones enlarge and secrete more sebum. The increased sebum plugs the opening of the hair shaft resulting in the earliest form of acne called the whitehead. This plug then becomes covered with skin cells and, upon constant exposure to the air, becomes a blackhead. These early blackheads and whiteheads are called **comedos** and represent the earliest and mildest form of acne. The comedo may become infected with bacteria and produce the unsightly pimple. The enlarging pimples give the appearance and feeling of ''pus under pressure'' prompting the adolescent to ''squeeze the zit.''

Some adolescents are more prone to acne than others because of their type of skin and the amount of oil in it. Some acne is to be expected as a normal fact of adolescent life. You can usually not prevent the mild form of acne such as whiteheads and blackheads (comedos). The real goal of acne management is to prevent these comedos from becoming pimples and the pimples from enlarging to form cysts within the skin, which can leave permanent scarring or ''pits'' in the skin. The following are some simple tips on keeping acne under control:

1. Good facial hygiene. Uncleanliness does not cause acne but it does aggravate it. Very oily areas of the skin should be washed frequently and dried well. Harsh, abrasive soaps and vigorous scrubbing may irritate the skin and are usually not necessary. Very oily areas should be washed more frequently. Less oily areas may be washed less frequently to avoid chapping. The type and strength of the soap depends upon how oily and sensitive the skin is and whether other creams and lotions are being used. Consult a doctor before using an abrasive soap. A back brush is useful for washing the areas difficult to get at on the back.

2. The skin should be allowed to breathe; don't block the pores. Acne tends to be aggravated by the custom of resting an oily face on an oily hand. Occlusive night creams should be avoided. Forehead acne is aggravated by long hair, bangs and tight sweat bands. If a ''cover-up'' is necessary, a water-based formula should be used.

3. Sunlight improves acne by causing the superficial layers of the skin to peel.

4. The many emotional stresses to which adolescents are prone may also aggravate their acne.

5. The tempting custom of pimple squeezing is one of the main contributors to permanent scarring from acne.

6. The role of diet in acne control is over-estimated and there is little evidence that certain foods cause acne. The saying ''greasy foods cause greasy skin'' is a myth, although the occasional teenager does report feeling that chocolate foods worsen his acne. The relationship of diet to acne may, however, be a healthy myth to perpetuate and to motivate good eating habits in teenagers.

If the above simple preventive measures do not keep your adolescent's acne under control, medical consultation is advised. Medical treatment of acne consists basically of cleansing the skin with various agents to remove excess oil, applying "peeling agents" which remove the "top of the plug" and prevent the comedos from becoming larger, removing large blackheads with a comedo extractor, and giving antibiotics which treat the infected pimple and also seem to have a beneficial effect on the composition of the oils.

Parenting the adolescent with acne involves treating not only his pimples but also his emotional reaction to these pimples. Acne "is in the eye of the beholder" and what is more important is how your adolescent's acne seems to him rather than to you. Your teenager is already painfully aware of his pimples every time he looks in the mirror and focusing parental attention on the teenager's acne will do little for his already shaky self-esteem.

● **Marijuana**

Marijuana (pot, grass) and the stronger drug hashish (hash) come from the plant cannabis sativa. The main psychoactive ingredient of marijuana is 9-THC and the intoxicating effect depends upon the amount of 9-THC in each cigarette. The amount of active ingredient that actually enters the bloodstream depends upon the strength of the street preparation, the mode of inhaling and the smoker's individual metabolism. Because there is a wide range in each of these variables, marijuana produces a wide range of effects in different people. Psychological and physical effects usually appear within several minutes after smoking; the peak effect occurs ten to twenty minutes later and lasts around one or two hours after smoking a single cigarette. This "instant turn-on" is one of the reasons for the increasing popularity of marijuana and hashish.

The main effect of marijuana is the change in sensory perception of one's environment. Visual images are more vivid. Hearing becomes more acute and there is a heightened awareness of the quality of musical sounds. Touch, taste and smell are subjectively enhanced. Laughter and "looseness" may enhance social interaction. High doses may actually cause social withdrawal. Although a positive emotional experience is described by most users, a temporary overwhelming and frightening nega tive emotional state may occur, especially when a potent preparation is given to a new user.

To what degree the psychological effect is real and to what degree it is imaginary is difficult to determine. There is a definite placebo effect, which reflects a learned set of expectations in experienced users or the effects that the group describes to a new user. The setting seems to enhance the psychological effects. Social interaction is enhanced in a group setting; sedative effects are experienced when smoking alone. An individual's behavioral temperament may determine sensitivity to the effects of marijuana.

Marijuana causes a dose-related impairment of scholastic mental performance, which interferes especially with short-term memory skills. Gross and fine motor coordination skills are diminished and the reflex motor reaction time is impaired. Of particular importance to the teenager are the detrimental effects of marijuana on driving performance. Specifically, marijuana may impair driving performance by increasing the braking time, by increasing the time required to visually recover from headlight glare of night driving, and by causing lapses of attention.

The impairment of mental and motor performance caused by smoking a marijuana cigarette is equivalent to that caused by consuming three bottles of beer or three ounces of 100 proof alcohol. When marijuana and alcohol are consumed together, the effects are additive. In addition to diminished mental acuity and motor coordination, reddening of the eyeballs may be the most easily recognizable sign that an adolescent has recently smoked marijuana.

The possibility of developing a physical dependence on marijuana does not apparently exist, certainly not to the extent of an addiction to alcohol or opium drugs. There are also no severe withdrawal features similar to those which occur with alcohol or opium drugs. However, with increased usage, higher doses are required to produce the same effects.

At this writing, there does not seem to be a definitely proven, permanently harmful physical effect of marijuana. Our present knowledge indicates that alcohol and tobacco have more proven harmful effects. However, our knowledge of the possible harmful effects of marijuana is far from complete and, therefore, we should not be lulled into considering marijuana safe.

The harmful physical effects of drugs should not be the major concern of parents and pediatricians. What should concern them is the development of drug habits at a particularly vulnerable age. At the very age the adolescent is searching for his identity ar evaluating various value systems, the use of drugs is programmir the teenager to use artificial stimulants, to turn on from withor rather than from within. This, and the possible predisposition using more addictive drugs, is of primary concern.

• Drug and Alcohol Abuse

Our main objective is to prevent drug abuse in the adolescen Most adventurous teenagers will occasionally smoke a joint have a drink. This is part of an adolescent's normal curiosity try all those forbidden things. This experimentation is a fact adolescent life and should not be considered a reflection of ine fective parenting or cause the "Where have I gone wrong?" fee ing in parents.

If your continuum of child-rearing has been successf your child should enter adolescence with the following found: tion: a secure meaningful family relationship; a positive sel image; involvement in meaningful activities in which he exper ences success and retains interest; secure peer relationships and respect for the value system presented to him by his environme of family, school, church and friends.

A child who enters adolescence without the above four dation is a high risk for drug abuse. Even a child who enters ad lescence with this foundation, and who seems to have his a together, may temporarily experiment with drugs. Howeve most of these adolescents eventually adopt the values which hav been instilled in them. They actually become a little wiser an more sure of these values from their experimentation, having ha the opportunity to decide for themselves what constitutes meaningful turn on.

What about the adolescent who has a drug or alcoh abuse problem? First, find out what purpose drugs serve in you adolescent's life and seek alternative stimulation. Get your ad lescent involved in meaningful activities at which he succeeds Your best defense against continued drug abuse is a good offens of involvement. Improve your parent-child relationship throug family recreation and meaningful discussions. Your goal is t build up your adolescent's trust in you so that he will be recep tive to a statement such as, "Drugs are bad for you, they are ille gal, and you should not use them."

The most effective drug education programs have bee those in which respected peers present the detrimental effects c drug abuse. In one California pilot study of this successful approach, participating students wore buttons that read "I'm na urally high." Since adolescents are more susceptible to peer advice than parental or adult authority advice, this peer education approach is a wise route. The use of sports figures or other heroes to speak against drugs is another successful method.

You may also take the "privilege-responsibility" approach as discussed in the section on discipline, page 244. In this approach you, as parents in authority, set down certain rules of responsible living. These include rules about teenage drinking or smoking. As your adolescent exhibits increasing responsibility and respects your wishes, his privileges also increase, for example, increased driving time or later hours. This approach works only if your adolescent trusts that your parental rules are in his own best interest.

Sexuality Education

The topic of sex education in the home and the schools has been the subject of much controversy and concern in recent years. I do not like the term sex education since it implies that purely physical considerations are involved. I prefer the term "sexuality," which covers not only the physical changes of various stages, but the emotions and attitudes associated with these physical changes.

Sexual Development from Infancy to Adolescence

Discovery of the genitals usually begins in the second year. The normal and healthy exploration of body parts begins with thumb sucking and finger-play in early infancy. The initial poking and tugging is followed by an awareness of genital sensitivity and the pleasure of self-stimulation. In fact, the exploration of body parts and the use of the body parts as a source of stress relief is considered by some researchers as evidence of a secure environment. Infants raised with a weak maternal-infant attachment (for example, those raised in institutions) exhibit less body exploration and genital play than infants with a secure parent-infant attachment. Toilet learning, the next genital milestone of infancy, gives an increased awareness of genital sensations, structure and function and the first realization in the child that he can control "how it works." Your attitudes and the feelings you convey toward your infant's toilet learning and genital exploration may be your earliest attempt at sexuality education.

Gender identity becomes apparent by age three when children begin calling other children "boys" and "girls." Little

girls and boys become aware that they urinate differently. Littl
girls wonder why they have no penis and where the urine come
from. At this point it is important to show little girls what the
have so that they are not preoccupied with what they don't have
Boys may wonder why girls have no penis and whether the
might lose their penis like the girls obviously did. If you notic
your child's genital bewilderment, eliminate his concern
through proper instruction. Call it like it is. Give your child th
proper names for genitalia—penis, vagina, vulva.

Gender-appropriate behavior is apparent at this age. Boy
are more aggressive and engage in more active play than girls a
this age. Much of this behavior difference may be a reflection c
parents' encouragement of gender-appropriate behavior. (Se
Gender Identity, page 280). I find myself slipping into thi
gender trap with my own patients, by eliciting a hug and kis
from a little girl and a handshake and ''give me five'' from a lit
tle boy. Also, I remember my own ridiculous attitude the firs
time I saw my three-year-old boy playing with a doll; the wisdor
of my wife fortunately saved the doll from immediate substitu
tion with a football. Perhaps parental programming of mor
aggressive behavior in boys may partially contribute to the muc
higher incidence of aggressive behavioral problems in boys. Th
show of affection and tenderness should be encouraged in botl
sexes. Assertiveness and physical activity should also be encour
aged in girls.

Most behavior differences between the sexes in infanc
and early childhood seem to be innate. We merely reinforce soci
ety's expectations of these innate sex differences. It is doubtfu
that differences in sexual behavior in infancy and early childhoo
are due to cultural factors alone.

Around three or four years of age, a child shifts from on
sex role to another, alternating between dolls and footballs, an
gradually adapts to the sex role that he or she is ''dressed'' in
For some children, such as the ''tomboy'' girl, sex-rol
adaptation is uneasy and prolonged. I feel that it is healthy fo
children to adjust to sexual behavior at their own pace. Parent
should take cues from their children rather than push sexual role
upon a child who is still finding his own way.

Around four years of age, most children realize the dif
ferent roles played by mother and father. Most mothers hav
babies and most fathers work. Girls want to grow up and be a
Mommy and have babies and boys want to grow up and be what
ever Daddy is. How effectively mothers are mothers, and father

are fathers, may leave valuable impressions upon your impressionable preschoolers.

A word about the infamous Oedipus complex seems in order here. This is the love triangle in which the boy wishes to replace the father, and the girl the mother. In the majority of homes, this idea is an insignificant and passing phase. Children seem more intent on becoming like the parent than replacing the parent.

"How-to-Tell" Techniques

Usually around four years of age the anticipated question, "Where do babies come from?" is usually asked and parents are called upon to begin their child's formal sexuality education. The following are some how-to-tell techniques for the young child:

1. Wait for openers. Seldom do children come right out and ask, "Where do babies come from?" They are more likely to look curiously at a pregnant lady or ask Mommy to go to the store and buy a baby.

2. Use correct terms and facts. Babies come from Mommy's uterus, not her tummy. The concept of a baby in a tummy eventually becomes inconceivable to the child and may make your teaching suspect. Give your child the correct terms for genitalia. If a child can say alligator and dinosaur he is certainly capable of saying penis, vagina and vulva.

3. Use books for visual aids, not as a substitute for parental instruction. A useful book for the young child is **How Babies Are Made**.

4. Use simple, short answers. Too much detail confuses the child. Do not volunteer more than he asks but let him satisfy his curiosity at his own pace. Young children have a limited ability to think abstractly and are prone to misinterpret statements. Their primitive ideas will prevail alongside the facts. Generally speaking, treat early sexuality education as part of the long list of body functions about which your child wants to learn.

Dirty Words

Children learn early that certain words have shock value. If you drop your fork at the dinner table the first time your four-year-old comes out with a four-letter word, your reactions may encourage the child to continue using his obscenities. Parental example is often the best deterrent to undesirable language in a child. If the parent uses a dirty word then this word is certainly not dirty in the eyes of the child. Sometimes an explanation of the real meaning of certain slang words and the use of alternative words help to defuse the shock value of slang.

Middle Childhood   The period from school entry to puberty is commonly referred to as the latency, or dormant, period because there is a gradual decrease in the rate of growth and, perhaps, sexual interest. While this may be a latent period for your child, it should not be a latent period for parents. Correcting sexuality information and forming sexual attitudes are the prerequisites to a smooth adolescent sexuality and are very critical during this period. During the latency stage, gender lines are seldom crossed. Boys stick with boys and girls stick with girls. This period is often described as the period of normal homosexuality. Play interests, "boy activities" and "girl activities" shape their future roles. Exhibition of genitals may occur at this age: "I'll show you mine if you show me yours."

Often around eight or ten years of age children become very private about their bodies and may become uncomfortable with parental nudity. If you sense these feelings, parental nudity should become discreet. During middle childhood and pre adolescence, your child may begin to get sexuality information from outside the home. Accurate sexuality information obtained in the home may eliminate this "blind leading the blind" sexuality education obtained from his equally poorly-informed peers. The following are specific guidelines for healthy sexuality education during middle childhood:

1. Teach your child at the rate he wants to learn, according to his own curiosity. Parents who are tuned into their children's needs usually know "when" and "how much" to teach.

2. Be comfortable with your own presentation. Rather than pick a method out of a book with which you might not be comfortable, devise a method of your own. The main purpose of books is to act as a visual aid to sexuality education. The philosophy and mode of presentation, however, must be yours. If you are comfortable, your child will be more comfortable. If you are not, your child will pick up your feelings.

3. Teach when your child is in a receptive mood. Don't suddenly announce one evening, "Tonight we are going to talk about sex." This is doomed to failure. Wait until your child gives you a cue that he is interested and receptive. Usually this cue will be a simple question. Effective home education is spontaneous, unstructured and mood-considered.

4. Besides providing accurate information, parents should teach attitudes about sexuality. Information may be taught, attitudes must be lived. Parental example means how you convey sexual attitudes. Does your body language convey how you love each other? Are you a ''hugs and kisses'' family? In a nutshell, the most meaningful sexuality education is conveyed by the day-to-day example of family living. The result of an effective sexuality education at home is that when a child enters adolescence, he trusts his home as a source of accurate information and comfortable example. Appreciate that usually children and adolescents do not easily approach their parents for information about sex. If your child does, this is an impressive compliment to your parent-child communication.

Sex Education in the School

Perhaps no subject has received more attention and been a subject of more controversy than sex education in schools. If you want to guarantee a large attendance at a PTA meeting, advertise the topic of the meeting as ''Discussion About Sex Education.'' Parents are concerned about too much, too soon and adolescents are concerned about too little, too late. Opponents of sex education in schools fear that information will foster more interest and therefore more sexually active behavior. They also believe that the parents' values will be undermined. Advocates of sex education in schools suggest that adolescents need a better understanding of sexuality in order to make more responsible decisions about their sexual behavior. In fact, a problem does exist. Today's adolescents are more sexually active than former generations and sexuality education is deficient. Can you imagine teen pregnancy and venereal disease being listed among the common problems of adolescents in current pediatric texts? But while parents and schools are theorizing about how to best teach the ''kids'' the facts of life, the ''kids'' are gaining practical experience (for which, in many instances, they are totally unprepared).

The school is faced with many dilemmas on the subject of sex education. The level of interest in already acquired information varies substantially among the class. How do you teach a class without under-teaching some and over-teaching others? Can you approach sexuality like any other subject in the biology curriculum? Should a student have a certain level of knowledge at a certain age? How does the school present accurate biological information (which I feel should be part of a high school biology class) without, of necessity, discussing questions of attitude and morality (which many parents feel should be the primary responsibility of the home)?

Parents are rightly concerned about who is teaching what in the school, and the school needs to know what the parents feel should be taught, when, and by whom. The key to effective sex-

uality education in schools depends, therefore, upon the parent
and the school creating a sexuality education program which bes
suits the needs of the adolescents in their own school. The fol
lowing are some suggestions about reaching an agreement on a
effective sex education program in your school:

The attitudes and ethics of adolescent sexuality should b
taught, or more correctly, lived at home. You cannot teach in
two-week high school course what has been lived for ten years a
home. School, however, can provide a further dimension to sex
uality education. Adolescent sexuality attitudes are influence
not only by the example in the home but by media, religiou
groups, and peers. The school affords the opportunity for pee
group discussions. Some adolescents feel more comfortable i
group discussions about sexuality rather than in a privat
discussion with their parents. Group discussions and the man
visual aids available to schools are the main benefits of sexualit
education in the schools.

The main question seems to be not whether sexuality edu
cation should be part of a school program but how it is taught.
feel sexuality education should be lived at home, taught i
schools and discussed in value-oriented groups (such as churc
youth groups). Input in these three areas will, hopefully, allo
the development of a sexually responsible adolescent.

1. Before deciding on a curriculum, parents should be involve
in the decision about who will teach what to which grades.

2. Sexuality education should be presented as part of a genera
biology course on "how the body works" and not marketed as
separate sex education course.

3. Certain elements of sex education such as menstruation, fen
inine hygiene, and wet dreams, may be more comfortably taugl
by separating boys and girls. The general topic of adolescent sex
ual changes in the body and reproductive organs should b
shared by both sexes and discussion should be encouraged.

4. Never lump sex education with a discussion on alcohol an
drug abuse. ("Today we are going to discuss three common add
lescent problems: drugs, alcohol and sex.") Sexuality, is a nor
mal, healthy part of maturing; drugs and alcohol are not.

The attitudes and ethics of adolescent sexuality should b
taught, or more correctly, lived at home. You cannot teach in
two-week high school course what has been lived for ten years a
home. School, however, can provide a further dimension to sex
uality education. Adolescent sexuality attitudes are influenced nc
only by the example in the home but by media, religious groups

and peers. The school affords the opportunity for peer group discussions. Some adolescents feel more comfortable in group discussions about sexuality rather than in a private discussion with their parents. Group discussions and the many visual aids available to schools are the main benefits of sexuality education in the schools.

The main question seems to be not whether sexuality education should be part of a school program but how it is taught. I feel sexuality education should be lived at home, taught in schools and discussed in value-oriented groups (such as church youth groups). Input in these three areas will, hopefully, allow the development of a sexually responsible adolescent.

CHAPTER VIII

PARENTING THE COMMON CHILDHOOD ILLNESSES

Parenting the Sick Child

Parents are normally so attuned to their child's behavior that they can recognize the early signs of illness. Parents will often say "He just doesn't look like himself." A term which I hear very often is "peaked." This old term escapes definition but mothers know what it means—a combination of pale, sad circles under sad droopy eyelids, and a generally tired and worn-out appearance. Young children often show regressive undesirable behavior during illnesses—bedwetting, temper tantrums, attention-getting antics, whining, and sleep disturbances. Your child may show diminished appetite, nausea and vomiting and generalized muscle aches and headaches. A sick child usually brings out the best in parental instincts and love—TLC (tender loving care) in medical jargon. Parents are naturals at providing this remedy.

Should he stay in bed? Children usually limit their own activity and it is seldom necessary to force them to stay in bed. What about fluids? (Chicken soup is grandmother's oldest remedy for all illnesses.) Sick children usually lose their appetite for solid foods. Cold symptoms and fever do increase a child's need for fluids so it is important to increase his fluid intake. Small, frequent feedings (just like feeding an infant) are usually the most tolerable means of providing nutrition for an ill child.

Giving Medicine

Even young toddlers begin to develop attitudes about takin
something to feel better. A toddler develops a fascination fc
bandaids, thinking he needs to seal even the tiniest leak in hi
body. A child will frequently approach his most available physi
cian, his mother, and request an ointment for his scratch. Th
desire for bandaids and ointments is a healthy and humorou
stage of childhood development and reflects a child's emergin
pride in the integrity of his body. When it comes to various col
syrups, it may be unwise to convey to your child that every tim
he develops a sniffle Mommy will reach in the medicine cabino
for a magic solution which will clear up his cold. It is much bet
ter to begin, at an early age, to teach your child good nasa
hygiene (blowing his own nose).

Most medicines are packaged in palatable syrup and chil
dren are no longer required to swallow large pills. However,
sick child is often an unreasonable and unwilling child and ma
refuse to take his medicine. Simply convey to him that this is
non-negotiable item, and get it down any way you can. You ma
have to resort to Mary Poppins' routine— "A spoonful of suga
makes the medicine go down." Crushing an aspirin in a spoonfu
of a favorite jam is a technique frequently used.

Most childhood medicines are prescribed to be taken b
the teaspoonful (5 ml). Since home teaspoons come in variou
sizes, it is wise to purchase a dropper or a teaspoon calibrated a
2.5 ml and 5 ml. Most drugstores carry various calibrate
devices for administering medicine. These are not only mor
accurate but make giving the medicine a bit easier.

Parenting the Child with Fever

Since you will probably spend more time parenting your chil
through fever than treating any other single childhood illness,
shall present this section on fever in much greater detail than tha
of many of the other childhood symptoms.

Your child's body temperature is regulated by an organ i
his brain called the **hypothalmus**. This is a thermostat whic
helps regulate the balance between heat production and heat los
in the body. For example, when your child is cold he shivers t
produce heat, and when he is warm he sweats to lose heat. Infec
tions release substances called **pyrogens** (heat producing sub

stances) into your child's blood stream, which elevate the body's temperature or cause fever. Your child's body thermostat reacts to reduce the heat, through dilation of the blood vessels, and an increased heartbeat. This brings more blood to the surface of his skin where the heat can dissipate and accounts for his flushed cheeks. He may sweat in order to cool by evaporation and he may breathe faster to get rid of the warm air.

In addition to being a signal of an underlying illness, fever itself causes a child to feel ill (headache, muscle aches and general tiredness). Besides seeking medical attention for the cause of the fever, the following are suggestions to help you parent your child through his illness.

ow To Use a hermometer

What is fever? Although normal temperature is usually stated to be 98.6° F (37° C), normal temperature may also vary among individuals from 97° F and 100.5° F (36° C-38° C). Also, the daily temperature may normally vary within the same individual, usually lower in the morning and during rest, and as much as a degree higher in late afternoon or during strenuous exercises. Generally, a temperature greater than 100.5° F, (38°C) no matter where, or when taken, may be considered a fever.

THERMOMETER CONVERSION CHART

93.3	95	96.8	98.6	100.4	102.2	104	105.8	Fahrenheit
34	35	36	37	38	39	40	41	Celsius

Your child's temperature may be taken in three locations—the rectum, the armpit or axillary, and the mouth. The rectal thermometer has a rounded stubby end which allows easy insertion into the rectum. The oral themometer has a longer, thinner shaft which holds the mercury. The thermometers are marked oral and rectal. Rectal thermometers are easiest and safest to use in most children under five years of age. After age five the oral thermometer may be used to take either the oral or axillary temperature. Buy the thermometer which is easiest for you to read (some are easier than others). The thermometer is graduated in long lines which mark each degree and short lines which mark each two-tenths of a degree, for example, 98.2° F, 98.4° F and 98.6° F. You may need some practice to find the mercury line. Hold the thermometer at the top, the end opposite from the mercury bulb. Slowly roll the thermometer between your thumb and forefinger until you notice the wide silver ribbon of mercury. Some thermometers have a red line marking 98.6° F. Before taking a temperature, hold the thermometer firmly at the top and shake it with a wrist-snapping motion in order to "shake down" the mercury column below the 95° F mark. (Shake it over a bed or soft surface in case you drop it.)

To take your child's rectal temperature:

1. Shake down the rectal thermometer and grease the bulb end with petroleum jelly.

2. Lay your child across your lap face down as in Figure 5.

Figure 5.
Rectal temperature

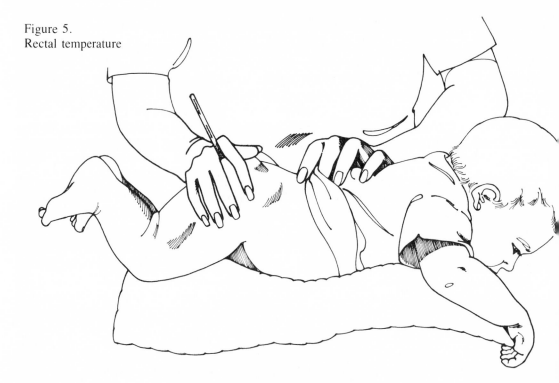

3. Gently insert the thermometer bulb about one inch into the rectum, allowing the thermometer to find its own path. Don't force it.

4. Hold the thermometer between your index and middle fingers with your palm down, so that you can grasp your child's buttocks together with your fingers. In this way you can control both his movements and the thermometer so that it will neither come out nor injure his rectum if he moves. Never leave a child alone with a thermometer in place.

5. Ideally, try to keep the rectal thermometer in place for three minutes. However, the rectal temperature reading will approach within a degree of the true temperature the first minute, so if your child is protesting, it is not necessary to leave it in more than a minute.

6. Write down the temperature reading. It is also a good practice to feel or kiss your child's forehead or body at the same time you are recording his temperature to educate your hand to act as a quick thermometer.

Rectal temperature is usually one half to one degree higher than oral temperature and axillary temperature is usually a degree lower than oral. Use a rectal thermometer unless you are sure your child is emotionally able to cooperate in oral temperature-taking.

To take your child's temperature orally, place the mercury end under your child's tongue slightly to one side and have him close his lips firmly. Instruct him to leave his mouth closed while the thermometer is in because the passage of air during breathing may make the temperature reading inaccurate. He may hold the outer end of the thermometer with his fingers to keep it in place but be sure he does not hold the thermometer with his teeth. Taking a temperature orally requires two to three minutes to achieve an accurate reading. It takes three to four minutes to achieve a stable reading when taking an axillary temperature.

When to Worry About Fever

What is often more important than the level of the fever is how sick your child generally seems to you. If his fever is high (103° F - 105° F) but he does not act as sick as his high fever would indicate, if you are able to bring the fever down easily by the methods suggested below, and if he seems better to you when you get the fever down, then this may be a less worrisome situation. However, if he looks and acts sick even with a slight fever and especially with a high fever, if he does not seem better to you when his fever subsides a little, or if his fever remains high after you apply the methods below, then this situation is certainly more worrisome and your doctor should be called immediately. The younger your infant, the more worrisome is his fever. **Any fever in an infant under four months of age should be immediately reported to your doctor.** Between the ages of six months and one year, infants commonly have a viral illness called **roseola** which produces a very high fever (103° F - 105° F) for three days. After the fever drops, a faint generalized rash appears and lasts usually for less than twenty-four hours. Parents often say, ''I am surprised his fever is so high because he does not look or act that sick." (See **Roseola**, page 411.)

When taking your child to a doctor for any illness, especially fever, remember that you are visiting the doctor for consultation and advice, not always for medication. For example, recently a mother who had brought her child to see me for assessment of the child's high fever was, upon leaving, asked by my nurse what I had said was wrong with her child. This mother replied, "Oh, she has nothing." Because I had not given her child any medicine for the fever (except the usual methods described below), she had incorrectly inferred that her child did not have any illness.

When your doctor examines your child for fever, in addition to determining the source of your child's fever, he is trying to make a judgment whether the fever is caused by a virus or bacteria. Certains infections, such as ear, throat, and urine infections are caused by bacteria and need antibiotics for proper treatment. Other infections are caused by viruses and your child may exhibit no symptoms other than a high fever. This is termed a **fever of unknown origin**. These FUOs are usually three- to five-day viral illnesses, subside without antibiotic treatment and need only the temperature control methods outlined below. If your child seems unusually sick for a viral illness, your doctor may wish to do some laboratory tests to help him make a diagnosis. The exact cause of your child's fever is often difficult to determine in the first twenty-four hours. Therefore, follow-up reporting to your doctor is necessary. This means that your doctor will ask you to report to him in twenty-four hours and, if your child develops any other symptoms such as ear pain or increasing drowsiness, he may need to reassess his initial opinion. Viral illnesses generally improve during the follow-up period. Untreated bacterial infections may gradually worsen or produce further symptoms and thus require a change of diagnosis and treatment.

I cannot overemphasize the importance of reporting to your doctor should your child's general condition worsen during this follow-up period.

Treating Your Child's Fever

What can you do to help your child get rid of fever? The use of antipyretic medications such as aspirin and acetaminophen (Tylenol and Tempra) will help to reset his thermostat. The methods outlined below will help to increase heat loss. **Both** of these procedures are necessary. Using heat removal procedures without first resetting his thermostat with medications is usually ineffective. For example, if your house is too warm, you lower the thermostat and open the windows. If you open the windows but do not reset the thermostat, heat production continues and your house remains warm. Aspirin and acetaminophen reset your child's thermostat so that when you bring his temperature down, using the methods below, his thermostat will not produce more heat.

Aspirin— Selecting the Proper Dosage

The dosage schedules below are based on a review of the medical research literature and upon my own experience, and are dosages designed to be both safe and effective. Also, the following dosage schedule is based on giving aspirin every four hours around the clock. Since it is usually unwise to awaken a sleeping child with fever, in reality most children miss one or two dosages each day and therefore even the following schedule is slightly conservative. Children's aspirin comes in 1-1/4 grain size (75 mg tablets). If you wish to be precise, you may calculate your child's dosage—10 mg of aspirin per kilogram of body weight (5 mg per pound of body weight) given every four hours. An easier calculation is according to your child's age:

Age in years	1	2	3	4	5	6	7	8	9	10	11	12
No. of 1½ gr. tablets given every 4-6 hours	1	2	2	3	3	4	4	4	5	5	6	8 or 2 adult aspirin

One adult aspirin (5 grains) is equivalent to four children's aspirins (1-1/4 grain). If you give your child aspirin around the clock for two days (forty-eight hours) it is best to check with your physician before giving any more aspirin, in order to prevent a possible overdose.

Acetaminophen (Tylenol and Tempra) is an antipyretic which is as effective as aspirin in lowering fever but is a less effective pain reliever. Acetaminophen has two advantages. It is available in tablet and liquid form and is therefore easier to administer to young children. (Aspirin may be crushed in a teaspoon of water but it is not as palatable as acetaminophen syrup. Aspirin is unstable in solution and therefore can only be produced in tablet form). Although an acetaminophen overdose is as serious as an aspirin overdose, acetaminophen does not have a cumulative effect after prolonged use in the young child and therefore is less likely to produce an overdose with routine use. The dosage for acetominophen is the same as aspirin (10 mg per

kg or 5 mg per lb). Acetaminophen is available in four forms:
1. Drops: 0.8 ml equals 80 mg
2. Elixir: 5 ml (1 teaspoon) equals 160 mg
3. Tablets (chewable): 1 tablet equals 80 mg
4. Adult tablets: 1 tablet equals 325 mg
The following is a dosage schedule for acetaminophen for children:

ACETAMINOPHEN								
Age Group	**0-3 mos**	**4-11 mos**	**12-23 mos**	**2-3 yrs**	**4-5 yrs**	**6-8 yrs**	**9-10 yrs**	**11-12 yrs**
Weight (lbs)	**6-11**	**12-17**	**18-23**	**24-35**	**36-47**	**48-59**	**60-71**	**72-95**
Dose of Tylenol in milligrams	40	80	120	160	240	320	400	480
Drops (80 mg/0.8 ml) dropperfuls	½	1	1½	2	3	4	5	—
Elixir (160 mg/5 ml) tsp.	—	½	¾	1	1½	2	2½	3
Chewable tablets (80 mg each)	—	—	1½	2	3	4	5	6

Doses should be administered 4 or 5 times daily — but not to exceed 5 doses in 24 hours.

(The above recommendations are for Tylenol. The dosage schedule for other brands of acetominophen may vary.)

Other Methods of Lowering Fever

In addition to using the above medications to reset your child's thermostat, the following are some simple ways to help lower your child's temperature and to make him more comfortable. First, undress your child completely or, at most, let him wear light, loose-fitting garments. This allows his body heat to radiate and be dissipated by his much cooler environment. There seems to be a natural parental tendency to want to bundle children up when they have a fever. This retains the already excessive body heat.

Keep your child's environment cool by turning down the temperature in his room. Allow circulation of air by opening a window slightly or by using an air conditioner or a nearby fan. A draft will not make him sick. He is already sick and the cool air around his body dissipates heat by convection. However, you child's environment should not be cool enough to make him shiver, since shivering produces more body heat. Give him plenty of fluids, preferably cool, clear liquids in small, frequent dosages.

● **Tub Baths**

If your child's temperature is over 103° F (39.5° C) or he seems very uncomfortable with his fever even after you have tried all the above methods, then place him in a tub of tepid water up to his neck (the temperature of the water should be just warm enough not to be uncomfortable). As long as the water is cooler than his body, it will absorb the heat. Since a young child is already excessively irritable and more easily frightened when he has fever, he may vigorously protest being put into a bathtub. Crying and struggling increase his temperature and this should be avoided. Your child may more willingly submit to the tub bath if you sit in the bathtub first, accompanied by a few of his favorite floating toys, and have someone else hand your child to you while you are sitting in the bathtub. Rubbing his body with wash-cloths while he is in the tub stimulates blood circulation to his skin and aids the absorption of his body heat by the cooler water.

To prevent shivering, which increases heat production, gradually lowering the water temperature is effective, and also more comfortable. A tub bath of thirty minutes will usually succeed in lowering the body temperature a couple of degrees. If your child's temperature is excessively high, you may have to repeat the tub bath several times. Using alcohol as a cooling agent is unnecessary and uncomfortable, may produce shivering, and may produce toxic vapors which might be inhaled. Therefore it should not be used. After he has finished his bath, pat him dry with a towel and then leave him exposed. Gentle patting, rather than thorough rubbing, leaves a slight amount of water on your child's skin. This will evaporate and cool him more.

Why Treat Your Child's Fever?

Besides generally making your child more comfortable during his illness, one of the main reasons for keeping your child's fever down is to prevent **febrile convulsions**. If your child is under five years of age his relatively immature brain may react to a sudden change in body temperature and produce convulsions. The younger the child, the more susceptible he is to febrile convulsions. Febrile convulsions are not the same as epileptic convulsions. It is usually the rapid increase in body temperature, and not so much the degree of fever, that produces convulsions. This is why it is important to properly control rapid temperature

341

swings by the above methods. If your child has a febrile convulsion it will often stop as soon as his temperature is brought down
(Further discussion of the emergency handling of convulsions is
presented in the chapter on First Aid, page 453.) If your child
has frequent febrile illnesses or has had febrile convulsions
before, it is usually wise to commit him to twenty-four hours of
anti-fever medication at the first sign of a fever, even if you find
his temperature normal when you take it again several hours
later. If your child has a fever, he is likely to have this fever for
at least twenty-four hours. It is therefore usually best to "stay
ahead" of the fever by giving the aspirin and acetaminophen
every four hours. Treating the fever after it occurs encourages
temperature swings and therefore does not effectively prevent
febrile convulsions. Unless your physician advises, do not
awaken your child in order to give him fever-lowering medications. One question which parents commonly ask is, "May he go
outside during a fever?" Yes, he may and, in fact, he often
should go outside during a fever because the fresh circulating air
often brings down his temperature.

It is important that parents do not develop a fever phobia.
Except for febrile convulsions, the fever produced by the usual
infection does not harm your child. In fact, some studies claim
that fever may actually increase your child's ability to fight
infection.

Your Child's Respiratory Infections

Colds

● **What is a Cold?**
Colds are usually called upper respiratory infections (URI) in
medical terms, which simply means an infection in the tissues
lining the respiratory passages, the nose, sinuses, throat, ears
and larynx. Micro-organisms, viruses or bacteria invade the lining of these respiratory passages and the lining tissue reacts to
this invasion by inflammation (swelling) and by secreting
mucus. This mucus accounts for the runny nose and the postnasal
drip (tickle in the throat). Sneezing and coughing are the body's
reflex defense mechanism to clear the mucus. Swelling of these
tissues plus the mucus discharge account for the discomfort and
general unwell appearance of a child with a cold (See general
signs of illnesses, page 333). A child usually has about five
colds per year, which is just a simple fact of life in a school-aged

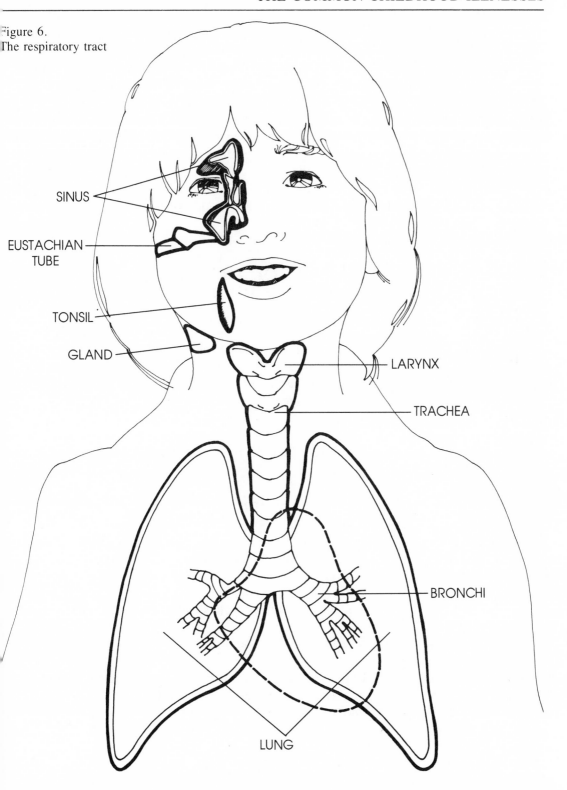

Figure 6.
The respiratory tract

SINUS

EUSTACHIAN
TUBE

TONSIL

GLAND

LARYNX

TRACHEA

BRONCHI

LUNG

child. As he grows, his immunity to various cold germs also develops, and the number and severity of colds usually decrease with age.

● **General Treatment of a Common Cold**

Treatment of a common cold should be aimed primarily at the mucus discharge produced. Keep the discharge thin and keep it moving. Using cool mist vaporizers or humidifiers, and drinking plenty of fluids help keep the discharge thin, thereby allowing the secretions to be more easily removed by the coughing and sneezing mechanisms. Cool mist vaporizers are more effective than the hot mist variety. The cool mist forms a finer particle and

---

SUMMARY OF TIPS TO CONTROL YOUR CHILD'S FEVER

You may wish to write in the correct aspirin and acetominophen dosage from the previous charts. Use a pencil and periodically change the dosage according to your child's age.

1. _____ children's aspirin every 4 hours. Do not use longer than 48 hours without consulting your physician.

2. _____ teaspoons or_____ tablets of acetominophen every 4 to 6 hours.

3. Undress your child completely except for diaper or underwear.

4. Encourage your child to drink plenty of fluids.

5. Keep the environment cool.

6. Place your child in a tub bath (tepid water), if you are unable to bring the fever below 103°F (39°C) with the above steps.

better penetrates the respiratory passages. Do not add anything to the water in the vaporizer since these substances may irritate the respiratory passages of a young child. Because a young child breathes primarily through his nose, clear nasal passages are very important to his general comfort. If he is too young to blow his own nose then do it for him. (Use the nasal aspirator and salt-water nose drops method described on page 179 .)

● **Medications for Colds**

Generally, over-the-counter remedies are designed either to dry up secretions (decongestants), or thin the secretions and make them more easily coughed up (expectorants or cough looseners). Bear in mind that even these non-prescription remedies often produce such side effects as drowsiness, hyperexcitability, nightmares and a rapid heart beat. In my experience, if a young child is given a high enough dosage to help the cold, he usually experiences undesirable side effects. Giving a low dosage (in desperation to give him something) may do no good. Some children are more susceptible to side effects than others so it is wise to check with your physician before using these over-the-counter medications.

There are two causes of colds: viruses and bacteria. Virus infections generally do not need to be treated with antibiotics; bacterial infections do. When your doctor examines your child, he makes a medical judgment whether or not your child needs an antibiotic for his cold. He may say, "His cold has settled in his ears and he needs an antibiotic" or he may say, "I think your child has a virus infection which will clear up without antibiotics, but call me if he gets worse." Again, you are going to the doctor primarily for consultation and advice, not necessarily for medicine. The last part of your doctor's statement, "Call me if he gets worse," is very important. A simple virus cold may progress into a bacterial cold (discharge becomes thicker, your child is more cranky, and generally looks and acts worse) and an antibiotic may be needed. Call your doctor and inform him of the progress of the illness so he can alter his judgment. Do not use left-over antibiotics without first checking with your doctor.

● **Treating the Complicated Cold**

When does a common cold become a more complicated cold? There are two general tips to assess the severity of your child's cold:

1. How much is it bothering him? Is he happy and playful? Does he eat well, sleep well and not seem particularly bothered by this

noisy and wet nuisance? Or is he cranky, irritable, quiet, "jus not himself," or complaining of pain anywhere (ears or throat)
2. What does the nasal discharge look like? Is it clear an watery, or thick and yellow or green? Generally, a clear water nasal discharge in a happy child indicates a virus cold an requires nothing more than the general care outlined above, plu a pinch of TLC and a "tincture of time." However, a thick yel low discharge and a cranky child (with or without fever) usuall means that a bacterial infection has set in and medical attention i needed. (It is usual for nasal discharge to appear yellow in th early morning, after the nasal secretions from a common col have accumulated during the night. If the nasal secretion become clear during the rest of the day and your baby is happy he probably does not have a significant cold.)

Other Types of Childhood Respiratory Infections

- **Rhinitis (runny nose)**

A runny nose is generally the first sign of a cold. If the discharg becomes thick and crusty, the lining of your child's nose ma become raw. A little petroleum jelly around the edges of his nos trils will soothe this irritation. If the skin around the nostr becomes reddened and crusty, a secondary bacterial infectio may be present and a topical antibiotic ointment may be neces sary. Nose drops should be used only on your doctor's advice Excessive use of nose drops may actually increase the nasal cor gestion. If drops are suggested, clear the nose before adminis tering them. (See **Pseudo-colds** page 179 and **Allergic Rhinitis** page 373.)

- **Sore Throat (pharyngitis)**

A sore throat may be part of a cold and may be caused by a viru or bacterial infection, or simply by the irritation of a postnas drip and cough. Your child's throat may look normal but "hurt lot" (characteristic of some viral infections) or it may be red dened and have whitish material on the tonsils (tonsillitis). Pain ful ulcers on the throat and inside the rest of the mouth are ofte caused by a virus called **herpes**. It may be difficult for your do tor to determine which type of throat infection your child ha without examining him and giving him a throat culture. Ver acidic juices may irritate certain types of sore throats (for exam ple, herpes) but generally let your child drink what he wishe Since vomiting is common with sore throats, (the stomach is irr tated by swallowing infected mucus) he may not wish to eat heavy meal. Gargling with salt water may help the older chil Humidified air will help the dryness. Aspirin or acetaminophe will relieve the pain or fever.

● **Strep Throat**

Strep throat is caused by the bacteria streptococcus and is characterized by a generally sick child (fever, flushed, vomiting, very
tired); a painful sore throat, which appears beefy red; and
swollen tonsils which are covered with a white, odorous material. Neck glands may be very swollen and tender, and your child
will become progressively worse if untreated. A ten-day course
of penicillin or other appropriate antibiotic is necessary to effectively treat strep throat. Strep throat is the most serious throat
infection for several reasons. It is highly contagious and therefore it is usually wise to also treat close contacts, such as siblings. Also, certain organs of the body (heart, joints, muscles,
kidneys) may react to the presence of the streptococcus bacteria,
which may result in rheumatic fever or nephritis. Rheumatic
fever, however, is becoming a rare disease because of the general improvement in health standards and the early recognition
and treatment of strep throat.

● **Scarlet Fever**

Scarlet fever accompanies strep throat and can be recognized by
a general sunburn-like scarlet rash. Scarlet fever is simply strep
throat with a rash. The toxin from the streptococcus has been
released into the blood stream causing a generalized rash. The
words ''scarlet fever'' no longer have the dreaded connotations
they used to. It is just an added feature of strep throat, it is treated
the same way, and is not necessarily any more serious than strep
throat without the rash. Streptococcal sore throats are unusual in
children under two years of age; they are usually a disease of the
school-aged child. It is highly contagious and the child should be
isolated from twenty-four to forty-eight hours after antibiotic
treatment begins.

● **Swollen Glands**

When your child has an upper respiratory infection, the infection
drains into the nearby lymph glands in his neck under his jaw
bone. These glands are just like the tonsils in his throat and they
enlarge to fight the infection. Generally, the more swollen and
tender the gland, the worse the infection. Because children have
so many URIs it is common for these glands to remain slightly
enlarged all during childhood. There are similar infection-
draining glands throughout your child's body, especially under
his arm, in his groin, and all around his neck. Sometimes these
glands can become very large around the back of the head. This
is usually due to the drainage of a scalp infection (often caused

by an insect bite), and is normally of no concern.

● **Laryngitis**

If a cold involves the larynx, the vocal cords become swollen and produce the characteristic hoarseness which accompanies colds especially in older children and adults. High humidity is the preferred treatment for this type of laryngitis.

● **Croup**

Croup is a type of respiratory infection which causes swelling of the vocal cords and often the adjacent airway (trachea). It can be recognized by the "seal bark" it produces when breathing and coughing. Croup is potentially one of the most serious types of respiratory infections because the swelling of the vocal cord obstructs the passage of air. The main goal in parenting the child with croup is to recognize when croup is serious and when it is not. How much trouble your child is experiencing getting air in is the main sign by which to judge the severity of croup. If his cough sounds "very croupy" but he is smiling, happy and playful, this is usually not serious. On the other hand, if he is having trouble getting air in, this is more serious and you should call your doctor immediately.

The following are signs that your child is experiencing difficulty getting air in:

1. A generally anxious, tired or even panicky child.

2. With each breath, the throat caves in just above the top of the breast bone (a feature called indrawing).

3. Labored respirations which produce a hoarse, musical noise

The severity of croup is not indicated by how much noise your child makes, because the most serious degree of airway obstruction may be the quietest. Croups should always be treated with concern. It is usually worse at night, it is more serious in the younger infant, and it may rapidly change in severity.

You can treat croup in two ways. Calm your child by using all your parental ingenuity to settle him (e.g. reading him a story). Anxiety aggravates his breathing difficulty. To maintain high humidity use a cool mist vaporizer, steam from a bathroom shower, or a croup tent (made by covering his crib with a sheet and running the vaporizer into this tent). Use whatever method you can to create the most humidity in the most comfortable way. Sometimes the security of sitting on your lap with his head against your shoulder while the vaporizer is blowing right at his nose may be the most effective method. Croup is usually caused by a virus and antibiotics are therefore not usually necessary. Over-the-counter remedies should not be used without your doctor's advice. If you are uncertain about the severity of your child's croup, or are uncomfortable with your home treatment, call your doctor or take your child to the hospital. The higher humidity outdoors often causes children with croup to improve en route to the hospital.

• Bronchitis

As we work our way down the respiratory tract, the next targets of infection are the **bronchi**, or lower airways. Because the lower airways are narrower, bronchial infections often produce noisy breathing as the air passes through inflamed airways. An infection or an allergy may cause the muscles around the bronchi to contract and further narrow the bronchi, thus producing a wheeze. Like croup, the severity of bronchitis depends upon how much your child is bothered and how much trouble he is having getting air in. Often a child wheezes only during expiration (when the airways are narrowest), but has no trouble getting air in (quiet inspiration). This is much less serious than if he also is having difficulty getting air in (recognized by retraction of the skin between his ribs during labored inspiration). Besides treating bronchitis with the general measures for URIs, medical attention should be obtained. Beware of the "happy wheezer" who is becoming progressively tired. Some children can wheeze for one or two days without apparent distress, but often they become progressively more tired and exhausted, at which point they can become ill very quickly.

• Pneumonia

Strictly speaking, any chest infection may be called pneumonia. Because of the dreadful connotation the term "pneumonia" had in grandmother's day, the term "lung infection" is often used today. Pneumonia (used here to mean an infection of the lower airways of the lung) is not as common, nor as serious as it used to be. Signs of pneumonia are a high fever, a severe cough, rapid respiration and a generally ill child. If your child's cold is worsening steadily and is accompanied by these signs, seek medical attention.

• Persistent Cough ("Doctor his cough isn't getting better")

A persistent cough in the otherwise well child is a common concern to parents. The main question, again, is how much is it bothering him? Is he getting worse or just not getting better? Is the cough accompanied by any other signs of illness?

The most common cause of these lingering coughs is a lingering virus (a virus which may take four to six weeks to clear), which is characterized by a parent's statement, "He seems perfectly well during the day but coughs at night." Many of these coughs are caused by postnasal drip and do not necessarily mean a chest infection. A child with a persistent cough should be examined by your doctor to eliminate the possibility of any serious illness.

In addition to the general methods of treatment, the proper use of cough medicines is very important. Your child's cough is his own mechanism for removing retained secretions and should not always be suppressed. Your first goal is to loosen these secretions (using fluids and humidity), not suppress the cough. Your doctor may prescribe an expectorant (cough loosener).

Children are seldom bothered by coughing during the day but may lose sleep at night. In this case, cough syrups, expectorants and/or cough suppressants may be used at night but not during the day. A lingering cough is often aggravated by strenuous exercise and your child should be advised to temporarily stop his exercise if a coughing spell occurs. Generally, a cough that is not bothering him and is not getting worse is more of a nuisance than a serious medical problem. Your doctor should, however, make that decision. (See **Allergic Coughs**, page 373, and **Smoking and Colds**, page 180.)

Ear Infections in Childhood

Middle ear infections (otitis media) are probably the most common childhood illness. Figure 7 is a diagram of the middle ear. Notice that the middle ear (the space behind the eardrum) is connected to the throat by the Eustachian tube. This tube periodically opens and closes and has three functions: 1. to equalize the air pressure on both sides of the eardrum, 2. to drain the middle ear of fluid which accumulates during a cold, and 3. to prevent germs from entering the middle ear from the throat. Young children are susceptible to middle ear infections because they harbor infectious organisms in their throats to which they have not yet become immune, and the Eustachian tubes are short and straight allowing easy entry of the organisms from the throat to the ear. When fluid accumulates in the middle ear during a simple cold, may be trapped because the Eustachian tube is also blocked. As general principle, fluid trapped anywhere in a child's upper respiratory tract (nose, sinuses, ears) may eventually become infected. This infected fluid accumulates behind the eardrum causing pressure against the drum and produces intense pain. pressure builds up too much, the eardrum may rupture, allowing the trapped fluid to drain out to the outside ear canal. This rupture allows the release of pressure and therefore the release of pain and may give a false sense of security that the ear is better. Even though your child feels better, the infection should still be appropriately treated to allow the perforated area of the eardrum to heal. Frequent ear infections produce a vicious cycle. Middle ear infections damage the lining of the Eustachian tube which further aggravates the already inefficient drainage system, causing more infections.

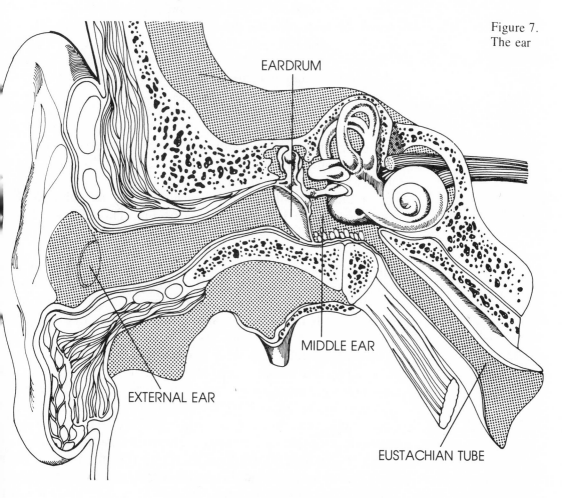

Figure 7.
The ear

EARDRUM

MIDDLE EAR

EXTERNAL EAR

EUSTACHIAN TUBE

How do you recognize an ear infection in your child? The older child has enough command of language to tell you his ear hurts. The ear infection in the infant is more difficult to diagnose but there are some signs: cold symptoms plus a cranky baby; thick, yellow discharge from nose or eyes, and a cranky baby; a

cranky, irritable baby for no apparent reason. Fever is not alway
present in a young infant. Ear pulling is an unreliable sign
because babies enjoy playing with their ears. Teething is often
confused with ear infections, but teething is usually associated
with throat secretions, not a thick, yellow, nasal discharge. Also
teething babies do not usually look generally ill. Ear infection
are commonly recognized at night. The pain is worse at night
because when your baby lies flat, the infected fluid presses
against his eardrums, causing pain. This is why he feels better
when he sits upright and you are holding him. Babies with ear
infections will often sit up or stand up in their crib, allowing
gravity to drain the fluid away from their eardrum, thereby
relieving the pain in their ears. Sometimes there is only
build-up of middle ear fluid (serous otitis media) which may no
produce pain nor be accompanied by other signs of cold, but you
may notice that your child's hearing is diminished. After suffer
ing through their child's frequent ear infections, most mother
notice a change in personality and can tell when an ear infection
is coming on. Some children have a high pain threshold and d
not always complain about ear pain. Because fluid build-up i
the middle ear will diminish hearing, nearly all children show
some **change in behavior** if this occurs. This change may b
your only warning sign.

Why is proper treatment of middle ear infections s
important? Besides affecting his hearing, improperly treated ea
infections make a child generally unhappy at a time when he i
rapidly graduating from one developmental stage to another. I
addition, diminished hearing may slow his languag
development.

● **Parenting the Child with Frequent Ear Infections**
After obtaining proper medical treatment for your child's ea
infections and the course of medication is finished, you shoul
ask your doctor to recheck his ears to be sure the infection
completely clear. Just because your child is free of pain does no
mean the infection is completely healed. A partially healed ea
infection can lead to eventual hearing problems, because som
fluid may remain behind the eardrum. To ease the pain, let you
child sleep upright on a couple of pillows or hold him upright i
your arms. The upright position allows the fluid to drain awa
from the eardrum and relieve the pressure and pain. Analgesic
(aspirin and acetaminophen) may be helpful. Analgesic ear drop
prescribed by your doctor may give your child temporary relie
but these drops only mask the pain and do not treat the infection

Keep these drops on hand for the middle-of-the-night infections, to tide him over until appropriate medical treatment can be obtained.

As your child becomes older, your doctor may show him some exercises to open his Eustachian tubes and "pop his ears." If the ear infections are increasing in frequency and lasting longer, your doctor may suggest a "prevention regimen," consisting of daily decongestants or antibiotics to prevent recurrent infections and to give the uninfected Eustachian tubes time to grow and drain the middle ear properly. Sometimes the fluid in the middle ear becomes so thick and glue-like it needs to be removed by an operation called a **myringotomy** (opening the eardrum). In some children who cannot be controlled on medical treatment alone, surgical implantation of tiny plastic tubes in the eardrum ventilates the middle ear and often decreases the frequency of ear infections. The aim of all these medical and surgical procedures is to simply bide time and preserve his normal hearing until later childhood, when most children do grow out of it.

● **Preventing Ear Infections**

Although most children will have an occasional ear infection during their early childhood, the following are tips to lessen the frequency and severity of ear infections:

1. Breastfeed your infant until he wishes to wean. Studies show that breastfed infants have fewer infections.

2. Control allergies. Allergies may cause fluid to accumulate in the middle ear. (See **Allergies,** page 373.)

3. Treat colds early. If your child has had frequent ear infections, learn to recognize the warning signs and treat the cold before it "goes into his ear." The most common sequence of colds leading to ear infections is the following:

Stage One. Runny nose. A clear, watery discharge in a happy baby. Treatment for this is usually just a good nose blow.

Stage Two. Snotty nose. The nasal discharge becomes thick and yellow and persists that way. At this point, call your doctor.

Stage Three. Cranky baby. The combination of a yellow nasal discharge and a cranky baby usually means the cold has settled in his ears. (See **Treating the Complicated Cold,** page 345.)

● **How to Check Your Child's Hearing**

Most hearing problems in childhood result from the accumulation of fluid behind the eardrum, which dampens the sound by

impairing the vibration of the eardrums (See Figure 7). I cann‹
overemphasize the importance of paying close attention to yo›
child's hearing. Besides risking impaired language developmen
a child with impaired hearing (especially from middle ear flui‹
is generally an unhappy child. The following signs should ale›
you to a possible hearing problem in your child:

1. Signs of speech delay or decreased response to usual soun‹
as listed on page 225 under **Language Development**.

2. A persistently cranky or ill-tempered child.

3. An unexplained "personality change," especially during
cold or following an ear infection.

4. Poor school performance.

5. An allergic child is prone to accumulation of fluid in his mi‹
dle ears and is at high risk for hearing problems.

Usually by three years of age, a child is able to coopera›
in simple hearing tests. The easiest test a parent can administer
the whisper test. Cover one ear with your hand and whisper in›
your child's other ear at a distance of around twelve inches, in›
tone just loud enough for you to hear your own whisper. Whisp›
simple questions such as, "How old are you?" "What is yo›
name?" Or ask him to repeat whispered numbers. The whisp›
test will not detect a minor hearing deficiency but is useful
noticing a discrepancy between the hearing in one ear and t
other ear. Similar results may be obtained by holding
wristwatch a few inches from your child's ear and comparing h
hearing in one ear with the other. If your child is prone to fr
quent ear infections and periodic fluid accumulation in his ear
it is wise to periodically check his ears with the whisper test ‹
the tick-tock of the watch. You should do this both when he h
an ear infection and when your doctor says his ears look norma
In this way you will develop a "feel" for knowing when h
hearing is impaired.

If you suspect your child's hearing is diminished, or if ▌
has any of the above indications of hearing impairment, it is wi
to have your child's hearing checked by means of an **audi‹
gram**. In one part of the audiogram, a small device the size of
hearing aid is placed in your child's ear canal. This measures t▌
vibration of the eardrum. An eardrum that is "stiff" indicates
possible chronic middle ear problem. The next part of the audi
gram tests your child's response to sounds of various freque›
cies. This is certainly a more accurate test than one with spok‹
words, since the whisper test and response to usual spoken wor‹

may not detect impaired high frequency hearing. The audiogram, in conjunction with examination of your child's ears by your doctor, should be performed without delay if you suspect your child's hearing is impaired. Prompt medical attention is important, because the longer the fluid is allowed to remain in the middle ear, the more thick and glue-like the fluid becomes and the more difficult it is to remove.

● **Swimmer's Ear**

Swimmer's ear (external ear infection, otitis externa) is an infection of the lining of the ear canal. (See Figure 7.) The lining of the ear canal contains secretory glands and surface cells which normally form a protective waxy coating. This lining is water-repellent and contains secretions too acidic for the survival of invading germs. An external ear infection occurs when this protective lining is broken down. This occurs from irritation of this lining by over-zealous wax removal with objects such as Q-tips and bobby pins, and prolonged contact with water (e.g. swimming) which washes away the protective coating of the ear canal and provides a warm, moist environment for the invasion of bacteria.

There are several ways to recognize when your child's ear infection is in the outer ear. Infection of the external canal usually occurs during the swimming season whereas middle ear infections (otitis media) usually occur during the winter months when colds are more common. Itching in the ear canal, usually the earliest sign of an external ear infection, rapidly progresses to varying degrees of pain. Pulling on your child's earlobe or pressing upward behind the ear lobe elicits pain; the child doesn't want his ear touched. A child's hearing is usually normal unless the infection also involves the eardrum or unless the ear canal is plugged with wax or drainage.

It may be difficult for your doctor to treat this type of ear infection over the phone since he cannot be sure of the severity of the infection or whether the infection is in the outer ear, middle ear or both. An external ear infection is usually treated with ear drops which contain an antibiotic to treat the infection, cortisone to lessen the itching and the swelling of the ear canal, and sometimes a topical anesthetic to ease the pain. When applying the eardrops, instruct the child to lie on his side with the infected ear upward. Gently pull the auricle up and back to straighten the ear canal and allow the drops to flow deeper into the canal. Gently pump on the ear cartilage just above the ear lobe to drive the eardrops further down into the canal. If the canal is plugged with

wax or drainage, your doctor may need to clean out the debris i
order for the drops to reach the infected lining of the canal. If th
canals are very swollen and the drops won't stay in, then yo
doctor may place a small, eardrop-saturated gauze wick into th
canal. This allows the drops to penetrate deeper. If the infectio
has extended into the eardrum, your doctor may prescribe an or:
antibiotic.

● **How to Prevent External Ear Infections**

1. To scratch the itching or to clean out wax, don't put an
irritating objects into the ear. If ear wax is a problem, consu
your doctor for appropriate methods of removing this wax.

2. After he swims, show your child how to tilt his head t
encourage the water to drain out through the ear canals b
gravity.

3. If water remains in the ear canal, roll a small piece of absorb
ent tissue between your thumb and forefinger and gently inse
the tissue a short distance into the canal in order to absorb th
remaining water.

4. If swimmer's ear is a recurrent problem, your doctor may pr
scribe a preventive ear drop (usually mild acetic acid solution) t
be used after swimming. Ear plugs are often effective but the
commonly irritate the lining of the ear canal and may increase th
risk of an external ear infection. They should not be used withou
your doctor's advice.

Tonsils and Adenoids—Should They Stay or Go?

Tonsils and adenoids are lymph glands which function to pro
duce infection-fighting cells. They are large in childhood an
usually shrink to a smaller size as your child grows older. Tonsi
and adenoids enlarge during throat infections and may becom
infected themselves (tonsillitis and adenoiditis). The tonsils are
mass of round, marble-sized, reddish tissue located on either sid
of the base of the tongue. Adenoids are located behind the nas:
passages and cannot be seen without a special mirror.

Due to the general improvement in the standards of pub
lic health and the discovery of new antibiotics, tonsillectomie
are not performed as readily today as years ago, but it is still
common operation. When should tonsils come out? If the so
throats are increasing in frequency and severity, if your child fr
quently misses school because of these infections or if the tonsi
are becoming so large that they obstruct his swallowing, then
tonsillectomy should be considered. The doctor who knows yo
total child is the one who should make the decision about
tonsillectomy.

Enlarged, frequently infected adenoids may present more of a problem than tonsils. The adenoids are located near the throat opening of the Eustachian tube. Large adenoids may obstruct this opening and predispose your child to frequent ear infections. Also, because they are located behind the nasal passages, enlarged adenoids may obstruct the flow of air from nose to throat, causing your child to be a "mouth breather." Prolonged adenoidal obstruction results in an "adenoidal child" (adenoidal fascies) who has a generally unwell facial appearance, nasal speech and open-mouth breathing which is particularly noisy at night. Your child snores loudly, you can hear him all over the house. If his adenoidal fascies and his ear infections are increasing in frequency and severity, and are interfering with his overall growth and development, then an adenoidectomy may be considered. Again, the doctor who knows your total child should make the decision.

The Child Who is "Not Completely Well"

Children have a remarkable ability to withstand chronic, low-grade respiratory infections without apparently being bothered by them. However, if you delve into the history of these children, they are never completely well and are often not completely happy. Their appetite is off, they sleep poorly, miss a fair amount of school and perhaps are not growing as they should. Their nose is always stuffy, their mouth is always open and they have circles under their eyes. These children often have chronic, low-grade sinusitis, adenoiditis, tonsillitis, ear infections, allergies or a combination of all of these. Sometimes he does not seem that sick and medical attention is not always sought. With today's sophisticated medical care system, a child who is not completely well deserves a chance to be healthy. He usually responds to a variety of treatments: allergy investigation and treatment, medications, tonsillectomy and adenoidectomy, etc. A child needs all of his available energy to graduate through his developmental stages and he should not always be left to his own resources to get himself well.

Colds in the Older Child—Sinusitis

Sinuses, part of the respiratory passages, are cavities in the bones adjacent to the nose and eyes. These cavities may fill with fluid and become infected. By the age of six years, your child's sinuses are developed to the point that a nose cold may settle in his sinuses. Sinusitis may be a very subtle illness and is one of the more common reasons an older child may not be "completely well." The usual signs of sinus infection are postnasal

drip, night cough, tenderness when touching the area over th
sinuses, headaches, circles under the eyes and general tirednes
If a cold lingers on in an older child and he is becoming progre
sively more tired, suspect sinusitis and seek medical attention

Common Childhood Intestinal Problems

**Normal
Variations in
Stools and Bowel
Habits**

In his first few days, the stools of your newborn, which contai
amniotic fluid debris, are dark green, tar-like and sticky. The
are called **meconium**. In the next few days, these "transition
stools" become greenish-brown, and by one or two weeks of ag
his stools assume a regular color and consistency. Breastfe
babies' stools tend to be passed frequently, are of yellow
mustard-like consistency, and usually do not have an offensiv
odor. Stools of formula-fed babies tend to be passed less fre
quently, are firmer, darker and have an unpleasant odor. If th
formula contains added iron, you can normally expect a green
ish, darker stool. The frequency and consistency of stools var
widely among babies and children; you will become accustome
to your baby's individual stool patterns and the circumstance
which cause changes. Generally speaking, if your baby appea
well, is gaining weight normally and is not in any discomfor
then the consistency and frequency of his stools should not be
major concern to you. Your infant's stools may occasionally b
green, if bile was not absorbed due to the fast passage of foo
This is not abnormal.

Constipation

Constipation, a very uncomfortable intestinal problem especiall
for the young infant, has nothing to do with the frequency
which his stools are passed but rather their consistency and th
difficulty of passing them. If your infant has a bowel moveme
only every three or four days but his stools are reasonably so
and he expresses no difficulty passing them, he is not const
pated. This is his normal bowel pattern. A constipated baby
periodically uncomfortable and passes hard, pellet-like stoo
with difficulty. The passage of these hard stools often causes
small tear in the rectal wall, called a **rectal fissure** and a fe
drops of blood may accompany this stool or be noticed on th
diaper. Because passage of a hard stool is a painful act, esp
cially if a fissure occurs, your child may voluntarily hold on
his stool. If the stool is retained within the intestines, the wat

content of the stool is reabsorbed, thus making the stools firmer and aggravating the constipation.

If your baby is formula-fed, a change of formula may produce a change in the stool consistency. Solids which tend to be constipating are rice and bananas. Temporarily stop all solids until you see an improvement in stool consistency, and reintroduce them one at a time until you have isolated the foods that cause constipation in your infant. Occasionally adding corn syrup (1 tablespoon for every 8 ounces) to his formula may loosen the consistency of his stools. If your baby is straining, has a distended abdomen, and is red in the face, insert a baby glycerine suppository gently into his rectum and hold the cheeks of his buttocks together for about five minutes, allowing the suppository to dissolve. Suppositories stimulate the act of defecation, soften the stool and lubricate the rectum (especially if a fissure is present), thus allowing the stool to be passed with less discomfort. Persistent constipation in a tiny infant should be reported to your doctor.

Constipation in the older child is the most common cause of recurrent abdominal pain and is often due to a toilet training problem in early infancy. Normally, the presence of stool in the large intestine gives an "urge to defecate" signal. Unlike urine, which a child usually cannot voluntarily hold on to, a child can voluntarily respond to his signal to defecate, or choose to ignore it. If he chooses to ignore it, the fluid in the retained stool is absorbed and the stools become harder. It then "hurts to go," he holds on to his stools longer and the vicious cycle begins, resulting in a constipated, uncomfortable child. Often, the fluid may leak out around the hard stool and soil his pants, a problem called **encopresis**. The paradox of soiled pants caused by constipation often comes as a surprise to parents, who consider soiled pants a "diarrhea" problem. Treatment of encopresis begins with treatment of constipation.

● **Treatment of Constipation in the Older Child**

Infant-led toilet training is the main step in preventing constipation in the older child (see **Toilet Training**, page 256). You should also counsel the child about how his bowels work. Teach him that training his bowel muscles is similar to training his other muscles to work properly. Show him, using diagrams, that voluntarily holding on to his stools makes them harder and that is why it hurts to pass them. Encourage him to try to go in the morning shortly after breakfeast, otherwise allow him to set his own pattern.

The main point you wish to convey to him is to "go whe[n] he has to go." Some children with a longstanding constipatio[n] problem say they don't know when they have to go. This mean[s] that the constipation has become so chronic that the usual intest[i]nal stretching signals of defecation no longer function. Th[e] embarrassment of soiled pants further complicates this problem[.] The combination of embarrassment and discomfort focuses [a] great deal of attention onto what should be a natural biologic[al] process. Before using laxatives and stool softeners, it is best t[o] consult your physician if the constipation problem has been [a] long standing one.

Stool softeners or laxatives (such as mineral oil) may b[e] prescribed by your physician. They are usually best given befor[e] bedtime to encourage bowel movement the next morning. Kee[p] in mind that chronic constipation takes a long time to cure. [It] may take at least a month of stool softening before your child ca[n] regain confidence in his intestinal signals. If the constipation [is] severe, an enema and a suppository may be necessary to sta[rt] him out with a clean slate.

The following are foods which act as laxatives: frui[t,] prune juice, corn syrup, vegetable roughage and bran cerea[l.] Potentially constipating foods are rice, cheese, bananas, choc[o]late, and sometimes milk.

Diarrhea

Diarrhea, which means "liquid stools," refers to the consistenc[y] of the stools, not the frequency with which they are passe[d.] Infants experience a change in stool consistency for many re[a]sons. Teething causes a temporary diarrhea which is more of [a] nuisance than a medical problem. Teething stools are looser an[d] are passed more frequently (because of the increased mucu[s] swallowed during teething) but the color and the odor of th[e] stools usually do not change.

Changes in diet are also often accompanied by changes i[n] stool consistency. An intestinal allergy to certain foods such a[s] cow's milk may produce diarrhea, which may continue chron[i]cally until the offending allergen is eliminated from the die[t.] Diarrhea usually accompanies upper respiratory infection[s.] Some antibiotics used to treat these infections may also produc[e] a diarrhea which clears up when the antibiotic is finished.

The most frequent and concerning cause of diarrhea i[n] childhood is termed **gastroenteritis**, a virus or bacterial infectio[n] of the intestines. The intestinal lining is very sensitive to infec[c]tions and heals very slowly. While this lining is infected an[d] healing, the intestines are unable to absorb food. Infected intestines loose water into the stools causing frequent, watery, mucousy stools, which are often greenish, foul-smelling and may be tinged with blood. This type of diarrhea is usually caused by a virus and commonly follows or accompanies a cold. Next to fever and colds, this type of diarrhea is the most common childhood illness.

Why, and when, is diarrhea potentially serious? Diarrhea stools contain a lot of water and body salts (called **electrolytes**). Normally, the body contains a balance of water and electrolytes, which is necessary for many organs to function. Diarrhea stools can cause the body to lose too much water and/or salts; when your child loses more water and salt than he takes in, a potentially serious condition called **dehydration** could result. Your main goal as parents is to distinguish between the diarrhea that is just a nuisance and the type severe enough to cause dehydration. Signs of dehydration are weight and water loss, drowsy and lethargic behavior, dry mouth, dry eyes, dry skin, little urine output and fever. If your baby is generally happy, bright-eyed, wet and has not lost any weight, he is not dehydrated.

A sudden onset of diarrhea accompanying or following a cold, without any apparent change in diet, is probably due to an intestinal infection. The following are ways to manage the diarrhea:

1. At the first sign of diarrhea, stop all solid foods, cow's milk and formula. If you are breastfeeding, do **not** stop nursing.

2. Weigh your baby with his clothes off. This is his baseline weight and subsequent weighings (on the same scale, undressed) will tell whether he is losing weight. If he is not losing weight, he is not becoming dehydrated.

3. Give him a clear fluid diet. These fluids should contain calories in the form of simple sugars. The following are appropriate fluids:

a) Sugar solution containing one level tablespoon of ordinary table sugar for 8 ounces of boiled water. Do not boil the sugar solution, as this may cause excessive evaporation and make the sugar solution stronger than needed.

b) Flat gingerale and cola.

c) Oral electrolyte solutions (e.g. Pedialyte or Lytren). These solutions, available at your pharmacy, are designed to replace the salts which are lost from the diarrhea. They should not be continued for more than twenty-four hours without checking with your doctor.

4. Give your child small, frequent feedings (e.g. 2 ounces to 4 ounces every one to two hours).

Your basic goal is to replace at one end the fluid that he
losing at the other. Clear fluids alone should not be continued f(
more than forty-eight hours because a straight sugar solution di(
will, itself, cause diarrhea.

If after twenty-four hours he is not losing weight, and th
frequency and consistency of the stools is improving, add sem(
solid foods (rice cereal without milk, mashed bananas) to the reg(
men of small, frequent, fluid feedings. If his stools continue t
improve, add applesauce, saltine crackers, gelatine and yogur
As a general rule, as your child's stools become more solid, so ca
his diet.

Resume milk or formula gradually, only after you hav
seen much improvement in your child's diarrhea. Begin b
diluting the formula twice as much as you usually do. Your doct(
may wish to change formulas during the recovery period. Certa(
formulas (e.g. soy and lactose-free formula) are often better tole(
ated by inflamed intestines. If your child has been taking cow
milk, then dilute the milk as recovery begins. Never boil milk (
give undiluted skim milk to a child who has diarrhea. It is too co(
centrated and may worsen the dehydration. Yogurt is often bett(
tolerated than milk. If the diarrhea worsens, go back a step—h(
intestines are not yet ready for milk or dairy products.

● **When to Call Your Doctor**

If, despite following the above steps, the diarrhea worsens the(
check with your doctor, especially if the diarrhea is accompanie(
by vomiting, fever, weight loss, dehydration (or the first signs (
it) or progressive abdominal pain. Over the phone your doct(
will want to know the consistency and frequency of the diarrhe(
how it is changing, whether it is accompanied by vomiting
whether there are signs of dehydration, if his weight ha
changed, what diet you have been offering him, and how muc
he has been eating. Be as accurate as you can so your doctor ca
assess the severity of the diarrhea and judge whether or not h
should see the child. Parents often want medication to stop th
diarrhea. Since most of these infections are caused by viruse(
the intestines will heal themselves. Most diarrhea in childhood
treated with diet, not drugs. The above suggestions are designe
to stop the effects of the diarrhea (i.e. fluid and salt loss) and (
rest the intestines from irritating foods. Narcotic medication
which appear to lessen the diarrhea because they slow down th
movement of the intestines, do exist. They give the false impre
sion that the diarrhea is lessening when, in reality, there is still

lot of fluid loss from the intestines which you may not see. These narcotic medications are a bit risky and often unnecessary, especially in infants and young children. The intestinal lining is very slow to heal following an infection and some of the enzymes necessary for milk absorption may not return for weeks or even months. A prolonged period of "loose stools" following an intestinal infection is common and may require dietary manipulation or a special milk product prescribed by your doctor. This is the "convalescent stage" of an intestinal infection. Be reassured that this is only a prolonged nuisance stage which, with help from your physician, will gradually disappear.

Vomiting

As a general rule vomiting, associated with pain or signs of fluid and weight loss in a generally unwell child, is cause for concern and medical attention should be obtained.

● **Vomiting in the Young Infant**

Most so-called vomiting in tiny babies is simply regurgitation, or spitting up, resulting from a temporary feeding problem or air swallowing. This type of vomiting is more of a nuisance than a medical illness, particularly if your baby is otherwise well and gaining weight normally. (See related sections **Regurgitation** and **Milk Allergy**, page 144.)

A condition which occurs primarily in male infants under two months of age is called **pyloric stenosis**. The pylorus is the intestinal end of the stomach and, if it is too narrow for the food to pass through, the food builds up in the stomach and is ejected under force, causing "projectile vomiting" (vomitus coming out several feet). Pyloric stenosis is suspected if a vomiting infant shows weight loss and signs of fluid loss or dehydration. A minor surgical procedure (enlargement of the opening of the pylorus) is necessary. Your main signal of a problem is weight loss. Generally, occasional vomiting in a child who appears well and who is not losing weight is a temporary nuisance rather than a medical or surgical problem.

Vomiting of green bile by a generally ill-appearing child, accompanied by the sudden onset of severe abdominal pain, may indicate an intestinal obstruction. Immediate medical attention should be obtained. (See related section **Abdominal Pain**, page 366.)

● **Vomiting in the Older Infant and Older Child**

Most vomiting in this age group is caused by an infection or irritation of the lining of the stomach, called **gastritis**. This is often accompanied by nausea, mild stomach discomfort and retching or "dry heaves." Anti-vomiting medications are not as effectiv or safe for children as they are for adults. Treatment should t directed at preventing the dehydration which results from the lo of body water and salts due to the loss of gastric juices.

● **To assess and treat the vomiting child:**

1. Be sure that the vomiting is not secondary to some other il ness which needs treatment, such as a cold, cough or earach severe abdominal pain, high fever or frequent urination. If you child looks generally ill or if the vomiting is accompanied b other concerning symptoms, call your doctor for advice.

2. Sips and Chips. Offer clear fluids very slowly and frequentl Ice chips, popsicles (made with frozen juices at home), clea soup broth, flat gingerale or cola are good choices. To sma infants who may refuse these liquids, offer from 2 ounces to ounces of a sugar solution (1 level tablespoon of ordinary tab sugar in 8 ounces to 10 ounces of water) every one to two hours.

3. Follow the same guidelines for observation of dehydratic and consultation with your physician as those listed in the sectio on **Diarrhea** (page 360).

4. Very gradually resume a regular diet as the vomiting sul sides, beginning with clear juices, saltine crackers, rice cere and bananas. Remember that small, frequent feedings are usuall tolerated best by a vomiting child.

Common Childhood Pains

I do not like term "overly concerned mother." Pain is the body signal that some problem exists in the system. When someon you love hurts, you will naturally be concerned. The purpose c this section is not to teach you to correctly diagnose these pair or to lull you into feeling that these pains are normal and shoul be ignored. This approach would be unwise, potentially dange ous and would deprive your child of a necessary medical opinio from his doctor. The purpose of this section is to present som common pains your child may experience during middl childhood.

About one-third of all children from six to ten years c age experience various recurrent pains which have no easil identifiable cause, do not harm your child if left untreated an usually disappear without treatment after varying lengths c time. In order of frequency, these pains include headache abdominal pains and muscle pains.

Headaches

Approximately 50 per cent of children between six and fifteen years of age have periods of unexplained headaches which disappear without treatment. Parents often think brain tumors cause their child's headache. Brain tumors are way down on the list of causes of headaches. Headaches are usually not an early sign of a brain tumor in a child. The following list of "normal" characteristics of headaches may be of some help to you in deciding which headaches you should worry about:

1. Headaches, unaccompanied by other signs such as vision disturbances, eye pain, colds (sinusitis), vomiting, a change in balance or weakness of one side of the body.

2. Children are vague in their description and localization of the headaches, they tell you "It hurts all over."

3. The headaches do not increase in frequency and severity and do not usually interfere with the child's daily activities.

4. The child is usually unable to identify a "trigger" for the headaches, i.e. what change in his environment starts the headache.

5. Headaches in young children (under four years of age) are of more concern than headaches in the older child.

Persistent headaches warrant a thorough medical examination by your child's physician. This should include checking your child's vision, blood pressure and urine. Usually a complete physical examination will detect any serious cause for the headaches. Your doctor may not be able to tell you what causes the headaches, but he can often reassure the parents about what does not cause them.

Childhood migraine headaches are cyclical headaches which are severe, usually accompanied by nausea and temporary vision disturbances, and precipitated by an identifiable trigger (e.g. loud noises, tension). There is often a family history of migraine headaches.

Mid- and late-afternoon headaches are common in the school-age child and usually result from a combination of eye strain, tension after a long day at school, hunger and low blood sugar. (See pages 268 and 282 .)

● **Parenting the Child with Headaches**

1. Obtain a complete medical examination. Your doctor will recommend treatment depending on the cause of the headaches.

2. Attempt to identify and eliminate what triggers the headaches—tension, certain foods, television, certain activities, menses.

3. Regardless of the cause, most childhood headaches are alleviated by advising your child to lie down in a dark, quiet room with his eyes closed and think pleasant thoughts until the aches disappear. To treat the mid-afternoon school-related headaches, it is advisable for the child to rest mind and body for a few minutes after school and to eat a nutritious snack before beginning his after-school activities.

Abdominal Pains

Between six and ten years of age, 10 per cent of children experience a type of abdominal pain called "unexplained recurrent abdominal pains of middle childhood." When evaluating children with these pains I am struck by one distinctive feature— they do not fit any known medical condition. However, these pains are real, your child hurts, and you are worried. These pains are characterized by the vagueness of their description, their reasonably consistent pattern, and the fact that they don't get worse but they don't get better. When these children are asked where it hurts, most point to the region around the umbilicus, but they do so in an indefinite manner. They seem to have difficulty determining the exact site of the pain, whereas children with an abdominal problem which has some underlying identifiable cause can often locate the exact site of this pain. If the pain is not of serious concern, your child may react as though it hurts when you press on his abdomen, but he does so with a smile on his face.

Usually these pains are mild and are seldom severe enough to make the child cry. Most children say these pains are a dull ache, but occasionally they say they are sharp as needles. The duration and time of onset of these pains vary. They are usually not associated with any other symptoms, but some children may experience associated headaches, pallor, vomiting or tiredness. Boys and girls experience these pains at a similar frequency, but around nine years of age, as many as 25 per cent of girls have recurrent lower abdominal pains. These are probably pre-puberty pains caused by the development of the pelvic organs.

Many theories exist about the origin of these recurrent abdominal pains but for most children there is no good explanation for the pain. In some, but certainly not all, of these children the cause of these pains may be emotional. Children who have these pains are more likely to have high-strung personalities, are often over-conscientious and anxious, and are prone to fears and sleep disorders. There is often a history of similar pains or personality traits in other family members, or an over-focusing o eating and bowel habits. In some children, these pains are pre-cipitated by some stressful situation. However, many children are normal, well-adjusted children from well-adjusted families. If you are worried, consult your doctor.

● **Medical Evaluation of a Child with Recurrent Abdominal Pain**

Your doctor is faced with a major decision about how far to pro-ceed in investigating these abdominal pains. He could perform every test possible to see what turns up. This approach may alle-viate parental concern and may also make your doctor feel more certain that he has not missed anything. But it is also uncomfort-able for your child and is usually an unnecessary medical expense. Your physician's main concern is whether your child has any illness such as a urine infection which, if left untreated, may cause him added harm. A careful history, a physical exami-nation and just a few laboratory tests can usually determine this risk. Medical follow-up studies found that if no specific medical illness was suspected after a careful office evaluation by a pedia-trician then an extensive in-hospital medical evaluation by a gas-trointestinal specialist rarely uncovers a cause. (See **Milk Allergy** as a cause of abdominal pains, page 144 .)

● **Parenting the Child with Recurrent Abdominal Pains**

There are certain factors which tend to cause abdominal discom-fort in most children, and eliminating these may lessen the fre-quency and severity of these pains. Constipation leads the list of causes of abdominal pain (see page 358). Stress can contribute to abdominal discomfort in children, the same way ''nerves'' do in adults. The muscles of the intestines are richly supplied with nerves and general anxiety may cause these nerves to contract the muscle, producing pain. Alleviating any unnecessary anxiety in your child may alleviate the ''anxiety'' in his intestines.

Certain foods may irritate the bowel and a careful history relating foods habits to these pains should be kept. Milk is one possible food allergen; you may try eliminating milk and dairy products. In most cases of unexplained abdominal pain, no food allergen is identified. Other frequently overlooked causes of abdominal pain and general fatigue are hunger and low blood sugar. I feel school-aged children should have mid-morning and mid-afternoon snacks, in order to prevent these problems. Exag-gerated concern by a family about general foods habits might also be a contributing factor.

In general, when your child has these pains, try to iden-tify those factors in his environment which differ on that particular day. You may discover that some unsuspected stressful situation causes the pain.

What about medication? Generally there are no useful medications for these unexplained pains. Parental support and sympathy are your child's best medications.

● More Serious Types of Abdominal Pain

Seldom a day goes by in a busy pediatrician's office when the doctor does not get a call from a worried parent who says, "I think he has appendicitis." Although appendicitis is low on the list of causes of abdominal pain I feel that a certain amount of caution about your child's pains is a natural consequence of loving your child. It is certainly safer to be overly concerned than to neglect what may turn out to be a serious medical problem. Your parental intuition will often tell you when your child's abdominal pain is more than just "a little indigestion." If your child is one of these children who has frequent, unexplained abdominal pains, but who experiences a pain which is "different," seek medical attention.

Specific signs that warrant prompt medical attention are the following:

1. Sudden onset of severe abdominal pain accompanied by a hard abdomen, incessant vomiting (especially if green) and a generally unwell child. These signs indicate a possible intestinal obstruction caused by loops of bowel twisting around each other (volvulus) or a small part of the bowel telescoping into a larger part of the bowel (an intussusception). Intestinal obstruction is more common in the younger child, who cannot accurately verbalize how sick he is. If your child shows the above signs, call your doctor immediately, even if the child seems well between these episodes of pain.

2. Abdominal pain that your child can accurately locate by pointing with one finger is of more concern than pain which your child locates only vaguely. There is an old medical axiom that the farther the site of pain is from the umbilicus the more concerned you should be. If your child winces when you press around the lower part of the abdomen, especially around the umbilicus and toward the right lower part of the abdomen, call your doctor immediately.

3. Abdominal pain associated with fever and chills. Children with other illnesses such as a sore throat or pneumonia may complain of abdominal pain first. One of the reasons for this is that there are tonsil-like glands throughout the abdomen which often swell and produce pain (tonsillitis of the abdomen) when there i a generalized infection. I have seen children with signs of abdominal pain, similar to those which indicate appendicitis, when the real problem was tonsillitis or strep throat.

4. Abdominal pain may sometimes be due to food poisoning. Vomiting is the main sign of food poisoning. The pain is usually in the upper mid-abdomen. The abdomen is generally soft when you press. Food poisoning usually begins two hours after the offending meal is eaten. Older children who can verbalize their feelings usually complain of a "sick to their stomach" feeling of nausea. Other signs include retching or "dry heaves," chills but no fever, and a general, all-over, unwell feeling.

5. Young children may experience vague abdominal pains due to a urinary tract infection, which is why pediatricians often check the urine when evaluating unexplained abdominal pains. An untreated urinary tract infection may later cause serious kidney problems. (See related section on **School Phobia**, page 309.)

Muscle Pains

Growing pains are common muscle aches of middle childhood. We do not know the cause of these pains but it is doubtful that they are due to growth. They do not coincide with periods of rapid growth in children and disappear prior to the onset of the adolescent growth spurt.

These pains usually occur in the front of the thigh muscles, in the calves, and behind the knees. The degree of pain may be very mild to severe. Growing pains usually occur late in the day or evening but may be severe enough to awaken the child and make him cry. Growing pain muscles do not hurt when touched and do not appear swollen. There are usually no external signs; the muscles just hurt. Children may experience muscle pain after strenuous exercise, especially if they failed to stretch their muscles prior to participating in competitive sports. (See **Sports Medicine**, page 396.)

What can you do to relieve your child's muscle aches? Most so-called growing pains are relieved by heat, rubbing and hot-water soaks, similar to the treatment of a muscle cramp. Many a good parent has spent an hour rubbing their child's sore legs until the pain disappeared.

How can you be sure that these aches are only growing pains and nothing more serious? Growing pains usually occur in both legs, in the muscles, not the joints. Your child is otherwise completely well. Growing pains are not worsened by moving the legs. The child is able to walk around without increasing the pain. The diagnosis of so-called growing pains should be made by your doctor, not yourself, and a thorough orthopedic examination should be carried out to exclude any underlying illness (such as foot problems).

Eye Problems

Discharging Eyes

The problem of discharging eyes in a baby in his first few months is usually due to a blocked tear duct. (See page 180 .) A yellow discharge in an older infant or child usually indicates an eye infection. The important point for parents to note is that discharging eyes in the older infant or child may be just the "tip of the iceberg," meaning that this may not only be a sign of an eye infection but also of an underlying sinus infection, nose and throat infection, or ear infection. If your child has discharging eyes and cold symptoms, this signifies that the problem is a cold. Discharging eyes in a cranky child usually mean an associated ear or sinus infection. Medical attention should be obtained.

Conjunctivitis

Conjunctivitis is an inflammation of the membrane lining of the white of the eyeball called the **conjunctiva**. The eyeball is red (caused by dilated blood vessels which branch out over the white of the eyeballs), it itches or burns and is often sensitive to light. Clear or yellow discharge may flow from the uncomfortable-looking eye. Conjunctivitis may accompany a viral illness such as measles or a cold. In this case, the eye may be sensitive to light. If your child's eye becomes increasingly more sensitive to light, he may have a more severe eye infection and should be examined by a doctor. A bacterial infection called **pinkeye** causes a yellow discharge and swollen eyelids. If allergic conjunctivitis is the problem, the discharge is usually clear and watery, and the eye itches.

Sties

A sty is a little, pimple-like boil that appears on the edge of the eyelid and is caused by an infection in the base of an eyelash. A true sty is soft and tender to touch. Treatment of a sty is basically the same as that of any boil or abscess. Warm moist soaks (use a cotton-tipped applicator, applied to the sty, for as often and as long as your child can tolerate) will usually cause the sty to open and drain its contents. Antibiotic eyedrops prescribed by your child's doctor often help control the infection. To prevent sties in children, wash crusted eyelashes, especially when the child awakens in the morning, before eyelash secretions are allowed to plug the base of the eyelash hair and become infected. Recurrent sties are common in children who frequently rub or pick their noses and then rub their eyes. Bacteria from their nose is transmitted into the eye, so discourage this habit. If this problems recurs, your doctor may wish to prescribe a medication to clear up the bacteria in the nose.

Sometimes a small, non-tender nodule, similar to a sty, may appear in the middle of the eyelid or near the border of the eyelid. This is called a **chalazion**, an inflammation of the glands in the eyelid. Eyelid nodules, more common in older children, are both a slight irritation and a cosmetic embarrassment. Chalazions do not usually respond to antibiotic drops and hot, moist soaks as sties do. They often need to be removed by an eye doctor.

Cross-Eyes

During his first few months, it is common for your baby's eyes not to be perfectly straight at all times. Your baby's doctor checks this during the well-baby exams. If your baby's eyes are severely crossed at all times, or remain crossed after six months, your doctor may wish to refer your baby to an eye specialist for further testing. The eyes of a young infant often appear crossed but actually are not. This illusion is due to two features. Some babies have wide nasal bridges (the space between the eyes) and a prominent fold of skin which extends outward from the nasal bridge slightly covering the white of the eye at the inner corner. Some babies also have a large iris (the colored portion of the eyeball). The combination of these two features means that a lot of the white of the eyeball is not showing, especially the part nearest the nose. Your child may thus appear cross-eyed but is really not. As your infant grows, the nasal bridge becomes more narrow and less flat, the iris becomes smaller and the eyes no longer appear crossed.

Cross-eyes in infancy is usually caused by a weakness in one of the eye muscles. Cross-eyes in the preschool child may be due to an underlying vision problem. If the eyes are crossed, one eye focuses on the intended object while the other focuses on a second object. In other words, your child is seeing double. In order to focus the lazy eye on the intended object, your infant or child may tilt his head to compensate, or he may simply mentally block out the unintended image in the lazy eye and use only his straight eye to see. Over a period of time, his vision in the lazy eye becomes weaker and, if left untreated, permanent impairment of his vision may result. Treatment of the lazy eye by an eye doctor consists of patching the "good eye" to force your infant to use his lazy eye, eyedrops, special glasses, eye exercises, or an operation on the muscles of the lazy eye. Early recognition of cross-eyes is very important. Some very mild cases of cross-eyes appear only when the infant or child is tired. Therefore they may appear straight when your baby's doctor examines them. Ask your doctor to show you how to shine a light in your baby's eyes (or look at a photograph of his eyes) to see if the reflected dot of light is in the same location in both eyes. If it is, then your baby's eyes are straight.

Vision Problems in Children

Your child's vision is primarily determined by the shape of the **cornea** (the covering of the eyeball over the iris), the shape of the lens and the shape of the entire globe. As your child grows, the shape of the eye changes and, therefore, so does his **visual acuity**. Visual acuity is usually measured on a scale of 20. Visual acuity of 20/20 (considered normal) means that your child can read at 20 feet what the child with normal vision can read at 20 feet. If he can read 20/30, this means that he can read at 20 feet what the normal child can read at 30 feet. The newborn's visual acuity is around 20/300. Gradually, as the entire visual apparatus matures, visual acuity usually reaches 20/20 by the age of six years. Some children may not reach normal visual acuity until age eight years. Children can usually cooperate enough to undergo a visual acuity test in your physician's office by the age of three or four. Because the child's eyeball structures grow as he grows, his visual acuity is subject to change anytime during childhood, until he is fully grown. This is why visual acuity is usually tested every year as part of the yearly physical examination.

Nearsightedness (myopia), the most common visual acuity problem in children, means that the child's visual acuity is normal when he looks at objects close to him, but his visual acuity lessens as he tries to see objects farther away.

Astigmatism (improper curvature of the cornea) is another cause for diminished visual acuity in childhood. It commonly produces fatigue, eyestrain and headaches if left uncorrected. **Farsightedness** is not as common in children. **Color blindness**, an inherited disorder usually in males, is a visual problem in which the ability to perceive one or more of the three basic colors is impaired or completely lost. Red-green color blindness is the most common. Rarely does color blindness significantly interfere with a child's learning.

How do you recognize if your child has a vision problem? First, many visual problems have a hereditary basis. If either or both parents developed visual problems in childhood, convey this important factor to your child's doctor and he will pay special attention to your child's visual development. Signs of diminishing visual acuity are excessive blinking and rubbing of eyes, squinting, tearing, "tired eyes," tilting the head to one side, stumbling in a toddler and eye strain headaches after reading or near the end of the school day. An observant parent or teacher will notice that a school child holds his book close to read, attempts to sit close to the blackboard, or uses a variety of visual contortions to clearly see the writing on the blackboard.

The Allergic Child

What is an Allergy?

What is an allergy and what causes an allergic reaction? The term "allergy" actually means altered reaction. The offending substance is called an allergen. It may be a pollen in the air, a substance in the food or a substance which touches the skin. Allergens enter the body through the respiratory tract, skin or gastrointestinal tract, and stimulate the body to produce an antibody. Non-allergic children do not produce an antibody to a specific allergen; allergic children do. The combination of the allergen and the antibody then settles on certain tissues such as the skin or the lining of the respiratory tract, where it stimulates the production of substances called histamines. These histamine substances cause the blood vessels to dilate (redness of the skin, hives), the mucus glands to secrete mucus (runny eyes, nose, cough and fluid in the middle ear) and the muscle around the respiratory airway to contract (wheezing or asthma).

Common Allergic Reactions in Children

• **Allergic Rhinitis (Runny Nose, Hayfever)**

Allergic rhinitis (runny nose, hayfever) is characterized by a clear nasal discharge; a stuffy nose; watery, itchy eyes; and sneezing. The nasal passages may become swollen and, since young children are primarily nose-breathers, this may cause your child to breathe with his mouth open and to snore at night. Like the child with chronic adenoid problems (see page 356), longstanding allergic rhinitis results in a typical "allergic facies'': mouth open, dark circles under the eyes (allergic shiners), and a crease across the bridge of the nose caused by rubbing the tip of the runny nose upward with the palm of the hand (called the allergic salute). Children have a remarkable tolerance for these chronic, nuisance-type illnesses and, according to many parents, they do not seem sick. I am, however, struck by their very uncomfortable appearance. Treatment for allergic rhinitis is discussed below.

● **Asthma**

Asthma (which means wheezing) is a breathing problem characterized by rapid, labored breathing, indrawing of the chest during inhalation and wheezing during exhalation. During an asthmatic attack, the lining of the bronchial tree reacts to the offending allergen by swelling and pouring out mucus fluid into the bronchi, thus narrowing the air passages. The muscles of the bronchi contract, which further narrows the air passages and further obstructs the flow of air. In order to move the amount of air necessary for breathing, your child must work harder. His chest muscles work harder to get air in through these narrowed airways (indrawing of the chest) and he breathes faster. When exhaling, the airways are even narrower, the obstruction increases, and a musical sound called ''wheezing'' (like a wind instrument) is produced. Indrawing of the chest during inhalation, coughing to dislodge the mucus, and wheezing during exhalation are your child's normal compensatory mechanisms to move air through his narrowed passages.

Parents of a wheezing child commonly ask, ''Is my child asthmatic?'' Not every child who wheezes is an asthmatic child. Asthma implies a long-standing, periodic problem which has an allergic basis. One type of infection, called bronchitis, may cause the bronchi to react in a manner similar to an asthmatic attack, but a child with this type of ''infectious asthma'' does not deserve the label ''asthmatic child.'' Periodic bronchitis, caused by infections and respiratory infections, usually lessens as your child grows older whereas bronchitis with an allergic basis tends to become more long-standing. Before pronouncing your child ''asthmatic,'' your child's physician will examine the frequency of his episodes and whether they seem to have an allergic basis. It is often difficult to tell whether your child's wheezing episodes have an allergic or infectious basis, or both. However, children nearly always outgrow the frequent bronchitis caused by infection and the majority of children eventually even outgrow allergic bronchitis.

When should you worry about your child's wheezing? Children can often wheeze for hours or days and exert a lot of energy moving their breathing muscles. You should be concerned with a wheezing child who is becoming exhausted. Is the wheezing bothering your child? An older child can usually tell you when he is having difficulty moving enough air, but an infant who cannot express himself may cause more concern. If your infant is alert, active and seems reasonably happy, then he is probably moving enough air. "Air hunger" makes an infant unhappy and fretful. The noise of the wheezing is also a guide to its severity. Children who are moving a lot of air tend to wheeze more, whereas a child who is indrawing and laboring to move air with a less audible wheeze ("tight" wheeze) is probably not moving a great deal of air and is cause for concern.

The happy wheezer is of less concern than the silent wheezer. Wheezing during exhalation only, is of less concern than the child who shows indrawing during inhalation. In other words, trouble getting air in is more concerning than trouble getting air out. (See **Bronchitis**, page 349 .)

Another form of asthma is called "exercise asthma." Not all children with exercise-induced "asthma" are truly asthmatic, because they are not generally allergic children and only wheeze during certain types of exercise. Exercise-induced asthma is easily controlled by taking medication immediately before the planned activity. The problem usually diminishes as the child grows older.

Treatment of the Allergic Child

Treatment of respiratory allergies is directed at removing the offending allergen, blocking the immune response which triggers histamine release and blocking the effect of the histamine substances throughout the respiratory tract.

● **Removal of the offending allergen (called the "trigger")**
If your child's respiratory problems seem to have an allergic cause, a careful search must be made for the offending allergens. The older child with a long-standing allergy often knows what he is allergic to, but the young child may need some detective work. The following are common inhalant allergens: outside allergens such as trees, grass, ragweed pollens; household allergens such as dust, feathers, molds, mildew, tobacco smoke, wool, animal danders, cooking odors, deodorizers, fireplace smoke, air fresheners, household plants, stuffed animals, aerosols and any dust collectors.

A child spends a great part of his life in his bedroom. If

your child is highly allergic, you should pay careful attention to maintaining a dust-free environment in his bedroom. Since your child spends more time in his bed than any other single place, attention should be placed on allergy-proofing his bed. Depending on the severity of your child's problem, your doctor may suggest that his bedroom only be used for sleeping, and should therefore contain nothing other than his bed and perhaps a wooden chair. If possible, he should dress, study, and play in another room, and the door to his bedroom should always be kept closed.

The mattress and the pillows should be foam rubber. Feather pillows should not be used. Mattress springs should be covered with dust proof, airtight covers and zippers (sealed with tape). This prevents dust from accumulating within the springs. Special non-allergenic mattresses and spring covers are available. Bed clothing should be cotton or synthetic, not fuzzy, and washed frequently. No wool or down blankets should be used.

To clean your child's bedroom, all furniture, rugs, clothes, books, toys and drapes must be taken out of his room and dusted. The walls, floors, ceiling and bed should be dusted and washed thoroughly. Dust-collecting drapes should be replaced with cotton or synthetic curtains or pull-down window shades. Allergic children should avoid fuzzy, stuffed toys. They can usually tolerate animals stuffed with foam rubber and covered with a synthetic such as nylon.

The main dust-collector in most homes is the wall-to-wall carpet, especially the shag variety. Ideally, this dust-collecting carpet should be removed and a few cotton throw-rugs used. These should be washed weekly. If this is not possible, attempt to get the carpet least likely to collect dust and vacuum it daily while your child is out of the house. Vacuum cleaners are notorious for spreading tiny dust particles to which your child may react. The contents of clothes closets should be kept to a minimum and clothing should be stored in tightly zippered garment bags. Books, stuffed toys and upholstered furniture should not be kept in his bedroom. During the winter months, a vaporizer or humidifier minimizes the effects of dry air. It is important to clean vaporizers and humidifiers frequently, since they are a common source of molds and mildew.

Since dust may enter through the heating system, especially a forced-air system, air filters should be cleaned and replaced frequently. Accessory filters should be placed in the registers in your child's bedroom. Air conditioning often helps to filter the dust particles in the air but some allergic children tolerate air conditioning poorly. Electric air filters, either a separate unit or part of an air conditioner, may remove some of the dust particles from your child's bedroom. Electronic air cleaners can be added to your central heating system and may help clear most of the dust from the central air system. Sprays which act as dust inhibitors may be used to spray rugs, upholstery and other household dust collectors. Upholstered furniture is often allergenic. The least allergenic types are wooden chairs or sofas with removable foam cushions covered with smooth, washable covers.

Furry or feathered pets are frequent allergens. This presents a problem because, given the choice, a child is likely to elect to keep his allergy rather than get rid of his pet. It is wise to be sure he is not allergic to an animal before you buy one. If your child's pet is already firmly established in the family, then the best you can do is not to allow the pet inside the house, and certainly not in your child's bedroom.

Molds and mildews are highly allergenic. Molds collect in damp places such as cellars and may often be difficult to see or smell. Mold growths can be prevented by the use of certain non-toxic sprays available in garden supply stores.

House plants are notoriously allergenic and they need to be removed or kept in areas of your house where your child spends little time.

Food allergies are discussed on page 147. The only treatment for food allergies is to avoid the allergen.

Most allergic children are very sensitive to inhalant irritants such as paint and it is therefore preferable to remodel or redecorate your home when your child is away (e.g. at summer camp). If your child is highly allergic to certain pollen inhalants such as those produced during the ragweed season, he should wash his hair frequently, preferably before going to bed, because pollen may collect in his hair and, as a potential inhalant allergen, may be the source of problems during the night.

● **Treatment aimed at blocking the immune response to the offending allergen (allergy shots)**

Evaluating an allergic child for allergy shots is difficult for the physician, the parents and the child. There is a wide variation in children's allergies and a widespread controversy among medical specialists about the benefits of some forms of treatment.

The first step in evaluating the allergic child is to establish whether your child has an allergy. Is there a family history of allergy? Can you relate his symptoms to specific allergens? If you and your child's physician are convinced that your child's symptoms are caused by an allergy, then the next step is to determine to what degree the allergies are bothering your child. How much does this medical problem interfere with the growth and development of your child as a happy individual? How much school does he miss? How much play does he miss? How much sleep does he miss? Does the allergy cause only an occasional runny nose and sneezing and is it therefore more of a nuisance than a medical problem? Or are his allergies seasonal (e.g. hayfever), which result in two months of severe discomfort every year? Does he have recurrent asthmatic attacks which are increasing in severity and frequency, or recurrent ear infections made worse by his allergies? The type of allergies your child has and how much they bother him will influence the extent of the evaluation your child's doctor may wish to undertake.

If your child's allergies tend to be a periodic nuisance but do not really bother him, your doctor may suggest that you attempt to detect what he seems to be allergic to by observing your child yourself. Your pediatrician may also offer guidelines for environmental control which may remove potential allergens such as those described on page 375. He may also suggest the periodic use of antihistamine decongestants, hoping your child will eventually outgrow the allergy (which many children do).

If your child has severe respiratory allergies, your physician will be compelled to pull out all stops in order to alleviate your child's allergic reactions. The process begins with a very detailed history to determine which inhalants you know your child is allergic to. This is followed by counselling on strict environmental control as previously described.

At some point your doctor may wish to refer your child to an allergist for further evaluation. The next step often involves "skin testing," which means the allergist or your pediatrician injects a series of allergens into your child's skin in order to see which ones your child reacts to. I find that making the decision to skin test a child is as uncomfortable for me as the testing is for the child. The physician is faced with a dilemma. He does not wish to submit the child to an uncomfortable and expensive procedure which is not 100 per cent reliable but, on the other hand, he wants more information on which to base a long-term treatment regimen. Recently a blood test called the RAST (radioallergosorbent test) has been developed which actually detects allergic antibodies in your child's blood. This test is expensive and not always used in every allergy evaluation.

The next medical decision concerns hyposensitization, or allergy shots. Theoretically, by receiving injections of increasing dosages of an allergen over a long period of time, your child develops a type of antibody to these allergens which helps prevent the allergic reaction to this allergen when he inhales it. Your physician must consider several factors to resolve the dilemma of whether to submit your child to allergy shots. First, the shots do not always work. In fact, there is controversy about whether allergy shots are effective in the majority of children. Your doctor is also concerned about the psychological effects on your child of visiting the doctor's office every week or two for several years. Your doctor must also weigh two sets of evidence. The first states that the majority of children with hayfever and asthma eventually outgrow their symptoms naturally, and the second that the untreated child runs an increased risk of developing more severe and lasting allergies. In the end, these concerns often give way to the desire to give your child the benefit of any treatment which may lessen the severity and duration of his allergies and may remove the problem which is interfering with his growth and development.

Allergy injections have been proven to be effective against allergies to insect stings. If your child has had a severe reaction to an insect sting then a course of injections is advisable. The value of shots has not been proven in the case of food allergies, infectious bronchitis or eczema.

• Medications to block the production or effects of the histamine substances

Medications for allergic rhinitis are called decongestants and antihistamines and, as their names imply, are designed to constrict the swollen lining of the respiratory tract and to control the outpouring of the mucous secretions. Basically, these medications "dry up" the nose and sinuses, and are usually effective if used according to your physician's advice. Unfortunately many of these medications are sold over the counter without prescriptions. Avoid abusing antihistamines. Remember, their purpose is to dry-up respiratory secretions and therefore they should be used only when the problem is in the upper respiratory tract, i.e. in the nose or sinuses. They should not be used for asthma because they dry up the secretions in the lower respiratory tract. This makes the secretions thicker and therefore more difficult to cough up, thus leading to what is called a mucous plug, a plug of mucous stuck in the bronchi which is difficult to dislodge by coughing, and may become infected. Antihistamines also have varying side-effects. They usually cause drowsiness in adults, but children often show the opposite effect and become "hyper." They sometimes have sleep difficulties, and undergo personality changes.

Nose drops and nasal sprays are designed to constrict the blood vessels in the nose and relieve the congestion. They should be used only with a physician's guidance since over-use of nose drops may actually contribute to nasal congestion rather than alleviate it. Medications for asthma are usually called bronchodilators, which are designed to relax muscle spasms of the bronchi and smaller airways, and to open the airways to make air flow easier. These may be given by inhalation, injection or orally, and are extremely effective for "breaking" an asthmatic attack and controlling the wheezing. There are also preventive medications which, taken daily, are designed to prevent histamine release. In severe cases of allergy and asthma, cortisone may be periodically prescribed by your doctor. In addition to prescribing medications for allergies, your doctor will show you the techniques of nasal hygiene and chest drainage which may clear the mucus from the air passages. The general rule in treating childhood allergies is to keep the secretions thin and moving. Stagnant fluid in children, like stagnant water in a pond, often becomes infected, which further complicates the allergy.

Skin Allergies

- **Eczema**

Eczema is a hereditary skin problem which has an allergic mechanism similar to that of respiratory allergies, except that the target organ is the skin. Itchy, scaly and crusty skin is the hallmark of eczema. Eczema in the young infant usually occurs on the face and neck and arms. The face is usually spared in the older child but the arms and legs, primarily the skin inside the elbows and knees, are affected. Itching causes the child to scratch, the scratch produces more skin irritation which causes more itching (called the itch-scratch cycle) and in time these scratched areas become very thick. The skin of the child with eczema is often sensitive to many irritants such as soap, detergents, fabrics (especially wool), excessive heat and sweating.

To treat a child with eczema, besides eliminating the offending allergens, the following suggestions will make your child more comfortable. Keep his environment cool to reduce sweating. Avoid those skin irritants which your experience has shown will irritate your child's skin. Minimize emotional stress as the skin is often the mirror of emotions and stress can cause eczema to flare up. Use mild non-allergenic soaps. Most eczema treatment is aimed at relieving the itching. Non-allergenic emollients, either applied directly to the skin or added to the bath, may soften the thickened skin. Medications such as cortisone cream are effective in alleviating the itch and reducing the inflammation of eczema, but they should be used only with your physician's guidance.

• Contact Dermatitis

Contact dermatitis produces a rash similar to an eczema rash except that it is not chronic and usually does not have a hereditary basis. Contact dermatitis may be due to an irritant such as a piece of clothing, due to a certain chemical (detergents) or to an allergic reaction within the skin to a plant such as poison ivy. Poison ivy is the most common and most uncomfortable type of contact dermatitis. The typical rash consists of many small blisters which itch intensely, and often appear in a line where the leaf has brushed over the skin. The allergic reaction is caused by the oleoresin in the poison ivy plant. Skin contact with the plant is not always necessary as the oleoresins may be carried by smoke or pollen from nearby burning poison ivy plants.

Treatment of poison ivy is directed at relieving the intense itching and slowing down the inflammation. Although calamine lotion is the usual stand-by, a prescription of cortisone cream from your doctor is the quickest, most effective treatment. Soothing solutions (Domeboro) may be used in the bath or as a compress. Excessive scratching of poison ivy or eczema-type skin rashes may produce a secondary bacterial infection and a topical antibiotic cream may also be necessary. If your child knows he has come in contact with a poison ivy plant, washing the skin and the clothing thoroughly may remove some of the oleoresin before the skin inflammation begins.

• Hives

Hives is an allergic skin rash characterized by raised, red "wheels" which often have circular, red, raised borders the size of a dime or a quarter, with pale centers. Unlike contact dermatitis, hives are an allergic reaction of the blood vessels of the skin to an allergen which has entered the system, either through pollen, food, drugs or insect bites. In most cases of hives, a child looks worse than it really is, but it does itch and causes the child to be generally uncomfortable. Mild hives is usually treated with antihistamines and disappears within four days. Certain types of hives, (e.g. insect bite sensitivity) may be very severe and, in addition to the rash, may cause swelling of the tissues throughout the body. Eyelids and hands may be affected, and if the tissues of the vocal cords and airway also react (as in croup and asthma) the child may experience an alarming inability to move enough air. This type of general allergic reaction requires immediate medical treatment. Usually an injection of adrenalin is given to alleviate the generalized swelling and breathing problems.

Parenting the Allergic Child

No caring parent wants to see their child uncomfortable day after day. The allergic facies of an uncomfortable child brings out similar feelings of discomfort in the parents. Children with chronic allergies, especially if they miss many of the fun things of life because of their allergies, frequently "get down" and develop the feelings, "Why am I always sick and why am I different?" This is where the art of parenting your allergic child comes in. Your child needs your sympathy and support but not your anxiety; he has enough of his own. Because of the necessity of environmental control and frequent trips to the doctor, focusing on his allergies may make your child feel his world revolves around his allergies. A natural consequence of loving your child is that you may tend to over-emphasize the illness. This, however, is not in the best interests of your allergic child. Parents, try to play down your child's allergies and focus on more enjoyable activities. In so doing, you are conveying the message to your child that his allergies are a problem but they should not greatly interfere with his life as an otherwise normal healthy child.

Urinary Tract Infections

Urinary tract infections (UTI) are one of the great masqueraders in the range of human infections. Most infections give a clue to their origin by signs and symptoms directly related to the infected area (e.g., a sore throat indicates a throat infection, a cough indicates a lung infection). However, the signs of an UTI may be just about anything. Figure 8 shows the major components of the urinary tract.

How Urinary Tract Infections Occur

Normally, the urine manufactured in the kidneys travels down the tubes (called ureters) connecting the kidneys to the bladder. When the bladder is sufficiently full, the bladder muscles squeeze the urine out the lower end into the urethra. The one

Figure 8.
The urinary tract

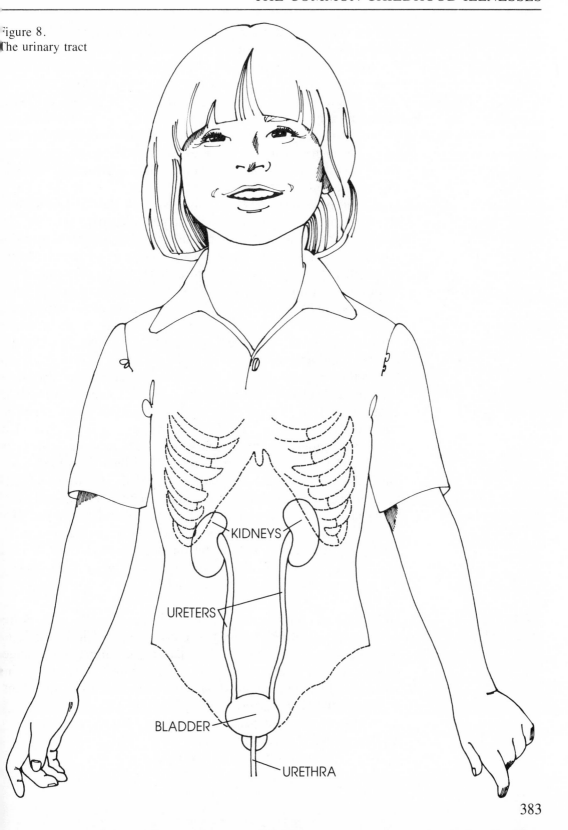

KIDNEYS

URETERS

BLADDER

URETHRA

way valves, located where the ureters enter the bladder, prevent urine from flowing back into the ureters and kidneys during bladder contraction. One principle of the human body, which is especially relevant to children, is that fluid which does not move often gets infected. The normal urinary tract is designed to keep urine moving.

Most urinary tract infections occur for one of two reasons. The urinary tract is "open to the outside" and bacteria may travel up into the bladder and multiply in the urine and lining of the bladder and urethra. Girls are more prone to urinary infections than boys because the urethra is much shorter. Also, there are often many bacteria in the vagina near the opening of the urethra. Since the normal urinary tract is designed to keep urine moving, any situation which causes stagnation of the urine may result in a urinary tract infection. Structural problems of the "plumbing" may interfere with proper drainage of urine. These problems usually occur in two locations: either in the valves or at the bladder neck. Infection may occur if the valves are incompetent, which means that they do not close completely when the bladder contracts and they thus allow the urine to flow back into the urethra instead of out the other end. Infection may also occur if there is an obstruction of the bladder neck where the bladder enters the urethra, thus preventing the bladder from emptying completely. These structural abnormalities cause stagnation of the urine (called residual urine) and back pressure within the bladder. This pressure is then transmitted back into the ureter and kidneys. The eventual result of repeated infections and back pressure is kidney damage which may not be detected until many years later, after irreversible damage has already occurred. The goals in managing urinary tract infections are to detect urinary tract infections early, before the infection ascends into the kidney, and to detect any structural abnormalities early in infancy before they result in kidney damage.

How Do You Recognize a UTI?

Older children may show more adult-like symptoms such as frequency of urination, burning on urination, difficulty holding onto the urine (urgency) or back pain. The infant and younger child may not show such obvious symptoms. The following signs may alert you to an urinary tract infection in your infant:
1. Recurrent unexplained fevers.
2. Vomiting and diarrhea.
3. Unexplained abdominal pain.
4. Not growing normally (failure to thrive).

5. Unexplained fatigue.

You will notice that these signs are not specific. They are the type that may often be passed off as the flu.

Parenting the Child with a Possible UTI

Don't always attribute vague illness to the flu or to "what is going around." This diagnosis should be made by your doctor, not you. I have seen many children who I thought had the "flu" or a "virus" when diagnosing over the phone but, upon examining their urine, discovered this "flu" was a urinary tract infection.

If you are taking your child to the doctor for any vague symptom, give your child a lot of fluids to drink just before going to the doctor's office and collect a urine sample as soon as you arrive in case your doctor wishes to examine your child's urine. Certain habits, particularly in females, which cause irritation of the vagina or urethra and promote urinary tract infections are excessive masturbation, especially "mounting"; the use of irritating soaps, especially certain bubblebaths; and lazy bladder-emptying habits such as waiting too long to go and dribbling a little, which leads to stagnation of residual urine. During bladder training, teach your child to respond immediately to his urge to urinate and not to hold on for a long time. Girls should be taught to wipe themselves from front to back after a bowel movement, instead of wiping themselves towards the vagina, which may allow bacteria from around the rectum to enter the vagina.

If there is a family history of urinary tract problems, especially in the siblings, parents should be especially vigilant about any signs of possible urinary tract infections.

Meatal stenosis (narrowing of the urethra where urine comes out of the penis) is a condition in males which may cause a mild obstruction of urine flow and thus lead to urinary tract infections. This condition cannot always be diagnosed simply by looking at the opening of the penis (the meatus) since the meatus may appear small but function normally. Signs that your child may have meatal stenosis are usually some unusual "piddle patterns" such as discomfort upon urination, a short urinary stream which "sprays" a lot, or dribbling a lot after urination. If your child has any of these signs, mention them to your doctor.

Orthopedic Problems

The purpose of this section is to help you appreciate the normal stages and variations in your child's leg and foot growth and to offer guidance about when to be concerned about your child's orthopedic development. Remember, just as in the human face, there are wide variations in the contours of the legs and feet.

How Children's Bones are Different

Infants and young children are more prone to "crooked bones" for two reasons:

The first is **joint laxity**. A child's ligaments (the tissues which connect bones together) are very stretchy and are called lax ligaments. When pressure is applied to bones during weight-bearing, these ligaments stretch and the joints bend. You will notice that you can bend your infant's fingers back almost to his wrist and, by holding one hand on his knee and the other on his ankle, you can move his lower legs from side to side a few inches. The ligaments of some children have more stretch than those of other children. Ligament laxity tends to be a family trait. As children grow, their ligaments normally tighten and become less stretchy, thus making the joints more stable.

The second reason infants and young children are more prone to crooked bones is **bone twisting**. The bones of a child are continually growing and may twist as they grow, especially if sustained pressure is applied to the bone. Since joint laxity and bone twisting are aggravated by sustained pressure in the wrong direction, treatment is aimed either at discouraging certain habits (e.g. sitting or sleeping in improper positions), which cause sustained pressure on the joints and bones, or at adding a device (e.g. supportive shoes, bars) which shifts the weight in the proper direction.

Your Newborn's Legs and Feet

Your newborn may have "bowed legs" and "inturned feet." This normal occurrence is due to the position of his legs and feet in utero. Because there is no "standing room" in utero, your baby naturally draws his legs up over his abdomen and curves his feet inward. This position causes the leg bones to be twisted inward, resulting in a combination of bowed legs and inturned feet. In the great majority of infants these curvatures correct themselves. One of the main reasons for frequent well-baby examinations during the first year is to check your baby's leg growth to be sure these curvatures are straightening o normally.

How can you help these bone curvatures? Babies often sleep in the fetal position (Figure 9). By repeatedly pulling his feet out from under him while sleeping you will help your baby stop this habit. Occasionally an infant will resist this correction. If the curvatures persist, either sew his pyjama legs together, or wrap a towel around his legs to prevent him from curling them underneath him. This should not be done without consulting your doctor.

Figure 9.
Sleeping in the fetal position may cause bowed legs and in-turned feet.

Usually a newborn's feet turn in mainly because of the above-mentioned normal curvature of the lower leg bones. Occasionally, one or both feet are themselves curved inward because the front of the foot is curved inward in relation to the back of the foot, a condition called **forefoot adduction**. Your doctor will discuss this incurved foot problem with you on your baby's first check-up. If, without a great deal of force, you can easily stretch the front of the foot in line with the back of the foot, then only a minor problem exists. This is easily treated by periodic stretching exercises which your doctor will demonstrate to you. If you stroke the skin on the outside of your infant's foot and he voluntarily straightens his foot, then no deformity exists and no treatment is necessary. Sometimes a newborn's foot shows a fixed curvature which cannot be easily stretched back to the midline and your doctor may recommend a treatment called **serial casts**. These look like little plaster boots. They are molded to your infant's feet and changed every few weeks until the incurved foot is straight. Orthopedic shoes, called **straight last** shoes are then worn for about a year. Babies tolerate these casts and shoes well. They usually are of more concern to the parents than to the infant. Fixed curvatures of the foot should be detected and treated early. Treating the condition after the child begins to walk is much more difficult.

Toeing-In (Pigeon Toes)

Most toddlers who toe-in have normal feet. The problem is inward curvature of the lower leg bone, and the feet simply follow the leg. Most in-toeing problems correct themselves by two or three years of age. What can you do to prevent in-toeing? Some infants will toe-in a bit even with normal legs, feet and hips. This usually does not interfere with walking and should no cause concern. Avoiding the sleeping and sitting postures which aggravate lower leg curvatures is usually all that is necessary to prevent the problem.

When should you worry about your child's toeing-in? As a general guide, seldom is any orthopedic correction necessary for a child under two years of age. If your child's in-toeing does not cause him to trip over his feet while walking or running, then no treatment is necessary for the child over two years. If by age two your child's legs are not beginning to straighten and he tripping a lot, your doctor may refer your child to an orthopedic specialist. Some older children may toe-in in order to compensate for the strain of flat feet (see **Flat Feet**, page 389). Again if your child's feet appear normal and he does not trip when walking, then time and proper sitting and sleeping postures will correct this variation.

Toeing-Out

Toeing-out is seldom due to any orthopedic problem and seldom disturbs a child's walking. Infants normally turn their legs outward when beginning to walk to increase their stability. Sleeping in the frog position usually prolongs this toeing-out. As your child grows, he will tend to bring his legs together more when he sleeps, and naturally bring his feet inward when he walks and runs.

Knock-Knees

All children, especially between the ages of two and six, show, to some degree, knock-knees. This is due to the lax ligaments supporting the inside of the knee joint. When a child stands, his legs seem to cave inward at the knee joint and stay apart at the ankles. As your child grows, the ligaments supporting the inside of his knees strengthen and his knees knock less. Knock-knees can also result from the "weak ankles" of flat feet. Although this problem is usually self-correcting, it should not be completely ignored. An older child who shows an increasing degree of knocked-knees may develop structural problems in the upper leg bones. To prevent orthopedic problems caused by knock-knees in later childhood, simply encourage your child to avoid the sitting postures which stretch the inner ligaments of the knee (see TV position, Figure 10). A knock-knee appearance is common in older, obese children with chubby thighs and flat feet.

Flat Feet

Flat feet are normal in infancy. Young infants have "fat pads" everywhere, including the arch of the foot. When you look at a baby's foot there is seldom any visible arch, only a pad of fat which obscures the arch. As the infant grows, this fat pad tends to disappear and an arch may appear by age two years, at least when your child is not standing. When the infant stands, the previously visible arch may disappear and the feet may again appear flat. This is because the lax ligaments that normally bind the bones of the arch together cannot support the weight on these bones and the arch "collapses." As the child grows, these ligaments strengthen enough to support the weight and the flat feet usually correct themselves by the age of three or four. Infants and children who have generally lax ligaments (fingers, wrists, knees) also tend to have a greater incidence of flat feet. This generalized ligament elasticity tends to be a family trait.

When should flat feed be treated? The decision to treat

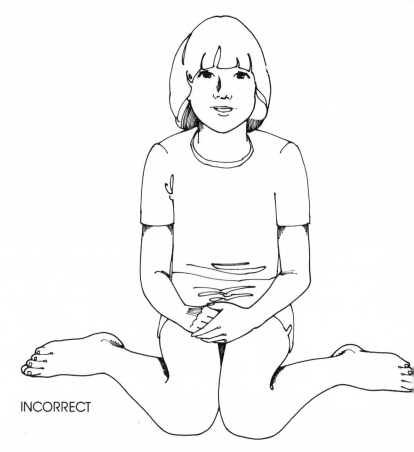

Figure 10.
The TV position.
Encourage your child
to avoid the sitting
postures which stretch
the inner ligaments of
the knee.

INCORRECT

flat feet depends upon whether there is undue strain on the lig
ments of the foot. The easiest guide is to look at your child's he
direction. If the heel (Achilles tendon) is straight (perpendicul
to the floor) then the axis of weight-bearing is normal and r
abnormal stress is placed on the flat foot. If your child's heel
slanted outward then unnecessary strain is placed upon the foo
which, if left untreated, may result in leg pains, aggravation (
knock-knees, and persistent out-turned heels and sore feet
later childhood.

A child's normal step consists of three parts. The heel
placed down onto the surface, the mid-foot adapts to the surfac
upon which it is placed, the forefoot turns in slightly and t
ankle joint locks, enabling the final step of pushing off, using t
ankle as a rigid lever. If, because of excessive ligament laxit
your child's heel and ankle bones do not lock into position durir
walking, there is excessive side-to-side movement of the join
This joint instability may result in unnecessary stress on t

CORRECT

bones and ligaments of the foot and lead to painful feet and poor walking habits.

Some children compensate for flat feet and heel slant by toeing-in, which is often a protective gait to guard against straining the foot ligaments. If your child has flat feet and begins to show out-turned heels then your doctor may suggest orthopedic shoes. These ''supportive shoes'' have a sponge rubber arch support and sometimes a wedge on the inside of the heel. These shoes support the lax ligaments of the arch until these ligaments strengthen and the heel straightens.

Many orthopedic specialists feel that so-called corrective shoes for flat feet are widely overused. Instead of corrective shoes, your doctor may recommend custom-molded plastic inserts called **orthotics**, which are worn inside regular shoes. These orthotics support both the heel and the arch and give the ankle stability while the child is walking. Older children and adolescents who complain of foot and leg pains from flat feet

391

may also be helped by orthotics with a reasonable heel. Ho
your child "wears out" his shoes may be a clue to abnorm
strain on the feet. If your child's feet are normal, his sho
should show most of their wear on the outer border of the he
and the inner border of the sole at the toe. Children with ou
turned ankles secondary to flat feet may show the opposite sig
of shoe wear.

How Sitting and Sleeping Positions Can Affect Your Child's Leg Curvatures

Peculiar sleeping and sitting positions probably do not har
orthopedic development in many children. However, in tho
children who have very elastic ligaments, certain postures ca
cause undue strain and result in problem curvatures of the leg
and feet. Sleeping in the fetal position (Figure 9) prolongs th
inward curvature of the legs and feet, which is normally prese
in newborns due to their position in utero. Unfolding the infant
legs from underneath is advisable. Sitting with the feet folde
inward underneath results in the same problem. Sleeping in th
frog position is normal during the first year and may actually b
the preferred position for proper hip development. Howeve
sleeping in this position after one year may contribute to ou
toeing. Sitting in the so-called "W" or TV position (Figure 1
causes improper stress in three areas. It causes the upper leg
turn in, the lower leg to turn out and the ankles to bend outwar
The result of this posture is knock-knees. The "tailor" o
"Indian" position (Figure 10) is the best sitting position f
proper leg development.

Shoes

"Doctor, when should he have shoes?" This is a question pa
ents ask about children around nine months of age. Your infa
and toddler do not need shoes for support. Shoes do not impro
the orthopedic development of most children. Children enjo
being barefoot. A toddler requires shoes only for protectio
when walking on an uncomfortable surface and for cold weathe
      What should you look for when buying shoes for yo
child? The following important features should be considered
1. The type of heel.
2. The flexibility and thickness of the sole.
3. The support of the counter (back of the shoe).
4. The flexibility of the shoe top.
5. The fit. (Shoes should be snug at the heel so the shoe sta
on, but there should be room at the toes and ball of the foot.
      For the young infant, simply get a shoe which is easy f
you to put on and take off, because you will be constant

engaged in this game. The infant who is just beginning to walk should have a shoe with a firm heel counter and a soft, thin, flexible sole. Infants bend their feet and toes to push off when beginning to walk and therefore need a very flexible sole which does not skid easily, and a very flexible leather top. Unless your toddler has very lax ankle ligaments, high top shoes are not necessary for ankle support, but they may be the only shoes which won't slip off his feet. Your child may be able to wear lower cut shoes as soon as his heel fits the back of his shoe, so that the shoe does not easily slip off his heel or rub up and down and cause blisters.

As your child masters walking, the sole of the shoe may be a little thicker, but it should still remain flexible at the forefoot. "The older the child, the higher the heel," is a reliable guide. Low-heeled shoes in the older child and adolescent frequently contribute to foot and leg pain. In fitting your child's shoe, be sure his heel is snug at the back and the toes have enough room. When your child is standing there should be one-half inch to one inch between his longest toe and the front of the shoe and the shoe should be loose enough to enable you to pinch a small fold of leather on the sides or top. The shoes should support the arch well but allow good flexibility of the forefoot. Young children grow out of their shoes long before they wear them out. Older children, however, usually wear out their shoes first. Be sure the counter of the older child's shoe is strong enough to resist being bent between your thumb and forefinger. If the counter is too soft, your child may soon wear out his shoes. (For further discussion see **Corrective and Uneven Shoe Wear**, page 391 and **Shoes**, page 209.)

Sports Medicine

Sports, either competitive or individual, are a necessary part of your child's physical and social development. An increasing awareness of safety in sports and a new medical speciality called sports medicine have emerged during the past ten years. In this section I will discuss the major topics of sports medicine which are relevant to the pre-adolescent and adolescent, with emphasis on minimizing the risk of sports-related injuries and parenting your child through his sports adventures.

The Sports Physical

Most schools require your child to have an annual sports physical examination before playing competitive sports. This is a law in many states and a requirement for school accident insurance. Sports physicals can be performed in a group or individually.

Group physicals (locker room exams) are impersonal, insensitive to privacy and usually fulfill only legal requirements rather than yield meaningful information. Group exams by sports medicine specialists are best reserved for college athletic programs, not for school-aged children.

An individual examination by your child's pediatrician is most meaningful since this doctor knows your child and your child's sports participation is just another milestone in childhood development. Sports physicals are necessary for the following reasons:

1. To detect any medical condition that may interfere with your child's participation in a particular sport.

2. To counsel both the parent and child about practices which may minimize the risk of injury, enhance performance and contribute to your child's enjoyment of the sport. These include conditioning, warm-up and stretching exercises, nutrition and safety measures.

3. To counsel the child about team relationships so that the sport will contribute not only to his physical but also to his social development.

4. To counsel the parents about their supportive role on the "team."

5. To fulfill legal and insurance requirements.

Sports physicals should be scheduled at least three weeks prior to sports participation for two reasons. In case a medical illness or contraindication to participation is detected, sufficient time remains for treatment. It also allows time for sufficient conditioning exercises to prepare growing muscles and joints for competitive sports.

"Doctor, is it all right for my child to play contact sports?" This is a valid question for concerned parents to ask and, again, I regard parental concern about sports injuries as just another symptom of loving your child. Whether your child chooses to play contact team sports depends upon many factors. Is the athletic program well-coached, well-supervised and well equipped? Is your child's temperament suited to such sports? Is he motivated? Does he really want to play? Do the potential benefits, such as physical and psychological development, outweigh the risk of injuries?

Concern about the effects of twisting forces on growing bones (e.g. Little League Elbow) and other potentially serious injuries are justified. Since pediatricians are frequently asked for their opinion on this matter I will offer mine. A child needs to play and nearly all play involves some risk of injury. I feel the risk of injury in a well-coached, well-supervised, well-equipped, weight-matched football game is less than the risk of an injury to a child who is "hanging around" an unsupervised playground, riding his bicycle around the neighborhood or on busy streets, or participating in unsupervised sandlot sports. Most children who can escape parental pressures to play a certain sport will choose a sport which matches their temperament. If your child is comfortable in the sport which he has selected, then he will profit both physically and emotionally from the sport. If, on the other hand, he plays football not because he wants to but because Dad wants him to, his self-esteem will suffer. Pressuring a shy, gentle child onto a football field of "gorillas" in order to "make a man out of him" is questionable parenting. His talents may better be channelled into other activities befitting his temperament.

Peer acceptance is a primary social need of most pre-adolescents and adolescents. The concept of the team fulfills this basic need. Team sports, such as soccer and football, may contribute more to the social development of these children than individual sports (e.g. tennis). Endurance sports, such as swimming and track, are usually safer than contact sports and provide both physical development and skill accomplishment. What your child may lose by not participating in a contact team sport, such as football, he gains by acquiring a skill. Team sports may contribute to a child's social development during his adolescent years, whereas individual skill sports may contribute to your child's self-esteem and be more beneficial to him for a longer period of time. In summary, a sport should give your child both enjoyment and learning. The sport should match the child's temperament. Parental guidance is more profitable than parental interference.

How to Reduce Sports Injuries and Enhance Performance

● Safety Equipment

In most organized league or school sports your child will be properly fitted with safety equipment. However, many injuries occur during unsupervised activities when safety equipment is often overlooked. In activities such as roller-skating and skateboarding, the knees, elbows and head are frequently injured, and therefore helmets as well as knee and elbow pads should be used. For ordinary bicycle riding, special pads are available which fit over the handlebars and crossbars, the two sites which children frequently fall against.

● **Shoes**

Short-cleated soccer-type shoes are certainly safer than baseball spikes. If your child does a lot of running (e.g. jogging), a shoe with an adequate heel which fits properly is essential. If he usually runs on a hard surface (e.g. a basketball surface) and complains of heel pain, a soft rubber pad may be inserted inside his shoe beneath his heel. This cushions the effect of pounding his soft, growing bones against a hard surface. Generally, prolonged running on any hard surface should be avoided by a growing child. They should jog on soft grass or on a field rather than on pavement. If your child has a history of ankle injuries, high-topped shoes plus preventive ankle taping may spare him further ankle strain. Rubber teeth guards should be worn for all contact sports such as hockey and football; these are often overlooked in unsupervised sports.

What Sports Activities Should Be Avoided?

The trampoline is a potentially hazardous piece of gymnastic equipment because of the risk of serious neck injury which can result in paralysis. Both the American Academy of Pediatrics and the NCAA (National Collegiate Athletics Association) have recommended that the trampoline be banned from school gymnastics. Parents would be wise to also follow the recommendation and ban the trampoline from the backyard. Skateboards are also potentially hazardous. In 1977, there were 375,000 skateboard accidents reported in the United States. If all the inventions designed to propel our children through their childhood faster (walkers, skateboards, and mopeds) were banned our children's world would be a lot safer, and their alternative activities would probably be more meaningful.

Conditioning

There is an old axiom in sports medicine: ''Get in shape to play don't play to get in shape.'' This advice is especially relevant to children. At least three weeks of gradual conditioning are advisable before you move into high gear in competitive sports. Too much too soon results in a variety of muscle aches and strains During the pre-adolescent and adolescent growth spurt, children's bones grow faster than their muscles. This is why pre stretching exercises are even more important for children than for adults. Sustained stretching exercise for at least fifteen second several times a day, and ten minutes before the game is ver important for the young athlete. Conditioning, stretching exercises and pre-game warm-ups decrease your child's risk of muscle injuries and also enhance his athletic performance.

Nutrition for the Young Athlete

Besides the nutrition he needs to sustain basic bodily functions and to increase growth, the young athlete needs extra calories to supply the increased energy he needs during exercise. The following are suggestions on how to meet the nutritional and energy needs of the adolescent athlete.

1. Each day a growing child (whether or not he is an athlete) should have a balanced diet consisting of food from the four basic food groups.

a) Milk and dairy products (2 servings). If your child has a milk intolerance (see page 144) then yogurt and unprocessed cheese are alternatives.

b) Meats and high protein foods (2 servings). Meat, poultry, fish, eggs.

c) Fruit and vegetable groups (4 servings). Green leafy vegetables, potatoes, citrus fruits.

d) Cereal and grain groups (4 servings). Whole grain cereal, bread, pasta.

2. Athletes need extra energy foods. Besides the basic nutritional requirements, the young athlete will need extra energy in proportion to the demands of his sport. For example, if a young athlete uses 1000 extra calories per day (the average amount used in two hours of sustained exercise) he needs to add 1000 calories of high energy food to his already balanced diet. These foods should be primarily carbohydrates such as fruits, juices and grains. These additional energy requirements cannot be met by vitamins, proteins or mineral supplements since these are not energy sources.

3. Athletes need a lot of extra water. Thirst often does not signal the amount of water needed. The young athlete should be encouraged to drink water until he is no longer thirsty and then drink two or more glasses after that. Both hunger and dehydration decrease athletic performance.

4. Athletes should eat an after-school snack of at least 500 calories, primarily carbohydrates (juice, fruit, yogurt, nutritious cookies). This avoids the low blood sugar feeling which may reduce athletic performance during the after-school practice.

5. Both adolescent males and females need extra iron, males because of their growing muscles and females because of menstruation. If an athlete's body is low in iron, his or her athletic performance may be compromised. This is why the doctor meas ures your adolescent's hemoglobin (blood count) as part of sports physical. The following suggested foods contain iron (i order of level of iron content): liver, beef, poultry, fish, prune iron-fortified cereals, raisins, beans, green leafy vegetables an egg yolk. The iron in animal foods (meat, poultry, fish) is mo efficiently absorbed through the intestines than the iron i vegetables.

6. The Pre-Game Meal. To provide high energy withou compromising performance, a pre-game meal should be low i fat since fatty foods stay in the stomach for a longer tim resulting in a feeling of fullness. A high carbohydrate meal eate two to three hours prior to the game will provide steady energ without leaving the athlete full and uncomfortable. Suggeste foods are a lean meat or chicken sandwich (without mayor naise), fruit and fruit juices, salad, sherbet, nutritious cookie much extra water. If travelling, the athlete should avoid food which carry a high risk of food poisoning (e.g. shellfish, han burger). Finally remember the old axiom, ''Saturday's game played on Thursday's food.'' Eating a high energy nutritious di for several days before the game, stores up energy.

- **Nutritional Misconceptions**

Athletes do not need extra vitamins if they eat a well-balance diet. Vitamins do not provide energy. Salt tablets should not b used. Sweat consists mostly of water. Athletes actually lose ver little salt. Their requirements can be adequately met by a ba anced diet. Too much salt interferes with normal body chemistr and may compromise performance.

A crash diet and rapid weight loss to make the team is common problem in weight-matched sports. Weight can b gained and lost in only two areas of the body—lean body mas (muscles) and the fat. Weight in a growing child should not b lost from his lean body mass, only from his excess fat. Sinc most children have at least 5 per cent to 10 per cent of their bod weight as excess fat, a weight loss of at least 5 to 10 per cent c their present body weight would be safe for most children. A obese child could lose more and a lean child should not lose any Weight loss in a growing child with a well-balanced diet shoul occur primarily by increased energy expenditure not by a restric ive diet.

''How much can my child lose without hurting himself? is a valid question. If your child must lose weight to make th team, here are some simple suggestions for a safe program c weight loss.

1. Discuss with your doctor during the sports physical how much your child is overweight.

2. Be sure your adolescent eats a well-balanced diet. (See page 397.) The average adolescent will need around 1800 calories per day to meet growth requirements.

3. Start a program to lose around two pounds per week, primarily by increased energy expenditure. About two hours of any sustained exercise will expend around 1000 calories. If your child's diet matches his basic needs, by expending 7000 calories, he will lose two pounds of body fat per week. Weight reduction in the adolescent should begin many weeks before the weigh-in day, in consultation with the doctor. If weight is lost mostly by increased energy expenditure rather than by restrictive diet, the loss will not interfere with normal growth.

4. Weight gain. Some athletes wish to gain weight, or rather to gain muscle (bulking up), prior to the football season. If this is desired, you should get proper nutritional guidance from your child's physician. To add an extra pound of muscle mass, your child must consume an extra 3000 calories. The important point is to limit the desired weight gain to muscle and not increase the fat. A gain of one and a half pounds per week is about the maximum amount of muscle which can be gained. Any more than this may appear as fat. In addition to an extra 500 to 700 calories in nutritious foods (low in saturated fats and cholesterol), he must increase his muscle work considerably. Increased food intake without increased muscle work will produce only fat, not muscle. Weightlifting is popular because it results in a rapid increase in muscle strength over a short period of time. However, each year I see many teenage boys in the office who complain of chest and muscle strains resulting from improper weightlifting. Weightlifting should be supervised, with programs designed by the athletic director. To be certain your child is not gaining fat, his physician can check any change in body fat by measuring skin-fold thickness at several points with calipers.

How to Recognize Common Sports Injuries

There are three common types of sports injuries: strains, sprains and fractures; contusions; and over-use injuries.

● **Fractures, sprains and strains**

How do children's bones and joints differ from adults'? Why are sprains and fractures of greater significance in children? Near the end of each bone, children have soft areas called **growth plates**. These growth plates are weaker than the ligaments which attach to the ends of the bone. When a sudden force is applied (e.g twisted ankle), the growth plate may separate. This produces type of "fracture" unique to growing bones. The same type c injury in an adult would result in a torn ligament because there i no growth plate and the ligament is the weakest part of the adu joint. If your child sustains an injury to a long bone (arm or leg) do not consider it just a sprain and wrap it. Parents should neve diagnose or treat joint injuries in children. If a growth plat injury is not properly treated, growth of the bone may be pai tially disturbed and shortening of the affected limb may result

The following are signs of problems which definitel warrant medical attention:

1. Point tenderness. If your child points to the area with one fin ger and can pinpoint the pain to a small area the size of a quarter an underlying fracture is very likely.

2. Pain when moving the joint. Children often hold their joint i a position of maximum comfort to avoid pain. For example, if a elbow injury has occurred, your child may carry the affected arr flexed near his body, as if he is making his own sling. In general pain, swelling, tenderness and limitation of motion are signs o problems which warrant medical attention.

Muscle strains (pulled muscles) are stretch injuries an tendons. The most common sports strains are to the muscles o the back and the thigh (pulled hamstrings) and to the hip muscle (pulled groin muscle). Mild strains often do not cause an athlet to leave the game, and the pain and stiffness may go unnotice until the next day. If the strain is severe, there may be associate injury to the muscle tissue and bleeding within the muscle resulting in immmediate swelling, stiffness and pain on move ment of the muscle .

A muscle cramp is a sudden, severe, incapacitating pai in a large muscle, usually the thigh or the calf, which is associa ted with a marked spasm or "tightening." Heat and massag usually give prompt relief to muscle cramps. There is usually n lingering pain and the athlete can resume his activity.

● **Contusions**

Contusion means "striking" and the injury is frequently called "charley horse." This is a common tackling injury in footba and occurs most frequently in the front thigh muscles. Contu sions result in pain and swelling at the site of the trauma; thi pain is exaggerated with flexion of the muscle. These signs ma occur immediately, or as late as twenty-four hours after th injury. Contusions over bony prominences (shoulders and hips) are called "pointers."

● **Over-Use Injuries**

Young athletes commonly complain, "The only time it hurts is when I run." The ends of children's bones, called epiphyses, are prone to inflammation if the joint is overused, especially if the motion involves twisting or pounding (e.g. "Little League Elbow" from throwing curve balls, "jogger's heel" pain from pounding on hard surfaces).

Shin splints is a very painful condition caused by inflammation and swelling in the muscles and tendons in the front of the leg, the muscles frequently used in running. This problem results from poorly conditioned muscles, running on hard surfaces and an improper running technique. Parents should remember that, if their child begins to complain of pain in a bone or muscle used frequently in his sport, he should stop the activity immediately and seek medical attention. Listen to your child's "joint signals." If he complains of pain or you notice a sudden decrease in his performance, seek medical attention. Don't think it will get better as the season goes on. Joint irritation caused by over-use usually worsens with time and may result in a permanent limitation if not attended to properly. (See treatment and rehabilitation below.)

First Aid Treatment for Strains, Sprains and Fractures

To help you remember how to administer first aid, remember the word ICES (Ice, Compression, Elevation and Support).

Ice decreases muscle spasm, local pain, bleeding and swelling. Crushed ice in a cloth bag or towel should be applied to the site of injury for twenty minutes. Ice should not be applied directly to the skin as it might cause frostbite. **Compression**, or pressure applied with elastic bandages may reduce the swelling from a muscle or joint injury. Begin wrapping at the point farthest away from the heart. This minimizes the swelling of tissues beyond the bandage. The bandage should be just snug enough to insert one finger beneath it. If the fingers or toes beyond the bandage begin to swell, turn blue, or feel numb, the bandage is too tight. **Elevating** the affected limb about six inches will also minimize swelling. Your child will normally flex his leg or arm in the position of comfort. Using a splint, crutch or sling for **support** will both lessen the pain and prevent further injury from unnecessary movement or weight bearing. If a neck or back injury, or a severely broken bone is suspected, do not move the the injured child. Tell him not to move and then call your local

Rescue Squad or someone who is expertly trained in supporting these types of injuries.

Proper first aid to muscle injuries will prevent further tearing of an already injured muscle and will thereby minimize bleeding in the muscle. Profuse bleeding within an injured muscle prolongs the time needed for recovery from muscle injuries.

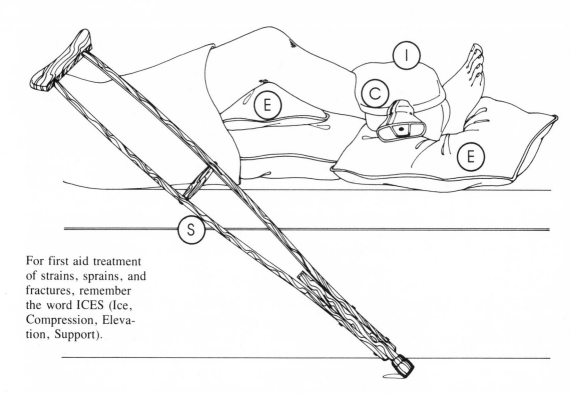

For first aid treatment of strains, sprains, and fractures, remember the word ICES (Ice, Compression, Elevation, Support).

Rehabilitation

The "rest it and forget it" treatment is not appropriate for the growing athlete. Conditioning has built your child's muscles for his particular sport. If a limb is injured and requires rest, the rested muscle loses its strength (called "disuse atrophy"). This weakened muscle not only delays your athlete's return to activity but increases his chance of reinjuring the muscle. An athlete's unused muscle may begin to lose strength as soon as four days after injury. This is why medical treatment for muscle and bone injury should include rehabilitation.

Rehabilitation attempts to restore normal range of motion and strength to the affected limb as quickly as possible, without aggravating the injury and slowing the healing. Your doctor should outline a program of rehabilitation for your child, either to be done at home, in the physiotherapy department of a hospital or at school. This program will consist of heat treatment, usually after the swelling subsides, either in a whirlpool bath or a shower at home, and muscle exercises. He should begin with isometric exercises (tensing the muscles without moving the joint) and gradually progressing to isotonic exercises (moving the muscles against a load, as in gradual weightlifting). Restoration of strength exercises may begin as soon as the joint can be moved without pain. Pain is the body's signal that the injured tissues are not yet ready to be overused. The adolescent athlete usually has great team spirit and may feel he is letting the team down by not returning to competition. He will therefore try to pin down his doctor by asking when he can play again. Your child's doctor may wisely not give him a definite date but rather give him a step-by-step program and say that "when your muscles have regained their original strength and you can move your joint fully without pain, you can resume competition." Often, a gradual, well-planned program of rehabilitation returns the child to the game sooner, and prevents a re-injury which may cause him to miss the entire season or permanently affect his sports career.

Parenting the Young Athlete

Parents, remember that you want your child's sports participation to enhance his physical development, to increase his social skills and to bolster his self-esteem. I am often astounded by the negative emotional reaction of grandstand parents to a child's mistake or a team loss. A child under pressure does not perform well. A child is painfully aware of his mistakes. He should not have to endure parental disappointment as well as his own. Support your child through his sports endeavors as you have supported him through his earlier developmental stages. Most children are naturally competitive and love to win but perhaps we place too much emphasis on winning. Children are forced to deal with adult pressures soon enough. Remember, your child is playing a sport, he is not working for the sport. At the end of a sport season, your child should emerge an improved athlete, happy with his performance and secure in his team relationship.

Common Childhood Infectious Diseases

What is an Infection?

What is happening in your child's body when he has an "infection"? Simply, a struggle is being waged between invading micro-organisms, viruses or bacteria, and your child's own defense mechanisms. Some viruses or bacteria invade your child's body and live harmoniously within the body. Other micro-organisms invade the tissues, cause harm and stimulate the body to mobilize its defenses against the infection. One example of the body reacting to infection is the common skin boil. Bacteria invade the skin. Blood flows to the infected area, producing the four classical signs of infection—redness, swelling, heat and tenderness. The white blood cells engulf the bacteria. The result of this battle is the leftover debris called **pus**. The local tissue walls off this battleground, forming an abscess, which in medical jargon is referred to as "pus under pressure." Besides these local signs there may be other signs, such as fever, that the body is fighting an infection. The white blood count may also change during an infection. Your doctor may use a white blood count test to help him determine what type of infection your child has.

Products from the infection are carried through the body's disposal system, the lymphatic channels, to local reservoirs called **lymph glands**. These glands, most noticeable in the neck, under the arm and in the groin, often enlarge and produce conspicuous lumps which give a clue as to where the infection is.

Your doctor must determine whether your child has a virus or a bacterial infection. The body's own defense mechanisms usually heal viral infections (e.g. measles, mumps). Your doctor simply treats the symptoms of the viral infection (pain, fever, diarrhea) until the body's defenses have cured the illness.

Bacterial infections are usually easier to determine because symptoms are more pronounced. Bacteria may even be seen under an ordinary laboratory microscope. Some can be grown from certain tissue (e.g. scraped off the tonsils), a process called a "culture." It is sometimes difficult for your doctor to be certain whether your child has a viral or a bacterial infection. He may order some laboratory tests to help make the correct diagnosis. If your doctor suspects a bacterial infection, he will prescribe the antibiotics to best fight your child's particular type of bacteria. Bacteria have the interesting ability to change their genetic make-up over time (survival of the fittest) so that they may eventually develop a resistance to certain antibiotics. If your child is not getting well, it may mean that the bacteria are resistant to the prescribed antibiotic and the doctor may decide to change to another antibiotic. Your doctor will usually not prescribe an antibiotic if he suspects a virus infection. Remember, you go to a doctor for consultation, not always for medication.

Immunizations   An immunization is the deliberate stimulation of the body's defenses (antibodies) against a particular germ by giving a person a vaccine of that germ. The vaccine is composed of the germ

---

RECOMMENDED SCHEDULE FOR IMMUNIZATIONS OF INFANTS AND CHILDREN*

2 months	**DPT[1], OPV[2]**
4 months	**DPT, OPV**
6 months	**DPT, (a 3rd OPV is optional)**
1 year	**Tuberculin test[3]**
15 months	**MMR[4]**
1½ years	**DPT, OPV**
4-6 years	**DPT, OPV**
14-16 years	**Td[5] — and repeat every 10 years**

[1] DPT equals Diptheria, Tetanus Toxoid combined with Pertussis (whooping cough).

[2] OPV equals Oral Polio Vaccine.

[3] Frequency of Tuberculin tests depends on the risk of Tuberculosis in a particular community.

[4] MMR equals Measles, Mumps and Rubella (German measles) vaccines, given together in one injection.

[5] Td equals combined Tetanus and Diptheria Toxoid. This type of Diptheria Toxoid is less potent and is used in children over 6 years of age. Tetanus boosters are necessary only every 10 years in a previously fully immunized child and for clean, minor wounds. For contaminated wounds, a booster dose should be given if more than 5 years have elapsed since the last dose.

*This is the current suggestion of the Committee on Infectious Diseases of the American Academy of Pediatrics, 1980.

---

itself and is prepared by changing the germ in such a way that it does not cause disease but stimulates the body to produce antibodies to the germ. If the "real germ" enters the body, the body will already be "immune" to that germ and no disease, or a milder disease will result.

● What Every Parent Should Know About Their Child's Immunizations

1. Many children have no reaction to any of their vaccines. With the DPT injection, some infants and children may experience pain, swelling and redness in the muscle at the site of injection and a low, moderate fever. Reactions to DPT vaccines usually occur within the first few hours after the injection, seldom last more than twenty-four hours, and can be treated with analgesics (aspirin and acetaminophen.) (See page 339 .) Reaction to the MMR vaccine occurs in approximately 5 per cent of children, does not occur until one or two weeks after the injection, and is usually limited to low grade fever and mild joint pain. Reactions to vaccines are entirely unpredictable and are usually caused by your child's own body immune mechanisms at the time of the injection. In no way should reactions be blamed on the person who gives the injection.

2. The immunization schedule provided is meant strictly as a guide which should be followed as closely as possible. The initial series of three DPT vaccines may be given as close as one month apart. Interruption of the recommended schedule does not interfere with the immunity. It is not necessary to start the series again, regardless of the time elapsed.

3. Immunizations should not be given while your child has a febrile illness. They may be given safely if your child has a minor infection such as a cold. Delaying your child's immunizations because "he always has a cold" is not usually necessary.

4. If your child does have a reaction to a vaccine be sure to accurately report the severity of the reaction to your doctor so that your child's future immunization program can be modified to minimize reactions.

5. Recommendations for immunization for foreign travel are periodically updated. If the risk of reaction to a vaccine outweighs the risk of contracting the disease, then immunization is not recommended. This is why the smallpox (routine) vaccination is no longer given in North America.

Recommendations change continually because of outbreaks of various communicable diseases in various countries. Contact your local health department for the immunizations currently required for the countries you are visiting. Immunizations required usually include smallpox, cholera, yellow fever, perhaps gamma globulin protection against hepatitis, medication for prevention of malaria and vaccination against typhoid. Be sure to carry a stamped immunization card, which states that you received the required vaccines. It may be required to re-enter your country. (See **Foreign Travel** page 472 .)

When is Your Child Contagious?

Contagious diseases, especially viruses, have an incubation period from at least one to fourteen days, (the period from the time the germ enters the body to the appearance of symptoms). During this period, the virus is growing in the body but produces no symptoms. In most cases the child is most contagious just before you notice any symptoms or when the symptoms are so mild they pass unrecognized. This is why quarantine is partially ineffective in controlling the spread of infectious diseases. Most viruses are communicated by oral and respiratory secretions, most commonly by a cough.

Measles (Rubeola)

Measles begin like a common cold with cough, runny nose, watery and reddened eyes which are sensitive to light and a low grade fever. The child is most contagious during this stage. In the next three or four days, the cold symptoms worsen and the fever rises to around 104° F. A rash, which appears at the height of the fever around the fourth or fifth day, begins on the forehead around the hairline and gradually spreads downward to cover the entire body by its third day. On the face and upper body, the rash becomes red and raised, and runs together (confluent), whereas on the lower extremities the rash may be in discrete patches. The rash begins to fade about the third day, disappearing in the same order it appeared. It may cause some peeling of the skin, usually not on the hands and feet, as in the case of scarlet fever. (See **Scarlet Fever**, page 347 .) The child is no longer considered contagious toward the last days of the rash, which usually disappears five days after it first appears. A cough is usually the most noteworthy sign of measles. The fever usually breaks shortly after the rash appears. The temperature returns to normal in about five days. Measles produce interesting spots, called Koplik spots, on the inside of the cheeks. These Koplik spots resemble grains of salt on a red base, begin just before the measles rash appears, and are used to confirm the diagnosis of measles.

There are no ''antibiotics'' to treat measles, because it is a virus. Physicians treat the symptoms and the child's own body defenses cure the disease. Treatment should consist primarily of taking analgesics and antipyretics (aspirin and acetaminophen) for the fever and generalized discomfort, avoiding bright light which is painful to the eyes, rest, drinking fluids and receiving emotional support.

Occasionally, toward the end of a viral illness, bacteria may invade certain tissues such as the ears and the lungs, and cause a bacterial infection. An antibiotic may be required. If your child's high fever lasts more than three days, recurs after it has broken, or your child seems to be increasingly drowsy, call your doctor.

On rare occasions, a child who has been vaccinated may contract measles. This may be because the vaccine used in the United States between 1962 and 1968, and in Canada until 1970, provided a shorter period of immunity than the vaccine now used.

In some cases the vaccination may not have taken because of improper storage of the vaccine.

Most children who are properly vaccinated usually show no signs of the disease but if they do, the case is usually milder, non-communicable and without the severe complications possible with the natural virus.

Mumps

Mumps is a virus localized in the saliva or parotid gland of the neck. Mumps begins as a vague, virus-like illness with fever, headache, nausea and vomiting, and general tiredness. A day after the first symptoms, the child may notice a pain beneath the earlobe. Usually by the third day of the illness the parotid gland is obviously swollen. The contagious period for mumps lasts from the onset of the symptoms (even before the neck swelling is noticed) until the swelling has disappeared, usually within seven days. Usually both sides of the neck are swollen, but in 25 per cent of children, swelling is apparent on only one side.

Parents may sometimes confuse mumps with other types of swollen glands such as the swollen glands associated with throat infections. These glands are lower and further forward, toward the middle of the jawbone. The parotid gland is higher and toward the back of the jawbone lying just beneath the earlobe and its swelling is more obvious.

Mumps is usually a mild disease whose symptoms disappear within seven days. Although swelling of the glands is the only sign of mumps you may see, mumps may involve many organs, mainly the brain, gastrointestinal organs, heart and testicles. When mumps involves the vital organs, serious complications, such as encephalitis, may result. The main reason for encouraging the mumps vaccine in all children is to prevent the complications which are possible with mumps. If your child contracts mumps, treat his symptoms, the fever and pain, with analgesics such as aspirin and acetaminophen. (See page 339.) Nausea and vomiting frequently accompany the mumps because the disease commonly involves the gastrointestinal organs. Therefore a clear fluid, bland diet is recommended in the early stages of the illness.

Many children who are exposed to mumps do not develop obvious signs, but are infected enough to develop a lasting immunity to mumps. It is estimated that 50 per cent of adults who think they never had mumps are immune to the disease.

Rubella (German Measles)

Rubella is a virus which usually begins as a vague flu-like illness—low fever (usually 100° F-101° F), general tiredness and a slight cold. Because of the mild signs, a significant illness is usually not suspected until several days later when the rash appears. The rubella rash is pink-red rather than purple-red like the measles rash. It develops, spreads, and disappears more quickly than the measles rash, usually disappearing by the third day. The measles rash tends to run together, especially on the face, whereas the rubella rash usually consists of distinct patches on the face. The diagnosis of rubella is not easy since the symptoms are mild, the rash is also often mild and the child is usually not very ill. The glands of the neck, especially those along the back of the neck and behind the ears, are often enlarged and tender but these symptoms are typical of many other viruses.

The contagious period for rubella is longer than that of many other viruses, lasting sometimes from seven days before the rash appears to five days after it appears. Rubella is more common among older children and adolescents than among pre-schoolers.

Rubella is such a mild disease that it seldom harms the child, but there is danger if it is transmitted to a pregnant woman. It can cause abnormalities in the fetus (the ''rubella syndrome''). If a pregnant mother has been exposed to rubella, how can she know if she has become infected? First, the doctor can do a blood test to determine whether you are already immune to rubella (about 85 per cent of women of childbearing age are immune to rubella). Secondly, if you are not already immune a further blood test (called ''antibody titer'') can detect if you have been recently infected with rubella. These tests are often necessary to alleviate the anxiety of a pregnant women.

Rubella vaccine, along with measles and mumps vaccine, is now given to infants around fifteen months of age. This vaccine is given both to render all children immune to rubella to prevent the possibility of transmitting rubella to a pregnant woman, and also to render young females immune before they reach childbearing age. The rubella vaccine itself does not produce communicable rubella, so your child can receive the vaccine if you are pregnant. Women who are susceptible to rubella are usually given the rubella vaccine immediately after delivery in order to prevent their infection in subsequent pregnancies. As a precaution, women are discouraged from becoming pregnant for two months after receiving the rubella vaccine. The necessity for this precaution is still being investigated.

Chickenpox

Since chickenpox is one of the most common contagious childhood diseases, parents should be familiar with it. Usually the chickenpox rash appears without warning in young children. Occasionally a child feels vaguely unwell and has a low grade fever one day before the spots appear. The most striking feature of chickenpox is how rapidly the eruptions change. In the first few hours, dot-like red areas about the size of a match head appear on the face and trunk. They can initially be confused with tiny insect bites. If you suspect chickenpox, pick out a few of these spots. If your suspicion is correct, you will notice, within a few hours, clear blister-like vesicles on red bases, plus the beginning of fever (usually 101°F-102°F), and this confirms chickenpox. Very rapidly, new crops of vesicles appear all over the trunk and face; fewer on the extremities. Eruptions can appear in different stages. As a new red dot appears some vesicles break, becoming ulcer-like in appearance, while others form a crust. Within a small area you may see small red dots, vesicles, ulcers and crusts. Around the seventh day of illness the fever disappears and all the eruptions crust over to form scabs. Your child is considered contagious from one to two days before the rash until all the vesicles have crusted. (The crusted vesicles may not totally disappear for a couple of weeks.) Some children may have only a mild form of chickenpox in which there may be very few vesicles and little or no itching.

The most distressing symptom of chickenpox is the intense itching. The vesicles of chickenpox may also erupt on particularly uncomfortable areas such as on the mucous membranes of the mouth or on the vagina.

The two main goals in parenting the child with chickenpox consists of relieving the intense itching and preventing permanent scarring. Itching may be relieved with soothing, anti-itch compounds such as Domeboro soaks and Calamine lotion. Sometimes an antihistamine may help, especially as a mild sedative at night. Although chickenpox does not usually cause permanent scarring, scratching may produce a secondary bacterial infection and may result in permanent or pitting discoloration on the skin, especially of the face. Cut your child's fingernails very short and explain to him that scratching his face may leave permanent scars.

The most common of the very few possible complications of chickenpox is a secondary bacterial infection of the eruptions which may need to be treated with antibiotic cream. Pneumonia and encephalitis are rare.

There is no vaccine available for chickenpox and quarantine usually proves unsuccessful. Chickenpox is spread chiefly by contact with the eruptions, and possibly also by the air-borne route. Chickenpox is usually a milder illness in children than in adolescents or adults, a fact which provides a rationale for not over-protecting the young child from catching chickenpox. A form of chickenpox called ''shingles'' can be particularly debilitating to the elderly person who may not be immune to chickenpox. It is therefore wise to keep an infected child away from a susceptible older person.

Roseola

Roseola, a common illness in infants, usually occurs between nine and fifteen months. Although probably a virus, its mode of spreading and the period of contagion is uncertain. Roseola is characterized by the sudden onset of a high temperature (104° F-105° F) in a previously well child. The parents are surprised that the infant has such a high fever, because he does not act that sick. Aspirin and acetaminophen cause a temporary drop in the fever. The child seems well when the fever drops, only to become somewhat irritable as soon as the fever rises again. These signs continue for about three days, when the fever drops as suddenly as it began. A rash appears after the fever disappears. The rash may appear immediately after the fever disappears or about a day later. The rose-pink roseola rash usually appears first on the trunk, fades on pressure, is much fainter than the rash of other viral illnesses and may not even be noticed. It usually lasts no more than twenty-four hours.

Diagnosis is the main problem with roseola. You take your child to the doctor because of high fever. Your doctor examines your infant and can find no identifying cause for the fever (called a FUO or fever of unknown origin in medical language, see page 338). He suspects roseola, he does not give an antibiotic (since antibiotics are not effective against viruses) and gives you advice on treating the fever. He says "I can find no cause for the fever. Your infant's ears, throat, lungs and urine are not infected and he does not act as sick as the high fever would indicate. I suspect he has roseola so be prepared for the fever to go up and down for three days. Follow my instruction on fever control. He should not act sicker. If he does, call me. Expect a faint rash to appear after the fever breaks. If the rash appears, only then will we be sure it is roseola." The important part of the doctor's advice is "If he gets sicker, call me." Viral infections usually do not worsen; they just may not improve for a few days. On the other hand, bacterial infections which need an antibiotic usually worsen if left untreated.

Your main goal in parenting the infant with roseola is to control the fever (see page 338). The sudden onset of a high fever may produce febrile convulsions. If the fever is controlled, roseola presents more of a concern to the physician and parents than to the infant.

Scarlet Fever

See page 347.

Scabies

Scabies (from the Latin "scabere," to itch) is an extremely contagious skin infection caused by a tiny mite the size of a pinpoint. The mite attaches itself to the skin (usually in moist skinfolds such as between the fingers, toes, under the arms, inside elbow creases), burrows under the skin where it sets up camp and hatches its eggs. In infants and children, scabies may appear just about anywhere on the body. The presence of the mite causes a hypersensitivity reaction resulting in intense itching, especially at night. The skin rash of scabies may resemble tiny flea bites, the vesicles of chickenpox, eczema, impetigo or a combination of all these rashes. Sometimes tiny, tunnel-like burrows can be seen on the skin surface. Diagnosing scabies is often difficult because of the secondary rashes caused by intense itching, but the condition may be suspected in any unusual skin sore which itches intensely, does not respond to the usual remedies, has been present for several weeks and seems to be spreading. Your doctor may confirm the diagnosis of scabies by scraping the rash and observing the mite under his microscope. If many of the child's care-givers have a rash which itches intensely, usually on their arms, and your baby shows signs of fussiness, this might be a clue to scabies.

Scabies is easily treated with a special prescription lotion. Be sure to follow your doctor's instructions since over-use of these lotions may be harmful. These lotions are best applied at night after a warm bath and after scrubbing of the lesion with a stiff brush to allow better penetration of the lotion. Even after the mite has been killed by one of two applications of the lotion, the itching may persist for weeks, but it gradually decreases. Parents should realize that, even though the itching persists, the scabies has probably been cured by the initial application of the lotion. Additional applications of the lotion and over-zealous skin scrubbing may be harmful. Soothing anti-itch compounds such as Domeboro may relieve the itching. Normal laundering of clothes and bedding will remove any mites from the source. You do not have to scrub the whole house because mites die within a few days if they don't find a warm nesting place. Scabies is spread through contact with the infected areas or by bedclothing and other "close contact" apparel, often making it necessary to treat an entire family.

Head Lice

The head louse is a tiny parasite which punctures the skin of the scalp where it feeds and deposits its excretory products. Itching may be the first symptom. Sometimes the itching may be the only symptom but often secondary bacterial infections may occur, resulting in impetigo-like rashes and tiny boils throughout the scalp. The head louse deposits its eggs (nits) on the base of the hair shaft where they can be seen as tiny, oval, grey, dandruff-like specks firmly cemented to the hair shaft. Nits are clearly visible whereas the adult louse is nearly impossible to spot. When the eggs hatch, after about one week, the mature louse is transmitted through shared clothing and combs.

If you suspect your child has head lice, examine the hairs on the back of his head for nits or evidence of itching and scratch marks. The nits are most likely to be found at the back of the head, within an inch of the hairline. Although they resemble dandruff, nits are firmly attached to the hair shaft. Dandruff flakes slide up and down easily on the hair. To treat head lice:

1. Comb the nits out of the hair with a fine toothed comb or pull the nits off the hair with a small tweezers.
2. Obtain a prescription shampoo or lotion and wash the hair

exactly as described.

3. Thoroughly wash personal articles such as combs, brushe and bedclothing.

Worms

● **Pinworms**

Pinworms, also called threadworms because they resemble smal pieces of white thread about one third of an inch long, are th most common childhood parasite.

To understand how these worms behave in your child you should understand the life cycle of the pinworm. Pinworm reside and mate in the child's intestines. The pregnant femal then travels down the intestines and out the rectum. She lays he eggs around the rectum, especially at night. All this activit around the rectum results in intense itching, causing the child t scratch the egg-infested area around his anus and buttocks. Thes eggs are then picked up on the fingers and beneath the fingernail and transmitted to the child's mouth, to other children or to othe members of the household. The swallowed eggs hatch in th intestines, mature, mate and repeat the life cycle.

Although these tiny parasites have been blamed for ever imaginable symptom from appendicitis to learning disabilities probably the only symptom they can be found truly guilty of i intense itching around the anus, buttocks or vagina. Pinworms therefore, constitute more of a nuisance than a real medica problem.

Sometimes the tiny, thread-like white worms can be see at night by spreading your child's buttocks and shining a light o the rectum. If the itch scratch symptoms indicate pinworms bu you cannot see them (which is usually the case), you can easil capture the eggs by placing the sticky side of a piece of tap around the anus in the area of the itch. This is best performe when your child awakes, before he takes a bath or has a bowe movement. Take the tape to your doctor. He can place it under microscope and examine it for pinworm eggs.

Treatment for pinworms is safe and simple. The child i given a single dose prescription medication which is repeated te days later. Treatment of the whole family is advisable to mini mize recurrence. The pinworm medication (pyrvinium pamoate is a red dye that colors the stool and vomitus bright red. Sinc vomiting occasionally occurs shortly after swallowing this medi cation, it is a wise precaution to administer it in a place wher vomiting or spilling of the dye containing medication won't stai anything.

● Roundworms

Roundworms are much less common than pinworms but are of greater medical concern. Roundworms are reddish-brown and about six inches long. Roundworms may multiply in the large intestine and, because of their relatively large size, cause severe abdominal discomfort and malnutrition, especially anemia. These worms are usually passed through the rectum or through vomiting, which may be the first clue that your child has roundworms. A special prescription medication eliminates these roundworms.

Impetigo

Impetigo, an infection of the skin caused by the bacterium streptoccus, begins as tiny red dots, which progress to become blisters which rupture, producing a honey-colored crust. These yellow crusts distinguish impetigo. These lesions itch a great deal and can be spread to other parts of the body or to other children by scratching fingers. Impetigo may occur anywhere on the body but the most common site is around the entrance to the nose where the skin around the nostrils appears raw, reddened and contains yellow crusts. Often, the small crusty areas may enlarge, producing patches of impetigo the size of a coin. To treat impetigo:

1. Decrease the itching by use of a soothing solution such as Domeboro, available without prescription.

2. If there are only a few small areas of impetigo, an antibiotic ointment may suffice. In most cases, ointments are ineffective and oral antibiotics may be necessary.

3. Cut your child's fingernails and advise him not to scratch. If the above treatments are followed, extreme isolation is often unnecessary except for a case of severe impetigo.

Ringworm

Ringworm, a fungus infection of the skin or scalp, produces a rash which at first is about the size of a dime. The rash gradually enlarges, resulting in the characteristic reddened, elevated, scaly border with a pale center. Skin lesions of ringworm may itch but not as intensely as other skin lesions. Ringworm is contagious by contact and by finger scratching but is not considered as contagious as impetigo. The child with ringworm need not be isolated.

Ringworm is a fungus infection, which requires a prescription cream for proper treatment. You should consult your doctor.

CHAPTER IX

CHILD SAFETY, ACCIDENT PREVENTION AND FIRST AID

Accidents are the most common cause of death in the healthy child. Car accidents are most often the cause of death, followed by fires and burns, drowning, falls, and poisoning. Parenting your child through his accident-prone years is a challenging task. This chapter presents tips on accident prevention and advice on dealing with accidents.

The Accident-Prone Environment

"Accident-prone child" is an unfair term. It implies that many children are, by nature, more likely to suffer accidents. In most of these cases, however, some factors in the environment, rather than within the child, predispose these children to accidents.

Tips on Accident Prevention

1. Avoid accident-prone family situations. Childhood accidents occur most often because of stress or a change in family routine. For example, when parents might be tired or ill the family might be rushed and, therefore, less cautious. There may be a sudden change in a child's normally secure environment as during vacation or a move. An unfamiliar care-taker or babysitter might cause stress in a child. If there is a change in your family routine or relationship, you should pay more attention to your child and his environment.
2. Have realistic expectations of your child's ability to distinguish safe from unsafe behavior at various stages of his development. In most developing children, the desire to perform a cer-

tain feat precedes both the ability to accomplish that feat and the understanding of its potential dangers. Some children are cautious and calculating. They do not attempt a task before they

MOST FREQUENT CHILDHOOD ACCIDENTS

Birth to 6 months	<ul><li>auto accidents (use infant car seat)</li><li>crib accidents</li><li>changing table accidents</li><li>bath water burns</li><li>falls — rolling out of infant seat or off changing tables</li></ul>
6 months — 12 months	<ul><li>auto accidents</li><li>falls against sharp table corners</li><li>electric burns — sockets and cords</li><li>toy accidents — strings, sharp edges, small mouthable parts</li><li>cigarette burns</li><li>grabbing accidents — hot coffee, breakable glass</li><li>high chair accidents</li><li>walker and stroller accidents</li></ul>
1 year — 2 years	<ul><li>auto accidents (use child car seat)</li><li>exploring accidents — storage cupboards, medicine cabinets, falling on stairs</li><li>climbing accidents</li><li>cuts from sharp knives</li><li>eating poisonous plants</li><li>unguarded water hazards (bathtubs, pools and ponds)</li></ul>
Preschool & school age	<ul><li>auto accidents (use seat belt)</li><li>tricycle and bicycle accidents</li><li>yard and street accidents</li><li>playground accidents</li><li>fire accidents — matches, lighters</li><li>water accidents</li></ul>
Teens	<ul><li>auto accidents (encourage driver education)</li><li>moped accidents (encourage first aid course)</li><li>sports accidents</li><li>drug and alcohol abuse</li></ul>

intuitively know they can safely manage it. The parents of these children might say, "He was slow to begin walking and then suddenly he was off and running." Other children are impulsive. They do not think before they act. Impulsive children are more likely to have accidents.

What is your child's behavior pattern? If he is calculating and you know his transition from one developmental stage to another is smooth, he has a lower risk of having accidents. If your child is impulsive and his transition between developmental stages is stressful, he is at a higher risk of having accidents.

Children need guidance rather than over-protection. Educating him is safer than restricting him. Teach your child to swim. Teach him rules of the road. Teach him which objects are dangerous and why. There is, however, often no substitute for supervision. Despite your instruction, the memory of a young child is often short and his behavior often impulsive.

Public information on household safety and specific hazardous products is available from the Consumer Product Safety Commission, Washington, D.C. 20207, or call toll free (800) 638-2666 or (800) 638-8326.

In Canada contact: Consumer and Corporate Affairs, Department of Product Safety, 1410 Stanley Street, Montreal, Que. H3A 1P8, (514) 283-2825.

Infant Equipment Safety

● **Cribs**

1. Crib slats should be no more than 2-3/8 inches (6 cm) apart to prevent the infant from slipping his body through the slats, hanging by his head and strangling.

2. The mattress should be firm and fit snugly against the side of the crib so that the infant's face cannot become wedged between the mattress and the sides of the crib, causing suffocation. The mattress that was designed by the manufacturer of the crib should not be substituted for another.

3. Check baby's height when he is standing on the mattress against the side rail. Once the height of the side rail is less than three quarters of the infant's height, the baby is then too tall to be safely left alone in the crib.

4. To prevent scratching the infant and catching his clothing, metal hardware should be smooth and should not protrude into the crib.

5. Latches on the drop side of the crib should be secure. You should not be able to release them from the inside.

6. Toys that could serve as steps for the infant to climb out of the crib should be removed.

7. The crib should not be placed against a window, near any dangling ropes, (Venetian blinds), nor near any furniture which could be used to help the infant climb out of his crib. The crib should be placed so that your infant would not fall against any sharp object, become entrapped and possibly strangled between the crib and the adjacent wall or furniture if he climbs out of the crib.

8. Any string longer than eight inches attached to a toy, mobile, pacifier or clothing should not be in the crib or within reach of the infant. Strings can strangle.

9. Avoid cribs with ornate tops. Infants have strangled in the concave space between the post and the crib.

10. If the nursery is not within hearing distance of every room in the house (mothers have exceptionally good hearing), an inter com may prove a valuable safety feature.

11. Do not leave a baby unattended with a bottle propped up to feed himself.

12. Buttons on clothing can become entangled in the mesh of a mesh crib or playpen.

13. Cribs should be painted with a lead-free paint. Cribs manu factured after 1974 should conform to the regulations of the Haz ardous Substance Act. Pamphlets concerning crib safety are available from the U.S. Consumer Product Safety Commission.

- **Infant Carriers**

Front carriers are the best for the young infant. From six to eight months, backpacks are usually easier. Consider the following features when using and selecting a carrier:

1. Be sure the straps and connectors are sturdy and properly attached.

2. The leg openings should be large enough not to pinch but small enough to keep the infant from slipping out.

3. The carrier should be deep enough to support the head of a baby under six months, and deep enough to support his back when older than six months.

4. Periodically check for frayed straps, loose snaps or ripped seams.

5. Use the restraining straps. Older infants may stand up in the carrier and fall out.

6. Be sure the covering over the frame is well-padded.

Figure 11.
Front carriers are best
for the young infant.

Figure 12.
After 6-8 months,
backpacks are usually
easier.

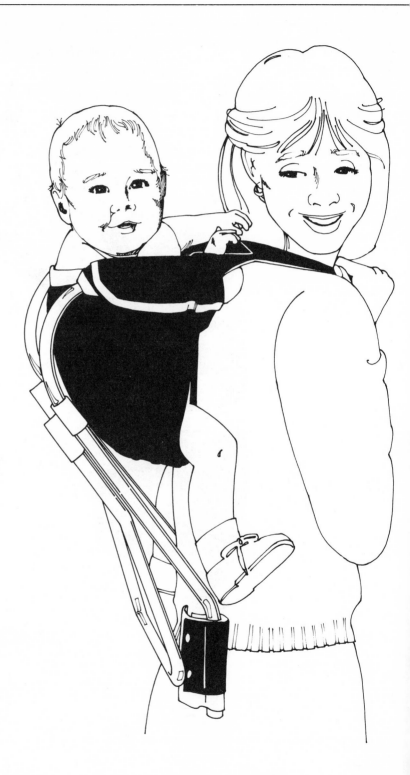

• Infant Seats

Falls are the most common accident which occur with infant seats. Do not leave a baby in a seat unattended (e.g. sitting on the changing table or on a counter top, while you do something else "just for a second"). Even a baby of three months can roll out of an infant seat. When babies are around five or six months, they may rock forward in the seat and topple over sideways. Other safety tips are:

1. The infant seat should have a wide, sturdy base.

2. Use the restraining belts, but don't rely on them if baby is sitting on a table or counter top.

3. Be sure the supporting bars are fastened securely. If they pop out of the sockets the seat will fall backwards.

4. Attach non-skid tape to the underneath surface to prevent slipping.

5. Do not use the infant seat as a substitute for a car seat.

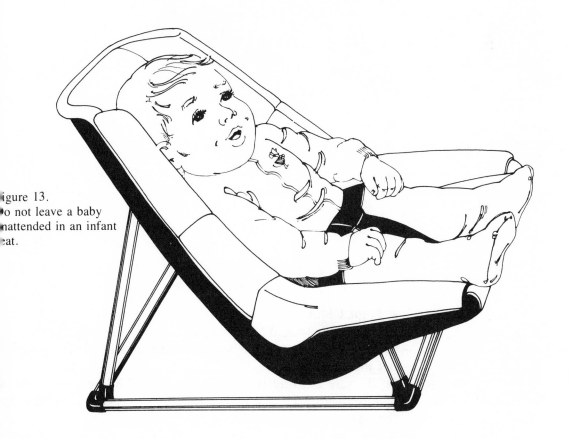

Figure 13.
Do not leave a baby unattended in an infant seat.

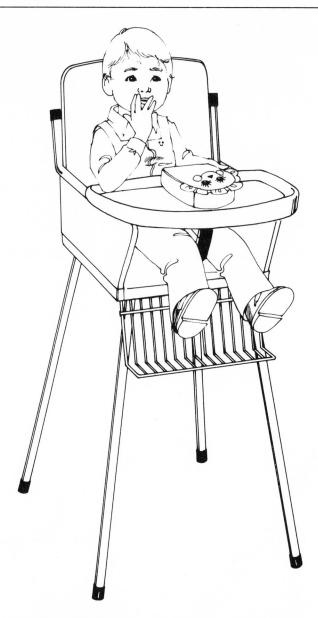

Figure 14.
Keep the high chair
away from hazards.

● **High Chairs**

1. The chair should have a wide base for stability.

2. Use the safety belt and be sure the belt attaches to the frame and not the tray.

3. Be sure the tray is properly secured. Children tend to push against the tray when seated or pull on the tray when climbing into the chair.

4. Be sure the chair and tray is free of sharp edges and splinters.

5. Keep the chair away from hazards, e.g. stoves.

● **Strollers**

1. The base should be wide enough to prevent tipping when baby leans over the side.

2. If the stroller adjusts to a reclining position, be sure it will not tip backward when baby lies down.

3. Two wheel brakes are safer than one.

4. Use the restraining belt.

5. Check for sharp edges. Be sure latching devices are securely fastened.

6. The shopping basket should be placed on the back of the stroller either directly over or in front of the axle of the rear wheels.

Figure 15.
The base of the stroller should be wide enough to prevent tipping when the child leans over the side.

● **Walkers**

Walkers provide the infant with a means of locomotion which they are not yet mentally able to handle. I do not advise their use. If you insist on a walker, observe the following safety suggestions:

1. Walkers tip easily. Be sure the wheel base is much larger than the frame that holds baby. A properly designed walker should not tip when baby leans over the side.

2. Be sure the wheels are sturdy. Flimsy wheels may bend, allowing the walker to tip.

3. Remove throw rugs and other obstacles which may become entangled in the wheels and cause the walker to tip.

4. Do not allow walkers near stairs. Do not rely on stair gates. An impetuous infant may get up enough momentum to cruise right through the gate.

5. Be sure all coiled springs and hinges are encased in protective covers. Avoid the older X-frame walkers which can pinch a child's finger.

● **Playpens**

1. Observe the same safety tips as for cribs.

2. The netting should be small enough that it cannot catch the buttons on the child's clothing.

3. If toys are hung from the sides, avoid string or cord that is longer than twelve inches.

4. Remove large toys or boxes that can be used as steps for climbing out.

5. Cover exposed nuts and bolts. Secure latching mechanisms that may act like scissors and pinch baby's fingers.

Home Safety

Since many childhood accidents occur in the home, walk around your house with this book in hand and check the following:

1. Are all drugs and chemicals (cleaning agents, insecticides, etc.) stored where your child cannot possibly reach them?

2. Are potentially harmful substances in their original safety containers, or did you transfer them to an "easier container"?

3. Do you leave caps off containers or leave potentially dangerous substances lying around until you are finished with them before putting them in their proper place?

4. Are all glasses used by your children unbreakable?

5. Do you turn pot handles toward the back of the stove?

6. Is your baby's night wear flame-resistant?

7. Are electric cords in good condition, not frayed, and out of reach so that your baby cannot trip on them, chew on them or use them to pull the appliance down upon himself?

8. Are your unused electrical outlets protected with dummy plugs?

9. Are hot radiator pipes covered?

10. Are windows properly locked? Are the screens secure?

11. Is furniture which the child could climb upon placed in front of a window?

12. Is the fireplace screened? Is the screen in place when the fireplace is in use?

13. Are your child's toys safe? (See following section on **Toy Safety**.)

14. Is all string, clothesline and dangling cord out of reach?

15. Are the stairs safe, not slippery, well-lighted, with safe hand rails?

16. Are electrical devices away from the bathroom?

17. Are guns, knives, scissors, sewing tools and cigarette lighters out of reach?

18. Are small objects, such as nuts, which your child could choke on, out of reach?

19. Do you have decals on large panes of clear glass such as sliding doors?

20. Is your yard safe? Have you removed boards with splinters and nails, toxic plants and berries, garden tools?

21. If you have a swimming pool, is it fenced properly?

22. If you have a swing set, has your child been taught not to walk behind the swing when someone else is swinging?

23. Has your child been instructed about not leaving the yard without permission?

24. If your child is a tree climber have you surveyed the limbs to determine which may be weak or rotten? Have you told your child exactly which limbs are off limits?

25. Have you gone through the usual ''Do not touch'' routine about lighters, fires, chemicals, sharp objects, stoves, and electrical outlets? By age two most toddlers are able to understand safety discipline. However, don't always rely on it, because toddlers have short memories and impulsive behavior. There is just no safer method than supervision.

26. How sturdy is your changing table? Are pins within reach of your curious baby? Never leave your baby unattended, even for a split second, on the changing table. Even tiny babies can suddenly turn over and roll off the changing table, even though their mother's back was ''turned just for a second.'' Don't rely on the safety strap on the changing table.

27. Is there a small night light in your child's bedroom to light the way during his nighttime trips to the bathroom? Night lights may prevent the drowsy child from banging into walls and furniture.

28. Is your home protected against fire and burns? Are there heat and smoke alarms appropriately placed about your house? Stickers called "Tot Finders" are available from your local fire department. They should be placed on your childrens' bedroom doors and windows. Many household burns occur when children are accidentally scalded by turning on the hot water faucet. This potential burn hazard can be minimized by setting the water at no higher than 130° F (72° C).

29. Don't leave garden hoses lying in the sunshine. The water in the hose may become hot enough to scald the curious child.

30. If your toddler is walking, has your home been toddler-proofed? Have you covered sharp edges (fireplace bricks and coffee table corners) with rubber protectors?

Toy Safety

Consumer and government concern about the safety of the toys has been growing rapidly. The common toy hazards are listed below:

1. Avoid sharp-edged toys.

2. Avoid those with small, removable objects (beads, buttons, etc.) which could be swallowed. The small metal or plastic island which produces the noise in squeak toys can come loose and be swallowed. Blocks should be too large to swallow.

3. Toys should fit your child's age and his temperament. If your child is a thrower, get him soft lightweight toys. Missile-type toys (darts and arrows) can cause eye injuries.

4. Many accidents occur when a younger child uses toys meant for an older sibling.

5. Certain toys, such as string toys, should be used only under supervision.

6. Put toy shelves in most rooms to encourage your child not to leave his toys lying where someone could trip over them.

7. Outdoor toys such as playground equipment and bicycles should be checked regularly for loose bolts and sharp edges.

According to Public Law 91-113, the Bureau of Product Safety can require that unsafe toys be removed from retailers shelves. This law also gives you the right to return any toys on the bureau's hazardous toys list for full reimbursement. If you purchase any items that you find are safety hazards, write: Consumer Product Safety Commission, 1750 K Street, N.W.

Washington, D.C. 20207. Describe the article completely, where it was purchased, its country of origin, what part of the toy is hazardous. Include your name, address and phone number. If you require information about the current list of hazardous toys, baby furniture and other baby products, call the Consumer Product Safety Commission toll free hotline at 800-638-2666.

In Canada contact: Consumer and Corporate Affairs, Department of Product Safety, 1410 Stanley Street, Montreal, Que. H3A 1P8, (514) 283-2825.

Car Safety

Car accidents head the list of causes of children's deaths. Many parents who are generally conscientious about the health of their children do not effectively use car safety devices, despite wide publicity about the subject. Studies have shown that deaths occur in car accidents ten times more often if the child is not restrained. The purpose of this section is threefold:
1. To present the rationale for car safety devices.
2. To offer guidelines on proper selection of car safety restraints for your child.
3. To present tips on making auto travel safer for your child.

● **Rationale for the Design of Car Restraints for Infants and Children**
Infants and small children need special protection. They are lightweight and, in the event of a sudden stop, may be hurled against the inside of the car or the windshield. Regular seatbelts do not fit over the bones of a small infant but rather concentrate all the force in a small area—the pelvis and abdomen. Car safety devices restrain the child from being thrown against something during a sudden stop. They also distribute the force of impact over a wider area of the body.

● **How to Select a Car Safety Device**
You should base your choice of a car safety device on the following factors: the age and weight of your child, whether the device has been crash-tested (which means the device has undergone dynamic testing with dummy occupants and has also been approved by the new and upgraded standards of the Department of Transportation), and how easy the device is to use. The latter is a very important consideration. The more complicated the device, the less willingly it is used.

I feel the main reason for the laxity in using car safety devices is a feeling that they are too complicated. Parents think, ''I am only driving a few blocks to the store, why bother?'' Actually, most of the protective devices on today's market are simple when you consider the valuable cargo you are transporting. The safest restraint is the one you will use properly every time without taking shortcuts. For a car safety device to be effective it must be used exactly according to the manufacturer's directions.

● **Types of Car Safety Devices Available and How To Use Them**

1. For infants from birth to twenty pounds. (Figure 16) Infant carriers are tub-like containers designed to be installed facing backwards in the semi-upright position. The seatbelt anchors the carrier and the safety harness secures the baby within the carrier. If you examine Figure 16 you will notice that most of the force is transmitted to the seatbelt and carrier if the car stops suddenly. The rear-facing direction and semi-upright position allow the remaining force to be distributed through the back of the baby (mostly on the bone, not on the organs) and the safety harness secures him within the carrier. This carrier can also be used to transport a sleeping baby outside the car. Traditional "car beds" are not effective car safety devices. Their design and fabric construction do not enable them to absorb the force of impact nor restrain the baby.

2. Infants weighing twenty pounds to forty pounds.

a) The protective shield. When your infant outgrows the infant carrier (usually by a year) he will graduate to an upright device which faces forward. The protective shield, which is perhaps the easiest car safety device to use, consists of a seat cushion and a plastic shield over the child's body. The seatbelt secures the shield. I do not recommend using this shield because there is no harness to secure the child within the shield. I find that most children can and do easily slip out of the shield and therefore render it ineffective. Also, side protection is poor with this device. Parents are constantly turning around to see if little Johnny has escaped his cage again. This reduces the driver's attentiveness, an additional safety hazard. If your child is self-disciplined enough to stay in a protective shield, you may find this device the easiest to use. Protective shields are not recommended for children with glasses.

b) The car seat (Figure 17) is safer than the shield because the safety harness restrains the child within the seat. Side protection is also better. Some car seats require a top anchorage strap to prevent them from pitching forward. This may pose a problem in some cars. Some models contain all three of the protective features. The carrier is used in the rear-facing position in early infancy. It is then turned forward and upright and used as a car seat in later infancy and childhood. An optional protective shield may be added. Some models can even be transformed into a stroller. The competition is really trying to blend safety, government regulations and contemporary parenting.

3. Children over forty pounds (usually over four years of age). These children should ride on a firm cushion just high enough to allow the seat belt to ride across their hips and the lower edge of the belt to touch their thighs. The seat belt should be at an angle of forty-five degrees for maximum effectiveness. The seat belt should not ride above the hip bones because the force of impact would then be transferred to the abdominal organs rather than to the hip bones. Across-the-shoulder straps usually do not fit the small, restless child properly. Seat belts alone are not recommended for children under the age of four or

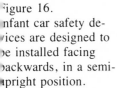

Figure 16.
Infant car safety devices are designed to be installed facing backwards, in a semi-upright position.

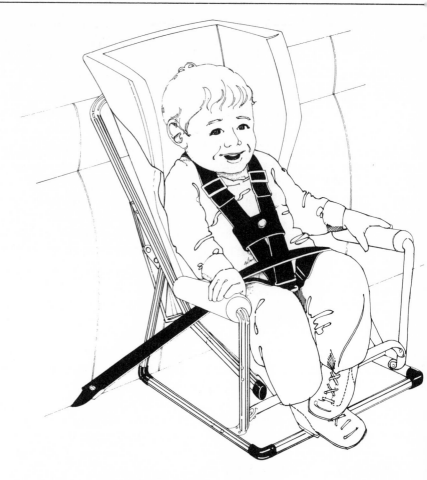

Figure 17.
This car seat offers a
safety harness and
good side protection.

those who weigh less than forty pounds. The safety harness and
cushion is more effective for the young child than just a seat belt.
A certain amount of discipline and instruction is necessary for
the child to remain quietly in the seat belt.

● **Additional Tips on Auto Safety for Children**

1. The center of the rear seat is the safest place for the child in
his car safety device.

2. A parent's lap is not an effective car safety device. Parents'
arms are not protective safety harnesses. Even if you are wearing
a seat belt or shoulder strap, your arms will not be able to protect
your child from the sudden force of a collision.

3. Two children, or a parent and a child, should not be strapped
into one seat belt.

4. To be effective, safety harnesses and seat belts must be
adjusted to properly fit the child in the safety device.

5. Children should not be allowed to play with sharp objects such as pencils or metal toys while the car is moving. Heavy objects and small metal toys should be secured or placed on the floor as these objects become dangerous projectiles if the car stops suddenly. The inside of a car is not meant to carry either unsecured passengers or unsecured cargo.

6. Disruptive behavior in a car is a common childhood problem. A fringe benefit of a car safety device is that your child's behavior may actually improve while in a safety restraint. An interesting study was conducted to determine the effects of car restraints on a group of infants who showed disruptive behavior (climbing, kicking, screaming) during car rides. While in the car seats the behavior of these infants actually showed improvement and generally they did not fuss about being restrained.

7. The economic necessity for car pools is increasing. Car safety must increase to keep pace with these necessities. To improve car pool safety and sanity:

a) Insist upon strict discipline. The more children you transport, the stricter your discipline must be. Mothers involved in car pools should agree upon a consistent game plan for car pool discipline. Consistency encourages desirable behavior.

b) Encourage desirable behavior before undesirable behavior turns the car into a moving wrestling ring. Songs, word games, riddles and interesting stories will usually hold young children's attention for a short period of time.

c) Doors and tailgate should be locked and secured with safety latches, if available.

d) Children leaving a confined space often immediately run to release energy; they may run into the path of an oncoming vehicle. It is wise to insist that when the car comes to a stop, the adult gets out first to insure that there are no oncoming vehicles before the child is allowed to open his door and get out.

e) Catching fingers in slamming car doors is a frequent childhood injury. To guard against this you may insist that doors be closed by the adult and not the children.

Car safety devices are to auto accidents what immunizations are to infectious diseases. I urge all motoring parents to be as conscientious about the use of proper car safety restraints as you are about immunizing your child.

Information on car safety devices can be obtained from the following sources:

1. A pamphlet called **Don't Risk Your Child's Life** can be obtained from Physicians For Automotive Safety, 50 Union Avenue, Irvington, New Jersey 07111.

2. A booklet entitled **A Detailed Review Of Currently Marketed Infant and Child Automobile Restraints**, Michigan Office of Highway Safety Planning, 7150 Harris Drive, Lansing, M.I. 48913. Phone (517) 322-1942.

Water Safety

● **Swimming Pool Safety Tips**

1. Maintain strict swimming pool discipline from the time your child is very young. Your child should grow up with a realistic respect for water, its enjoyment and its dangers. If you have a backyard pool write a list of regulations and outline the consequences of breaking these rules. Adhere to your statements. Include rules about not swimming alone, diving, horse-play and running around the pool as well as any other safety measures relevant to your situation.

2. Backyard pools pose a special safety hazard for toddlers and small children. A fence and self-latching gate are required by law in many communities. To comply with the fence law some families enclose the entire backyard, but the pool is easily accessible from their home. Neighboring children may be protected from your pool, but your own child may not be. It is nearly impossible, even for the most caring and cautious parents, to watch their toddler or young child constantly. Added swimming pool safety measures are required for the toddler and young child.

a) Install safety latches on the doors in your home so that your child cannot get out of the house without your knowledge.

b) Never leave a young child unsupervised around a pool.

3. Do not rely on the fact that your child knows how to swim. Supervision is still the best safety precaution.

● **Teach Your Child to Swim**

Since a panicky infant can drown in less than seven seconds, teach your baby how to relax in the water and not to panic.

How to start? Tiny infants, especially newborns, need a warm water temperature (around 90° F) in which to relax. To get into the water, hold your infant firmly in your arms with his head at the same level as your head or higher. Lower yourself until your shoulders are submerged. The water will be at about baby's chest. His face should never be lower than yours because you won't be able to watch his reactions to know when to continue or when to stop.

When baby seems relaxed and happy, proceed to the next step, blowing bubbles. Hold your baby facing you upright. Blow slightly against his face, then lower your mouth into the water so baby can see the bubbles you make. Maybe let his hand feel the bubbles. He will copy you when he is ready. Practice this play-time and bubble-blowing time frequently. Going in the water six times a day for ten minutes is much better than going in once for sixty minutes. Remember to have fun. No infant or child can learn if he is unhappy. A happy, confident child is less likely to panic in a difficult situation. Retreat at the first sign of tension. Remember the child's feelings and happiness come first. Swimming is a much later step.

Once your infant is comfortable in the water and does not fear playing in the water (such as blowing bubbles) the next step is to teach your infant how to hold his breath under water for longer lengths of time. Never teach by force. When you are ready to proceed to the next step of breath-holding and swimming, it is wise to obtain some professional instruction. I also recommend the book **How To Teach Your Baby To Swim** by Claire Timmermans, Stein and Day, New York.

● **Boating Safety**

Boating safety requires additional discipline. If you are a boating family, teach your child at a very young age that boating means wearing a life jacket. There is no compromise. If you begin when your child is young and if you are firm enough, your child will accept the rule. Unfortunately, so-called approved life jackets have become so cumbersome that many children refuse to wear them. Attempt to fit your child with a flotation device that he will accept and introduce this as the required standard for boating. Besides a personal flotation device, a leash and safety harness may be used to protect a roving toddler on a boat.

Cycle Safety

There was a time when "motor milestone" referred to the time when a child crawled, walked or ran. Parents were naturally very excited that their child could move from point A to point B under his own power. In today's mobile world, motor milestones may refer to the age at which the child progresses from walker to tyke bike, to tricycle, to bicycle, to moped and so on. Since we have cycled our children into a high risk motor world, parents should teach their children the safe use of these vehicles.

1. How safe is the bike? Be sure the bike meets the required federal safety standards. Exposed bolts should have protective covers. The bike should have side, rear and front reflectors. Handlebars should have handgrips. Pads should be placed around the crossbar in the center of the handlebars. Parents should periodically check their children's bike for loose wheels, bolts, chain guards, seats and especially handlebars. Bikes of

435

recent design with higher handlebars and smaller wheels are more difficult to control and may increase the spiralling number of bicycle accidents. Encourage the use and the construction of bike paths in your community.

2. The Bike Should Fit the Child.

a) While your child is sitting on the seat with hands on the handlebars, he must be able to place the balls of both feet on the ground.

b) Your child should be able to straddle the center bar with both feet flat on the ground and about one inch clearance between the crotch and the bar (See Figure 18).

3. Night Riding. If night riding cannot be discouraged, ankle lights which produce a moving warning light should be worn. Reflectors should be visible from all sides. Reflectorized orange vests like those used by hunters provide additional protection for night cyclers.

4. Teach your child the cycling rules of the road.

a) A bicycle driven in traffic is considered a traffic vehicle and is

Figure 18.
Be sure your child's bicycle meets the required safety standards.

subject to the same laws and traffic control signals as motor vehicles.

b) Come to a full stop at intersections and busy streets. It is often safer to walk the bike across the intersection rather than to ride across.

c) Ride in single file at all times in the direction of the traffic on the right edge of the road.

d) Test the brakes frequently to be sure they are in good condition. If the bike has hand brakes, add a coaster brake for extra security. Apply brake pressure evenly to front and rear brakes, slightly favoring the rear brake first, especially when braking on gravel or wet pavement.

e) Keep your hand on the handlebars and your seat on the seat.

f) Do not hitch a ride by holding on to other vehicles. Do not carry passengers or heavy objects on the bike. This makes the bike very difficult to control.

g) Test the road condition. Be extremely cautious on wet pavements, gravel and roads with potholes and bridges.

h) Use a guard clip on trouser cuffs.

i) Keep tires properly inflated.

j) When passing a parked car, beware of opening car doors.

● **Cycling with Infants and Small Children**

The following guidelines will help you cyle more safely with your child:

1. Infants under six months should not be carried on a bicycle.

2. Infants from six to twelve months old should be carried in a backpack.

3. Children from one to four (up to forty pounds) should be carried in a special child carrier which is mounted over the rear wheel and has built-in safety harnesses and foot rests which keep the child's feet away from the spokes.

● **Minibikes and Mopeds**

The Department of Transportation cites two major reasons for minibike accidents. Their low profile and small size make young riders hard to spot in traffic. The small wheels, small base and limited capacity for braking and accelerating result in poor handling characteristics. The American Academy of Pediatrics and the Academy's Joint Commission on Physical Fitness and Recreation in Sports Medicine have strongly advised parents not to buy minibikes for their children. In addition to the obvious lack of safety features, I feel that minibikes and motorized mopeds encourage a potentially dangerous behavior. They are the forerunner to the ultimate in adolescent cycling risk, the motorcycle.

The motorcycling trends exploit children at a stage when their basic irresponsibility is coupled with a basic tendency for daring and risk-taking.

I advise you to discourage your child's use of motorized cycles. If your child does ride a motorized cycle, be sure he has the proper instructions on using the vehicle as safely as possible. Do not permit him to ride on highways, sidewalks or streets. Require your child to wear a safety helmet, sturdy shoes and protective clothing. Check your home owner and automobile insurance policies. They do not necessarily cover minibike and moped accidents.

Poisoning

The environment of a curious child is loaded with potentially harmful chemicals to eat, drink or inhale. Parents should know the following:

1. Tips on poison prevention.

2. The phone number and resources available at your local Poison Control Center.

3. The substances which are harmful and those which are not.

4. First aid treatment in case your child ingests or inhales a potential poison.

● **Tips on Poison Prevention**

1. Safety caps. Be certain all medicine and potentially harmful substances are packaged in safety containers. Avoid the temptation to transfer chemicals to an "easier container." If a potentially harmful substance does not have a safety cap, transfer the substance to a safer container and label it. Many accidents occur when the cap is left off and poisonous substances are inadvertently left within reach of a curious child (e.g. leaving the furniture polish container open while cleaning). Safety caps are a help but don't rely on them completely, because children often overcome the challenge by pulling off the cap with their teeth.

2. Put safety latches on cupboards and medicine cabinets containing potentially toxic substances.

3. Store insecticides, petroleum products and potentially harmful chemicals in a safe place.

4. Avoid referring to medicine as candy.

5. If your child shows an interest in a potentially harmful substance, teach your child about its harmful effects with vivid words and gestures. Attempts have been made, with questionable success, to market paste-on labels such as "Mister Yuck" and "Officer Ugg" to discourage the curious child. The "out of reach" approach may be effective in your own home, but education is necessary to protect the young child in someone else's home which may be less child-considered.

Household Agents That are Either Not Harmful, or Only Mildly Harmful and Usually Require no Treatment Are:

batteries
bath soap
candles
chalk
cigarettes[1]
modeling clay
shaving cream
Silly Putty
ink
crayons labeled with A.P., C.P., or C.S. 130-46 designation

cosmetics[2]
oral contraceptives
detergents[3]
mercury from broken thermometers
newspaper
matches
pencil lead
putty
vitamins with or without fluoride[4]

---

[1] **Cigarettes:** Although one cigarette theoretically contains enough nicotine to be toxic, ingested tobacco is not easily absorbed from the intestines and protective vomiting frequently occurs.

[2] **Cosmetics:** Most cosmetics such as liquid make-up, eye make-up, vegetable hair dyes, cleansing or conditioning creams, non-alcoholic hair dressings, hand lotions and creams, lipstick, shampoos, deodorants, most perfumes and shaving creams are not generally harmful. However, permanent wave neutralizer and fingernail polish are extremely harmful. Mouthwashes contain a large amount of alcohol and therefore can harm your child if ingested in large quantities.

[3] **Detergents:** Most household laundry detergents, cleansers and dishwashing cleansers are non-toxic. However, bleaches, ammonias and electric dishwashing detergent granules may be highly toxic.

[4] **Vitamins containing iron:** The iron may be highly toxic if ingested in large amounts.

CAUTION: The above list is meant only as a guide. Consult your Poison Control Center for definitive advice.

6. Read the label before giving medicine. Don't give medicine in the dark.

7. Learn which plants in your yard, home and community are poisonous.

8. Keep first aid supplies easily accessible.

● **How to Effectively Use Your Local Poison Control Center**

In the past ten years, an effective poison control center network has been established throughout the United States and Canada. These centers keep up-to-date information on all potential poisons and their treatments as well as a 24-hour physician consultation service. Nearly every local hospital has access to these centers or you can call them directly. Consult your local hospital or the Yellow Pages to find your nearest Poison Control Center. Display the phone number in a conspicuous place. The establishment of poison control centers with staff specially trained in emergency medicine has made the greatest contribution to the marked reduction in deaths by poisonings in the past ten years.

LOCAL POISON CONTROL CENTER
PHONE NUMBER:

So they can advise you on the treatment of your child, your Poison Control Center needs the following information:

1. Name of substance and the listed ingredients.

2. Time of ingestion.

3. Amount ingested.

4. Age and weight of your child.

5. Symptoms: Did he cough or vomit immediately? Is he acting any differently after ingestion and, if so, what exactly are his symptoms?

6. Your telephone number. Many poison control centers call back after a few hours to check the condition of your child.

Consult your Poison Control Center for appropriate information. Do not rely on this book for the most recent facts. Poison Control Centers keep up-to-date information on the newer products. Each case is unique. A book cannot deal with each case. The precise information required can be more quickly obtained by calling a center than by looking up the information in a book. For these reasons, I will not list treatment for all possible poisons but rather will present guidelines to help you effectively use home treatment with the help of your local Poison Control Center.

• If Your Child Swallows a Potentially Harmful Substance

1. Encourage him to drink lots of water. (Dilute the poison.)

2. Call your Poison Control Center. Follow their instructions.

3. If advised to induce vomiting, use your poison prevention kit. Syrup of ipecac, a safe and effective agent for inducing vomiting, is available without prescription and should be kept in all households which have small children. You cannot always run to the nearest drug store when you need it. The sooner vomiting is induced the better. To induce vomiting, give your child 1 tablespoon (15 cc.) of syrup of ipecac, in 8 ounces of water or non-carbonated fruit juice. Jostling or bouncing your infant on your knee may hasten the vomiting. If vomiting does not occur within 20 minutes, give 1 more tablespoon of ipecac in juice or water. This method is effective at least 90 per cent of the time. Since prolonged vomiting may occasionally occur following a dose of ipecac, observe your child for 45 minutes after he first vomits. Perform this ritual in the bathroom. "Stomach pumping" (gastric lavage) is seldom necessary in a conscious child. Ipecac-induced vomiting is equally effective, safe and certainly less traumatic. Inducing vomiting by encouraging gagging with a finger or blunt object is not as safe or as effective as using ipecac.

Figure 19.
Poison prevention kit

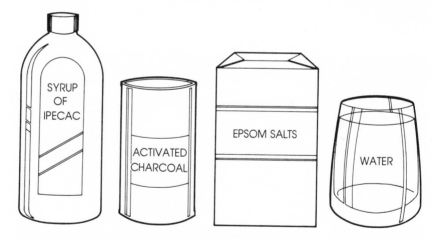

1. Syrup of Ipecac (to induce vomiting)
   Dosage: 1 tbsp. (3 tsps.) in a glass of water or juice.
2. Activated Charcoal (to absorb poison)
   Dosage: 1 tbsp. in a glass of water or juice.
3. Epsom Salts (laxative)
   Dosage: 1 tsp. in a glass of water.

4. Follow the guidelines given to you by your Poison Control Center. If a potential poison has been ingested in large enough quantities, the center may advise you to take your child to the hospital after giving the ipecac at home. Always take the container of the poison with you to the hospital. Vomiting often occurs en route to the hospital so take appropriate precautions in your car. At the hospital your child may be given additional med-

---

PARENTS' FIRST AID KIT

- Absorbent Cotton
- Adhesive Tape — ½" and 1"
- Bandaids — various sizes
- Steri-strips (butterfly bandages)
- Cotton-tipped Swabs
- Sterile Gauze Squares — 2" × 2" and 4" × 4" — individually wrapped
- Roll of Gauze Bandage — 2" wide
- Tourniquet
- Flashlight — small penlight
- Tweezers and Splinter Forceps
- Scissors
- Thermometer
- Tongue Depressors
- Measuring Spoons
- Elastic Bandage — 2" and 4"
- Large Cloth — 3 × 3 ft. (useful as large bandage or sling)
- Vaporizer — cool mist
- Acetaminophen (children's Tylenol, Tempra)
- Children's Aspirin
- Syrup of Ipecac
- Activated Charcoal Solution (2 tbsp. A.C. and 8 ozs. water and flavoring)
- Epsom Salts
- Hydrogen Peroxide
- Petroleum Jelly
- Rubbing Alcohol
- Antibiotic Ointment — Neosporin
- Analgesic Eardrops (Auralgan) — by prescription
- Antiseptic Solution — Betadine, Effodine
- Domeboro Powder (soothing solution as directed by physician)
- Cortisone Cream (as directed by physician only)
- Calamine Lotion
- Cough Medicine (as recommended by physician)

---

ication to neutralize the poison or decrease the absorption of potential poison. Activated charcoal absorbs the poison, while magnesium sulfate (Epsom salts) causes it to pass through the intestines faster. A specific antidote may be given. The Poison Control Center may advise you to give these agents at home. If milk is recommended on packages as a neutralizer of certain detergents and poisons, especially lyes, it should not be given before the ipecac since milk may delay the action of the ipecac and slow the vomiting.

● **When Not to Induce Vomiting**

It is important not to induce vomiting before consultation with your Poison Control Center. The substance may not be harmful and therefore need no treatment. Certain chemicals, such as hydrocarbons, cause more danger to the lungs than the intestines and the risk of getting the substance into the lungs is greater if vomiting is induced.

Do **not** induce vomiting for:

1. Strong corrosives: lye, strong acids, drain cleaners.
2. Petroleum products: gasoline, kerosene, Benzine, turpentine.
3. Polishes: furniture, car.
4. Cleaning fluids: bleach, ammonia.

● **Aspirin Poisoning**

Since aspirin poisoning is still the number one cause of poisoning in children, parents need to know the following about aspirin poisonings. The present restrictions on the strength and number of children's aspirin per container are safe. Even if a child under five years of age ingested the whole bottle, aspirin poisoning would be unlikely. Sudden ingestion of two grains per pound may result in moderate asperin poisoning. Less than two grains per pound, usually produces no symptoms. Adult aspirin preparations pose a greater accidental poisoning hazard than children's tablets. You should take greater precautions with your bottles of aspirin than with your children's aspirin.

Therapeutic aspirin poisoning may occur if your child is given a regular dosage of aspirin for too long, especially if your child is slightly dehydrated and not urinating enough to excrete the aspirin. A safe guide is not to exceed the dosage recommended by your doctor or that listed on page 339. Do not give aspirin around the clock for more than forty-eight hours without checking with your doctor. Acetaminophen (Tylenol, Tempra) is as effective as aspirin in lowering fever and is safer because it does not accumulate in the body if given over a long period of time.

• Inhaled Poison

If your child inhales a potentially poisonous gas, such as chlorine or pesticide spray, give him plenty of fresh air and call your doctor or Poison Control Center.

Poisons which contact the eyes or skin should be washed out immediately with water. Contaminated clothing should be removed and your doctor consulted. (See page 455 for treatment of eye emergencies.)

• Lead Poisoning

Children ingest lead mainly by chewing on old paint chipped from the surfaces of older furniture painted with lead paint. These sweet-tasting chips appeal to children. Even a small amount of paint chips (the size of a postage stamp) with high lead content may be toxic to the child and should be removed by inducing vomiting. Although the law requires the newer paints to have lower lead content, old paint underneath repainted furniture may be high in lead. Keep your little beaver from chewing on old painted wood.

• Poisonous Plants—Don't Eat the Berries

Of approximately 300,000 plants in the United States and Canada, 525 are suspected to be poisonous. The following is a list of common potentially harmful plants: azalea, castor bean, holly berries, English ivy, bird of paradise, daffodil, hyacinth, lily of the valley, buttercup, elderberry, hydrangea, mistletoe, morning glory, mushrooms(wild), jonquil, oleander, philodendron, poinsettia, poppy and rhododendron.

If your child has swallowed some leaves or berries, try to identify the plant and call your Poison Control Center. If you are uncertain whether the plants are poisonous, vomiting may be induced if they have been ingested within the previous two hours. A handy reference about poisonous plants is **Poisonous Plants of the United States and Canada** by J. Kingsbury, Englewood Cliffs, N.J., Prentice-Hall, Inc., 1964.

Head Injuries

Head injuries from falls, rocks and baseball games are to be expected in the active child. Nature anticipated these many insults to the head; your child's skull is a protective helmet and the great majority of blows to the head do not injure the brain.

Bleeding and concussion are the two main concerns in head injuries. When the small blood vessels between the skull and the brain have been broken, bleeding occurs between the brain and the skull. The skull is a rigid box. The bleeding, therefore, occupies space and compresses the brain. A blow to the head may also ''shake'' the brain, resulting in an injury called a concussion. Pressure upon the brain from bleeding or swelling of the brain from a concussion produces the symptoms of head injury mentioned below.

To deal with head injuries, you should know a few important facts about the scalp. The scalp contains a very rich supply of blood vessels. For this reason, even a small laceration bleeds profusely. When a tissue rich in blood vessels such as the scalp is suddenly compressed between two hard objects (the floor and the skull) small blood vessels within the scalp are easily broken and produce the characteristic ''goose-egg.'' Don't be alarmed at the large size of these lumps. Also, because of the rich blood supply, scalp wounds do not become infected as easily as do wounds to other parts of the body.

A head injury does not mean a brain injury. A blow to the head, which causes a large ''goose-egg'' and a crying child, should be parented with a warm hug and a cold ice pack. The sooner the ice pack is applied, the smaller the goose-egg. Pressure and ice will control the anticipated bleeding from scalp vessels. After a period of crying and pain, most children will resume playing and no further symptoms will develop. This is a head injury, not a brain injury. If your child is unconscious, even momentarily, following a blow to his head this is a more concerning sign. Call your doctor immediately.

- **Parenting the Child with a Head Injury—A Step-by-Step Approach**

   Step 1. First Aid

a) If the child is unconscious but breathing normally and his color is good (lips are not blue) place the child flat, head down, and call the Rescue Squad for transportation to the local hospital. If a neck injury is suspected, do not move the child until experts in the transportation of subjects with head and neck injuries arrive. If the child is not breathing, or convulsion occurs, follow the guidelines in the section on resuscitation and treatment of convulsions below.

b) If a child has a laceration or abrasion, or you can see the site of his injury, apply ice and pressure for twenty minutes. This will reduce the size of the eventual lump.

   Step 2. Period of Observation. If your child is conscious, alert, and does not seem to be having any immediate problem, administer the usual parental sympathy and begin the most important task, the period of observation. If pressure is going to develop on the brain either from bleeding or from swelling, time is required and symptoms may not develop for several hours. Observe your child for the following signs:

1. Change in his level of alertness. Is he alert, talking well, responding to simple questions, and does he seem aware of his environment? Sleep is the normal state of refuge for the upset child, so the desire to fall asleep may complicate your assessment. Let your child sleep but awaken him every two hours. During his sleep, observe him for a change in his usual color or breathing patterns. Parents are usually so attuned to their child's normal sleep patterns that any change in his usual behavior or sleep state should be a cause for concern.

2. Watch his eyes. The eyes are the mirror of the brain, in health and also in disease, especially in a head injury. Does he look at you with the bright, penetrating look so typical of children's normal visual expression toward their parents? Are his eyes straight? Are his pupils the same size in both eyes and can he see objects clearly? Hold up your hand and ask him how many fingers he sees. Point to known objects and ask him to name them. Cover one eye at a time. Does he complain of seeing double?

3. Is his walking steady? Do you notice any change in his walking style or balance, as if a weakness exists in one arm or leg?

4. Is your child vomiting consistently? Children will often vomit once or twice soon after a head injury, even if there is no brain injury. If vomiting persists or begins again several hours after the injury occurs, there is cause for concern. It is wise to feed your child only clear fluids for a few hours, in case vomiting occurs.

5. Headaches are to be expected, but they usually subside within a few hours. If the headaches increase in severity, be concerned. Aspirin should not be given as it may aggravate bleeding. Acetaminophen is safe.

There are many more signs and symptoms of a possible brain injury, but the above symptoms are the easiest for an intuitive parent to recognize.

Step 3. When to call your doctor. Certainly, if any of the above five signs occur, call your doctor immediately or take your child to the hospital. Even if no injury is apparent, you may wish to check with your doctor soon after the accident. He will emphasize the necessity for the period of observation outlined in Step 2 and may wish to modify the signs to watch for to fit your situation. For example, it may or may not be necessary to awaken your child during the night. Remember, children who are sick, act sick. If there is any persistent change in your child's behavior following a head injury, call your doctor.

Most children's head injuries do not need skull X-rays. Your doctor will advise whether or not your child should have this test. Generally, a child who has none of the above symptoms does not require a skull X-ray. A period of observation and a medical examination is more useful than a skull X-ray. How your child acts is more important than what an X-ray shows. A skull fracture in itself is not harmful if there is no injury to the brain.

What To Do If Your Child Stops Breathing

After you have shouted to someone nearby to call the local Emergency Squad:

Step 1. Clear your child's throat of any fluid, mucus, vomitus or foreign body. Do this by momentarily holding your child's head down to allow gravity to drain the fluid and by possibly applying chest blows and back blows as described in the **Strangulation** section below. (See Figure 21.)

Step 2. Mouth-to-mouth breathing.

a) Place the child on his back and slightly bend (flex) the neck forward and bend (extend) the head backward in the so-called sniffing position. Do not extend the head of an infant or small child backward as much as you would a larger child's or adult's,

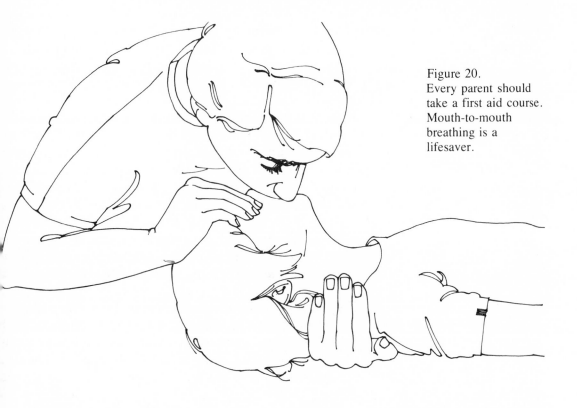

Figure 20.
Every parent should take a first aid course. Mouth-to-mouth breathing is a lifesaver.

447

as this will obstruct breathing. A towel rolled up beneath the neck will help maintain the correct position.

b) Hold your child's head straight with your hand on his forehead and use your thumb and index finger to compress his nostrils to prevent air leaking from the nose. (See Figure 20.) An alternative is to press your cheek against your child's nostrils during inflation. The other hand can be placed under his neck or upon his chest to feel the rise of his chest during breathing.

c) Fit your mouth snugly around your child's lips and blow into his mouth with just enough force to see his chest rise when you blow. Twenty to thirty breaths per minute (every two to three seconds) is adequate for infants and children. In a small infant you may obtain better air inflation by placing your mouth over both his nose and his mouth.

d) Continue mouth-to-mouth breathing until trained help arrives or until your child resumes breathing himself.

I strongly advise every parent to take a first aid course, preferably during your pregnancy or very soon after childbirth. Courses are usually available from your local Red Cross. First aid is a skill you hope you will never have to use but, if you do, you will save your child's life.

Choking (Strangulation)

Obstruction of the airway by a foreign body is one of the leading causes of accidental death in infants. Infants and small children like to "mouth" everything and small objects may become caught in their throats and obstruct their breathing. What do you do if your child starts choking?

Step 1. If your child is coughing vigorously but he is not blue, he is obviously breathing and he does not seem to be panicky, simply give him emotional support. His own cough reflex may handle the problem. This is especially true in the usual cases of "the fluid that has gone down the wrong way." If your child can speak, cry, or cough, then the airway is not obstructed and you should not interfere with his efforts to dislodge the material.

Step 2. If your child is having difficulty getting air, is blue or is losing consciousness, place him head down and administer four back blows between the shoulder blades. (See Figure 21.)

Step 3. If your child's airway is still obstructed, flip your child over on his back and administer four chest thrusts. With your child lying on the floor or across your lap, place your hands across the front and sides of the child's lower chest. Quickly compress the chest downward with the thrust of the arms and upwards with the thrust of the hands. The back blow procedure gives a higher instantaneous expelling pressure, whereas the chest thrust provides lower initial expelling pressure, but it is more sustained. The combination of back blows and chest thrusts

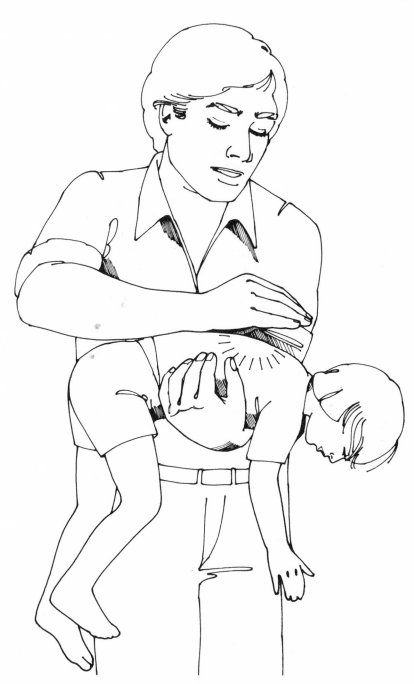

Figure 21.
your child is having difficulty getting air , is blue, or is losing consciousness, place m head down and dminister four back ows between the oulder blades.

449

will usually dislodge foreign bodies in the child's airway. If this does not work repeat both procedures again.

Step 4. You should not use your finger to dislodge foreign bodies from the back of a child's throat, unless you can see the foreign body and you are certain you can get your finger around it. Inserting a large adult finger in a child's small throat may push the foreign body farther back into the throat or may cause the child to panic and suck the object into the lungs rather than swallow the object.

The Heimlich maneuver is a procedure developed by Dr. Henry J. Heimlich in the early 1970s. It has gained popularity as a first aid maneuver for dislodging foreign bodies caught in the airway of a choking person. The Heimlich maneuver is performed as follows: Standing behind the choking victim, wrap your arms around the victim's waist, making a fist with one hand and grasping the fist with the other hand. Place the thumb side of your fist toward the upper abdomen and compress with a quick upward thrust, repeating several times if necessary. The pressure on the abdomen is transmitted to the lungs, thus compressing the air within the lungs and working the object up out of the airway. The Heimlich maneuver is generally not recommended for infants and small children because of the danger of damage to the abdominal organs. In children, the combination of back blows and chest thrusts is equally effective.

Swallowed Objects

Children often swallow small objects such as coins. These nearly always pass through the intestines and are eliminated in twenty-four to forty-eight hours without causing any harm. Occasionally an object such as rock candy may lodge in a child's esophagus (the tube running from the mouth to the stomach). Pain in the area where the object is stuck plus excessive drooling (the inability to swallow saliva) are signs of this type of obstruction. Call your doctor for advice or take your child to the hospital.

Near-Drowning

The term near-drowning refers to a person who has suffered some degree of suffocation under water but responds to first aid resuscitation. First aid for a near-drowning child follows the same principles of artificial respiration as outlined on page 447. In addition, the following suggestions may be helpful when giving first aid to the near-drowning child:

1. If a neck injury is suspected, keep the child's head as still and straight as possible. A fracture of the cervical spine (broken neck) is a common aquatic injury usually caused by diving in shallow water.

2. Attempt to clear the airway of debris, such as leaves or grass, that may be lodged in the back of the throat if the victim was swimming in a pond.

3. In many near-drownings, the lungs are not full of water because the vocal cords tighten up, sealing the airway and preventing water from entering the lungs. Therefore, pumping on a child's chest to dislodge water from the lungs may not be necessary. Do not pump on a child's stomach or use the Heimlich maneuver to dislodge water because you may cause water and vomitus to be regurgitated from the stomach and drawn into the child's lungs.

4. The very first step in managing the near-drowning child is to administer mouth-to-mouth resuscitation as soon as possible, even before you pull the child out of the water. Follow the steps on mouth-to-mouth breathing as outlined on page 447. Since water may be sitting in the airway, administering mouth-to-mouth to the near-drowning victim may require much more force than administering it to a person who is not breathing for other causes. If the child does not respond immediately to mouth-to-mouth breathing (some life signs such as crying, breathing on his own or independent movements), a brief attempt to dislodge water from the airway by chest compression may be tried. However, mouth-to-mouth resuscitation is the primary, life-saving first aid.

Even though a drowning child may initially appear to be without any signs of life, a thorough attempt should be made to revive the child, especially by administering mouth-to-mouth breathing. The protective effect of cold water on vital organs and certain protective reflexes within the body, allow near-drowning victims to be revived after many minutes of suffocation under water.

5. As emergency first aid or mouth-to-mouth breathing is being administered, call for help immediately, so that trained emergency medical technicians can arrive quickly to continue the first aid treatment and take the child immediately to the hospital. Many medical problems such as collapse of a lung, cold stress, or chemistry changes within the blood can occur immediately after the drowning victim is revived. These need immediate hospital treatment.

Nose Bleeds

In a well child, nose bleeds are usually due to nose picking with resulting injury to the small blood vessels lining the inside of the nose. Nose bleeds are more common in the wintertime, when central heating and low humidity cause excessive dryness in the lining of the nose and formation of a crust along the lining. This crust irritates the child, causing him to pick at it. This problem is usually alleviated by increasing the humidity of his bedroom air when central heating is on. The nasal crust can also be softened by applying petroleum jelly with a cotton tipped applicator. If there is a weakness of some of the vessels lining the inside of the nose, anything which causes the face to flush (exercise or anxiety), also causes the blood vessels in the nose to dilate and sometimes to bleed. Nose bleeds usually occur in the front part of the nose and are easily controlled by the following measures:

1. Your child should sit, leaning slightly forward.

2. Apply pressure by pinching his nostrils together. Nostril pinching is much more effective if you insert a twisted piece of wet cotton into the bleeding nostril. This piece of cotton should fit snugly and be large enough to cover the front two-thirds of the nose. This allows the pressure from the nostril pinching to be transmitted to the nasal septum, the middle portion of the nose which contains many of the blood vessels prone to bleeding. Pressure may also be applied to the major vessels supplying the nose which are located where the upper lip joins the gum, just below the nostrils. To do this place a piece of wet cotton underneath the upper lip and apply pressure with two fingers upward in the direction of the nostrils. Compressing the upper lip from the gum toward the outside may also be effective. Pressure should be applied for ten minutes.

3. Your child should remain upright to prevent blood from dripping into his throat. Persistent swallowing of blood may cause a child to feel nauseated and vomit the blood. After the nose bleed has been controlled, discourage the child from sniffing or sneezing through his nose as this may dislodge the clot and cause the bleeding to recur. Once the bleeding stops, it is often wise to leave the piece of cotton lodged in his nostril for twenty-four hours to allow a clot to form over the vessel, particularly if your child suffers from recurrent nose bleeds. The cotton plug should be removed gently in order not to dislodge the clot and cause bleeding to recur.

If you are unable to stop your child's nose bleeds with the above measures, the nose bleed may require nasal packing or cauterization of the bleeding vessel. Your child should be taken to the hospital.

Trauma to the Nose

If your child is struck very hard on the nose, an ice pack should be applied to the nose for at least one-half hour in order to minimize swelling of the tissues of the nose. After the bleeding is controlled, check the nose for the two signs of a fracture: cosmetic distortion of the nasal bones and obstruction of breathing through either nostril. If either of these signs are present, obtain medical attention immediately.

Foreign Objects in the Nose

Children sometimes place small objects such as peas or beans into their nose. Even if your child does not complain of discomfort in the nose, you may suspect the problem if there is a very foul-smelling discharge from one nostril.

If you can see the object, you may attempt to remove it with tweezers. If the object is lodged far back in the nose, take your child to the hospital, where a doctor will remove it with a special instrument.

Convulsions

Convulsions, a result of abnormal electrical activity of the brain, cause many of the muscles throughout the body to jerk, the eyes to roll back, and sometimes a loss of consciousness.

If your child has a convulsion, you must try to keep him from falling or biting his tongue, and ensure that he continues breathing (a child may stop breathing during a severe convulsion). To parent your child through a convulsion:

1. Place him horizontally, preferably in the prone position with his head turned to one side. This allows the secretions in his throat to drain out through gravity. Make certain that he is not near objects he could strike or with which he could hurt himself when thrashing.

2. Some children will momentarily stop breathing and turn blue during a convulsion. If your child is not breathing, begin mouth-to-mouth breathing as outlined on page 447. This is important since decreased oxygen in the brain encourages the convulsion to continue. Most convulsions in a child under five are due to a sudden high fever, although the fever may go unnoticed. If this seems to be the cause of your child's convulsion, reduce the fever as quickly as possible. Undress your child completely, place cold towels over him and cool his environment. The convulsions will usually stop when the fever declines. It is usually unnecessary and often unwise to force a child's mouth open and place a blunt object between his teeth. As long as the above steps are followed, the child is prevented from hurting himself, and he continues breathing, then convulsions seldom harm a child.

3. While most convulsions stop within a few minutes, some wil continue for ten to twenty minutes while others may recur afte the initial convulsion. For this reason, emergency help shoul always be called immediately. Your child should be taken to th hospital to determine the cause of the convulsion and what fur ther treatment may be necessary. (See **Fever Control** page 344 .)

Burns

Thermal burns are one of the leading causes of death and disabil ity in children. To treat burns.

1. Submerge the burned area in **cold water** immediately, for a least five minutes. This alleviates pain and cools the burned area thereby slowing tissue damage. Do not use ice packs as thes may increase tissue damage. Cold water packs or a cold showe may be continued to relieve the pain.

2. Cover the burned area with a clean cloth such as a sheet o towel. Do not apply oils or butter.

3. Call your doctor or take your child to the hospital. Furthe treatment may be necessary to prevent infection or loss of valua ble body fluids from the burned area. Even if the burned area i as small as a postage stamp, if it is severe enough to cause blis tering (a second degree burn), you should call your doctor fo advice. An improperly cared-for burn may cause poor cosmeti healing or interfere with the function of the burned area.

The general principles of minor burn care aim at pre venting infection, alleviating pain, improving cosmetic healin and preventing contracture (shortening) of the tissue as it heals The following guidelines will help you in the general care c your child's minor burns, but it is very important to consult you physician.

1. Do not break the blisters without your doctor's advice. Thes are biological dressings which are best left intact unless the occur over a joint or flexion crease.

2. Wash the burn frequently to keep it clean. The best method i a jet of water, such as a tap or shower jet. Dry thoroughly with clean cloth.

3. Keep the burn covered with appropriate antibiotic ointmer such as a Betadine ointment.

4. If the burn is over a joint or a flexion crease, such as the palr of the hand or fingers, movement and stretching of the burne area should be encouraged to avoid contracture (shortening) c the tissue as it heals.

5. Burns are acutely painful. Cold water is the best initial pai reliever. Further analgesics may be prescribed by your doctor.

6. As the burned tissue heals, it may be necessary for your doctor to remove some of the scarred tissue to minimize infection. This procedure is called debridement.

7. Consult your doctor about applying a burn dressing. Some areas heal better without a dressing as long as the area is kept clean, washed frequently and covered with an appropriate antibiotic ointment.

unburns

Sunburns are usually first degree burns which cause the skin to redden. Occasionally a sunburn may be a second degree burn and cause blistering. Relieve the pain of sunburns by immersing the burned area in cool water. Caine medications are topical anaesthetics which may afford some temporary pain relief but should be used only on a first degree burn, never on a second or third degree burn. Sometimes a sunburn may produce a very uncomfortable skin reaction similar to hives, called "sunpoisoning." Prescription medications are necessary to control this reaction so you should consult your doctor. Excessive drying of the skin which may follow a severe sunburn may be minimized with a moisturizer cream containing Vitamin A.

ye Injuries

Foreign bodies in the eye cause redness, a burning sensation and excess tearing. Besides being extremely aggravating, foreign bodies may scratch the surface of the eye and therefore should be removed as soon as possible. Foreign bodies may be removed from your child's eye in the following ways:

1. Carefully hold the child's eye open and wash it out with a gentle stream from a pitcher of water.

2. If you cannot remove the foreign body with water, try to locate the object and determine whether it is on the eyeball itself or underneath the upper or lower eyelid. Pull down the lower lid to see if the object is there. If you suspect it is under the upper lid, tell your child to look down and then pull his upper eyelid down over the lower eyelid. In so doing, the lashes of the lower eyelid may dislodge the foreign body from beneath the upper eyelid. If this method is unsuccessful, tell your child to look down and then grasp the upper eyelash with your thumb and index finger and gently pull the lid away from the eyeball. Place a cotton tipped applicator or cotton tipped match stick horizontally along the center of the upper lid. Pull the lid forward and upward, thereby causing it to fold back over the applicator. The under surface of the upper eyelid will then be exposed, thus

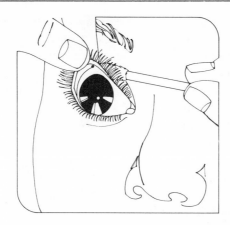

Figure 22.
Removing a foreign
body from the eye.

enabling you to see the foreign body. (See Figure 22.)

3. Remove the foreign body from the surface of the eyelid with the edge of a clean, moist handkerchief, tissue or moist cotton. Do not use dry cotton on the eye. Do not attempt to remove a foreign body from the surface of the eyeball. This should be done by your doctor.

4. If your child feels no itching or painful sensation in his eyeball after you have removed the foreign body from the surface of the eyelid, then you may safely assume there has been no injury to the eyeball. If, however, he still has pain in his eyeball, either the foreign body has not been completely removed or the eyeball has been scratched. In this case medical attention should be obtained.

Chemical burns to the eyeball, which can result from splashing a caustic substance in the eye, should be treated immediately by irrigating the eye with running water. You should either pour a glass of water over your child's eye, have him hold his eye under a running stream from a faucet or immerse his eye in a pan of water. Chemical irritations are extremely painful. Your child may be unwilling to open his eyelids. You may have to forcefully hold his eyelids open while you are irrigating the eye. Water irrigation should continue for at least ten minutes. After you have irrigated your child's eye and lessened the irritation, call your doctor for follow-up advice.

If your child feels any pain en route to the hospital for an eye injury, it is best to cover both eyes. This prevents eye movement, which may aggravate both the pain and the injury. You must explain to a young child why you are covering his eyes since children frighten easily when their eyes are covered without explanation.

Pulled Elbow

Suddenly jerking a young child's outstretched arm (see Figure 23) may cause a temporary dislocation of the arm bone near the elbow joint, a condition called "pulled elbow" (subluxation). You can recognize pulled elbow by the following signs: Following a sudden jerk on a young child's arm, he complains of pain, the arm hangs limp at his side and he refuses to use it. A child may also protect his elbow by holding his arm bent across his chest as if it were in a sling. Medical attention should be sought immediately. Even though your child's elbow may slip back into place easily, (the child will be free of pain and will use his arm again) allow the ligament to heal by placing the child's arm in a sling for two weeks. A young child's elbow is extremely susceptible to subluxation and parents should avoid a sudden "come along Johnny" jerk of his arm.

Figure 23.
Suddenly jerking a
young child's arm may
cause "pulled elbow."

Cuts and Scratches

Your main objectives in parenting the child with a laceration (cut) are the following:

1. Stop the bleeding. Apply pressure until the bleeding stops, which may take as long as ten minutes. If a major blood vessel has been cut apply a pressure bandage as follows: Place a thick pad of sterile gauze or clear cloth directly over the wound. If the blood soaks through this cloth do not remove it, because the clot that forms under the initial dressing helps to seal the wound. Simply add more layers of gauze over the initial one. Maintain steady pressure on the center of the bandage, keeping the pad firmly in place as you wrap more gauze over the pad. Keep pressure on the wound for at least ten miutes. Secure the bandage by tying the ends or using adhesive tape. Ice packs may help stop the bleeding and lessen the swelling. **Never apply bare ice to a bare wound** as this may cause frostbite and further damage the tissue.

2. Keep the wound clean. Ordinary soap and water from a gentle jet stream such as a shower or faucet will help wash out the dirt and debris from the wound.

3. Apply a moist gauze to the wound to keep the edges from drying out (gauze saturated with antibiotic ointment is best).

4. Elevate the wound area so that it is higher than the level of the

457

heart. This helps control bleeding and swelling.

5. Give your child emotional support. Seek medical attention fo stitches and the proper dressing of the wound. You can help you doctor improve the healing by applying first aid properly an seeking medical attention quickly. The sooner the wound i attended to and whatever stitches necessary are applied, th lower the chances of infection and the better the cosmetic results

6. Be sure you understand your doctor's follow-u instructions—how to take care of the bandages, what to put o the wound, whether to wash it and how and when the stitche should come out. A well-healed laceration is the result of goo professional care and good parental care.

Scratches (abrasions) result from scraping off the oute layer of skin. Abrasions do not usually need stitches but are ofte very painful and become easily infected because of the debri that may be imbedded in the wound. The following ar guidelines for home treatment of abrasions:

1. The abrasion should be cleansed of all debris such as sand dirt or pieces of glass. Abrasions are often more painful tha cuts, and the cleansing solutions which burn (e.g. alcohol should not be used.

2. Remove imbedded foreign material from the abrasion wit clean tweezers.

3. Depending on the wound, either apply an antibiotic ointmer directly to the abrasion and leave the abrasion uncovered, or appl a gauze impregnated with antibiotic ointment.

4. Wash frequently (preferably with a jet of water) and dry th wound well with a clean gauze. Keep it covered with antibioti ointment until the wound is well healed.

Abrasion, burns and lacerations often heal with irregula skin pigmentation. To improve the cosmetic result, avoid prolor ged exposure of the wound to the sunlight for six months.

Splinters

Good splinter tweezers should be part of your first aid kit. T remove splinters, cleanse the puncture site well with an antisep tic solution. To avoid breaking off part of the splinter, try t place the tips of the splinter tweezers as far as possible aroun the splinter. Try to remove the splinter along the same path as went in. Soak the puncture wound in an antiseptic solution for few minutes, dry the area well and cover it with an antibioti ointment. As with all puncture wounds, a tetanus shot should b administered if your child has not had one in the previous te years. Splinter wounds may become infected. If you see th signs of infection (swelling, redness, warmth and tendernes:

consult your physician for treatment. Occasionally the splinters are very large, deep or close to important structures within the hand or foot. In this case, it is wise to take your child to your physician or to the emergency room at your local hospital for removal of the splinter.

Insect Stings (bees, wasps, hornets and yellowjackets)

Stinging insects cause both localized pain and swelling due to the stinger and the injected venom.

Bees leave their stinger and its attached venom sac in the wound. Scrape away the protruding poison sac with a sharp knife before removing the rest of the stinger. Squeezing the sac with forceps will only inject more venom. Wasp stingers do not have an attached venom sac. Ice will ease the pain of the sting and may slow down the migration of the venom.

Swelling of the hands, eyelids and eyes, watery eyes, and breathing difficulties can occur within minutes of an insect sting. Approximately five per cent of people are hypersensitive to the stings of the bee and other members of the bee family. If these symptoms appear take your child to the hospital immediately as an allergic reaction to these insect stings can be fatal. If your child has previously had an allergic reaction to an insect sting and he is stung again, consider the following steps:

1. Apply a tourniquet above the site if it occurs on the arm or the leg. The tourniquet should be just tight enough to allow you to slip your index finger under the constricting band. Apply ice. Keep the level of the affected limb below the level of the heart.

2. Take your child to the hospital emergency room immediately, even before the allergic reaction occurs.

3. Children who have had a severe allergic reaction to a stinging insect should receive allergy shots (hyposensitization) against all four members of the stinging insect family. These shots are usually very effective.

4. Your doctor may prescribe a bee sting emergency kit (adrenalin) in case you are a long distance from medical facilities.

Tick Bites

A tick fastens itself to the skin with its teeth and reinforces this attachment with a cement-like secretion. Although the tick can voluntarily detach itself quickly, if you attempt to remove the tick (with tweezers, for example), the head or mouth parts will usually remain imbedded in the skin. To encourage the tick to voluntarily release itself from the skin, cover it with a heavy oil or petroleum jelly to plug its breathing pores. If the tick does not fall off in a half hour, carefully remove it with a pair of tweezers. You should try to remove all the body parts. Grabbing the tick securely and rotating it counter-clockwise may cause it to release its grip. If any mouth parts remain in the skin, they may be pried out with a needle or small lancet. Tick bites, and leaving tick parts in the skin, can result in local infection or the very unusual, but nevertheless concerning illness called Tick Fever.

Animal Bites

Animal bites, such as dog bites can cause infection due to the bacteria carried in the animal's mouth. For this reason, animal bites should be cleansed well and treated with either topical antibiotic ointment or systemic antibiotics prescribed by your doctor. Parents usually fear two types of infection from dog bites: tetanus and rabies. Tetanus vaccine is often over-used. A tetanus booster is not required more than once every ten years (see **Immunization**, page 405). Rabies is a viral disease found mainly in wild animals such as the skunk, foxes, raccoons and bats, but it may also infect domestic dogs who have been exposed to rabid wild animals. The disease is very rare in rodents such as squirrels and rats.

Contact your local health department to find out if rabies is prevalent in your community. If your child is bitten by a dog, try the following before beginning rabies surveillance:

1. Attempt to corral the dog and locate its owner to see if the dog has been properly immunized.

2. If there is a question about the dog's immunization, you should report this to the local health department and the dog should be quarantined for a period of ten days. If the dog shows any signs of rabies (unprovoked aggression, snapping at anything in its path, excessive drooling or any bizarre behavior) the animal is sacrificed and examined for rabies. A series of injections of anti-rabies vaccine is then usually given to the child. A wild animal that bites the child should be killed and its head submitted for laboratory examination of the brain.

Snake Bites

The most common poisonous snakes of North America are the copperhead, the rattlesnake, the cottonmouth water moccasins and the coral snake. Parents should be familiar with the poisonous snakes found in their community and should also teach their child how to recognize them. One or two puncture wounds caused by the fangs, very rapid swelling, discoloration and extreme pain at the wound site are signs that the snake bite is probably poisonous.

To treat a suspected poisonous snake bite proceed as follows:

1. Quiet the child, make him lie down and refrain from moving as much as possible.

2. Flush the wound with copious amounts of water.

3. Apply a tourniquet two to four inches above the wound (between the wound and the heart). The tourniquet should be loose enough to allow one finger to slip underneath.

4. Do not pack the wound area in ice, as this may increase tissue damage.

5. Take your child to the hospital immediately. If the snake was not captured, try to describe the species as accurately as possible to the hospital personnel.

6. Do not make any cuts across the fang site and attempt to suck out venom. In inexperienced hands, this procedure may do more harm than good.

Death from a snake bite is now very unusual because of rapid first aid treatment and emergency medical transportation systems. Morbidity and severe limb damage is still a major threat which can be minimized by proper first aid treatment.

Marine Animal Stings

Marine animal stings (jellyfish) cause extreme pain, swelling, redness and heat at the site of the sting. The intense burning pain of a jellyfish sting may be minimized by applying alcohol and placing ice packs on the area. Most local emergency rooms in seaside areas keep a concoction (made of a meat tenderizer) which neutralizes the toxin from the sting.

CHAPTER X

SPECIAL SITUATIONS

Adoption

The telephone rings one day and a person from a local adoption agency announces that you have the chance to suddenly become parents. This long-awaited beautiful news may catch many childless couples unprepared. The following are factors you might want to consider before adopting your first child:

1. What should you know about the biological birth-parents? Most adoption agencies provide the adoptive parents with the essentials such as the age of the birth parents, medical status, history of hereditary diseases, the relationship of the birth parents to their child at the time of the adoption and any other significant information which the adoptive parents have a right to know. Consider what you should know and also what the adopted child may wish to know about his birth parents later in life.

2. What should you know about the child you are considering to adopt ? You should know the age and perhaps the reason for the separation from his birth parents. What was the length and quality of foster care? Obviously a healthy newborn adopted out of the hospital nursery is the ideal. However, the availability of these "first choices" has recently declined due to contraception, the availability of abortion and the fact that more unwed mothers now keep their babies. If you are fortunate enough to receive a newborn, you will usually be given the significant details of the birth history including any complications which may influence the adoptee's health. Couples seeking to adopt will find older children more abundant. If you adopt an older child, it is very important to find out all the details about the quality of foster care, the child's medical and psychological history and specific features of his temperament.

3. What particular behavior can you expect from an older adopted child? Many older children have spent varying lengths of time in different foster homes and consequently they may not have developed secure "roots" so important in the early formative years. Don't be disappointed if your adopted child experiences initial difficulty in forming strong attachments with you. Soon he will understand the permanency of this home and gradually develop an attachment to his adoptive parents. It is usual for an adopted child to periodically show symptoms of non-attachment and emotional swings. These are caused by periodical questioning about his security with your family.

The adolescent adoptee may show particular sensitivity during his identity crisis. Who am I? What are my roots? What were my real parents like? Who are they? Where are they? These are feelings which only an adopted person can fully understand. Adopting parents must realize that this identity searching is common in nearly all adopted children and has nothing to do with the quality of your parent-child relationship. If an adopted child senses your insecurity, this reinforces his own insecurity and a vicious cycle is created. Convey all the signs of parental love to your child that I have mentioned so frequently in this book such as eye-to-eye contact, touching and family recreation. Your child will eventually show his love and attachment to you as "Mom and Dad." "Bonding" is a lifelong process. Although an adopted child may have been temporarily deprived in infancy of strong bonding, caring adoptive parents can, to a large extent, make up for this early deprivation.

Adopting parents commonly compensate for this insecurity by becoming over-indulgent, over-protective and over-permissive, and are consequently unable to effectively discipline the child. If you recognize that your child's feelings are normal identity conflicts which occur at various stages of his development and that your feelings are simply a symptom of your love for your long-awaited child, then you will be able to effectively discipline your child.

4. When should I tell my child that he is adopted? In most cases tell him as soon as he is old enough to understand, which is usually by age three years. Your responsibility, however, does not end with one simple explanation. At various stages of development your child will begin fantasizing about his origin (''Whose tummy did I come out of?'') and, therefore, repeated explanations of the details of his adoption and what you know of his roots should be given to him according to his curiosity and level of maturity. Encourage your child to express his feelings and let him know that you understand that his frequent identity searching is normal and will be respected.

5. The ''sealed records'' problem. Adopting parents can no longer be guaranteed that the identity of the birth parents will remain confidential. Normally, in a legal adoption, the child's original birth certificate is replaced with the new legal name of the child and the original birth certificate is sealed and classified as confidential. Recognizing that some adopted children may eventually be intent on searching for their identity and locating their birth parents, most states have passed ''sealed records'' laws. These stipulate that the identity of the birth parents be kept confidential and be made available to adult adoptees only by court order after assessment of each individual case. These laws are designed to protect the rights of birth parents and adopting parents but have recently been challenged by adolescent and adult adoptees as not being sensitive to their rights. Many adoptees have succeeded in obtaining a reunion with their birth parents and studies have shown that these reunions have had positive effects. The adoptees' identity conflicts diminished following reunion with the birth parents, since many of their questions were answered and fantasizing was no longer necessary. Also, although adopting parents naturally fear a loss of their child or a weakening of their relationship, the contrary seems true. Following the reunion with their birth parents, the adoptees' relationship with their adopting parents seemed more secure.

Children of Divorce

The number of children caught in the crossfire of family separation is increasing at an alarming rate. In the 1980s, 30 per cent to 40 per cent of all children will grow up in a home with one parent.

Preparing Your Child For the Divorce

Parents are understandably apprehensive about how to tell the children about an impending divorce. The following are some general guidelines which you should modify according to your situation and the ages of your children.

1. Tell your children as soon as the decision to separate is final. This allows them some time for adjustment between the initial shock and the actual departure of one parent from the home. Telling your child early allows time for continued questions and dialogue about a divorce, and enables both parents to support the child's adjustment anxieties.

2. Tell your child what divorce actually means in your situation. He should understand that one parent will no longer live in the house. Tell him who will have custodial care and where the non-custodial parent will be living. Because mother **usually** has custody, we will use the term mother to mean custodial parent for ease of discussion.

3. The father should define exactly what his role will be in the child's care. Children are bound to feel that not only is ''Mommy losing Daddy'' but they are ''losing Daddy also.'' It is important for a father to impress upon his children that they have not lost a Daddy. A child needs to understand how the father-child relationship will continue (e.g., where Daddy will live, how often he will see him). Defining father's role exactly may of course be difficult, since many fathers may not have yet answered this question in their own mind.

4. The mother (custodial parent) needs to define what changes will occur within the household. Will she be working? Will they continue to live in the same house? Children need to be reassured that family life will go on. They should understand that the family has not been competely destroyed, only severely changed, and some adjustments need to be made.

5. Tell your children the reason for the divorce, in language and detail appropriate to their age and level of understanding. The rationalization that divorce is ''so common'' has no meaning to the child. He is concerned about his own family, and not general social customs. It is important that children feel reassured that they are not the cause of the divorce. Details of marital infidelity should be withheld from the child as they serve no useful purpose.

6. Children should be instructed not to take sides against either parent. They should be encouraged to vent their feelings about the divorce in general and each parent in particular.

7. Tell your child how often you plan to visit. The younger the child, the more frequent should be your visits. Younger children cannot really conceptualize time, so the statement "once a week" may not mean much to the child under five. Ideally, visiting a young child should be like his feeding schedule—small, frequent visits on a demand basis.

Older children should be consulted in working out a visiting arrangement that respects the busy schedule of a school-aged child. Scheduled visiting rights are somewhat artificial, especially for older children. The children may have some important activity and may be ambivalent about spending a "weekend" with Dad. Perhaps an open visiting arrangement is more realistic for older children.

For example, Dad could call up and say, "How would you like to go to dinner or go to the ballgame tonight?" thus giving the child the option.

Spending every weekend with Dad is a situation far removed from the reality of family life and can be confusing to the child. These weekends may also be unrealistic because they often consist entirely of fun and games, which is totally different from a child's "other life" at home. The occasional "Disneyland Daddy" is fun for a child, but a steady diet is not a realistic way of life. To avoid these problems, during their time with their children, non-custodial parents should maintain a discipline similar to the one which prevails at home. Otherwise the child becomes confused and, worse, learns to play one parent against the other.

These visiting dilemmas are not all negative. I have seen father-child communication actually improve following a divorce because, during the visiting periods, the child has the father's undivided attention. Quality time, not quantity time, is what counts.

Child-considered visiting rights necessitate communication between the divorced parents. It is important not to vie with each other for the child's love.

What Common Problems Can You Anticipate in Your Child Following a Divorce?

The feelings that children experience after parents divorce depend upon the age of the child and the parent-child relationship before and after the divorce. The most common feeling in both children and parents is one of uncertainty, about their own future and about the future of the remaining family. There are, however, some other common feelings and behaviors that children experience following a divorce:

1. Feelings in the pre-school child (three to five years)

Because pre-school children may not verbalize their feelings, they may show regressive behavior. These are behavior disturbances which result from a sense of loss and insecurity and consist of thumb sucking, masturbation, mood swings and sleep disturbances (caused by a fear of wakening and seeing Mommy gone too). Children may also regress in developmental progress such as toilet training. The pre-school child may cling to the custodial parent for fear of losing Mommy too. He may crave attention and not let you out of his sight. The young child may also feel he is to blame for Daddy's departure. The child's energy demands and behavioral changes put an added strain on the custodial parent who, at the same time, is struggling with her own adjustment. If possible, delay for a few months any sudden changes in your parent-child relationship such as a return to work or school. Your pre-school child may be too young to understand your needs and may interpret your departures as abandonment. Try to accept your child's desire to sleep with you and go with you wherever you go. Let him be near you as often as possible.

2. Feelings of school-aged children (five to twelve years)

Children at this age are apt to verbalize their feelings and bombard you with questions regarding the departed parent. Where does Daddy live? When is he coming back? Will Daddy get a new little girl or new Mommy? They may grieve overtly, with tears and signs of sorrow. They may refuse to accept the permanency of the divorce and fantasize that Daddy will be coming back. The child may carry these fantasies and disturbing thoughts into the classroom and school performance may decline.

The older child may start trying to figure out which parent is the "bad guy." He may become an ally of one parent and become angry at the other. The older child may also be more sensitive to the loneliness of his parents and may try to assume the role of friend and companion or even partner substitute to an unhappy parent. These are not always unhealthy roles as long as the compassionate child does not keep too much inside himself while attempting to comfort another.

Vague aches and pains such as fatigue, headaches, and stomach aches are common at this age and are related to attention-getting and reactions to stress. Anticipate a few visits to the doctor during the year following a divorce.

3. Adolescents

Adolescents are themselves going through an identity crisis, and are particularly vulnerable to the effects of a divorce. The adolescent can think abstractly and is even more prone to fantasize about marriage in general. The adolescent may become very judgmental about who is at fault and may wonder what kind of people his parents are. The behavioral problems of the adolescent are more likely to involve his peer relationships and minor delinquencies. Sexual gratification and sudden love affairs may occur. Adolescents are particularly judgmental about the possible sexual activities of the parents, and both the mother and the visiting father should exercise some discretion about their sexual pursuits. Do not count upon your adolescents to welcome a household free of marriage conflicts and tensions because, unless there has been excessive physical violence during the marriage, children do not usually view divorce as something which improves the family situation.

Common Problems the Custodial Parent May Experience

The custodial parent, whether the situation results from divorce or death, is faced with one of the most difficult of all parenting dilemmas. Your child needs an immense amount of attention and support to overcome the feelings we previously discussed. The increased demands on your energy of both your child and the household occur at a time when you need your energy to re-direct your own life. It is a time of dilemma and compromise. If you are continually unhappy as a person, you will not be happy or effective as a parent. Seeking support systems, such as a single parent group or a therapist, may help you cope during this difficult time.

Another dilemma the custodial parent must face is the difficulty she will have sympathizing with the child's feelings of loss because of her own feelings of hostility toward the child's father. One of the most common mistakes that divorced parents make, either consciously or subconsciously, is to vent their hostility through the child. It is easy to fall into the habit of devaluing the absent parent in the eyes of the child. This unfortunate practice only confuses the child and everybody suffers.

● **Discipline and the single parent**

The custodial parent must continue household routines and enforce family discipline. Depending on the previous involvement of the husband, many mothers find coping by themselves exceedingly difficult. Following a divorce, househould routines often become disorganized and discipline is relaxed. Just at a time when organization and consistent discipline are needed, your capacity to parent the whole household diminishes. The fol-

469

lowing suggestions may help you cope with this dilemma:

1. Children do not adapt well to many rapid changes. If some changes (e.g. different house, school, city) are necessary, attempt these gradually, with preparation.

2. Family life must go on and obviously some changes are necessary. If your children are at least school age, call a family council (see **Family Council**, page 246). Your child will have to accept some increased responsibility. This is a non-negotiable fact of single parent family life. Who will now do what, can be negotiated at the family council. You may make a list of the new responsibilities to be shared and let each child choose his contribution. Forcing too many responsibilities upon your child at this time may make him rebel and further resent the divorce. Organization in the household will make the child's total adjustment and your discipline much easier.

3. Single parents find it necessary to run a "tight ship." Remember that discipline also implies emotional support. If you increase both your expectations of your child and your methods of conveying your love to him, your child will most likely respect the changes in discipline.

4. Following a divorce or death, a single parent may frequently move back to the town of the grandparents. Grandparents can provide valuable support, both for the parent who needs love and companionship and for the children who may need the love and care only a blood relative can offer. The child may initially gravitate to the grandfather as a father figure, which is usually healthy behavior. Single parent organizations and church groups may also provide social contacts and valuable support.

5. You cannot be a "mother and father" to your children. This cliché is unrealistic. If you are the mother, be a good mother; if you are the father, be a good father. But what about some male figures in your child's life? Mothers are not expected to become football players and fishermen overnight. You can provide opportunities for your child to meet males who will act as role models at school clubs and church and sports events. Appreciate that the male role model is not a substitute for a continued father-child relationship.

It is wise to seek the counselling and support of your child's pediatrician prior to the divorce and periodically during the year or two following the divorce. The primary goal in parenting your child through a divorce is to preserve the child's sense of security within the divided family.

Travelling with Children

Travelling with children should be enjoyable. It can also be a time of stress if medical illness occurs or wise plans have not been made. The following are suggestions for enjoyable travelling with your children:

1. Be aware. The risk of childhood accidents increases during travel. Your child is out of his familiar, secure environment and parents often relax their surveillance. By simply increasing awareness of your children during your trip, you will increase your family's enjoyment and safety.

2. Be safe. Car safety and car discipline are especially important on long trips (see **Car Safety**, page 429). Bring along car games appropriate for your children. Engage your child in family games, riddles, naming cars, license plate games, billboard games. To entertain a busy toddler, take along a ''fun bag'' full of his favorite toys. Involvement is the key to preventing disruptive behavior during a long car ride. Frequent stops to let a young child release energy may be necessary. In our family, we call these ''pit stops.'' The children are admonished not to stray away from the car without a parent, are told just how long we are going to stop and are encouraged to go to the bathroom at this time. Carry a potty chair for the young child when you face a long stretch of highway.

3. Be prepared. If your child has a chronic illness and is on medication, take along an adequate supply of medication and consult your pharmacist about proper storage of these medications. If your child is susceptible to ear infections, take along an antibiotic (ask your pharmacist to dispense the antibiotic in powder form with instructions on how much water to add) and some analgesic ear drops in case you are in some area where medical attention is not readily available. Bring along your first aid kit. (See **Parents' First Aid Kit**, page 442 .)

4. Motion sickness can be minimized by taking along some medication given by your doctor, encouraging involvement in car games, avoiding heavy and greasy foods, carrying nutritious snacking foods, ensuring that the car is adequately ventilated and stopping frequently.

5. Food during travel. Breastfeeding makes travelling with infants easier. The breast is a travelling infant's best friend, both for nutrition and comfort. If you are formula feeding, carry an adequate supply of ready-to-use formula and baby food. Traveller's diarrhea is common in children. This may be minimized by drinking bottled water and eating foods that are peeled and cooked. Fast food outlets and food dispensing machines may not be well received by the young child's discriminating intestines. A hungry child is usually a disruptive child. Encourage car snacking.

6. Air travel tips. When travelling with an infant, request a seat with a lot of leg room. The change in air pressure may produce ear pain in tiny babies. To lessen the pain, give your infant a breast or a bottle on which to nurse during take-off and landing.

7. Medical help for the young traveller. Your child's doctor is always as close as the nearest telephone. Often, talking to a familiar doctor who knows him can help relieve some of your child's anxiety about being sick away from home. Your doctor can then guide you by phone by giving medical advice on using some of the medications you have brought along or about how to find a doctor to examine your child. To obtain medical care for your child while travelling.

a) Call the local children's hospital if you are in a large city. These hospitals have emergency services staffed by pediatricians or they can recommend a near-by pediatrician.

b) Ask a friend to recommend a pediatrician.

c) If you are a stranger in town, ask the local pharmacist to recommend a pediatrician.

d) If you are in a foreign country, ask your embassy for their list of competent physicians who speak your language.

Foreign Travel If you and your child are travelling outside the country, you should make the following preparations:

1. Contact your local health department for information about which vaccines are required to enter the countries you will visit or to return to your own country. Tell the department which countries you will be visiting and in what order. The United States Public Health Services publishes a monthly updated booklet "Health Information for International Travel" which contains the immunizations required for each country and information about any recent epidemics of contagious diseases in each country. Similar information is available from the Canadian government. The vaccines to consider are smallpox, cholera, yellow fever, gamma globulin prevention for hepatitis, typhoid and malaria prevention medication. Your local health department and your physician will advise you which vaccines and preventive medications are necessary. Documentation of these vaccines is important. An International Certificate of Vaccination can be obtained from your local health department. It must bear an official stamp certifying that you received the required vaccine.

If there are medical reasons why you or your child should not receive a required vaccine (e.g. allergy to eggs, pregnancy, eczema) you should receive a signed physician's statement on his letterhead indicating that you cannot receive the vaccination for health reasons. Have the letter validated with the official stamp from your local health department in order to avoid problems when entering a country. Most countries do not require vaccination of infants under one year of age.

2. Teenagers and many adults like to "go native" when visiting places such as South America, Africa and southeast Asia. This custom increases your risk of contacting an infectious disease. Food which you peel yourself, cooked food and well-done meat are the safest. Avoid salads made with low-growing vegetables such as lettuces. Drinking soda and bottled water is safer than drinking the town water and may minimize the severity of traveller's diarrhea. Milk is often unpasteurized in rural areas of developing countries and therefore should be avoided. Canned milk is safer.

3. If you are travelling to remote areas of developing countries, take a first aid kit, an extra pair of glasses and medications which your physician may advise you to have. The embassy of your country usually has lists of competent doctors who speak your language should you need medical attention.

Genetic Counselling

One of the newest and most interesting fields of medical science is genetic counselling. Couples who are at high risk of having a baby with an inherited disease can receive prenatal counselling and sometimes a prenatal diagnosis. The following is a list of considerations for parents who are at risk of transmitting genetic diseases.

1. If your concern is an inherited disease, prepare a family tree which shows as accurately as possible which family member carries what disease.

2. Make an appointment with your physician, or a specialist in genetic counselling if referred to one by your physician. The counsellor will attempt to determine if you carry the disease and, if so, what the risk is that you may transmit the disease to your offspring. A blood test may detect whether one or both parents are carriers of certain diseases such as Tay Sachs. A carrier is a person who does not actually have the disease but carries it in his genetic make-up. If two carriers mate, the disease may appear in their offspring. In many instances, parents cannot be diagnosed as carriers but the disease has either occurred in a previous child or within the family. A genetic counsellor puts all of the available information together and attempts to give you a risk factor, i.e., the percentage chance that your baby may have the disease. For example, in the case of spina bifida, a defect in the spinal cord development, if parents have had a previous child with spina bifida, the risk of having a similarly affected child is 5 per cent.

3. If you are pregnant how can you tell if your baby has a genetic disease? What is involved in a prenatal diagnosis? Many inherited diseases as well as diseases caused by changes in chromosomes (e.g. mongolism) can be diagnosed prenatally by a procedure called **amniocentesis**. In this procedure, performed around the fourteenth or sixteenth week of pregnancy, the doctor inserts a needle through the abdomen into the amniotic cavity and obtains a large amount of fluid. Amniotic fluid is like fetal urine. It contains the actual cells of the fetus and much chemical information about the fetus. This fluid is analyzed for abnormalities in fetal chromosomes, the sex of the baby, and certain chemical information that may suggest the presence of a certain disease.

Amniocentesis is advisable in the following three cases:
a) to detect defects in brain or spinal cord development if a close relative or previous child is affected.
b) if there is a risk of abnormal chromosomes (e.g. mongolism). You are advised to take this test if you are over forty years of age (some physicians recommend thirty-five years), if you have a previously infected child or close relative affected with this condition, or if you are a carrier of this condition.
c) if you have a child affected with, or you are a carrier of, a metabolic disease such as Tay Sachs.

Amniocentesis is generally a safe procedure. The risk of injury to the fetus is around 0.5 per cent. Due to this slight risk, your physician may not recommend amniocentesis unless the risk that your baby has an illness is greater than the risk of the procedure itself. For example, amniocentesis to diagnose mongolism is not advised until parents reach the age of thirty-five or forty, at which time the risk of mongolism is one per cent, or greater than the risk of undergoing amniocentesis. If you have already decided not to terminate the pregnancy regardless of the findings, then amniocentesis is unnecessary.

Parenting Twins

A family blessed with twins has twice the trouble and twice the fun. Twins occur about once in ninety births. The chance of having twins increases if there are twins in either the mother's or father's family. Mothers who are having twins often experience more severe symptoms of pregnancy than single birth mothers (e.g. more morning sickness). Another sign of twins is excessive weight gain which cannot be adequately explained by diet. It is usually not until the last three months of pregnancy that twins may be suspected by your doctor and confirmed by a special diagnostic test called ultrasound. Some mothers do not appear to be excessively large and the twins may be an unexpected bonus at delivery. In fact, in about 40 per cent of the births, the delivery of twins is a complete surprise to both doctor and parents.

There are two types of twins, fraternal and identical. Fraternal twins, which occur if two different eggs are fertilized by two different sperm, are about four times more common than identical twins. This type of twinning is considered hereditary because some women tend to ovulate more than one egg each month and some men may produce sperm cells in greater number or with a greater ability to fertilize the ova. Each fraternal twin has a different genetic make-up and, except that they are the same age, they may appear no more alike than any two siblings of the same family. Identical twins derive from a single fertilized ovum. Very early in embryonic life, the developing ova splits in two and each half forms a baby. These two babies are genetically identical, are always of the same sex and have the same blood type, but they may not look exactly alike. They may have the same hair color and texture, eye color, teeth, shape of ears, nose and mouth, but even identical twins show subtle physical differences. Their finger prints are similar but not identical. Occasionally, identical twins may show a phenomenon called **mirror imaging** in which the physical characteristics of one side of the child's body are reflected on the opposite of the other's body. For example, one child is right-handed and the other is left-handed, and certain facial characteristics appearing on one side of one child's face appear on the other's opposite side. Identical twinning is thought to be due completely to chance, unlike fraternal twinning which has a hereditary basis.

If the babies are of the same sex at birth, it may be difficult for the doctor to immediately tell whether they are fraternal or identical. The placentas of identical twins tend to be fused whereas fraternal twins tend to have separate placentas. However, often the placentas are so closely placed that they appear as one and the doctor cannot be certain by placental examination alone whether the twins are fraternal or identical. Special blood typing is often required to answer if the twins are fraternal or identical if they are of the same sex. If an uncertainty still exists the question is usually answered when the twins are older and their features become more distinct.

Twins do have a higher risk of medical problems in the newborn period. Twin pregnancies seldom go to full term and prematurity is the common complication of twin births. The second most common complication is called twin-twin transfusion, whereby one twin robs the other of some placental blood supply. This results in one larger twin, often born with too much blood volume, and one smaller twin born with too little blood volume. The possibility of these problems may cause your doctor to suggest that you deliver in a hospital which has adequate newborn intensive care facilities.

Suggestions for Parenting Twins

1. Preparation. If you know ahead of delivery that you are going to have twins, be prepared. Contact support groups in your community (e.g. The International Childbirth Education Association and The La Leche League International, see page 30). You may inquire if there is a Mother of Twins Club in your community. For advice on parenting twins and becoming a member of the Mother of Twins Club, contact Mother of Twins Club, Inc., 5402 Amberwood Lane, Rockville, Maryland, 20853. In Canada, contact Parents of Multiple Births Association of Canada, Box 129, Stirling, Alberta, Canada T0K 2E0.

Do you feel that you have more than the average new-parent anxieties? Do you have any risk factors which predispose you to postpartum depression (see page 74) which will lessen your effectiveness as a parent? Make an appointment with your prospective pediatrician before delivery to discuss these concerns. Many pediatricians will offer you the names of parents of twins in their practice. I have found that the practical advice and

Parenting twins demands the resourcefulness, organization and involvement of both parents.

support of other parents of twins is a valuable resource.

2. Parents of twins need help. While twins can be a beautiful blessing, they can also overtax the reserves of most parents. Obtain help for the household duties, especially for the first few months. As I have emphasized in the section on **The Adjustment Period** (page 75), ideal postpartum adjustment occurs when the mother is free of household chores and can devote all her energies to her baby. With twins, this advice is not a luxury, it is a necessity. Fatigue dampens the enjoyment of twins. Obtain help from anyone you can, friends, relatives, hired help. The best gifts well-meaning friends can give to parents of twins are housekeeping help, care of other siblings or an occasional dinner.

3. Father involvement. Father involvement is not an option, it is a must. Most fathers willingly see their role as a co-mother. I don't really think that twins get ''less mothering'' than single infants, but I think that they may get more fathering.

4. Be organized. Parenting twins demands resourcefulness and organization. You will devise shortcuts in food preparation, feeding your twins, dressing, bathing, shopping, and household management. Your efficiency will surprisingly increase. One of the benefits of allying yourself to other mothers of twins is the myriad of advice you will receive on organizing your time.

5. Breastfeeding twins. Remember the basic law of breastmilk production is that supply equals demand. If you have two little suckling infants who demand milk, you certainly will be able to

477

adequately supply their needs. If you do decide to breastfeed your twins, it is doubly important to follow the tips to successful breastfeeding discussed on page 99 .

Mothers who successfully nurse their twins seem to have three outstanding characteristics. They are intensely motivated and do not even consider that they "can't do it." They organize their time well. Housework is delegated, husband involvement is active and support groups in their community are used wisely. They are flexible and relaxed. Many mothers find that nursing the twins at different times is easier than nursing them together, but this varies from day to day. On some days both babies are content to nurse at the same time, and other days they wish their own time. Successful breastfeeding mothers adapt to this.

6. You are parenting individuals, not twins. There are no absolute do's and don'ts about treating twins as individuals. It is occasionally fun for you and fun for them to be dressed alike. However, from the moment of birth, treat each child as an individual with different needs and a distinctive personality. One of the joys of twins is to see two children of the same age growing up with different developmental patterns, emotional needs, strengths and weaknesses. Each one has a unique personality which needs unique nurturing. Call them by their names. "Bobby and Jimmy" is much more individual and personal than "the twins."

7. Expect certain behaviors in their individual search for identity. Twins grow up both as a "twin" and as an individual. With proper parental guidance, the twin aspect of identity can be a bonus. For most twins there is a certain added "identity comfort" in this close blood relationship with another person of the same age with similar features, a constant companion who adds an extra dimension to growing up. However, you can expect your children to have some ambivalent feelings about being a twin. The normal search for individual identity is often intensified in a twin and can lead to competition between them. This is usually a healthy competition which each child must periodically show in order to mature into an independent person. As long as this competition does not result in animosity between them, no parental interference is needed. You need not be overly concerned about playing favorites or worrying that one twin will think you are devoting too much time to the other. Simply parent each child according to your intuition about their individual needs. You will probably find that one or the other child needs a little extra parenting at different times, according to his individual developmental pattern. Parenting twins through these competitive phases means creating an environment which allows their individual strengths to flourish. The fatigue of the early years of parenting twins is usually rewarded in later years when you witness the emergence of a very special relationship.

Your Child's Pets

Pets provide companionship. They are love objects which usually enrich the life of a growing child. Like toys, pets provide enjoyment and also dangers to the child. In this discussion I will offer suggestions on selecting and caring for pets and about how to avoid many of the medical problems caused by pets.

Selecting a Pet

Animals that have been bred to be pets usually make the best pets. Exotic wild animals bred in captivity do not usually make good pets. Wild animals exhibit unpredictable behavior in captivity and are difficult to care for since we know less about their nutritional, medical and behavioral needs. Stick to the old reliable dog or cat. Select a breed which is known to be gentle with children, such as the Labrador retriever. Avoid breeds which have high strung personalities, such as the little "yappers" who compensate for their size with their unpredictable and unpleasant behavior. If a pet turns out to be a behavioral problem get rid of it, as it will turn out to be a liability to the entire family. To select a healthy pet, watch for discharge from the eyes, diarrhea, a cough, patches of missing hair or skin problems. Let your child play with the prospective pet for awhile before selecting it. If you are uncertain about the pet's health, ask a veterinarian to check over the animal before you purchase it.

Care of Pets

A pet requires as much care as a member of the family. In fact, children often become as attached to their pet as they are to a sibling. The following list of pet needs should be attended to: proper nutrition, good hygiene (bathing, hair and skin care), fresh water, exercise, a discipline which is kind but firm, and veterinarian care including vaccinations, worming, spaying and heartworm.

Medical Problems Associated with Pets

Allergies and infections are the two general medical problem associated with keeping pets.

● **Allergies**

If your child is an allergic child (eczema, asthma, hayfever), it i best to avoid house pets, especially long-haired dogs and cats Even though your child may not seem allergic to the pet at first if he is allergy-prone he will probably eventually become allergi to the hairy animal. If the pet is already established as a famil member and the child would just as soon keep both the pet an his allergy, at least keep the pet outside, not in the child' bedroom.

● **Infections caused by animal bites**

The wounds of animal bites are particularly concerning becaus of the chance of infection being transmitted by the bite. What d you do if your child is bitten by an animal?

1. Clean the wound well. Wash it with a jet of water. Becaus dogs harbor bacteria in their mouths, it is important to appl some antiseptic solution (such as Betadine) and an antibioti ointment (such as Neosporin). If the wound is large and dirty your doctor may wish to treat your child with an antibiotic.

2. Tetanus immunization lasts ten years. If your child has ha his full complement of tetanus shots, he does not need a tetanu booster if he has had one within the previous ten years.

3. Rabies is the infection most feared from an animal bite. I there is any suspicion that the animal may be rabid, your physi cian may advise that your child receive anti-rabies shots. Th treatment used to consist of a series of twenty-one very painfu injections. The newer anti-rabies vaccine is a series of five injec tions which are not as unpleasant as the older vaccine. By mak ing certain that your dog has received his rabies shots and by no allowing him to roam through the woods, you can lessen th chance of its contracting rabies. (See page 460 for a furthe discussion.)

4. Salmonella, an intestinal bacteria causing diarrhea, can b transmitted from the stools of your pet. The chance of con tracting this can be lessened by carefully washing your hand after handling litter boxes or cleaning up your pet's stools. Mos pets can carry salmonella and transmit this bacteria to your child

5. Worms. Dogs are often blamed for the worms children carry In fact, the majority of worms seen in children (pinworms an roundworms) are transmitted by a person, not by an animal Dogs do carry worms that may be transmitted to people, but thi is unusual.

6. Fleas are year-round pesky little insects which reside deep in the hair of animals and cause intense itching. If your pet is constantly biting or scratching himself, suspect fleas. Fleas lay their eggs off the host (e.g. in the carpet). To completely eliminate fleas from your home, both the animal and the carpet need to be treated. Flea bites on children cause intense itching but do not transmit any disease.

7. Ticks are warm weather pests that burrow into the flesh of the animal and swell to several times their original size by ingesting blood. Ticks can transmit a disease called tick fever (Rocky Mountain Spotted Fever). (See **Tick Bites**, page 459.)

There are many other less common illnesses transmitted from pets to children. It is wise to check with your veterinarian for advice regarding control of animal illnesses prevalent in your community.

Child Abuse

A discussion of the entire field of child abuse is beyond the scope of this book. In this section, I wish to present the following two messages: the importance of reporting child abuse should you suspect this in another person, and how to recognize if you, as a parent, are at a risk of abusing of your child.

If You Suspect Child Abuse

If you suspect child abuse, even if your suspicions are unconfirmed, you have the legal and moral obligation to report it. Laws are designed to protect both the child and the "reporter" of child abuse. Even if your suspicions prove incorrect, you cannot be sued for incorrectly reporting a case of child abuse. In fact, the reverse is true. A person who suspects child abuse and does not report it may be guilty of a misdemeanor. Reporting child abuse is important for the following reasons:

1. The safety of the child. If a case of child abuse goes unreported and no counselling action is taken, the chance of that child being harmed more is five to ten times greater than if some intervention has occurred. In other words, uncorrected child abuse tends to worsen, not improve.

2. The benefit of the abuser (parent, teacher, babysitter, etc.). The abuser needs help and wants help. Child abuse is usually the tip of the iceberg of some underlying personal or family problem.

All states and provinces have professionals trained to counsel child abusers and help the families. If you suspect child abuse, report this immediately either to the authorities or to your own or the child's physician.

How to Recognize Potentially Abusive Families

Child abuse is much more common than most people realize. It occurs at all socio-economic levels of family life. The following are characteristics of families that are at risk of child abuse:

1. The abusive parent was abused as a child.

2. The abusive parent is a product of a home with a defective parent model, a home in which he or she received consistently negative input from the parents and never developed a secure love relationship with either parent.

3. Prolonged parent-infant separation after birth, e.g., prematurity and prolonged hospitalization. There is an increased incidence of child abuse if the bonding relationship has been interrupted for a long period of time.

4. Unrealistic expectations of children (e.g. parent-child role reversals, wanting children to improve the marriage, etc.). A misconception is that abused children are not wanted. They are wanted, but often for the wrong reasons.

5. A multi-problem family, e.g., unsupporting spouse relationship, marital tension, alcoholism, drug abuse.

6. Increasing frequency and severity of spanking as the primary mode of discipline.

7. The difficult child, the hyperactive child, any child who taxes the frustration tolerance of the family, is a child who, abusive parents feel, invites abuse.

Child abuse naturally creates hostility toward the abuser because the child cannot defend himself. Child abusers need and want help. Studies on child abuse have often traced the roots of this abuse back into the abuser's childhood (as in 2 above). The most effective way of preventing child abuse, in either yourself or in your children as future parents, is to practice the philosophy of continuum parenting advocated in this book.

Parenting The Hospitalized Child

Leaving the security of his own environment and entering a strange room with strange people and sleeping in a strange bed may be very traumatic for a child. This anxiety is compounded if he is sick. He may not understand why he feels badly (if he is hospitalized for emergency treatment of an illness) or why he has to be in the hospital in the first place if he is not sick (an elective procedure, such as a tonsillectomy). The following are suggestions on parenting the sick and hospitalized child, especially the child under six years of age.

1. Parents, prepare yourselves. Be sure you understand the hospital visiting or care-by-parent policies. What procedures will be carried out on your child? What type of operation or medical test will he have? Doctors and nurses realize that fear of the unknown is a problem for both the parent and the child and are eager to communicate the necessary information to you. The policy which we have mentioned many times in this book, "understanding increases effectiveness," is also true in parenting the hospitalized child.

2. Prepare your child. If your child is in hospital for an elective procedure, visit the hospital for a tour the day before he is admitted. Most children's hospitals actually offer tours just to acquaint the child with the hospital. Read your child a short, simple book about children in the hospital. Many such books are available and can usually be found in the hospital gift shop. Fear of the unknown is a basic fear in children. The more they understand and are prepared for the hospital in general, and their procedures or operations in particular, the less fear they will experience. For example, if your child is having a tonsillectomy, show him pictures of where his tonsils are, tell him that he will be put to sleep by some medicine injected into his arm or by a mask placed over his face, and that he will wake up with a sore throat but that he may eat lots of ice cream afterwards to make his throat better. Young children often distort or fantasize information you may give them about certain procedures or operations, so try to keep it as simple and free of fantasy as possible.

3. What are your child's feelings about his impending hospitalization? Ask him to talk about his feelings, although children seldom do. Ask him to draw pictures about what he imagines the hospital to be like. You will learn a lot about his specific fears by this exercise.

4. Stay with your child. The younger the child, the more important his parents' presence and support. Most hospitals encourage parents to spend time with their child depending on the type of room and illness. You may have a rooming-in arrangement whereby you can sleep on a cot in your child's room. Most children's hospitals encourage **care-by-parent** which means you feed, and bathe him, care for his simple medical needs (under instructions from your doctor or nurse) and comfort him in periods of pain or stress. It has been my experience that children recuperate faster and have much less fear of hospitals when their parents are intimately involved in their care. Some large children's hospitals have multiple-bed wards. Depending on the nature of the medical illness, children are less apprehensive in wards where they can receive comfort without being alone. Parents are encouraged to give bedside care but may not usually spend the night in these wards.

5. Work **with** medical personnel. An illness in a child usually brings out the best in a caring parent, but it may also bring out little annoyances which may antagonize the medical staff. Parents are understandably anxious about their child's illness and want him to receive the best care. Doctors and nurses are aware of these normal feelings. Your child will ultimately profit if you make a conscious effort to communicate and work constructively with your child's doctor and nurse. Doctors and nurses are proud professionals. If your doctor and nurse feel that you have a sincere confidence in their ability to care for your child, then your child will ultimately benefit. (If you are breastfeeding, see the related section on **Breastfeeding Your Premature and Hospitalized Infant**, page 118 .)

Sudden Infant Death Syndrome

The sudden infant death syndrome (SIDS), or "crib death," is one of the most tragic of all family crises. In the usual case, an apparently healthy infant is put to bed and found dead the next morning, for no apparent reason. The incidence of SIDS is approximately one in 350 babies. It is more prevalent in the winter months and usually occurs in infants between one and six months of age. The peak risk period is between two and four months. SIDS is rare after seven months of age.

The cause of SIDS is unknown. Researchers feel there is more than one cause of death in these babies. It is not caused by suffocation, bedclothing, aspiration of food or vomitus, choking, milk allergy or bottle feeding. Infants with SIDS often have a slight cold preceding death but the relationship is unclear. The current theory is that SIDS is due to an abnormality in the part of the brain which governs breathing and heart rate patterns. SIDS might be caused by a malfunction in the neurostimuli which automatically control breathing and heart rate patterns. There is increasing attention being given to identifying an infant at risk and to the so-called near-miss baby (a baby who has had unexplained stop-breathing episodes but resumes breathing following stimulation by the parents). Premature babies and especially infants with these stop-breathing episodes have an increased risk of SIDS, possible due to a temporary immaturity of their cardiorespiratory regulating mechanisms. There is also a very slightly increased risk if there has been a previous incident of SIDS in the family. If you are concerned about whether your infant has any special risk factors, consult your physician. Even thinking about this tragic possibility causes much parental anxiety which may be alleviated by discussing your worries with your physician. After the initial shock of this tragedy, parents often go through a state of depression and experience guilt feelings. They need understanding, support and professional counselling. Pediatricians usually have the names of parents in your community who have experienced a SIDS in their home. These parents can be a valuable support resource during your grieving period. (See following section on grieving.)

Further information regarding SIDS can be obtained from The National Sudden Infant Death Foundation, 310 South Michigan Avenue, Chicago, Illinois 60604 (312-663-0650). In Canada contact The Canadian Foundation for the Study of Infant Death, 4 Lawton Blvd., Toronto, Ontario M4B 1Z4 (416-488-3260).

Grieving

Grieving is the emotional feeling resulting from the loss of a loved person. It is the internal as well as the external mechanism that enables parents to cope with the death of their child. I am writing this section not only to assist parents in their grieving but also to help friends of the grieving parent understand the mourning process and therefore be able to more effectively help the bereaved parents.

The bond of attachment between parent and child is the strongest of all human attachments. It follows that the grief associated with the loss of this attachment is also one of the deepest and most long-lasting of all human feelings. How parents approach the mourning process can have a profound effect on whether grieving becomes a healthy mechanism for coping with death, or an unbearable drain which empties the grieving parents of their ability to continue their normal social functions. Because the bonds of human attachment are individual, the way parents grieve is also individual. The grieving process will vary considerably in different individuals and the following discussion is intended only as a guide to understand the major components of grieving.

How the child died has a dramatic effect on how parents grieve. Grieving may be considered in three broad categories.

1. Anticipatory grief. If a child died as a result of a long-term illness the parents are allowed time to prepare themselves for the death of their child. This preparation usually makes grieving a bit easier.

2. Sudden unexpected death (e.g. SIDS) provokes a more intense grief reaction because of the shock of death and the sudden loss of a child without the benefit of some preparation.

3. Accidental death (e.g. drowning) often produces the most unbearable grief because it carries not only the shock of suddenness but also the intense guilt that "it was my fault, I was negligent." Irrational guilt is one of the most intense feelings and often undermines an otherwise healthy grieving process. Understanding, support and, often, professional guidance are needed to cope with accidental death.

The Grieving Process

The usual grief reaction begins with a feeling of shock and possibly denial. Did it really happen? For some parents, temporary denial makes overwhelming feelings of loss more bearable. Once the reality of death is accepted, parents experience feelings of intense sadness, helplessness, hostility and anger. Why did it happen? How could I have prevented it? Bodily feelings of "pressure" and "numbness" are common. Parents, especially the mother, experience feelings of emptiness, the loss of part of one's self.

In addition to losing part of one's self, parents become painfully aware that they have lost another person, a person in whom they have invested themselves. This human investment is now gone, leaving a feeling of emptiness that can never again be filled. Grief is never completely overcome but only gradually lessened enough to allow the parent to resume normal social functions.

As the grieving parents accept the reality of death and begin the **period of detachment**, their dead child will continue to live on in the parents' minds. Each vivid memory and bond must be painfully relived and painfully loosened. Each time the parent comes to grips with this detachment, they are one step closer to coping with this loss.

During this detachment phase of grieving, parents may attempt to immerse themselves in escape activities, father in his world of work and mother in many social functions. Other parents show just the opposite behavior, withdrawing themselves from normal social and work activities for a prolonged period.

A mother seems to experience more of the loss of herself. When a child dies the emptiness can affect her self-image, lead to depression and a feeling that she is no longer a complete person. Often the focus of sympathy is so overly directed toward the mother that the grieving father is deprived of much needed support.

Helping Siblings Grieve

Parents are often concerned about how to tell the other children about the death of a sibling. Realize that the feelings about the loss of a sibling are much different from your feelings about the loss of a child because a sibling relationship is different from the parent-child relationship. Sibling grieving depends a great deal on the age of the surviving children. Preschoolers are often more concerned with "What will happen to me?" and "What will happen to Mommy?" than "What happened to baby brother?" Children under age eight may regard death as a temporary absence and not an irreversible state.

Surviving children may misinterpret their parents' preoccupation with grieving as signs of withdrawal of love for them. Some parents, during the normal grieving process, may overprotect other children and be excessively concerned with otherwise minor illnesses. Children sense these feelings and this adds further confusion to their already shaky concept of what happened to their little brother or sister.

Encourage open dialogues about your child's death with the other children. Encourage them to express their own feelings and ask them direct questions which may bring out their own feelings. Children may also feel guilt and hostility, "It was my fault," or "It was your fault." They should be allowed to express these feelings. Parents know their children best and should use terms most comfortable to themselves and to the children. You may wish to use a religious theme such as: Baby

487

brother is in heaven. No, he will not be coming back. Why did he die? He got sick. Will I die if I get sick? No, only tiny babies die of this sickness and you are a big boy. Avoid ambiguous terms which may confuse your child. For example, the phrase "baby never woke up from his sleep" is confusing to the child and it is guaranteed to precipitate sleep problems in your surviving children. Whatever term you choose, the important point is to draw out your child's feelings and talk about his feelings with him as only an intuitive parent can. Helping the surviving children grieve and understand death contributes to the parents' own healthy grieving process by lessening their feelings of helplessness. For this reason, friends and professionals should usually not take over this job from the parents but rather support the parents in using their best intuition in telling the surviving children about the death of the sibling.

Suggestions on Helping Parents Grieve

1. Mourning does not follow a set pattern. How parents grieve is an individual question. It is vitally important that this individuality be respected. Friends should sense the cues of the grieving parents and support their ways of coping with death. The feeling of a loss of part of one's self is a feeling that no other person, however caring, can fully understand. A consoling phrase like "I know how you feel" is meaningless because you don't know how she feels. It is not a loss of part of yourself. The grieving parents will understand that their friends are also having difficulty coming to terms with their grieving process. If you feel you must say something to the parents, be attuned to whether your dialogue is supporting the parents' grief or adding to their discomfort.

2. The circumstances leading to the child's death should be truthfully explained to the parents. Full details of how the child died, why he died (if known) and detailed medical information about the illness should be given to the parents. An intellectual appreciation of the events contributing to the child's death helps ease the emotional drain of a loss they cannot understand. This is the reason doctors often suggest an autopsy. They can then explain the important medical findings to the parents. One of the reasons SIDS causes such intense grief is that parents cannot understand why their baby died.

3. Involvement makes grieving easier. Well-meaning friends and relatives may wish to spare the bereaved parents certain uncomfortable tasks such as removing the infants belongings from the nursery. This may often deprive the parents of a valuable mechanism to soothe the pain of detachment. Involvement in the ceremonies and burial preparations helps one overcome the feeling of helplessness and emptiness. Parents feel "There is something I can still do for my child." Friends and relatives can better help by alleviating the parents of the minor intrusions in their grieving process, by helping with the preparations and decisions not intimately related to the deceased child, such as feeding and organizing the multitude of mourners who may arrive at the house, each also having difficulty coming to terms with their grieving.

4. Grieving parents have the urge to do something. For example, a mother in my practice wanted to write a book on SIDS after her baby died of the Sudden Infant Death Syndrome. I encouraged this. The desire to help others enables parents to overcome their feelings of helplessness and restore their self-esteem. A common grief reaction feeling is to want to replace their baby. "I'll get pregnant right away," or "I'll adopt a baby." A dead baby cannot be "replaced." Parents may initially verbalize these feelings but it would be unwise for a well-meaning friend to suggest that a mother should get pregnant again. Time is the great healer of the pain of loss and eventually the parents will put these initial feelings into a more rational perspective.

5. Support Groups. In the case of SIDS, there is a SID-Parent organization in most large cities. It is wise to let the grieving parents know that such groups are available, but not to push them into joining. Only in an organization such as this does the phrase "I know how you feel" really have some meaning. Support groups are good for some parents and not good for others. These groups may help parents regain much of their lost confidence and resume normal social functioning. The desire to help similarly afflicted parents is a healthy mechanism by which the grieving parents can come to grips with their loss.

6. Be supportive during sensitive periods. The acute grief reaction may often begin as a period of shock during which the reality of death is not completely accepted. After this period of shock wears off, the grief reaction sets in and it is during this period that the parents need the most help. The acute grief reaction usually lasts two to four months and thereafter periodically surfaces for the next six to twelve months. Parents may be particularly sensitive to grieving reactions on the child's birthday, the anniversary of his death or during holidays such as Christmas. Friends should be aware of these sensitive periods and be especially supportive during these grieving days.

7. Recognize the signs of unhealthy grieving early and suggest professional guidance. Because grieving is a very individual feeling it is often difficult to spot unhealthy signs. The following are some signals to alert you to weaknesses in the usual grieving process:

a) A parent who does not wish to be or is deprived of being involved in the burial preparations.

b) A parent who shows no curiosity about the details of the death.

c) A parent who is showing very little outward emotion, or is "being strong."

d) A husband and wife who do not support each other's way of grieving. Marital discord is common after a child dies and is usually the result of poor understanding of each other's grieving.

e) Continued disorganized pattern of living; inability to complete simple household tasks, withdrawal from society and the inability to resume social functioning within a reasonable time, such as six months.

The above symptoms suggest that a grieving parent has not allowed himself to work through the process of the painful loosening of the bonds of attachment and the acceptance of the reality of death.

APPENDIX I

DRUGS IN BREAST MILK

The two main considerations in taking a drug during breastfeeding are: (1) will the drug harm the baby and (2) will the drug diminish milk production and thus indirectly harm the baby? I wish to add a third consideration (especially for over-the-counter remedies) — do you really need the medication or could you handle your illness (e.g., colds) without medication? Almost every drug taken by the mother will appear, to some degree, in her milk. However, most drugs appear in the milk in very small amounts (usually less than 1 per cent of the amount taken by the mother) and therefore have no harmful effect on the baby. The following list of drugs and their safety in breastfeeding is meant only as a guide. It is best to consult with your physician before taking any medication before breastfeeding.

DRUG	USUALLY SAFE DURING BREASTFEEDING	COMMENTS
1. Acetominophen	Yes	Avoid for 1 week postpartum.
2. Alcohol	Yes	Taken in excess can suppress lactation but usually does not affect infant.
3. Allergy medications, antihistamines, decongestants	Yes	May cause sedation or hyperexcitability in infant, may occasionally decrease milk supply. Avoid long-acting preparations unless advised by physician.
4. Amphetamines	No	Unless advised by physician.
5. Antibiotics: Penicillin	Yes	May sensitize infant to penicillin allergy.
Erythromycin	Yes	High levels found in milk — not recommended over other antibiotics.
Keflex	Yes	Not excreted in milk — safest for infant — good 'mastitis' antibiotic.
Sulfa	Yes	Not safe in newborn period.
Furadantin	Yes	No harmful effect known.
Tetracycline	No	May stain infant teeth if used for more than 10 days.
Flagyl	No	Unless advised by physician.
6. Antacids	Yes	Very little enters milk.

7. Anticonvulsants: Dilantin	Yes	With physician's supervision.
Phenobarb	Yes	With physician's supervision.
Tegretol	No	Safety not yet proven.
Mysoline	No	Depressant effect on infant.
8. Caffeine	Yes	Excess may cause irritable baby.
9. Cannabis	No	May impair brain growth in infant and impair maternal care.
10. Contraceptives	No	Suppresses lactation, alters natural composition of milk, possible hormonal effects on infant.
11. Diuretics: Lasix	Yes	Safe — not excreted in milk.
Thiazides	Yes	Usually safe — may suppress lactation if dehydration occurs.
12. Laxatives: Senna (Senakot)	Yes	No effect on infant.
Milk of Magnesia	Yes	No effect on infant.
13. Narcotics: Codeine	Yes	Small doses not harmful, larger doses may depress or excite infant. Use with physician's advice only.
Demerol	No	Unless advised by physician.

Heroin	No	Affects infant. Addiction possible.
Morphine	Yes	Single dose, if medically directed, usually does not affect infant.
14. Nicotine	No	Heavy smoking (20/day) suppresses milk ejection reflex; danger of second-hand smoke in infant's lungs.
15. Sedatives: Barbituates	Yes	Under physician's supervision; can cause depression or excitability in infant.
Valium	Yes	Not in first week postpartum.
Chloralhydrate	Yes	Usually safe in 5 mg. doses. Safe for infant.
16. Anticoagulants	Yes	Under physician's supervision.
17. Atropine	No	Inhibits lactation, affects infant.
18. Chloroquin (antimalarial)	Yes	No harmful effect on infant.
19. Cromolyn	Yes	No harmful effect on infant.
20. Digitalis	Yes	No harmful effect on infant.
21. Ergotamine (Cafergot)	No	May be toxic to infant.
22. Heparin	Yes	Not excreted in milk.
23. Insulin	Yes	Destroyed in infant's GI tract.

24. Iodides (Radioactive)	No	Discontinue breastfeeding for 24 hours after iodides, then safely resume.
25. Isoniazid	Yes	Under physician's supervision.
26. Keopectate	Yes	No harmful effects on infant.
27. Lithium	Yes	Under physician's supervision.
28. Methadone	Yes	No harmful effects on infant.
29. Phenactin	Yes	No harmful effects on infant.
30. Piperazine	Yes	No harmful effects on infant.
31. Propanolol	Yes	No harmful effects on infant.
32. Radioactive diagnostic materials	No	Discontinue breastfeeding for 24 hours after test, then safely resume.
33. Theophylline	Yes	Under physician's supervision.
34. Thyroxine	Yes	Under physician's supervision.
35. Vaccines	Yes	Vaccines taken by mother usually do not affect infant — under physician's supervision.
36. Vitamins	Yes	Usually does not affect infant.

Environmental Contaminants in Human Milk

In the past decade a flurry of articles appeared about the contamination of breast milk by industrial chemicals, such as DDT, which was withdrawn from the market in 1972. Now pesticides and industrial chemicals which pollute the water are under scrutiny. These chemicals, which have an affinity for animal fat, tend to concentrate in breast milk because of its high fat content. Although the concern is justified, you should not decide against breastfeeding because of it. I do not know of any cases in which infants become sick because of environmental chemicals in breast milk. Most reports of infant illnesses caused by contaminants in breast milk have been reported from Japan where the illnesses resulted from exposure to occupational chemicals during pregnancy and lactation. Since the benefits of breastfeeding far outweigh the risks of environmental contamination of breast milk, pregnant and lactating mothers can take the following steps to protect themselves and their babies from environmental pollutants:

---

1. **Avoid occupations in which you work in close contact with occupational chemicals during pregnancy and lactation.**

2. **Avoid eating fish from waters known to be contamined with industrial chemicals.**

3. **If pesticide contamination is suspected, fruits and vegetables should be peeled and washed thoroughly.**

4. **Avoid excessive weight loss during lactation. This may mobilize the chemicals from fat stores into your breast milk.**

APPENDIX II

MEDICAL RECORDS

It is very important for you to keep family medical records. If you move to another city or change doctors, these records can be invaluable reference sources if maintained consistently and accurately. The following pages can be used as a guide to keeping your own family medical records.

MEDICAL RECORD FOR _____
(name of child)

BIRTH RECORD

Date of Birth: _____

Length of Pregnancy: _____

Mother's Health During Pregnancy: _____

    drugs used: _____

    problems: _____

    illnesses: _____

Delivery:

    normal: _____ Caesarian: _____

    labor medications: _____

    other notes: _____

Measurements at Birth:

    weight: _____

    length: _____

General Health at Birth:

_____

_____

Type of Feeding:

    breast: _____ bottle: _____

Blood Type: _____

Other Information: _____

_____

_____

FAMILY MEDICAL HISTORY

List family illnesses, allergies, chronic conditions etc.

Illness	**Relationship to child**
e.g. (Asthma)	(maternal aunt, brother)
_____	_____
_____	_____
_____	_____
_____	_____

NOTES

ILLNESS/INJURY/HOSPITALIZATION RECORD

Illness/ Injury	Hospitalization (if applicable)	Date	Physician

Other Information:_____

IMMUNIZATION RECORD

Immunization	Date	Physician
DPT		
DPT		
DPT		
OPV		
OPV		
OPV		
DT Booster		
Td		
MMR		
Tuberculin test		
Others:		

INDEX

505

DATE DUE